IT SEEMS LIKE ONLY YESTERDAY

IT
SEEMS
LIKE ONLY
YESTERDAY

Memoirs of Writing,
Presidential Politics,
and the Diplomatic Life

JOHN BARTLOW MARTIN

William Morrow and Company, Inc.
New York

Library of Congress Cataloging-in-Publication Data

Martin, John Bartlow, 1915–
  It seems like only yesterday.

  1. Martin, John Bartlow, 1915–   —Biography.
2. Authors, American—20th century—Biography.   3. United
States—Politics and government—1945–   .   I. Title.
PS3525.A7525Z465   1986   818'.5409 [B]   86-12417
ISBN 0-688-06209-1

Printed in the United States of America

First Edition

1 2 3 4 5 6 7 8 9 10

BOOK DESIGN BY RICHARD ORIOLO

TO OUR CHILDREN, CINDY, DAN, AND FRED

CONTENTS

PART ONE

FAREWELL
TO INDIANAPOLIS

ONE

BACK HOME IN INDIANA

1.

On a warm spring morning in 1938, I was sitting on the sand at Fort Myers Beach, Florida, with my then wife, Barbara. We had been married a little more than a year; I was only twenty-two, less than a year out of college. The sand at Fort Myers Beach is white and powdery, and when trod by many feet it compacts until it is like concrete, as nowadays, when thousands of people jam Fort Myers Beach; but at that time we were almost the only ones there. A couple who looked a little older than we, maybe thirty, came along and sat down to talk. The man's name was Jack DeWitt and it turned out he was a writer. All my life I had wanted to be a writer, but I had never even met one. I asked what he wrote and how he did it. He wrote for the fact detective magazines, which I had never heard of. They were not the pulps—not, that is, fiction magazines containing mystery and western fiction printed on rough pulp paper—nor the big slicks like *The Saturday Evening Post*. Instead, the fact detective magazines published true accounts of criminal cases (or so they claimed). DeWitt gave me the name of an editor of two fact detective magazines in Chicago who was open to suggestions from unknown writers, Harry Keller. I had been covering police for the

11

Indianapolis Times; I'd try Keller. I told DeWitt we were on our way home after spending several months in the Dominican Republic and I had thought I'd try to write a piece about Generalissimo Trujillo, the Dominican dictator. I told him Trujillo was running a true totalitarian state—secret police, torture chambers, prisons full of political prisoners. Recently Trujillo's troops had massacred some twelve thousand Haitians.

DeWitt thought this sounded like something that would interest *Ken,* then a magazine published by *Esquire,* a magazine of liberal bent, opposed to all dictators, and given to exposés. DeWitt asked what I meant when I said the soldiers under Trujillo were all-powerful. They could, I said, do anything; and I related how one night at a dance in a small town in the interior I had seen a soldier take a teen-age girl by the hand and disappear with her into the darkness. (Actually I had no way of knowing whether she was afraid of him or enamored of him.) DeWitt told me to embellish that story and use it to personify the military's power.

He went on to tell me how to organize the piece—start with the Haitian massacre or the girl episode, give a few paragraphs on the republic's history, relate Trujillo's origins and how he came to power, describe his regime, and end by explaining the United States' policy toward him.

Soon Barbara and I took a bus back to Indianapolis. I don't believe I ever saw Jack DeWitt again. But that was for me the start of a lifelong career of writing.

2.

I had been raised in Indiana and gone to DePauw University, a small Methodist college in Greencastle, Indiana. Barbara and I had met there when she was a freshman and I a junior. I had attended a big public high school in Indianapolis that was mostly vocational, for the children of workingmen; she had attended what was then called a small exclusive girls' school in Evanston, Illinois. She was the only freshman girl at DePauw who wore a full-length mink coat. She lived with her wealthy parents in Evanston, the first suburb on the North Shore north of Chicago, then fashionable. Her house seemed to me a mansion; her father was a wealthy manufacturer who drove a big Packard, her mother was formal and distant, neither of them drank. Barbara's older sister had made her debut at the Stevens Hotel, later the Conrad Hilton, and Benny Goodman had played for it, and she had married a rich young man, all according to her parents' plan. Barbara and I broke up her parents' well-ordered world. Barbara took me to the Blackhawk Restaurant in the Chicago Loop, where one of the big swing bands of that period, Bing Crosby's brother's band, was playing and where the waiters spoke with Italian and East European accents I had never heard in Indiana; an exotic place. Chicago, so big, so gorgeous, so powerful, so exciting, so glistening by the shore of the inland sea—Barbara undertook to show me Chicago. I discovered later that she knew little about the real Chicago—only the nightclubs and the shops like Saks on upper Michigan Avenue. But at the time she seemed to be ushering me into a wonderland, and I fell in love with Chicago, a love affair that never ended.

Barbara was not beautiful but she was a gorgeous lascivious blonde. We became engaged. We were wildly in love—or so we thought: How we knew at that age I cannot now imagine. She was vulnerable, easily hurt, and she had an almost childlike manner. She came from what was called polite society; I did not; she taught me manners and how gentlefolk talk—when asked a question, for example, you respond, "No, I don't," not with the flat twangy boorish Indiana "Nah." She was no intellectual and she dropped out of college after one year. She feared her father was trying to prevent our marriage so she came to Greencastle and wanted to get married at once, and we did—were married on a bitter February night in 1937 by a justice of the peace in his shabby quarters upstairs over a saloon on the deserted town square. I went to Chicago and told her father we were married. He said only, "You married her, now support her." My own parents obtained a divorce at about that same time.

As editor of the DePauw newspaper and string correspondent for the *Indianapolis Times,* I was earning enough money to rent a small furnished room for us off the campus. In May the *Times* offered me a full-time job as a reporter; I arranged to complete my courses in absentia and Barbara and I moved to Indianapolis. I was making $22.50 a week at the *Times.* Barbara's father relented and gave us money to buy furniture for a one-room apartment.

My first assignment at the *Times* was to cover police. The city editor said only, "Report to Heze Clark at the police station at 4 A.M. tomorrow. He'll tell you what to do." Clark had been the *Times*'s police reporter for as long as anyone could remember, a gruff, squat man who couldn't write an English sentence but was probably the most thorough collector of facts on police cases I ever knew. He was switching to the afternoon shift; I would replace him on the 4-A.M.-to-noon shift. In a few days he taught me all I needed to cover police. Years later, when I was teaching at Northwestern University's Medill School of Journalism, I marveled how a student could spend ten thousand dollars and a full year learning less than Heze Clark taught me in a few days free. And I am sure the same could be said of any other journalism school.

The *Times,* a Scripps-Howard paper, was the third paper in town. The other two, Republican and stodgy, were bigger and more profitable; the *Times* was lively, aggressive, liberal, and leaning Democratic, more fun to read and to work on. The *Times* hired you young, paid you little, and promoted you fast. At twenty-three I was covering the Indianapolis City Hall.

That fall I fell ill with pneumonia, and the doctor advised me to spend the winter in a warm climate. Barbara's father gave us money and her uncle, a travel agent, booked us for a thirty-day Caribbean cruise on a freighter that carried about eight passengers. I was feeling so expansive that I bought a copy of *Harper's* magazine, at fifty cents; a luxury I could not ordinarily afford, and we took a train to Louisiana. I had never been so far from home. Our ship called at several ports in Puerto Rico, then headed homeward, but we didn't want to go back to the Indianapolis winter that soon, so when the boat stopped at Ciudad Trujillo—as Santo Domingo, the capital of the Dominican Republic, was then called—we got off. We knew nothing whatever about the Dominican Republic; we picked it only because the other passengers on our boat were Texans getting off there to drill for oil. All this was pure chance, and it led us to Jack DeWitt, the writer in Florida, and to writing an article on Trujillo for *Ken.*

3.

When we returned to Indianapolis early that spring, I went back to the *Times,* reporting and also doing rewrite, that is, working on the city desk, taking telephone calls from reporters, making notes on what they reported, and writing the stories for the paper. I wrote fast and apparently satisfactorily, and Norman Isaacs, the managing editor, later a well-known editor and educator, told me I should be writing magazine, not newspaper, pieces.

I was trying, writing weekends and nights, not an easy task with a full-time job. I wanted to write a novel and a Caribbean travelogue but I needed money. Using Jack DeWitt's name, I wrote to Harry Keller, the editor in Chicago of *Official Detective Stories* and *Actual Detective Stories of Women in Crime,* and he invited me to submit outlines of criminal cases I might write for him. I wrote to the editor of *Ken*—Arnold Gingrich, founder of *Esquire*—and outlined the piece on Trujillo. He said he'd been looking for a piece on Trujillo. I did the piece fast and sent it in. He sent it back for rewrite. This time I took my time, and I elicited the aid of my *Times* city editor, Vern Boxell, who taught me something about tightening up writing. I did as DeWitt had suggested: invented a girl who was raped by a soldier. I never again invented an episode in a serious magazine piece, for it is a shabby trick, a counterfeit substitute for solid reporting. This time *Ken* bought the piece for $150. I carried the voucher from that first story check in my wallet until it wore out. As the years pass, patterns emerge in one's life. Here was one in mine: writing, and traveling to the Dominican Republic. That doomed beautiful island republic played a crucial role for me lifelong.

Late that summer Barbara's mother died, and her father asked us to come and live with him in Evanston. The *Times* refused me a leave of absence so I resigned, and moved with Barbara into her father's house. A mistake.

Her father was a self-made conservative Republican businessman. He was fond of saying, "I went to the college of hard knocks," and capable of singing a jingle to the tune from *Snow White and the Seven Dwarfs:*

> *Heigh ho, heigh ho,*
> *We're in the CIO,*
> *We pay our dues*
> *To the goddamned Jews,*
> *Heigh ho.*

I was trying to write but finding it hard going in that house. I had several ideas for stories for *Ken;* I went down to Chicago to the towering lakefront Palmolive Building at the head of Michigan Avenue and talked to the editors of *Ken.* They were not enthusiastic—the ideas were not really worked out, were only glimmerings of ideas. I went also to see Harry Keller of *Official Detective.* By contrast to the glistening tower of *Esquire-Ken,* Keller's office was in a dingy warehouse district on Plymouth Court near the Dearborn Street railroad station. Keller was a tall bald man who looked to be in his forties. He encouraged me to write for him—at present he had no reliable contributor in the Chicago area. I told him about an old murder case in Indianapolis, and he thought it sounded promising. He introduced me to his two associate editors, Mickey Maloney and Phil Weck, and after work I went across the street with them to drink beer in a dark little saloon.

I wanted to write for Keller but did not know how to get started. I had no sources in Chicago, knew no detectives or lawyers. And I didn't know Chicago itself at all except for the Loop and that glittery strip on Michigan Avenue that Barbara knew. Occasionally she and I went down to the Loop to drink and dine and dance. But it wasn't much fun, perhaps because we were spending her father's money, not mine.

One morning when I woke up, Barbara was not in her bed beside mine. I dressed and went downstairs and after the maid brought coffee, I asked Barbara's father where she was. "She's gone," he said. I asked where. "To Columbus." That was the hometown of the young man she had intended to marry before she met me.

When she came home a couple of days later, she told me she no longer loved me and had gone to Columbus to see if she could marry her old flame but had found him married to somebody else. She didn't know what she was going to do. But she thought I should leave and she and I should get a divorce. That night in our bedroom I pleaded with her to change her mind. She would not. Then she laughed at me and said I was being silly, she didn't love me anymore. I did not understand it but accepted it as though I did. Again, I wonder how we thought we knew—she was then, I believe, not quite twenty-one, I twenty-three. I have since come to someone else's definition of love—love is what you've been through together

—and we had been through little then. (And yet for a long time I could not shake the memory of her lying naked with me in an apartment fold-down bed in the hot Indianapolis summer night.) In any case, next day I packed and she drove me down to Chicago, to the office of Harry Keller. We said goodbye, she in the car, I standing in the cobblestone gutter, and she drove off.

I went into Keller's office and told him I was leaving my wife. He thought it might be hasty. I told him it wasn't my idea and I had no choice. I told him I wanted to go to Indianapolis, do legwork on the old murder case there, then come back to Chicago, and he indicated that if I did the story well he'd buy it. I thought I could—by this time, from reading his magazines and talking at length with Mickey Maloney and Phil Weck, I had learned a good deal about how stories for these magazines were put together. Then Keller said he could see I was taking this pretty hard and he told Maloney to take the rest of the afternoon off and go across the street and drink beer with me until train time. I never forgave Barbara's defection but never ceased being grateful to her for introducing me to a wider world than Indianapolis.

4.

Most people who write their memoirs seem to have had happy childhoods. I hated mine. Many seem to regard the years of their youth as the easiest years of their lives. Mine were the hardest. Therefore, of both childhood and youth, I will say only what is necessary. My parents' forebears had come from the rural part of the crucial pioneer triangle where Indiana, Ohio, and Kentucky come together, and I was born on August 4, 1915, in a house in Hamilton, Ohio, but we moved to Indianapolis when I was three or four. My father was a contractor. I did not like him much when I was young, and he was disappointed in me, for I read all the time. Although he himself read nothing but the *Engineering News-Record,* he nonetheless bought me books for Christmas. He was a tall angular man just over six feet, a willful stubborn man, a bluff loud man in a noisy and rough industry from which I shrank. One afternoon he came home early, his face scratched, his nose and mouth bleeding, his eye puffed up, his suit torn and dirty. "I got whupped," he said and told my mother and me how: An ironworkers' union boss had come to his job to organize the workers, my father had "run him off the job," the union boss had refused to go, they had fought, and the union boss had knocked my father down and beaten him up and stomped him.

He had not finished high school; the eldest of three sons, he had had to quit school and go to work at thirteen when his father died. He began as a carpenter, became a carpenter contractor, became a general contractor, and in the 1920's became well-to-do. Even more to his credit, he refused to join the Ku Klux Klan, not easy in Indiana in the 1920's, for the Klan controlled Indiana, some of my early boyhood memories are of watching a seemingly endless parade of robed and hooded Klansmen marching around Monument Circle in Indianapolis in dead silence. The grand dragon of Indiana proclaimed, "I am the law in Indiana," and he was. Nearly every businessman belonged to the Klan. My father disliked everything about it, just why he never explained. He was a lifelong Democrat, as his father had been. Some Saturday nights my father, accompanied by my mother and me, would drive down to Indiana Avenue, the heart of Indianapolis's segregated Negro district, and pull up grandly in his long blue Buick touring car in front of a crowd of Negroes hanging around outside a pool hall and call out, "Which ones of you niggers wants to go to work on Monday?" There was no malice in it; it was his way of hiring labor. One of his regular workers asked him for a loan on Monday; my father said, "But you just got paid on Saturday—what'd you do with it?" The Negro said, "Mr. Martin, you ain't never been a nigger on Saturday night."

The buzz of insects, the whir of the lawnmower, the swish of the garden hose in the long summer evening, the fireflies over the dew-wet grass—this was my Indiana boyhood. This, and "niggers." Because of segregated housing, few Negroes went to grade school where I did; as a boy I feared the few, they could fight too well. My mother taught me that Catholics always build their churches on the tops of hills; she had been taught they were preparing to take over the country and the churches would be their military strongpoints. We lived in a small house on Brookside Avenue. Brookside Avenue—a mean street in a mean city. It was a wide brick street with streetcar tracks and trolley wires, the houses small and wooden, a tumbledown wreck of some stucco "flats," scattered neighborhood stores. When I was growing up there, our neighbors were a brick-layer, a railroad freight conductor, a minor-league baseball umpire, a painter. Across the street lived a family of Negroes but they did not show themselves on Brookside Avenue; they knew they were not welcome there. Later I brought my college friends to our house by a roundabout route so they would not see the meanness of Brookside Avenue; I was ashamed. My father planned to build for my mother a new house of stone in a "good"neighborhood on the North Side far from Brookside Avenue, but he lost everything in the De-pression.

I suppose my childhood was not all bad—my father took me fish-ing in the spring and summer, and in the fall we went to the country to gather walnuts and hickory nuts, and every Thanksgiving we drove to Anderson, Indiana, to have dinner with my grandmother Bartlow and my mother's sister, Aunt Verl. But most of my child-hood memories are dark. My mother was small, quiet, soft, sweet, and always sad. She was a romantic but romantic about her chil-dren, life, God, not about her husband—the few times I saw him try to demonstrate affection toward her, she fended him off. For nine years I was an only child. Then my brother Billy was born. Not long after that another brother, Dickie, was born. One Sunday morning when Dickie was about six months old, I found him dead in his crib. My mother dressed his body in his best white dress and a lacy bon-net and brought it downstairs to the front porch, where I was sitting in the wicker swing shaded by the awning, and put his body in my lap and told me to hold it. At least this is what she wrote in the "baby book" she was keeping; my present wife has read it, I have not.

My father doted on my brother Billy, perhaps because there was something wrong with him. I think now he was retarded, but I never heard the word until many years later. He was late learning to walk, he scarcely talked at six and did not enter first grade then. We rarely spoke of his condition except when he learned something like how to clean his hands by wiping them on his overalls—I taught him that playing with him in our sandpile in the backyard, and proudly showed my mother, who said, "See, he's getting better. He's heal-ing." She was a devout Christian Scientist. That was why we never knew what was wrong with Billy—she refused to let a doctor see him. She would say, "He's God's child," as people called the afflicted in the Dark Ages, and add a Christian Science homily, "God is love."*

In 1931, when I was fifteen, I fell ill with scarlet fever, then a dread disease. I was deathly sick but my mother refused to have a doctor, instead she called her Christian Scientist practitioner and asked him "to work on it." I recovered, but before I did Billy caught it from me. He became even sicker than I, delirious, his body burning red. Again she refused to call a doctor and prayed and she took the streetcar downtown to see the practitioner. Finally, past midnight at the climax, when Billy seemed about to die, my father, unable to stand by doing nothing any longer, burst out, "I'm going to get some medicine," and though my mother protested, he went— alone. When he returned my mother met him at the top of the stairs and said to him, "He's gone, John." I always thought she spoke almost in triumph but surely I was wrong. I was huddled in my bed in my room behind her. Never before had I seen my father, that big strong man, cry. I thought I had killed Billy.

I think it was Billy's death that broke my parents' marriage. It had been in trouble for several years. In the 1920's, my father had had several big construction jobs in Cincinnati and he had taken up with a woman there, he had taken her to the opera at the Cincinnati Zoo and to the Latonia racetrack and to the Hotel Gibson roof garden, where Jan Garber played and where they danced and drank bootleg whiskey, all things my mother abjured, things alien to Brookside Avenue, they had taken me with them. But I do not think it was his woman friend that broke his marriage; it was, rather, losing his business and his son. He had to get away—away from my brother's death, away from Christian Science and my mother, away from failure and no job, away from Brookside Avenue. Though he wanted a divorce he could not afford to keep two households so we three lived together a year and a half with almost the only dialogue among us being carried on by my mother, who was trying to convince me that it was all my father's fault. They quarreled often, "fighting," they called it, and seemed to enjoy it, sometimes she tried to hit him with

---

* Many years later, my present wife and I discovered that we have what is called Rh factor incompatibility—a blood incompatibility that sometimes results in the birth of deformed or defective children. (First children escape, I believe; subsequent ones do not.) She thinks my brother's condition may have resulted from the same Rh factor incompatibility in my parents, at that time unknown.

her fists, and I have memories of violent scenes, though I may have invented them—I was aways making things up. It is of course possible I have this all wrong, all this about Billy's death and its effect upon my father and upon me.

When Billy died, I was in my third year of high school, and an English teacher had opened a new world for me—modern literature. Throughout high school, and even in grade school, I wanted to write. I tried to write poetry and I sent it to my aunt Verl, who I imagined, wrongly, knew more about poetry than my parents. I had always read a lot but now I put aside Zane Grey and James Oliver Curwood for the authors my teacher sent me to—Hemingway, Dos Passos, Dreiser, O'Neill, Sherwood Anderson, Sinclair Lewis, Faulkner, Mencken, and more. I read them all, some several times, especially Dos Passos' *42nd Parallel* and Thomas Wolfe's *Look Homeward, Angel,* for in the first I found a world I aspired to know and in the second I thought I could see myself. (And also especially *The Sun Also Rises* and *A Farewell to Arms*—later when I met Barbara I thought she resembled the nymphomaniac heroine of *The Sun Also Rises,* Lady Brett Ashley, and perhaps I was right.) I read *The American Mercury* every month. My father called me, derisively, the bookworm. I began writing short stories and a novel and even a play, all imitative of those authors, no doubt, all unpublished and forgotten till now. I studied *Writer's Digest.* It must have been along in here that I knew I wanted to spend my life writing.

Something else happened too. A boy I knew in high school who lived in a working-class neighborhood was the son of a German immigrant ironworker, the first authentic proletarian I had ever known. Wolfgang, as I shall call him here, introduced me to Marx and Spengler, Kant and Nietzsche and Schopenhauer. I could not manage the *Critique of Pure Reason* or *Das Kapital* but I read the others. Wolfgang could roll his own cigarettes with one hand while walking down a railroad track, explaining to me what a gandy dancer was (one was mentioned in a Dos Passos novel). He liked to recite the life histories of Big Bill Haywood and Joe Hill. On many nights he and I sat up late at his house, drinking his father's home brew and talking about the Depression, the union movement, and the Communist party. He tried to convert me to communism. Wolfgang was a member of the Young Communists' League and wanted me to join. Once he urged me to accompany him to a Communist march in another Indiana town, a "Red Parade," and I intended to go but for some reason did not; the marchers were beaten and jailed. I used to say I didn't go because I had a date with a girl, but to be honest I don't remember why. Actually Wolfgang was more mature than I in many ways and used to explain things to me that I hadn't understood when my girl and I were fumbling around. He was, I now suppose, brilliant. He used to take me walking through the slums of Indianapolis, on the South Side and the West Side, among the unemployed and derelicts, talking about "when the revolution comes." He thought it not far off if the Depression continued. Many people agreed. I had always heard my father talking politics, but Democratic-Republican politics. This was a new political awakening.

I lost track of Wolfgang for many years. One Sunday after World War II he came to see me in my house in a Chicago suburb. He had gone to college, became a nuclear physicist, and during the war worked on the Manhattan Project, developing the atomic bomb. I don't know whether he was still a Communist. He was full of awe at the bomb, "the most important development since the discovery of fire"; but he must have been repelled by our quiet Sunday suburban life, for I never saw him again.

5.

I graduated from high school at sixteen—I had skipped two grades in elementary school. My father had always wanted me to go to an engineering school and go into his business. I had always refused—I wanted to be a writer. He doubted—sensibly—that anything much could come of a career so odd as writing. Now we had to decide. It was not really his decision—he could not afford to send me to college at all, my grandmother Bartlow would have to send me. I applied for admission to Indiana University, but one day shortly before school started a high school friend's older brother, Tom Ochiltree, an upperclassman at DePauw University, told me that if I would go to DePauw instead of Indiana he would get me into his fraternity. So I did. College admission was neither so difficult nor so carefully considered as later, when my own chidren went to school. (Cheaper too—I believe tuition at DePauw was $125 per semester.)

So far as I know, no other member of my family on either side had ever graduated from college.

That first year in college I behaved like a fool—went drinking and whoring in Terre Haute on Saturday nights, played poker and drank in the Delta Chi house and speakeasies on week nights, cut chapel and cut classes. I think now that I had come of age intellectually the last two years in high school but not emotionally and that I simply couldn't handle being away from home, happy as I was to escape Brookside Avenue. In any case, one morning near the end of the year I got drunk alone in my room and made a fool of myself; a fraternity brother who was studying to be a minister reported me to the dean of men, and he expelled me from school.

I went home and told my parents. My father said nothing. My mother said we mustn't tell my grandmother, it would kill her. My father was at home all the time. He had no work. In the 1920's he had plowed his large earnings back into his business and invested them in common stocks. He lost everything in the stock market crash and ultimately he had to put his business through receivership. He refused to declare bankruptcy, considering it dishonorable; eventually he paid off his creditors. That summer he was looking for work, any kind of work. Sometimes he took me with him—they might hire a young fellow where they wouldn't an older man. Once we went at dawn to the Real Silk Hosiery mill not far from Brookside Avenue to be first in line at the employment gate, only to see at opening time the foreman put up a sign on the gate, NO HELP WANTED. In the past, when I have told this story, I have said we went out together at dawn every morning to stand in line at factory gates, but the truth is that we only did it once, it was useless. The lines were long that summer. My father thought things would get better now that Franklin Roosevelt was president, and every time the president gave one of his "fireside chats" my father sat in front of the old Atwater-Kent radio, listening to every word, agreeing vehemently. My father was right. Roosevelt—*there* was a leader! All he did was save our house—the mortgage banker would have foreclosed if Roosevelt's HOLC (Home Owner's Loan Corporation) had not stepped in. All he did was give my father a job—my father, who had bossed so many men on big construction projects, got a job on WPA (the federal Works Progress Administration) as foreman of a small crew that was making a topographical map of Marion County (Indianapolis). (How you make a topographic map of anything as flat as central Indiana is beyond me, but the WPA worked many wonders.) Roosevelt saved us all.

I was looking desultorily for work myself that summer and a miracle happened: I found it. The father of my school friends was Sam Ochiltree; he was chief of the Indianapolis bureau of the Associated Press and he gave me a job as a stock gummer. My task was to take stock market quotations off a ticker tape and gum, or paste, them onto sheets of paper containing the names of stocks. I was paid nine dollars a week. For several months that was the only money coming into our household. My father bore it silently.

When the NRA—the National Recovery Act—was enacted it set a national minimum wage of $14.50 a week, as I recall, and so I got a raise. I also got promoted to night copyboy. I worked from 3 P.M. till 11 P.M. in the stark bare office filled with chattering Teletype machines. My job was to tear the copy from the machines and distribute it, one copy to the telegraph editor of the *Indianapolis Star,* one to the head of the night AP office who edited it for the Indiana state wire, one to the pony editor who edited it for small newspapers, and so on. If the story was hot I delivered it at a dead run. I loved it. I was working with editors and reporters. Indoors I wore my hat on the back of my head, as had Hildy Johnson in the Hecht-MacArthur play *The Front Page.* I learned to punch a Teletype machine, and they let me punch relief on the state wire when the regular puncher took a coffee break. Once in a while they let me edit copy for the pony editor. I even went to a state political convention with the AP political writer; my job was to run his copy back to the office, but sitting at a press table down front in the big convention hall, I felt as though I were covering the convention. I have seldom been happier than at this time. I hoped it would last forever. But when I asked Sam Ochiltree to make me an editor or a reporter, he said he would not until I had gone back to DePauw and graduated.

So in January or February of 1935, at the start of the spring term, I went back to DePauw. I was glad to leave Brookside Avenue again—my mother and father were both living there but it was hardly a marriage, they slept in separate bedrooms and seldom spoke to each other, often eating dinner with each other in silence;

they were only waiting for him to make enough money to afford a divorce. But though glad to get away, I disdained college. I had been out of school a year and a half and had held a job. I put a good deal of energy into becoming editor of the school paper and working as a string correspondent for the *Indianapolis Times* but I also bore down hard on my studies. I took no more English than was required, concentrated instead on political science, history, and economics. I learned some history and a little economics. But I think I learned less in my entire three and a half years of college than in my last two in high school. And I did graduate (being by then married to Barbara). At about the time we were married, my parents were divorced. Barbara and I were married in 1937. This, I now realize, was only six years after my brother Billy had died. A good deal had happened to me.

6.

So now in the fall of 1938, having left Barbara in Evanston, I was back at my mother's house on Brookside Avenue. I did the legwork on the old Indianapolis murder case I had described to Keller and wrote it and sent it to him, and while awaiting reply I did preliminary legwork on two story ideas I had for *Ken*—a piece on Paul V. McNutt, formerly governor of Indiana, then high commissioner to the Philippines, and an exposé of the Indianapolis 500 race. I visited my father and his new wife in their apartment on the North Side. I liked her, so much jollier than my poor sad mother, now left alone on Brookside Avenue, the scene for us of so much conflict and woe. My father was dubious about my going to Chicago to write; his wife said, "Let him go, John." At about that time the issue of *Ken* that carried my Trujillo piece came out. My father said nothing to me about it, but I learned later that he took a copy downtown and showed it off to his lawyer and his banker and the construction cronies with whom he ate lunch, and years later I found his copy— the Trujillo page number written on the cover in his longhand— among his things when he died. He did not like me much in my teens and my early twenties, nor I him, but long before he died I realized he'd been right at that time, I'd been a fool, and I regained my love and even my respect for my father.

Keller bought the murder story and sent me a check for $175, about $25 over the going rate. I took the money and went to Chicago alone to become a freelance writer.

The end of a marriage, the start of a career—I thought at the time I simply wanted to get away from Indianapolis and go to the big town, but I think now that I went to Chicago because I wanted to show my divorcing wife that I could succeed in the big town at my chosen work and without her—as though she'd care—and perhaps too because for a time I wanted to be near her and hoped she would change her mind about having fallen out of love. She did not, probably best for both of us; I never saw her again, and a year later I married Fran—and in the forty-six years since, *we* have been through quite a bit together, and I think I can say with more confidence than when we were twenty-two and twenty-four that we're in love.

TWO

CHICAGO: A LONG WAY FROM BROOKSIDE AVENUE

1.

In Chicago, I moved into the Hotel Milner, a sooty old brick hulk at the foot of Rush Street down by the river, a hotel that advertised, "$1 a day, laundry free, we pay cab fare from the railroad station, $5 a week on a monthly basis." It suited me fine. I had nothing but one suitcase and a portable typewriter. I had a room with a bed and through the dirty window a view of the fire escape. For a brief time I again acted like a fool as I had my first year in college—slept most of the day, wrote at night, and drank beer while I wrote. I soon leaned I couldn't make a living that way, and for the next forty-odd years of writing I worked from 9 A.M. to 5 P.M. and never drank between those hours.

I was writing everything—a book-length Caribbean travelogue that I never sold, the two Indiana pieces for *Ken*, a piece on the Black Hand, precursor of the Mafia, for *Esquire*. Those sold. But fact detective stories—Keller's magazines, *Official Detective* and *Actual Detective* (*OD* and *AD*, as we called them)—were the meal ticket. At first, a little timid about going out on the street to do legwork among the forbidding police in the big city, I wrote older cases that I could research in the library. Gradually, I began to work on current stories. Many were byliners for *AD*—stories ghostwritten for women involved in crimes. For example, a young Polish stickup man shot a man during a robbery; I persuaded his wife to tell me her life story and wrote it under her name. Keller paid her $50, paid me $150. I did a good many of these.

In such pieces, I had to check the facts of the crime with the police and at the criminal court. Doing so I built up a small network of sources who would talk to me—detectives, court clerks, assistant state's attorneys, the coroner. And I began to write fewer byliners and more straight crime stories. Chicago detectives were under standing orders not to talk to reporters without authorization by the police commissioner. They talked to reporters from Chicago papers anyway but not to me. I began hanging around outlying district police stations, then, when I had met some officers, hanging around the Detective Bureau at downtown headquarters. They got used to me, people are always hanging around police stations; Jack Ruby, who killed Lee Harvey Oswald, did. Sometimes I took a bottle of good brandy to a detective or promised to "buy you a hat"—give him a twenty dollar bill. I soon learned that some of my best sources were assistant state's attorneys, who would let me see police reports when detectives wouldn't, and the coroner, since his questioning elicited testimony from detectives that they otherwise would reserve for the trial. Newspaper reporters, naturally, tend to neglect such sources; I cultivated them assiduously, and through them met detectives in the Robbery Detail at headquarters, the "heavy men"—they went after armed robbers who held up banks and currency exchanges at gunpoint.

In all these fact-detective-magazine stories the bare facts were true—So-and-So really had killed someone on x date, and on y date he was convicted and sentenced to z number of years in the penitentiary. Plus the names of the detectives and the state's attorney. All this I checked most meticulously, mindful of libel. The two nightmares in this business were libel and what we called "post office." Post office: At that time the U.S. postal authorities had the power to decide what was obscene and to deny second-class mailing privileges to its publisher. The post office could put a magazine out of business. The trick was to write right up to the edge of the obscene and stop.

Except for the descriptions and a few bare facts of the case, the rest of a seventy-five-hundred-word story was almost pure fiction—invented dialogue, invented or embellished episodes, invented clues, rhetoric. None of this is to say that I could do it with my left hand. Not at all. I worked as hard at this writing as at any I ever did and, given the constrictions of the genre, made it as good as I could. And I thought of what I was writing not as articles but as stories. Thus I learned the uses of description, dialogue, characterization, and perhaps above all narrative pull—that mysterious invisible force that pulls the reader onward. (I still think of my pieces as stories.)

This work was almost perfect training for someone who aspired to write serious fact pieces. After all, I was learning to do legwork, how to interview people. I was learning the real Chicago—the vast checkerboard wards spreading for miles back westward from the lakeshore where dwell both the millions of workingmen in "two-flats"—two-family dwellings—who built Chicago and the thousands of criminals in slums who have given Chicago its reputation. And probably most important of all, I was writing. And slanting stories straight at a market. I have always believed, even later while teaching at journalism school, that writing cannot be taught. It can, however, be learned, by reading and writing. I was learning. And I had the added advantage of talking evenings with Mickey Maloney and Phil Weck; they could tell me why they had rejected a story.

Soon I no longer needed to read *OD* and *AD* but could read what I pleased. What I was reading was almost as important for my future as what I was writing. New books by Steinbeck and Hemingway and Faulkner, old ones by Forster and Huxley. I tried to adapt fictional devices to my crime writing and I began hanging around bookstores, especially Ben Abramson's Argus Bookshop. I was reading *Harper's* and *Life* and dreaming of the day when they would lie on my desk not because I enjoyed them but because I was working for them.

After a time I arranged for an experienced Chicago police reporter to do some of the legwork for me. When I hit my stride, I was writing a million words a year and at first selling a third of them at two cents a word, then selling half, which brought me ten thousand dollars a year, a good income at that prewar time. The two-cents-a-word market, as we called it, wasn't bad. Often, under assumed names, I had three or even four stories in one issue of Keller's magazine. Toward the end Keller was taking just about everything I could write. But by then I was spending more and more time on serious writing. None of this seemed extraordinary to me. I had set out to be a freelance writer and I was one. Looking back, I wonder at my temerity in moving to Chicago to write. Groucho Marx used to tell a relevant story. He related how his father had taught him to swim by throwing him off a dock into deep water. His straight man asked, of course, "Wasn't that hard?" Groucho: "Nothing to it once I got out of that burlap bag." All I needed was to get out of the burlap bag called Brookside Avenue.

2.

OD and *AD* were owned by M. L. Annenberg. Moe Annenberg also owned the *Daily Racing Form,* and it was published in the same place on Plymouth Court as *OD* and *AD,* the only authentic record of the past performances of racehorses in America. At that time, about 1940, there were in Chicago some five hundred illegal handbooks—gambling joints that accepted bets on horses—and they were owned by Al Capone's heirs, called by criminals the Mob or simply the Outfit, by outsiders the Syndicate and today the Mafia. The Syndicate's handbooks were dependent on Annenberg's *Daily Racing Form* and on a telephone and telegraph network that hooked up every handbook in the country with every racetrack in the country. The Syndicate killed the man who had run that network.

During my time at *OD* and *AD,* Annenberg was expanding his publishing enterprises. He started two new magazines—a third crime magazine, *Intimate Detective,* and a "true confession" magazine, *Living Romances.* I now wrote confession stories as well as crime, and for a time I wrote a monthly advice-to-the-lovelorn column for *Living Romances.* Annenberg was also starting *TV Guide;* it became one of the most successful of all magazines. And he bought the *Philadelphia Inquirer.* Keller used to play poker with his son Walter Annenberg and other Annenberg corporate executives. (Walter later became President Nixon's ambassador to the Court of St. James's and frequent host to President Reagan.) I played with them once, but the stakes were far too high for me.

Moe Annenberg became interested in the history of the Molly Maguires, a post–Civil War organization in the Pennsylvania coal fields that has been variously described as a secret fraternal order, a nascent labor union, and a terrorist and murder gang. Annenberg suggested that Keller send a writer to do a series of stories on the Mollies for *OD,* and Keller sent me. Keller and I had intended perhaps three pieces. But Annenberg became so engrossed in them that he could not get enough, and I believe I strung it out for eleven months. At about this same time Annenberg was convicted of income tax evasion. Before he went to the penitentiary, he asked for advance *OD* galleys to see how the Mollies story came out.

3.

Rush Street, where I lived on the Near North Side, was jammed with little bars, expensive nightclubs, jazz clubs, and gambling joints. Many stayed open all night. Gambling was wide open, protected by the police and politicians and controlled by the Syndicate. Living there you felt the Syndicate was never far away. Harry Keller's wife had been a nightclub singer there, and one night while she was sitting out a number a customer had asked her to dance. The dance ended, and as she walked back alone to her table, gunfire broke out behind her. The man she had just danced with lay dead on the dance floor. When the police came, she told them she never had seen him in her life. In the expensive nightclubs you could see not only well-to-do suburbanites but big-shot Syndicate men with their show girls. Ever since Capone's time, Chicagoans have enjoyed gangster watching. To me it was all new and all exciting, a long way from Brookside Avenue. I am afraid at times I was a little foolish about it. I took up briefly with a man in my hotel who said he was a police reporter. He drove a Cadillac and carried a huge roll of bills and loved to drive close to traffic policemen on rainy nights and splash them and curse them, then speed away. When I discovered he carried a gun, I stopped seeing him.

The rest of the Near North Side lay along Michigan Avenue and up the Outer Drive along the lake to Lincoln Park—the famous Gold Coast. At that time I knew nobody who lived there. West of the Rush Street strip and the Gold Coast, the night plunged into the criminal slums that had spawned the bootleg gangs and the Mafia: Little Italy, hard by the scene of the St. Valentine's Day Massacre, then only ten years into history. These were not the little slums of Wolfgang's and my Indianapolis. These were big, the real thing, mile after splotchy mile of them scattered over the enormous city.

At that time, Chicago was Mecca for all the yearning young men in all the mean little towns all over the Midwest, as it once had been Mecca for their mothers and fathers, now back in the little towns, defeated; the young men didn't know what they were yearning for, standing in the evening by the garden gate, but they felt it every time they heard the evening train go whistling by—somewhere there must be something more than the town they lived in. Chicago? Sherwood Anderson must have felt it too. And now I'd made it to Chicago. I used to walk up Michigan Avenue alone at night, across the river on the drawbridge, past the white-spotlighted Wrigley Building and the Tribune Tower and up the glistening avenue with its lofty spires and serrated skyline under the black night over the lake, traffic flowing, a great dynamo; and I used to think about Chicago: There's a lot of power and money here, a lot going on. I ached to write about it all for serious magazines. I couldn't do it for *OD-AD-ID*. But someday, somehow.

I must be careful here. I am not sure how consciously I was thinking all this. Perhaps it was more of an inchoate longing.

At that time I was consorting with two entirely different sets of friends. One consisted of the *OD-AD-ID* editors, married, with children and suburban houses or outlying apartments. Often on Saturday nights we ate supper in one of their homes and played nickel-and-dime poker and talked about our work. Sometimes Keller and his wife joined us. Keller was a difficult man. He was moody and he often drank too much. Imperious, highly opinionated, he ran his employee's lives to the extent he could. He himself had been married several times. He took his work very seriously and demanded that we do too. When he was not there, we make jokes about it. Keller always chose the titles of stories, and one of his favorites was "The Clew's in the Barrel with Julia"—he insisted on spelling it "clew"—and one of the staff invented a limerick:

> *This murder is mighty peculia,*
> *The Motive in it would foolya;*
> *Hate past endurance?*
> *Or simply insurance?*
> *The Clew's in the Barrel with Julia.*

Mickey Maloney and Phil Weck wanted to write. Weck was a natural writer, with a creative bent, and Maloney had worked several years for United Press. But they were afraid to attempt what I was doing, freelancing—they had mortgages, wives, children; they could not gamble. Eventually Maloney did try it but it didn't work out and he went back to United Press. He and I spent many evenings together, drinking beer and talking about writing. And about politics and the war—when Hitler sent his panzers into Poland, I heard his speech on the radio in my hotel lobby. In the summer Maloney rented a cottage on a lake in far northern Wisconsin and took his family there, and I visited them. All my life I had loved fishing and in Indiana as a boy had dreamed of someday fishing in the northwoods.

My other group of friends at that time consisted of several young married couples, childless, living on the Near North Side or the far South Side. They were jazz enthusiasts but seldom went to nightclubs, being unable to afford it and anyway preferring to sit on the floor in each others' dim-lit living rooms, drinking and playing jazz recordings. They were gay and frivolous. The jobs they held had little to do with their lives, were only ways to earn enough money to pay the rent and buy the beer and the recordings. I enjoyed my frivolous friends but I felt intuitively that my own direction lay more in that of the *OD-AD-ID* editors.

At that time too, usually alone, I was listening to jazz in nightclubs. In high school in Indianapolis I had gone often to what were then called black-and-tans—dance halls that were predominantly Negro but that welcomed white people—in order to listen to big Negro bands playing one-night stands, Louis Armstrong and Fletcher Henderson; and in college late at night we would gather around the radio in the fraternity house to listen to broadcasts of big-name bands from Chicago. And now here I was on the Near North Side of Chicago right in the middle of it. Jimmy McPartland and Wingy Manone and Muggsy Spanier were succeeding each other at the Three Deuces, and Cab Calloway was at a black-and-tan on the South Side, and Benny Goodman at the Stevens or Congress. Anita O'Day was singing at the Three Deuces, my favorite place, and she usually sat with me between sets and several times I took her out before or after her night's work. She was the only girl vocalist I ever saw who sang more to the band than to the audience. Billie Holiday came to the Three Deuces for a guest appearance, and when she heard Anita sing, she said to me, "Give that lady my purse." I wrote the lyrics of two songs for Anita and I told her if she didn't make it to the big time by the time she was thirty, she was finished. The last I heard she was still going strong in the big time past sixty.

4.

On the rebound from Barbara, I suppose, I was having a string of brief affairs. Some of the girls I met in the jazz clubs, more in the little Rush Street bars, a few in northern Wisconsin. About none was I serious nor, I am sure, were they about me. But on an October Sunday night that year, 1939, something different occurred. I was in The Pub, a little bar across Rush Street from my hotel with sawdust on the floor, frequented by students and young professional people. I was drinking scotch at the end of the bar with Grant Robbins, who in college had introduced me to Barbara. He went over to two couples at the bar. Presently he returned and told me they were trying to remember the Ernest Dowson poem "Cynara"—they had the first line or two but couldn't remember the rest, and he'd told them I'd know it. It happened that I did, and he and I joined the others. Thus, he introduced me to the second of my two wives—the one trying to remember the poem, a pretty little girl called Fran. She was with her date and her brother and his wife. I recited the poem and we stayed for a drink and I got Fran aside and got her telephone number. Next day I called her and on Tuesday took her to dinner at a Near North Side restaurant. That day my divorce from Barbara became final. Fran remembers the date clearly as October 10 because exactly ten years before, James Oliver Curwood had lectured at her grade school and adjured the students to go home and write in their Bibles, "What will I be doing ten years from today?" Fran was conventional enough to do it. She was still growing up, was twenty-one, two years younger than I, but in some ways more mature—and stable—than I. She was slight, not quite five feet tall and one hundred pounds, with brown hair and brown eyes and a strong jaw which, on occasion, she set. Her name was Frances Rose Smethurst, and her parents called her Frances Rose but I called her Fran. She had gone to Lawrence College in Appleton, Wisconsin, for two years. We began to see each other regularly that winter. She lived with her parents in an old ramshackle but attractive house on a shady street in Elmhurst, a middle-class suburb west of Chicago. Her father was old and stooped, with a white mustache—he had been fifty-one when Fran was born and he was a Spanish-American War veteran—and her mother seventeen years younger. Her father was traffic manager for a can manufacturer. He had had a heart attack many years earlier and his family had regarded him as a semi-invalid ever since. He did not drink and smoked only a few cigars; Fran's mother neither smoked nor drank and strongly disapproved of both. They never raised their voices.

Fran introduced me to her friends from high school and college in Chicago and Elmhurst; I thought them conventional and dull. I introduced her to my friends; she did not like the hard-drinking frivolous set and thought the editors lower middle class. Her family had little money but traced its lineage straight to London. (Her mother teased her father about being descended from the infamous English mass murderer Dr. Smethurst; he teased her about being descended from John Wilkes Booth; neither was true.) Fran liked to sing and dance; I did neither well; she taught me. I taught her to listen to jazz that winter, to play poker that spring, to fish that summer in northern Wisconsin. I took her to Indianapolis to meet my parents—separately—and my aunt Verl in Anderson, and when she returned she told her own mother that my parents were divorced, my aunt was divorced, and so of course was I. It must have been quite a shock. Her mother did not think much of me at the outset.

Having been burned by Barbara, I held something of myself in reserve, I had determined never to fall in love again, in our foolish idiom then, which seemed strange to Fran, though she said little about it, just looked knowing. One night, while I was taking her home, I said to her, "Why don't we get married?" She agreed. I said we'd have to do it this week; I wanted to go north, fishing. She agreed. I took her to her house in Elmhurst, and we wakened her mother and told her the wedding would be Saturday—this was Tuesday—and her mother said she'd have to paint the porch. We were married in the Congregational church in Elmhurst. Today, forty-six years later, we are still married, an idea that would have astonished me at that time (but not Fran). My own mother and father came to our wedding together. My father had rebuilt his business, made a second start after fifty; whatever it was that had hurt him had healed, and he had come back to my mother, and about the time Fran's and my first child was born, he remarried my mother and took her away from Brookside Avenue and built for her the stone ranchhouse on the North Side on Kessler Boulevard she had always wanted.

The morning after our wedding, Fran and I started driving north. I didn't want to go to Wisconsin, too many tourists; I wanted to go farther north to more remote country, the Upper Peninsula of Michigan, and we picked out an isolated town on the map with a name we liked, Michigamme. The day was cold and rainy. Passing through Wisconsin, Fran fell asleep beside me, covered with a topcoat. Near the town of Pembine the road crossed a narrow bridge at the bottom of a little rise of land, and as we hit the bridge the car skidded. I righted it, nothing happened. I looked at Fran. She was sleeping peacefully. Suddenly I felt a terrifying sense of responsibility. Now I really *was* responsible for her. I had never felt that way about Barbara. As I have said, Barbara had, when I first knew her, reminded me of Lady Brett Ashley in *The Sun Also Rises.* Later, when I read Somerset Maugham's *Of Human Bondage,* she reminded me of that novel's principal female character, Mildred, dumb, unreliable, cruel. And obsessive. Men write novels about the Lady Ashleys and the Mildreds of the world. But, if they are lucky, they marry the Frans. And live happily ever after.

We rented a camp, as cottages and cabins are called in Upper Michigan, at Three Lakes, five miles west of Michigamme. The camp was not much—no electricity, kerosene lamps, no running water, a hand pump, an outhouse. Some honeymoon! But it was on the shore of a beautiful lake and it shared the shore with only a few other camps, and the fishing was excellent, and we met people who remained our friends until they died. We were, without knowing it, setting another lifelong pattern—summers in Upper Michigan.

5.

Two months after Pearl Harbor, our daughter Cindy was born and we rented a little house on a secluded street in Winnetka, Illinois. Something happened: I doubt that Winnetka itself had anything to do with it, except that it was our first house and we were happier there than before; but the fact remains that it was during these years in Winnetka, 1942–1944, that I began to write my way out of the fact detective field. We began seeing a man I had known in high school, Francis S. Nipp. He had come to Chicago to teach English and work on his Ph.D. at the University of Chicago. In high school he had given me lists of modern American writers and their novels and, like Wolfgang, had spent long evenings with me talking about books. Now he became important to my writing and he stayed important for many years. He and his wife Mary Ellen spent long weekends with us in Winnetka, listening to music and talking about writing. He set me to reading *The New Yorker* regularly—"the best-written and best-edited magazine of all." Francis himself had when younger tried to write but he was no writer (whatever that means). He was, however, a natural editor. More than anyone else at this stage he encouraged me to write serious nonfiction for *Harper's*.

Eight German agents landed on the east coast from submarines with the intention of sabotaging the American light metals industry. They were captured and convicted. One of them, Herbert Haupt, had been raised in Chicago. I proposed to the *Harper's* editors a piece on Haupt's Chicago background. They responded as any magazine would to an unknown writer: They would not make an assignment but they would be interested in reading the piece if I wanted to do it on speculation. I did. And they bought it, my first piece for *Harper's*, published in April 1943.

I am mortified to admit that I didn't do much legwork on that story. I cannot remember that I so much as interviewed Haupt's parents and friends. I fear I wrote the piece mainly from newspaper clippings or from trial transcripts, plus legwork in the Chicago neighborhood where Haupt grew up. At that time I did not really understand what a serious "heavy fact" piece is. It is not a rehash of material taken from newspaper clippings and other magazine pieces, nor a piece based on telephone interviews. Instead, it is an original work and it is based on documents—trial transcripts, congressional hearings, other official papers, correspondence—and above all on personal interviews—long face-to-face interviews with everybody involved, often, in the case of key figures such as Haupt's parents, several interviews each lasting two hours or more. But I didn't know that then.

Soon I did another piece for *Harper's,* this time with more leg-work. A gang of young men and a woman called the Polkadot Gang held up several Chicago taverns and in one robbery shot an off-duty policeman dead. In doing a story on the case for Keller, I had found in court records a probation officer's report on the criminals. Background on their lives for *Harper's*—I pursued its leads. They had lived in a Near West Side slum; it happened I knew a detective there from my fact detective legwork; he supplied more details, took me on a tour of the neighborhood, and taught me about police work and criminal life. All this found its way into the *Harper's* piece, which sold. Still I did not myself interview the robbers themselves, as I did in later years.

At about this time I went to New York and met Frederick Lewis Allen, the editor of *Harper's,* and his associate editors, Russell Lynes, George Leighton, John Kouwenhoven, Jack Fischer, and Eric Larrabee. George Leighton had been handling my pieces. He was an excellent writer and reporter himself and had written a wonderful book about America, *Five Cities.* He had started out to the left of Roosevelt but during the isolationist debate had switched to the side of Senator Robert Taft, and he ended up leaving *Harper's* and working for the Republican Policy Committee in the Senate. (He was the first of several far-left liberals I came to know who over the years switched 180 degrees to far-right conservative. I've never really understood the switch but have wondered if it did not result from some personality instability as well as ideological conversion.) In connection with the Polkadot Gang piece, Leighton suggested I start writing what he called "crime in its social context"—take one of my fact detective cases and flesh it out with heavy fact, throw away the phony detective work, and develop the lives and social backgrounds of the criminals and their victims. Eventually George Leighton's idea of "crime in context" became an important base for my writing career—crime became, for me, simply a way of writing about human beings and our society, a matrix, a prism through which one viewed life.

But at that time, I was still writing a little of this, a little of that—occasional pieces for *Outdoor Life* and *Esquire,* minor pieces for *Harper's.* And always I wrote for the money market—Keller's *OD-AD-ID.* It therefore came as a shock when Keller announced one night at our house that he and the magazines were moving to Philadelphia permanently. He asked me to go with them. I asked for time to think it over.

I believed we should go. I didn't know how I was to make a living cut off from Keller's *OD-AD-ID*. True, I could stay in Chicago and write crime stories for his magazines. But the market would shrink. I couldn't make a living in other magazines—*Harper's* was paying $250 or $350 for a piece, and while that was more than Keller's 2 cents a word, it took far longer to do a *Harper's* piece. *Outdoor Life* was paying $100 or $150, *Esquire* $150, the same as Keller. Living in Winnetka, we were spending more money than ever before. And we had a child. I didn't see how we could risk it.

Fran disagreed. She had never liked or trusted Keller—it turned out she was right—and now she saw a chance to get free of him. She had confidence that I could make a living by writing, either writing for him at long distance or not writing for him at all, which is what she really preferred. Fran is small but she can be tenacious. She won—I reluctantly agreed to stay. Keller didn't like it. I wondered if I had made the mistake of my life.

6.

Ben Abramson, the Chicago bookseller, not only sold books but also read them and he liked to encourage young writers. At that time some booksellers used to call themselves bookmen, as booksellers no longer do or can. Ben gave me a book I'd never heard of, H. W. Fowler's *Modern English Usage,* and told me to read the article on rhythm. I had never read anything about writing so exciting. I use it yet. I was beginning to take writing seriously, under the guidance of Ben Abramson and Francis Nipp in Chicago, of Frederick Lewis Allen and George Leighton in New York. I had begun to think vaguely of writing a book about the Upper Peninsula of Michigan. Ben Abramson said it might fit into a series of regional books that Alfred A. Knopf was publishing. He would write to Knopf.

When I had been in high school, Alfred Knopf had been one of my idols—Knopf, colleague of H. L. Mencken, publisher of Mencken's *American Mercury* and of European novelists, probably the most distinguished publisher in America. Never had I dreamed I might write for him, might even meet him. I sent him an outline for a book on Upper Michigan; he sent me a contract, itself as beautifully printed as Knopf's books, and that summer Fran and I went to Upper Michigan to do the research.

I did a lot of it in bars in the mining and logging towns, talking to miners and lumberjacks and trappers and union men. Often Cal Olson, an old man who stayed with us at Three Lakes, took me, introducing me to men who remembered the old days. We concentrated on the Marquette Iron Range and the copper range and the forestland between. Fran and I did research in the Marquette County Historical Library. The Marquette County district attorney, John D. Voelker, had just published, under his pen name Robert Traver, *Troubleshooter,* a book about some of his cases, and I went to see him in his hometown, Ishpeming. There was not much law to practice in Ishpeming unless you worked for Cleveland Cliffs, the big iron-mining company, or the Northwestern Railroad; and Voelker, a liberal Democrat, was intuitively on the other side of the table, on the side of the workingmen and their unions. So he ran for district attorney and was reelected several times. Voelker was the only *natural* writer I ever knew. He published rough drafts. His writing was, basically, yarn spinning. He wrote many books, none in my opinion, so good as his first, *Troubleshooter.* When he finally was defeated for reelection, Governor G. Mennen Williams, urged by labor, appointed him to the Michigan Supreme Court, where he did a liberal's work in workmen's compensation cases. While there he published his first novel, *Anatomy of a Murder;* the Book-of-the-Month Club took it, Otto Preminger made a film of it, and Voelker, rolling in dough for the first time in his life, resigned from the court to devote himself full-time to fishing. I felt he had betrayed labor but who am I to say what he or anyone else should do with his only life? We remained close friends, and this led by chance to a chain of events that had an important effect on my life, as we shall see.

Knopf responded promptly and briefly to my manuscript (he was always prompt and brief)—it was satisfactory and he was putting it into production. I was disappointed; I'd hoped he would be enthusiastic. Francis Nipp said, "He's published books before." The first time I met Alfred Knopf he seemed forbidding, even intimidating, with his memorable head, his dark distinguished face, his Continental manner, his carefully chosen clothes. But as I came to know him,

I liked the Algonquin for a more practical reason: It was within walking distance of almost everywhere I had to go. Virtually the whole United States communications system was crammed into a postage-stamp-sized patch of midtown Manhattan, roughly from *Harper's* down on Thirty-third Street up to Knopf in the Fifties, with most of the magazines and, later, television networks, in between. I'm afraid I've come to think that New York is not a good place to be unless you are either young—young enough not to mind the tense jostling crowds, the hopeless traffic jams, the harum-scarum taxi rides—or unless you are rich—rich enough to keep a car and driver. At that time I was not rich but I was young and I loved it.

Sometimes I went to lunch with Frederick Lewis Allen. In high school or college, I had read Allen's *Only Yesterday,* the best book till then on the 1920s in America, and, like Knopf, he had long represented to me something unattainable. But here I was having a drink with him and his wife in their home, an old narrow three-story brownstown on Murray Hill. Allen was a slight man, so slight he looked almost frail, with sparkling eyes and a ready laugh, a wise man with an endlessly inquiring mind. He taught me much, most of it by the editing he did on my stories, cutting, tightening, endlessly tightening, and pointing up. Now and then he pronounced a dictum, such as: Never be afraid to address the reader directly, to write, "As we shall see," or "Let us first study the slum itself."

I was learning something else. New York editors, at least the good ones, felt cooped up in New York, isolated from the rest of the country. Time and again they asked me, "What's the mood of the Midwest these days?" Or "What's going on out there?" Just as farm boys yearn to go to New York, so do New York editors yearn to know what's on the farm boy's mind. Sometimes they sounded almost anxious. I myself had a strong sense of place, a sense that I belonged to the Midwest. I have always done a lot of place writing, that is, descriptions of places, setting of scenes, using place as a character in the story. I began to see that living in the Midwest, not in the East, was, for me as a freelance writer, a tremendous advantage. The Midwest was where things happened, it was, almost, the locomotive of America. And I as a writer almost had it all to myself, while in New York little happened and writers were scrambling all over each other. I was receiving an unanticipated bonus for staying in Chicago instead of going east with Keller.

And something else was happening. Just as New York editors got a new perspective on the Midwest from me, so was I, in New York, getting from them a sense of the nation that was new to me. Having grown up and worked only in the Midwest, my view of the nation had been parochial. Suddenly, as I talked to New York editors about their concerns, I began to develop a new and more spacious view of the nation—its problems, its politics, its concerns. From editors I got something more valuable than editing—insight and perspective.

8.

It is therefore not surprising that my next *Harper's* piece was on Muncie, Indiana, which, in the 1920s, had been studied by two sociologists as "Middletown," a typical small Midwest city. Now in wartime I went there to see what was going on. I found Muncie a three-shift war-plant boomtown, with all its irritations and wrenching change, all its crowded raw rough living, all the influx of hillbillies from Kentucky, all the misgivings about the future. This was my quintessential American heartland. For the first time, on this story I did true heavy-fact legwork. I interviewed at length all sorts of people—local United Autoworkers union leaders, rank-and-file workers, businessmen, farmers in their fields, the county agricultural agent, courthouse politicians, soldiers on furlough, people in cafeterias, the editor of a local newspaper, a professor at the local college, a banker. From several I drew their life stories. And repeatedly I asked: "What do you hear people talking about these days?" This was the heart of my story—what Midwesterners were thinking in wartime. I was working on such issues as labor, wartime strikes, national politics, postwar international relations. I thought then and I still think that you can get a more accurate sample of public opinion by that kind of lengthy interviewing than by the so-called scientific public-opinion polling so pervasive today. Certainly you can get nothing reliable whatsoever by a telephone poll. The *Literary Digest* went under because its telephone poll predicted FDR's defeat. Time and again today's polls are wrong—they missed the Reagan landslide—and yet ordinary people and even politicians who should know better continue to rely on them. Even face-to-face polling is unreliable—all too often it is done not by trained reporters but by inexperienced young people and housewives spitting out questions from a questionnaire fastened to a clipboard; nobody talks to a clipboard. But the greatest problem with polling is that if you ask a man directly to state his opinion on specific issues, he may or may not give you a straight answer. And he may even say he doesn't know because, privately, he thinks it's none of your business—many "undecideds" or "don't knows" are really so firmly decided that they don't want you to know it. On the other hand, if in a careful, probing, hour-long interview you ask him not what he thinks but, rather, what he hears his neighbors and friends saying, he will tell you what he himself is really talking and thinking about. Often at the end of an interview, I would ask about issues he had omitted. Highest on that list was postwar international affairs; almost nobody was thinking about that.

I was beginning to think about writing another regional book, one on Indiana. Alfred Knopf was interested. But in November of 1944 I was drafted into the Army.

THREE

UP FROM SLAVERY— MAYBE

1.

At the time, the Army seemed to me a total waste of time. Looking back, I don't quite think so, and I only wish I had given a little more of myself to it. I couldn't; I hated it; it was the force that was tearing me apart from Fran and Cindy and tearing up my writing career just as it seemed to be getting started. (Too bad about me!) I was sent to a camp near Little Rock, Arkansas, for infantry basic training. In my memory it rained or sleeted every day down there that winter, and Arkansas was nothing but an ocean of freezing mud. In Europe the Battle of the Bulge began, and the training cycle just ahead of mine was cut short and the troops flown directly into the Bulge only about twelve weeks from civilian life. We expected the same. I declined an opportunity to apply for Officer Candidate School—I had the romantic notion or an underdog's instinct that I preferred to remain an ordinary soldier, and I had acquired the enlisted man's dislike of officers, a dislike not diminished by a young second lieutenant who kicked me while I was lying prone firing a rifle. I shed no tears when, later, a grenade blew off his hand.

Fran and Cindy came down to Little Rock and lived in a rooming house run by a woman who drank paregoric and turned their gas heater down when she thought they were asleep. After basic training, I was sent not to the Bulge but to a school for military police and then to CID School—the Criminal Investigation Division. It made sense; criminal investigation differs little from reporting. Spring came, the war in Europe ended, and the Army formed its first CID platoon; I was assigned to it and we were shipped to Camp Boerne, Texas, a tent camp outside San Antonio in hilly desert country. Fran and Cindy lived in a tourist cabin. The manager gouged them on the rent. People in Texas and Arkansas resented the influx of Yankee soldiers and profiteered on them. Nevertheless, to me, after the winter mud of Arkansas, the CID in Texas seemed like paradise. The others in the platoon were about my age, thirty, professional men, a New York lawyer, several FBI men, a Border Patrol officer, several detectives. I had more in common with them than with the eighteen-year-olds in basic training. Mostly we played poker and drank whiskey and went on "jeep training marches"— actually long trips to resort hotels in the Texas hills or along the Mexican border. Every one of us was made a noncommissioned officer. The lieutenant in command explained to me that he gave me the lowest grade, T-5, technician fifth grade, because he knew I was writing pieces for Keller and for *Harper's* to supplement my Army pay and, if I didn't have heavy duties, as a staff sergeant would, I would have more time to write. It was fine with me. Fran too—I had been in the Army only a few months and was already almost a full corporal.

We were transferred to Houston and assigned to work with various Houston detective squads, I with homicide. Soon we were ordered overseas but first given a short furlough. Fran and I went to New York and stayed at the Algonquin and went to the theater, a last fling. We went to the Stork Club or "21," I forget which, and when we entered the maître d' greeted me coolly, "Good evening, Corporal," but I gave him a large tip, ten or twenty (my Army pay was about thirty dollars a month); and when we departed, he bowed and said, "Good night, sir." I wrote another *Harper's* piece, the only piece of pure rhetoric I ever wrote, called "Anything Bothering You, Soldier?" It is the question that an examining officer periodically asks each enlisted man. Nearly always the answer is "No, sir," for the soldier knows the taunting rejoinder of comrades if he complains: "Your story is very touching. Would you like to see the chaplain? Or use the crying room?" My piece voiced all the enlisted man's complaints about the Army and about civilians profiting from war. Frederick Lewis Allen thought it bespoke the bewilderment and discontent so many Americans felt. Fran and I were having lunch with him and his wife the day President Truman announced we had dropped the bomb on Hiroshima, and Fran said she thought that, to secure peace, we should share the bomb secrets with the Soviets, and Fred Allen looked at her as though he thought she'd lost her mind.

I went to a shipping depot in California, prepared to go to the Pacific, but almost at the last minute I was taken off the shipping order and in February of 1946 discharged. I came out resolved never again to write for fact detective magazines, a form of slavery. Reality soon overcame that resolve. But only briefly.

2.

The editors at *Life* had read my *Harper's* stuff and asked me to travel the Midwest and do a long piece about its postwar mood. I spent six weeks crisscrossing the territory between Columbus, Ohio, and Smith Center, Kansas, between Louisville and Bismarck, North Dakota. I did several trick things, like taking a train from Chicago to Waterloo, Iowa, called *The Land of Corn*, but I also did a lot of serious reporting—the life story of a young combat veteran who was marrying a girl and buying a farm in Nebraska; the economics and politics of farmers' cooperatives in Minnesota; an assembly line in Kansas City; race relations in Lousiville and Indianapolis; conversion from tank building to auto building in Michigan; anti-Semitism in Indianapolis; the small-town clubrooms of beer-drinking legionnaires; strikes and lockouts in Ohio and Indiana. Everywhere I asked, "What are people talking about?" and "Who runs this town anyway?" and "How'd it change during the war—will it go back to the way it was?" It was an extension of what I'd done on Muncie for *Harper's*. Finished, I sent some five hundred pages of notes to *Life* and asked what they wanted me to carve out of them. Nothing, it turned out—*Life* simply did not know what to do with this flood of facts and paid me five-hundred dollars and kept but never published the manuscript. But I never considered the work wasted.

I learned a lot about the Midwest. So did *Life*—years later a friend on *Time*, John Steele, told me *Time* and *Life* were still consulting my Midwest notes. And some of that legwork came to inform other things I wrote. I was getting my Midwest into national perspective.

I went back to Muncie and did a piece for *Harper's* called "Middletown Revisited"—Muncie in transition from war to peace. In Muncie too I found a man, Court Asher, who had been a kleagle of the Ku Klux Klan and was the publisher of a hate newspaper containing anti-Negro and anti-Semitic articles; and I did a separate piece for *Harper's* about him. And I went back to my second regional book for Knopf, *Indiana: An Interpretation.* It became quite a different book from the Michigan book. Instead of the earlier book's picturesque explorers and lumberjacks and miners, the leading characters of *Indiana* were politicians, union leaders, industrialists, writers. Instead of the wilderness, the atmosphere was that of farm revolt, strikes, violence, industrialization, and bored farm-town life. Since I had hated my childhood, one would have assumed I would hate Indiana and I was therefore surprised to find a certain affection suffusing parts of the book; and when I quoted the old saw "Many good men come from Indiana, and the better they are the quicker they come," it was more in jest than in bitterness. I wrote about Theodore Dreiser and Hoagy Carmichael and Cole Porter, who had come from Indiana, and James Whitcomb Riley and Booth Tarkington, who had stayed there. I tried to re-create the down-to-earth hard-to-beat Hoosier, a shrewd salesman at heart, who emerged in this century. I resurrected several Indiana politicians from the Civil War period, for it was the Civil War that had put Indiana into business—made the Indiana Republican party one of the most powerful in the nation, while native American capitalism flourished. The longest single chapter in the book was on Eugene V. Debs, the Indiana railroader turned Socialist; indeed, Debs almost ran away with the book (and that may explain why the conservative booksellers of Indianapolis did little to sell the book). But though *Indiana* sold poorly, for me it was not wasted. Just as the *Harper's* pieces on Muncie and the Klan and Asher and the *Life* legwork had helped prepare me to do *Indiana,* so did *Indiana* prepare me for my future work and for politics.

3.

Fran and I bought a house on Sunset Road in Highland Park, Illinois. This changed our lives. We had hoped to find a house in Winnetka but couldn't. Although both Highland Park and Winnetka were North Shore suburbs of Chicago, they differed vastly. Winnetka was inhabited mainly by well-to-do Anglo-Saxon Republican Protestants. Highland Park was equally well-to-do but, although normally Republican, in recent years it had been casting a surprising number of Democratic votes. Moreover, it was far more heterogeneous than Winnetka, and it had a large Jewish population. Indeed, although the population was less than a third Jewish, many people thought Highland Park overwhelmingly Jewish, I suppose because the Jews were highly visible, being successful and influential—prominent doctors and lawyers and businessmen. The town's bookstore was owned, as a hobby, by the wives of two successful Jewish lawyers and two successful Jewish businessmen; the husband of one was a leader in national Jewish affairs, especially the Anti-Defamation League of B'nai B'rith. We initially became acquainted because of the bookstore, to which I naturally gravitated, and when the ladies who owned it learned I was a writer, they and their husbands welcomed us and they became our close friends and many of their friends became ours. All these people and many more whom we met were readers; all were better educated and better traveled than I; all were thoughtful people interested in ideas. Many years later, one of them paid us the ultimate compliment: Chatting with Fran on the phone, she caught herself short and said, "Oh, I forgot—you're not Jewish." If Fran and I had settled among the conservative Protestants of Winnetka, I do not know how our lifeiight have turned out but I am sure it would have been far different from what it became under the liberating influence of our new Jewish friends.

The house on Sunset Road had the look of a low cottage snuggled into the side of a slight rise of land. White clapboard, it had two closed-in porches, a thirty-foot low-ceilinged living room with a fireplace. Across the street was a big park, and Cindy walked through it to school. I have always worked at home—one of the principal attractions of freelancing is that you don't have to go to an office. I appropriated the big downstairs bedroom—Fran says I always get the best room in the house—and installed my fifteen-dollar oak desk, which Fran had bought secondhand, and my secondhand typewriter, and my father built bookcases to line the walls. A good place to work. I always referred to it simply as "my room," not "my study," just as I referred to "my work," not "my writing." And Sunset Road was a good place to live, the first home Fran and I had had for our marriage. Always before it had been a string of hotels and apartments, motels and parents' houses, one rented house, all temporary, transient. Now we had a solid base. E. M. Forster wrote in *Howard's End:* "London was but a foretaste of this nomadic civilization which is altering human nature so profoundly, and throws upon personal relations a stress greater than they have ever borne before. Under cosmopolitanism, if it comes, we shall receive no help from the earth. Trees and meadows and mountains will only be a spectacle, and the binding force that they once exercised on character must be entrusted to Love alone. May Love be equal to the task!"

When I proposed marriage to Fran, I had told her not to expect a little white house in the suburbs with a picket fence. (No doubt I was playing Jake Barnes in *The Sun Also Rises*—trying to protect myself against too deep a commitment because of Barbara's betrayal.) Now our little white house in Highland Park had a picket fence. I took care of the yard myself, mowing the grass, planting a garden, raking leaves, doing all the things that a conventional young father in the suburbs does. One Saturday while I was atop a ladder putting up storm windows, wearing my old Army fatigue shirt, an Army captain from the nearby fort came by and called up to me, "You own this house, soldier?" I replied, "Yes, Captain" (not "Yes, sir"). He said, "My wife and I want to rent a room in it." "No, Captain," I said and went back to putting up storm windows, avenged at last on the officer corps.

I was buying and reading a lot of books, especially modern European fiction—Camus and Sartre, Dostoevsky and Kafka, Forster and Celine, Koestler and Malraux. I read F. Scott Fitzgerald and Mark Twain and Ring Lardner, *The Scarlet Letter* and *Moby Dick*. And *Madam Bovary* and *Of Human Bondage*. Why I had not read them sooner I do not know. They seemed to speak to me directly, especially Camus and Kafka.

In these years, however, I was too careerist, and too preoccupied with getting my private life organized at last, to integrate all this closely into my work and my life. Twice married, now with a permanent wife and child, with mortgage payments and car payments, I was almost obsessively concerned with the precarious existence of a freelance writer. Whether I might have as a young man written serious fiction, I'll never know, though I doubt it. By the time many years later that I could afford to risk attempting a novel, I had written heavy fact so long that the novel I wrote was highly topical—I had a vision, but it was a vision not of life but of a particular political situation. Similarly, I now think it was careerism that prevented me from becoming seriously interested in politics until I was thirty-seven years old. Even in college in the 1930s, I had been so preoccupied with getting a diploma and a job that I took no part in the peace marches and other campus protests of the time. World War II largely passed me by. I was aware that I was living through great events but even though I was in the Army, I was not really engaged with those great events—was intent on getting out of the Army and getting on with my writing and my private life. After the war, even writing for serious magazines about public events and public officials did not engage me in politics—they were stories to be written, not events to be myself involved with. Not until Adlai Stevenson first ran for president in 1952 did I really become engaged in politics and public life. I have remained so ever since.

Often Francis and Mary Ellen Nipp came out to our house on Sunset Road from Chicago for long weekends, and again we talked about writing and listened to recordings. I was buying and savoring old jazz—Bix Beiderbecke and Benny Goodman, Mezz Mezzerow and Sidney Bechet, Jack Teagarden, Duke Ellington and Fletcher Henderson and Jelly Roll Morton and above all Louis Armstrong. As a bachelor in Chicago, I had scorned jazz vocalists, except for Anita O'Day, had liked only instrumental jazz. But now on Sunset Road after Fran and I were married, I also came to enjoy Bing Crosby and Russ Colombo and Frank Sinatra (his songs, not the man). Fran had taught me to sing and when our children came along we taught them to sing, family singing.

And Francis Nipp brought me now to serious music—Beethoven and Mahler, Stravinsky and Moussorgsky, Debussy and Ravel and Sibelius. I took to it immediately. Why this should be so is mysterious. I remember as a child on Brookside Avenue listening to Caruso records my father brought home and played on the old Victrola. I hated it. Why my father, uneducated, a carpenter and contractor in a rough business, the son of a rural man, loved music I have never known; but he did. Where he got it I do not know. Perhaps from his parents. But I never knew his father—he died before I was born—and I remember his mother only when, in her dotage and incontinent, she came to live with us briefly before she died. Her daughter Ethel played the piano in a neighborhood theater near Brookside Avenue and she played beautifully, another aunt tells me, especially, for her own enjoyment, serious music. In any case, I had nothing to do with serious music from childhood till I was about thirty-two, living on Sunset Road. (Francis Nipp even brought me to chamber music, which I would not have thought possible.) Great music moves me deeply, as does good writing, and to this day, listening to certain passages of Beethoven, I find myself weeping for human aspiration.

Late too I came to looking at paintings. I think it was not long after Fran and I were married that I took to going to the Chicago Art Institute, with its marvelous collection of French Impressionism, and to the Museum of Modern Art in New York. Why I went, I have no idea. Nothing in my childhood or youth presaged it. But I found I responded to Picasso and Matisse and Cezanne somewhat as I did to Kafka and Camus and Beethoven, and after I became a collaborator and friend of Ben Shahn, I spent more and more time in museums and galleries.

All this, I now see—literature, politics, music, art—was a late education and late coming of age. I have no idea why it took so long—nor why it happened. But I have often wondered whether Fran is not the key to it. When I met her, she read no serious literature, she knew nothing about politics, she liked only popular music and even that only if she could sing or dance to it. She knew nothing of art. Yet it is possible that, by giving me an emotional base to build a stable private life on, and by attending to my writing, she set free something in me that had up till then been locked up.

4.

In Peoria, a tough railroad and industrial town in downstate Illinois, two powerful homegrown Midwestern forces collided as they had throughout the bitter strikes of the 1930s and '40s, management and labor, in this case a stubborn, Roosevelt-hating railroad president with his anti-union fervor and his armed strikebreakers ranged against quiet determined hometown strikers; a union man was shot dead on the picket line and the railroad president was later ambushed and killed near his home. I did a piece about it for *Harper's* that went further in the direction of George Leighton's crime-in-context than anything I had yet done. *Reader's Digest* picked it up, and then the *Digest* editor who handled it, Paul Palmer, suggested I look into the recent Centralia mine disaster; he had heard that none of the people involved, including the union officials and the governor of Illinois, seemed to have done anything to prevent it. I had been dimly aware that a coal mine at Centralia, Illinois, had exploded and killed more than one hundred men earlier that year, in March of 1947. I checked clippings. I would do the Centralia piece; the *Digest* would pay me twenty-five hundred dollars plus expenses. The *Digest*, with a big circulation and plenty of money, often planted stories in smaller magazines, including *Harper's*, then picked them up; with the *Digest's* encouragement, I told Fred Allen of *Harper's* about Centralia. He was dubious but agreed to read it. I set forth, driving away alone from our house on Sunset Road and heading downstate, thinking, "I've got a hell of a nerve, starting out single-handed, with nothing but my typewriter, to overthrow the political machine of the governor of Illinois." It turned out that the Centralia story changed the course of my career.

FOUR

A MINE DISASTER

1.

Whenever I started out to do the legwork on a story, I was afraid. I knew so little about the story; the people I would interview knew so much. Moreover, far from the brash reporter of *The Front Page*, I was diffident, at times almost shy. And when working for a newspaper, I had felt I had a right to ask questions, since a newspaper has an inherent right to keep the public record; but as a magazine writer, I did not feel equally privileged, I was after all writing a story which I hoped to sell at a profit to a magazine, whose publisher hoped it would entertain his readers and thus attract advertisers. Had I the right to question a coal miner's widow?

The only way to cure my hesitancy was to master the facts—to study the public record until I knew more about the case than anybody directly involved. (Some years later, when I had to make public speeches, the only way I could make my knees stop trembling was to remind myself, "You know more about this subject than anybody else in the room.") A law school maxim says, "On cross-examination, never ask a question that you don't already know the answer to." Interviewing a person reluctant to talk is like that. You already know the answer, the facts; what you want from him is how he sees those facts, and you want it in his own words. From this flow not only flavor and atmosphere but also character. (The lawyer wants only the answer that he already knows to come out; I want everything to come out, especially the human details that make the bald facts real.) And another interviewing rule on a difficult story like Centralia: First you study the printed public record before you interview anybody, then you interview the people involved who are likely to want the story told, and finally you interview those who are likely not to want it told, the hostile witnesses. I was learning that the success of an interview depends upon your advance preparation—on how well you know the facts before starting the interview, on whether you know when you arrive what questions you want to ask and in what order (if you ask the hardest first, that may end the interview).

Over the years I developed certain interviewing techniques. I learned it's best to interview a person in his home, since he will be at ease there and the objects that surround him will suggest questions to you and remind him of details. If this is not possible, see him at his office, or at a restaurant he knows, but almost never in your own home. If you want to interview a man of high position, such as a governor or the president of General Motors, you will have to arrange an interview formally through a secretary, but if you telephone the secretary and cannot reach him, never leave word for him to call you back—he won't. Just keep calling him. If you want to interview an ordinary private citizen, such as a miner's widow, it is best to do nothing by telephone—simply knock on the door. (It is hard to say no to someone face to face, easy on the telephone.) I always used a notebook and pen or pencil, not a tape recorder. A recorder tends to put a person on stage, as a TV camera does, and you want him to speak to you in his own idiom, not a stagy idiom. Nonetheless, never walk in on him with notebook and pen in hand; you may frighten him. Instead, keep them in your pocket when you start the interview. How to get them out? Simple—ask a first question that requires a numeral for an answer, such as "When were you born?" Nobody would expect you to remember his birth date; you take out your notebook and write it down, and from then on the notebook is out. I write down everything he says. If I don't, he will notice what I'm making note of and what I'm skipping; he will then start talking to the notebook, not to me, and there again we introduce a stagy note. Of course, I have encountered people who absolutely forbade any note-taking; I developed a memory trick for dealing with them. Another device: If you want someone's life story and he is reluctant, tell him your own life story; he may find threads in your life that match his own, and soon he is telling his. You should always try to establish an understanding, a sympathy even, with everyone you interview, even the villains; they're not totally evil, only human, and what you want to discover if you can is why they behaved the way they did.

2.

In the case of Centralia I went first to St. Louis since the *St. Louis Post-Dispatch,* being nearer, had covered the mine disaster better than the Chicago papers. The *Post-Dispatch* had taken the lead in exposing the failure of Governor Dwight Green to do anything to prevent the disaster though he had had ample warning that the mine was dangerous. It also had exposed how Illinois mine safety inspectors collected political contributions to the Green machine from coal mine operators (but not at Centralia). The *Post-Dispatch* editors gave me access to their files. They were proud of what they had done and well they should have been; they helped me, for they wanted the story told.

What had happened at Centralia was, briefly, this: The coal dust raised by cutting coal in a soft-coal mine is explosive. If it is allowed to accumulate on the floor and walls of an underground tunnel, any spark, such as one from an electric motor, can ignite it; the first small explosion throws more dust into the air, and that dust explodes, and so on—a self-propagating chain reaction of explosions that can reach throughout the mine. To minimize the danger, federal and state safety regulations require rock-dusting—sprinkling pulverized rock on top of the coal dust, thus damping it down. Rock-dusting will not prevent but it will limit an explosion. For years, the miners who worked in the mine called Centralia No. 5 had known that it was dangerously dusty, and that the company was rock-dusting inadequately. The state mine inspector, Driscoll O. Scanlan, agreed and repeatedly reported that the company was violating the state mining regulations, but his superior, Robert M.

Medill, director of the Department of Mines and Minerals in Springfield, handled his reports as routine. Medill told Scanlan to ask the miners to be patient. They refused. The union, Local 52 of the United Mine Workers of America, instructed William E. Rowekamp, a miner and the local's recording secretary, to write direct to Medill and finally to Governor Green himself. The letter to the governor said Inspector Scanlan had tried to get the mine cleaned up, but his superiors had done nothing and the mine was still dangerous—"In fact, Governor Green, this is a plea to you, to please save our lives." Nothing resulted. Less than a year later, on March 25, 1947, the mine blew up, killing 111 men.

I could not document all this in St. Louis but I saw enough to prepare me for interviewing in Centralia and to tell me that I must nail down each document in Springfield—if I could.

Centralia, a town of sixteen thousand, was no coal camp like the dismal company towns of West Virginia. It looked like any Midwest farm town—wide main street lined with low flat-faced stores, sprawling railroad shops and the ungainly black coal-mine tipple on the edge of town. I began by doing background legwork on the town itself—talked, as I had in Muncie, to farmers, businessmen, housewives. Only after that did I interview the people directly involved. And I began with the miners and miners' widows, for they were the victims, the aggrieved, and would want the world to know. I did not want the story to turn into debate among the powerful—Governor Green, and John L. Lewis of the UMWA, and the coal company. I wanted it to be the miners' story, the story of helpless ordinary people, what Spaniards call *los de abajo*, "those from below."

I went to see William Rowekamp, the miner, a tall lanky man in overalls, in his little house on a small plot of ground where he kept a garden. I told him what I was doing and said I'd like to talk to him. He said something like "Go ahead." He was by nature taciturn but soon he was talking freely, explaining mining to me, talking about his life, about the town, the mine, the union. He told me* how he, as recording secretary of Local 52, had written the "save our lives" letter, as it came to be known, to Governor Green, written it at his

---

* I am uncomfortable writing "he told me." In writing my stories, I kept myself entirely out of them and never used the first person unless it was unavoidable. In these memoirs, however, I feel I must, for here I need to show how I did the legwork and wrote the stories. My purpose then was to tell stories about other people; now it is to reveal myself. Which is why writing memoirs is harder.

cluttered little desk in the living room, typing it carefully and affixing the union seal—"I dassen't use the seal without it's official." When we finished, I asked him whom else I should talk to, as I always do, and he gave me the names of other miners. For the next few days, I went from one to another and I took to hanging around the bare upstairs union hall and they became so used to seeing me that they paid little heed, always what a reporter wants. I came to understand that the miners considered themselves a breed apart, superior to men who toiled on assembly lines or farms. The danger they were always in was part of the fascination. They were fierce fighters for their rights. They had a strong sense of being the underdog; talking about the hearse that had taken the body of a man killed in the disaster away from the scene, another told me, "I'll bet it's the only time he ever rode in a Cadillac." I felt as he did. Whence came my own underdog feeling I don't know. Perhaps from my size—as a kid I'd been small. Perhaps from seeing what the Depression did to my father and hearing Roosevelt talk about "the forgotten man." Perhaps from Wolfgang the Communist and his ironworker father. Perhaps from starting my own work at the bottom—stock gummer and copyboy for the Associated Press, cub reporter for the *Times,* and early member of the first newspaperman's union. Perhaps from my legwork in the Chicago slums on criminals and their victims. Wherever it came from, it remained a powerful force in my life and my writing.

To bring the disaster home to the reader, I needed to talk to the miners' widows, and several miners suggested I talk to Joe Bryant's widow: She had lost both her husband and her son. I found her four-room house near the railroad tracks in a cluster of houses around another mine shaft. She was a big woman, forty-four years old, sitting on a sofa in her parlor. She had borne eleven children. Two had died in infancy. Her husband, Joe, had gone to work in the mine at fourteen. When their oldest son, Harold, got out of the Army, Joe had helped him get a job in the mine, and Harold married a girl of fifteen named Ruth. Twice Harold was hurt in the mine. It frightened Ruth. She told me, "He always said if he was going to die he might as well die in the mine." (I interviewed her separately from Mrs. Bryant. I tried never to interview two people together.)

I asked Mrs. Bryant to tell me everything she had done the day of the explosion. Her second son had heard about it soon after he got off work at 3:30. He picked up his wife and went to his mother's house. She had heard nothing, was frying potatoes and sausage for supper. He went to Harold's house and told Ruth there'd been an accident in the mine and took her to Mrs. Bryant's house. They all sat down to wait for news.

As word of the disaster spread through town, some of the miners' wives went out to the mine. Cold rain turned to sleet toward dark; for warmth they went into the washhouse, a dim-lit barnlike structure where each morning their husbands took off their street clothing and put on their miners' clothing and each afternoon showered and changed again. Each of the wives, many of them already widows though they didn't know it, found her husband's clothing hanging from high racks and each sat down under her husband's clothing to wait. Mrs. Bryant and Ruth stayed at Mrs. Bryant's house. Throughout the long evening, neighbors kept coming in to see if she'd heard anything, and her son kept driving back and forth to the mine, but there was no news. They waited all night. At 9 A.M. Ruth's sister came to the house. She took Mrs. Bryant's oldest daughter into the kitchen and whispered to her, then she took Mrs. Bryant to the kitchen. "It was Harold," Mrs. Bryant told me. "They'd found him, they'd talked to a man who had seen him. I just said, well, I guess that's true." Nobody knew how to tell Ruth, so nobody did tell her, and when she came into the kitchen the whispering stopped, until "two merchant men" from town came to the house and told her. Mrs. Bryant waited all week and heard nothing. Past midnight on Saturday the two businessmen returned and asked how Joe had been dressed. Overalls and a white sweatshirt, she said—she knew because she'd just mended them. It made her cry, remembering for me. She told them he'd been carrying a pocketknife, a white cigarette case, and a whistle with a chain on it. They left. Not until nine o'clock the next morning did they return. They had Joe's cigarette case and his whistle. And they also brought some notes he had written. Harold had been right at the heart of the explosion, he had died instantly and violently. But Joe and thirteen other men had been some distance away, and they ran into the maze of tunnels, looking for a way out, deadly fumes pursuing them, till they came to a dead end, trapped. Here they lay down on the floor—breathable air would last longest down low. Waiting, they wrote notes to their wives. It must have taken Joe Bryant a long time to die; his notes were carefully lettered, not scribbled. Mrs. Bryant showed them to me. In one, on a page torn from a time book, he wrote: "Dear Wife fro Give [forgive] me Please all love you Be shure and don't sign any Paper see Vic Ostero [a warning against signing away her compensation rights] My Dear wife good By. Name Baby Joe so you will have a Joe love all dad." The baby was born three months later, a girl, and Mrs. Bryant named her Joedy.

While Mrs. Bryant was talking to me, several small children were playing around her legs, pulling her dress to distract her. On the wall hung two new pictures tinted in color and gilt-framed, one of her husband and one of Harold, and to each was affixed a little plaque: "Know Ye These Presents Certify That This is an Heirroom [*sic*] Portrait of Joe Bryant made from a photograph taken in the year 1935 and faithfully portrayed by the artist in a manner and quality befitting a work to be passed on to future generations as a priceless heirloom." She told me "a man from Chicago came round selling them." She paid $18 for each frame and $18.75 for Joe's picture; the man from Chicago "threw the boy's picture in." She received $1,000 from the union's welfare fund and nearly $1,000 from other welfare sources; the funeral took most all of this. For five years she would also receive $44 a week from state industrial compensation and Social Security combined. After five years the industrial compensation would stop, and after her children reached eighteen the Social Security would stop too until she herself reached sixty-five.

I asked her whom she blamed. She said, "I don't know nothin' about the mine, I wouldn't blame no one, them accidents happen, seems like it just has to be." And she said, "There ain't much to say. It don't pay to say much." But her young daughter-in-law Ruth said, "Everybody says it was just one of those things, it was their time to go, but I don't believe it. If that mine'd been safe they'd still be here."

When I left her and drove away down the black dusty road, I thought that from her and Rowekamp I'd gotten half the story. The other half I would get in Springfield—politics and the government bureaucracy.

The sources there would be unfriendly but by now I knew so much that I was prepared. What I needed most was access to the files of the Department of Mines and Minerals and an interview with its director, Robert Medill. When I went to his office in the cavernous statehouse, he was not there but his deputy told me I could go through the files—they'd all been published anyway during various investigations, he said. But it turned out they hadn't. I found a mountain of paper accumulated over five years. Piled up, the evidence was devastating. Every three months for three years, Inspector Scanlan had visited the Centralia mine and written a report listing many violations of the mining laws and regulations and sent it to the Department of Mines and Minerals in Springfield. His constant finding was that the mine was dangerously dusty and should be rock-dusted. I was able to trace the progress of his reports almost hour by hour as they wound their way through the bureaucracy. The department director, Medill, a genial politician, had not seen Scanlan's first thirteen reports (1942 through 1944); his deputy handled them. When a report arrived in the department's high-ceilinged old office, Medill's secretary stamped it "Received" with a time and date and put it on the deputy's desk. He read some but not all the reports and gave them to a girl in the typing pool; she corrected them for grammar and spelling and compressed their recommendations into a form letter addressed to the mining company, beginning, "The Department endorses" Scanlan's recommendations, and hoping the company would comply with them and let the department know. Medill's deputy signed the forms and they were mailed to the company's Chicago office. Not only did the company not comply with Scanlan's recommendations, it did not even bother to reply. In 1942 federal mine inspections started, and the federal inspector found the same violations and made the same recommendations as Scanlan. The company ignored them too.

In November of 1944 the union local instructed its recording secretary, Rowekamp, to complain directly to Medill that the tunnels were "very dusty and dirty.... They are getting dangerous." Medill's deputy sent Scanlan to investigate; he reported as he had all along. This time the company did sprinkle some of the tunnels, and in early December Rowekamp thanked Medill, but by the end of December the mine was as dusty as ever—the company's mine manager explained that in the winter "you can sell all the coal you can get out. So you want top production, you don't want to stop to rock-dust." Early in 1945 Scanlan telephoned Medill, who told him to write to him, and Scanlan did, saying that the mine should be shut down long enough to dust because "the coal dust in this mine is highly explosive." (This letter too was duly stamped "Received" with the time.) This time Medill acted—himself wrote a letter to his friend William P. Young of Chicago, the operating vice-president of the Centralia mine's parent company, Bell and Zoller, one of the big Illinois coal companies. "Dear Bill," Medill's letter began, and he recited Scanlan's and the miners' complaints and closed, "Please let me have any comments you wish to make. . . . Very kindest personal regards." Young replied to "Dear Bob," pleading the wartime demand for coal and a shortage of manpower and hoping things would improve so they could do what Scanlan wanted—"With kindest personal regards." Medill sent the correspondence to Scanlan and told him to ask the miners to be patient. They told Scanlan they'd wait till April, a hint of a wildcat strike.

In mid-March Scanlan took the unusual step of seeking Medill out at a statewide mine-safety meeting. Scanlan said to me, "I told him that the mine was in such condition if the dust became ignited that it would sweep from one end of the mine to another and probably kill every miner in the mine." Medill replied, according to Scanlan (Medill later denied it), "We will just have to take that chance."

The union local brought charges against the mine manager and asked the state Mining Board to revoke his certificate. Medill's deputy investigated and the board rejected the charge. Then the local voted to prefer charges against both the mine manager and mine superintendent. This paper too was stamped "Received." Medill convened the Mining Board and told Scanlan to come to Springfield. But there he shunted Scanlan aside to a coal operator, who tried to persuade Scanlan to withdraw one of his recommendations. Scanlan refused. Scanlan had been told he could go before the board, but though he waited all day in the outer office, the board never called him and it dismissed the union's charges.

Next the miners turned to their own union, to district headquarters in Springfield. Its bureaucracy proved as impenetrable as the state's, and its ties to management equally as close as the state's. It did nothing, contending it could do nothing. Actually the union could have called Medill and told him to get the mine cleaned up within *x* number of days or they'd strike every mine in the state. The Centralia miners made one further try—they voted to authorize their local's recording secretary, Bill Rowekamp, to write directly to Governor Green, and he did, the "save our lives" letter. The four officers of the local union signed the letter in the mine washhouse. Of the four, only one, Rowekamp, lived through the explosion. It is doubtful that Governor Green ever saw the letter until after the disaster; one of his aides sent it to Medill with a memo asking for a careful investigation—in effect, Medill should investigate himself. It is only sixty yards from the governor's office in the statehouse to the Department of Mines and Minerals office but this journey took the memo and the miners' letter two days. (By now I knew the importance of what is called telling detail and I knew you get it only by looking for it so I paced off that sixty yards.) Medill's reply cited the war effort and the Mining Board's actions and said conditions were no different from what they had been for the last ten or fifteen years. Medill suggested the governor tell the miners that he was calling their letter to the attention of the Mining Board. This apparently satisfied Governor Green's aid, for he dictated, over the governor's signature, such a letter. Medill summoned Scanlan to Springfield and "severely reprimanded" him, as Scanlan remembered it, and he also told Scanlan's political sponsor, a state representative, that he was going to fire Scanlan, Scanlan was convinced that only his sponsor saved his job.

In an unrelated action, the coal miners struck nationwide, and President Truman ordered the mines operated by the federal government under an enforceable safety code. This generated another mountain of paperwork, and federal authorities wrote to the company, requesting compliance with the inspector's recommendations, and the company said that "a substantial" number of the reported violations had been corrected and more would be when possible. The federal officials renewed their request, the company promised fuller details soon—but, as I wrote in the *Harper's* piece, "before any other correspondence arrived to enrich file CMA81-swr, the mine blew up." Copies of Scanlan's last report and the federal inspector's were still thumbtacked to the bulletin board outside the washhouse.

I spent days in the department's office, making notes on scores of federal and state inspection reports, correspondence, transcripts of the six hearings and investigations into the Centralia disaster. When I finished, I went to see Medill in his home on Lake Springfield. He was a large jovial man with a loud blustering voice. He offered me a drink—"I know you reporters"—but I declined. To bring him alive in the piece, I led him through his life story—how he started as a miner but switched to management, his gay life in the 1920s, his entrance into Republican politics. He had worked in 1940 for the election of Governor Green, and Green had rewarded him by appointing him director of the department.

When I left him, I thought that his interview, plus the heavy documentation, gave me the other half of my story. I stayed on in Springfield, interviewing legislators, union men, lobbyists, coal operators. All seemed to agree that coal mining could never be made safe until we stopped sending miners underground and instead developed the process of converting coal into gas in place—"underground gasification." I tried to see Governor Green but could not get an appointment. I went up to Chicago and interviewed an executive at Bell and Zoller, operator of the Centralia mine. I sent a telegram to John L. Lewis in Washington asking for an interview; I received no answer. So I started to write.

It was not that simple. The story was big and complex, jumbled up in my head, all disorganized and out of order. Once a writer had told me, "We always send our stories in too soon," before we've made them the best we can. (The temptation is almost overpowering: The minute a writer finishes a draft he can hardly wait to have someone read it.) Not only that—we also begin to write them too soon, before we have really digested the materials. I took a few days off, drove alone to Upper Michigan, and went fishing, trying not to think about Centralia, letting it marinate. This succeeded. Driving home I began to see the story. The principal elements were the town of Centralia, the miners, their union, the mine operators, and state and federal authorities. The story's impact would depend on two things: bringing the characters alive, and piling up the evidence of the history of the disaster. I dumped my notes and documents on my desk in the house on Sunset Road. In writing *Indiana,* I had organized research material on three-by-five cards but now I was developing a new organizing system. I went through my notes and documents, giving each a code number and numbering the pages, and when I came across something I wanted to use, I typed it out, triple-spaced, keying it to code and page numbers. I then cut up the typing line by line into slips of paper. I moved the slips around, arranging and rearranging them. Thus I was able to fit a striking quotation or telling detail into its proper place in the main narrative line. When I had the slips all arranged as I wanted, I pasted them together. The result was a long scroll. I rolled it up and put it on my typing table and began writing, letting it unroll and fall to the floor as I used it, and when I came to the end of the scroll, the rough draft was done. A few years later, when one of these scrolls became more than 150 feet long, running out of my room and out the front door and across the lawn, I abandoned the system and used 5-by-8 cards.

Francis Nipp had once remarked that he didn't see why a factual article couldn't be constructed as a work of fiction is constructed—according to the three Cs: Conflict, Characters tightly related to conflict, and Controlling idea. (By the last he meant that you must absorb the material well enough to be able to say what the story is about in a single sentence. If you can't do that, you haven't sufficiently conceptualized the story.) On Centralia, as I shuffled the bits of paper into the scroll, the complicated parts of the story began to fall into place. I decided to structure the piece like Beethoven's Fifth. The first movement should strike all the principal themes, with the explosion itself dominant; each succeeding movement should develop the themes one by one, until at the climax we return to the explosion. If the story worked, you should get narrative pull and even suspense—not the suspense of surprise, as in a mystery novel, but what Francis Nipp called the suspense of fine inevitability, as when you see a boxer get hit hard just once during the first round and you watch him in successive rounds knowing that though he tries to stay on his feet he is surely going down—and he does, about the sixth round.

I write a rough draft on the typewriter, never in longhand, never dictating. I do my thinking at the typewriter. I write a very long, very awkward, very loose rough draft and I write it fast—probably fifty pages a day on the average (triple-spaced). In rough draft, I am mainly trying to string the material together in an organized way, sometimes doing little more than eliding a document or an interview. Over the years I taught myself to cut about one for six. That is, if I want to end with a final draft of 20 pages, I write about 120 pages of rough draft. I put most pieces through six rewrites. Just before I do the final rewrite, I ask Fran to read the draft to me aloud, for by then I've marked it up so heavily that it is hard to read, and I have become too close to it—I can no longer see an awkward sentence or a dull passage but I can hear one. To me, writing is more like carpentry than art.

I get to my desk between 9 and 9:30 A.M. and work till 5 or 5:30 P.M.; I do not work evenings; I take Saturday off, and on Sunday deal with correspondence and other accumulated afflictions and plan the next week's work. I never end a day written out, with nothing more to say; instead I stop at quitting time by the clock and type out a quarter or half page of notes about what exactly is coming next; thus in the morning I can readily take up where I left off—getting started, on a story or on a day's work, is hardest. I make a carbon of everything, especially the rough draft, and at the end of each day I get the carbon to a safe place out of the house, for fire is the nightmare—I once knew a writer who worked two years on a novel in a cabin in the Minnesota woods, and the cabin burned down and, with it, the only copy of his novel.

Although in the rewrite I move sentences and paragraphs around and do heavy rewrite, trying to allow no rough-draft sentence to survive to the final draft, cutting every line that I am especially pleased with, doing the real polished writing on rewrite, not rough—in spite of all this the basic organization remains about the same because the basic conception remains the same. It takes me about as long to rewrite as to write the rough. Talking to Arthur Schlesinger and Dick Rovere, I found that they wrote entirely differently, only a few pages a day, slow writing, tight writing, and their rough drafts resembled final drafts far more closely than mine. But it took all of us about the same overall length of time to do a story from start to finish; I spent my time on rewriting, they on rough drafting. There is no "right" way to write; there is only *your* way.

Francis and Mary Ellen Nipp chanced to come out for the weekend just as I finished the Centralia rough draft. He read it and said, "If *Harper's* publishes this in anything like its present form, it'll make your reputation." It was the longest piece I had yet written, some eighteen thousand five hundred words in final draft. What made it so long and what made it so powerful was the relentless documentation—I kept piling it up and piling it up and piling it up—showing that for years everybody had known the mine was going to blow up but nobody had stopped it. After it was published, another editor told me, "As I started to read it I thought it was going on and on, but then I realized you knew exactly what you were doing." When Frederick Lewis Allen read it, he wrote me an extraordinarily (for him) long letter, which ended, "This office is rocking with cheers." He paid me five hundred dollars for it and made it the lead story in his March 1948 issue, the longest story *Harper's* had ever published in its hundred-odd years. *Reader's Digest* paid me twenty-five hundred dollars and published it at unusual length in its April issue. Allen tried to nominate it for a Pulitzer Prize but the Pulitzer Committee had no magazine category. Russell Lynes of *Harper's* got Ben Shahn to do some drawings to illustrate it. They published twenty-four of his drawings but he kept making more and in the end developed the material into several major paintings. Later Fran and I bought his collection of thirty-two Centralia drawings.

3.

Years later a Hollywood agent who had become interested in my work asked, "Don't you ever write any happy stories?" I'm afraid not, or almost never. It bothered me, however, that it is the fate of the writer of heavy fact to thrive on other people's troubles. This can be justified if one argues that serious heavy fact is intended not only to entertain the reader but to educate him, to alert him to something amiss in our society, even to bring about reform. And I was bursting to tell the world the awful truth about the mine disaster. But such efforts rarely bring about real reform. The Centralia story may have helped Adlai Stevenson defeat Governor Green, who was up for re-election that year, and it helped bring about a new federal safety code with teeth in it. But today, more than thirty years later, coal mines are still blowing up for roughly the same reason that Centralia blew up, and gentlemen in executive suites are still talking about underground gasification of coal. It is true that a later piece of mine in *The Saturday Evening Post* helped defeat a venal politician and still another got a man out of prison, where he had been sent wrongfully. But such things are rare. I have always interviewed and sympathized with *los de abajo,* as I have said, but I have no illusions about being the Sir Galahad of the downtrodden. No doubt Joe Bryant's widow got not one cent more in compensation for her husband's death than she would have had I never written the Centralia story.

What, then, can be the justification of heavy fact writing that, in effect, exploits misery? I am afraid it has to be literary. Only rarely did I work as an "investigative reporter," that recently overused and misunderstood term—produce evidence of a crime before the authorities knew there's anything wrong. Rather, I came along after the event; I studied all the available evidence and interviewed everybody I could find and I put the whole thing together. This is what a magazine writer can do that a newspaper reporter cannot—put a story in perspective, conceptualize it. Thus what began as a story about a mine disaster became a study of heedless immovable government bureaucracy, politics, profit-seeking business, indifferent unions, indifferent public officials, and a general breakdown in the machinery that runs our lives. I conceived the story in a sense that a hard news story cannot be conceived. It is a literary notion. I do not mean to compare the sublime with the ordinary, but Napoleon's retreat from Moscow existed as a fact but did not exist as an epic event until Tolstoy created it in *War and Peace.* Nor did the retreat from Caporetto exist until Hemingway wrote *Farewell to Arms.* Nor, if I may say so, did the Centralia mine disaster exist in that sense until I conceived and wrote my piece.

PART TWO

FREELANCE WRITER

FIVE

THE BIG SLICKS

1.

The 1940s and 1950s were in the United States the great days of magazine journalism. *Life* and *Look, The Saturday Evening Post* and *Collier's, Harper's* and *The Atlantic, Reader's Digest,* yes and the women's magazines, *McCall's* and *Cosmopolitan* and *Redbook*— each stood for something, each had its own character, and all published serious nonfiction—what was called heavy fact. They influenced our lives until the 1960s, when television drove them from the temple.

It was my good luck to come along when the "big slicks," as mass circulation magazines printed on glossy paper were called, were at the peak of their circulation and their profits, their prestige, and their power. I wrote for all of them.*

Francis Nipp had been right—publication of the Centralia story in *Harper's* did make my reputation, not with the reading public at large but with what counted more to a writer: with editors of other magazines. *Harper's* was one of the high-quality, low-circulation (and low-pay) magazines that the editors of the big slicks read seeking new writers. Editors' doors theretofore closed suddenly opened;

---

* Some of these magazines folded; some were later revived; some are still being published but they are vastly different from what they were then.

73

indeed, editors began coming to me. And in working this miracle, the Centralia story had considerable help. Frederick Lewis Allen told me that *Harper's* could not publish all the pieces I could write (one year I had pieces in eight of its twelve issues) and, furthermore, *Harper's* could not pay as much as I would need if I intended to make a living as a freelance writer of heavy fact. The big slicks, Fred Allen thought, were the answer. I needed to spread my work among them. To do this, he said, I needed an agent, and he offered to help me find one, though he hoped that in the future I would continue to write for *Harper's* as well as the big slicks. He spoke to Harold Ober, the agent, on my behalf.

At that time there were, I suppose, several hundred men in the United States who called themselves literary agents. Most were of utterly no use to a writer and the reputation of some with editors was so bad that they were actually a hindrance. Many advertised for clients, charged fees to read manuscripts, and prated about "helping" unknown writers, whereas what they did in fact was exploit them. Only a handful of agents was effective and professional. They never took on unknown writers, would not even read their work unless an editor or another client introduced them. The literary business in New York is a small, tightly knit world. No figure in it commanded more respect than Harold Ober. He had formed his own agency in 1929; by the time I came along he had two associates, Ivan von Auw and Dorothy Olding. Ivan handled books, and nobody paid much heed, since in those days books made no money, the big money was in the magazine market. Dorothy Olding handled magazines but so did Harold Ober himself. (Today the situation is reversed—the money is in books, not magazines.) Harold Ober had been F. Scott Fitzgerald's agent (and had helped raise his daughter). He was agent for William Faulkner, Philip Wylie, Catherine Drinker Bowen, J. D. Salinger, James M. Cain, John Gunther, Paul Gallico, and a long list of other well-known writers. He handled the best-selling novels of Agathie Christie; he also handled the poetry of Langston Hughes.

As I moved along, I developed associations with editors, particularly with Ben Hibbs and Stuart Rose of *The Saturday Evening Post,* that closely resembled a staff writer's relationship, and frequently I dealt directly with them on a piece, with little intervention by

Harold Ober.* But I always kept him informed, I always submitted the completed manuscript first to him and asked him to pass it along to the editor if it seemed all right, and I always paid his 10 % commission. Some writers in similar situations, like Richard Rovere, could see no reason to employ an agent, and once when an editor asked Rovere to come in and discuss a piece she wanted written and she offered him, let us say, a thousand dollars, he replied, "Let's pretend I have an agent. He would get ten percent. Why don't you pay me eleven hundred?" But my situation was different from his. For me, an agent can do many things. He can talk money to an editor, which I am not good at. When he thinks I am due for a rise in rates, he can ask the editor for it (and he knows what the market rates are). He can handle subsidiary rights—paperback rights to a book, foreign rights, film and dramatic rights. He can handle important administrative matters such as obtaining copyrights and renewing them. He can read a contract expertly, and film contracts are extremely complicated. He is in the market—and I am in Highland Park. He is talking to editors all the time; he goes to them with manuscripts and they come to him with ideas for pieces they want written. He knows what editor will want which piece. A good agent can introduce you to editors who would not otherwise see you. Soon I was going to New York about five times a year to have lunch with editors or visit them in their offices, discussing story ideas; Harold arranged it.

But above all, an agent gives an author support. Freelance writing is at best a risky, lonely business. The writer is all alone at his typewriter or in the editor's office. He needs support. He needs someone to turn to in difficult times. An agent like Harold Ober can be a rock to cling to in a stormy sea. The Ober agency became my agent in 1948 and it is still my agent, though we never had so much as a handshake agreement.

When people hear the term "literary agent," they probably think, if at all, of a flashy figure who talks glibly and rapidly, wears checkered vests, and commutes between Hollywood and New York. Harold Ober looked more like a banker than an agent. He had a modest suite of offices on Forty-ninth Street just off Madison Ave-

---

* Hibbs was the editor in chief of the *Post*. Rose was a senior editor.

nue, but he himself was a million miles removed from Madison Avenue and all it stands for. A white-haired New Hampshire man, with a dour manner but wide-open sparkling blue eyes, he was courteous almost to the point of seeming deferential—but not quite. He said little but listened to everything. I sometimes met editors in his office, and while we talked, Harold sat silent, looking down at his desk and doodling with a delicate letter opener, only rarely looking up at us from under his bushy eyebrows to make a comment in a low monotone (or more likely answer a question). After Harold's death and von Auw's retirement, Dorothy Olding became head of the agency.

Sometimes my pieces were my ideas, sometimes an editor's. When I submitted an outline showing the bare bones of a story and telling the editor how I would handle it, he would either decline it or tell me to go ahead. *The Saturday Evening Post* never made an assignment. But if the *Post* liked the proposal, it was almost certain to buy the final manuscript unless you blew it, for the *Post* editors, unlike many, knew what they wanted. And they not only bought pieces; they also published them—and the point of anybody's writing is, of course, to publish. I would always rather have a *Post* expression of interest than a firm assignment from several other magazines. Over the years, *Life* gave me a number of assignments but not until 1965 did they actually pay the full price for and publish anything I wrote. (*Life* and other magazines, if they made an assignment but decided not to publish the story, would pay a "kill fee" for it, usually about 15 % of the agreed full price.) Full price was between fifteen hundred and twenty-five hundred dollars plus travel expenses, and Harold Ober persuaded the *Post* editors to raise my rate and they also began paying me a generous bonus on nearly every piece. Moreover, the *Post* would give you a decision in a week and pay you in another, important to a freelance.

Advice to would-be writers usually includes advice to "slant" your story at a particular magazine. I would put it a little differently. I have always written with a reader over my shoulder—an editor who, while I was writing, in my mind was peering over my shoulder, watching; and if I was tempted to overwrite a sentence, or leave one loose, or collapse upon a cliché, or otherwise write something idiotic, the imaginary reader would frown; I would fix it. Early he was Frederick Lewis Allen of *Harper's* or Alfred Knopf, and then Stuart

Rose of *The Saturday Evening Post,* and there have been others. A generation of *New Yorker* writers must have written with the painfully gentle face of William Shawn peering over their shoulders. I wonder if editors really know how all-pervasive they are.

Many readers who remember *The Saturday Evening Post* at all remember it as a magazine that published pleasant stories by Clarence Budington Kelland and about the super tractor salesman Alexander Botts, articles about motion picture stars, cartoons, and color photographs. It did. But it also published fiction by William Faulkner and F. Scott Fitzgerald and serious nonfiction by Jack Alexander and Alva Johnson, two of the best journalists of our generation, and the rather somber pieces that I wrote. The *Post* was, in a few words, not unlike the network television that took away its audience—both frothy and serious.

In Harold's office I would meet Stuart Rose of the *Post* on his regular Tuesday trip to New York from the *Post* offices in Philadelphia in search of manuscripts. Stuart Rose remained my editor at the *Post* throughout my career there, and we became good friends. Yet he was in many ways a rather unlikely collaborator for me. He had begun his own career by writing a column on men's clothing for *The New Yorker.* He himself was a fancy dresser—derby hat, tightly furled umbrella, splendid neckties. He looked the classic man-about-town. In New York he stayed at the St. Regis and he lunched at Voisin and other then fashionable and expensive East Side restaurants. He was primarily a fiction editor. The *Post* had editors who were themselves expert nonfiction reporters and writers, like Jack Alexander; Stuart chanced to handle me because he was the man the *Post* sent to New York to see writers and agents. He lived in the country outside Philadelphia and kept a stable, went riding early every morning, and every weekend went fox hunting. He had been a U.S. Army cavalry officer and had never lost his love for the military life. And he was a Republican. Stuart Rose and I had little in common except a love of writing and a confidence that, as he put it, a good reporter could report anything. This was the way he handled me: not restricting me to a single narrow category of stories, such as crime, but rather giving me leeway to report and write what I wanted to or what he was interested in. It was, really, an ideal editor-author relationship.

Not only did he know what he wanted; he knew how it ought to be put together. Twice he returned manuscripts to me with memos telling me how to reorganize them, almost paragraph by paragraph, and I did his bidding without understanding it at all, and only when I saw the stories in proof did I realize how right he had been. Stuart Rose and Ben Hibbs and their associates at the *Post,* Fred Allen and George Leighton and their associates at *Harper's*—Rose and Hibbs and Allen and Leighton are all dead now, and it may be that other great editors like that are still alive, but I know of none. (Of course, it may be possible that in those days I myself was more open to editors' suggestions than later, after hardening of the writing arteries set in.)

2.

During the next fourteen years, I wrote for the big slicks. Many of the stories were the sort of thing I'd begun doing for *Harper's*— George Leighton's crime-in-context. But now I was really doing it—doing the hard interviewing it requires, collecting all the evidence I could about the crime, its actors, and their world. Many of these stories could as well have appeared in *Harper's* as in the *Post* or *Cosmopolitan.* Indeed, several of them did.

A few examples:

I did a story about a Chicago boy of twelve who killed his seven-year-old playmate. His mother had been married several times and was often absent. The story somewhat resembled the Centralia story—I found a thick file of correspondence between her and the school, where her boy had gotten in trouble time after time. Repeatedly she had appealed to Chicago's ponderous legal and educational machinery to take him and raise him; nothing resulted; the street raised him. Now what to do with him? The jury found him guilty of murder, and the judge sentenced him to twenty-two years in the penitentiary—the state of Illinois had no reformatory, no proper place to put him. As at Centralia, the state had failed.*

For some time I had wanted to do a story about capital punishment. I found a recent Ohio case, and Dorothy Olding took the idea to Herbert Mayes, editor of *Cosmopolitan.* Murl Daniels was

---

*I lost track of him but I have the impression that efforts were made to find a place for him in other institutions. I don't know what finally became of him.

twenty-four, the son of poor, unlettered hill people in a Columbus, Ohio, slum. He had suffered brain damage at thirteen when a truck hit him and soon he began getting in trouble—sexual delinquency, petty thievery, stealing cars. He was bounced around by the courts and by doctors and social workers and put in a reform school. Though not psychotic, he was diagnosed as a psychopathic personality, that wastebasket of psychiatry which contains so many dangerous men, men whom the psychiatrists cannot label psychotic or mentally defective but who have some inexplicable emotional and mental problem that drives them to make war on society. When at twenty he held up a storekeeper, the court sentenced him to an institution at Mansfield that was called a reformatory but was really a harsh maximum-security prison. Paroled after three and a half years, he teamed up with a violent moron he had met there, and they began holding up taverns. In one they killed the owner. They decided to get even with a prison guard who had, they thought, mistreated them at Mansfield. They couldn't find him but found his superior, one of the head guards, and they executed him and his wife and daughter. On the run, they killed a young man to get his car. At a roadblock, police captured Daniels and killed his partner. Daniels was sentenced to death by electrocution.

I wrote the Daniels story largely from interviews—interviews with everybody I could find who survived the crimes. His father told me, "Society raised him and now they'll kill him." He was right. Society knew of nothing to do with him but to execute him. I went to the Ohio State Penitentiary and witnessed the electrocution, lined up in the death chamber with the prison warden and other witnesses about eight feet in front of the electric chair while the chaplain and two guards half dragged him in, praying with the chaplain, mumbling while he was strapped into the chair, "Our Father who art . . ."; then a little blue light over his head went off and a red one on and a dynamo hummed, and his body jerked once, hard, and he strained forward against the heavy straps, a little wisp of blue smoke curling up from the electrode on his bare white leg. I never witnessed another electrocution.

"The Chair" was a grim story. In publishing it, Herbert Mayes of *Cosmopolitan* showed considerable courage. I doubt that anybody who has witnessed an execution favors capital punishment. I never knew a prison warden who did. No one, of course, can condone what Murl Daniels did; the world lost little when it lost him. Nonetheless, the idea of the state's closing in to take the life of a man it helped to raise is difficult to support.

Killers do not always come from the slums. Teen-age children of the middle class kill too. And sometimes, writing about them, I was struck by the parallels between their lives and my own. Milton Babich was nineteen, the son of respectable parents in a suburb of Milwaukee. The Babich and Birmingham families lived only a few blocks apart; their children went to high school together. Kathleen Birmingham was not quite eighteen. She fell in love with Milton Babich. They planned to get married. Kathleen became pregnant. They could not bear to tell their parents. They decided to elope. But Kathleen had a kid sister, Pat, who was a great tease. Kathleen and Milton came to believe that Pat knew Kathleen was pregnant. They thought she was teasing them about it. They feared she would tell their parents. Milt told her that she must stop talking about Kathleen's pregnancy because the neighbors would talk and embarrass their parents. She just giggled. He killed her. He was sentenced to life imprisonment.

My piece consisted almost entirely in the texture of the lives of these youngsters and their families—hardworking father, mother with few interests outside her children, the honor roll, a long dress for the senior prom, college plans, strict parental rules. After Kathleen became pregnant she and Milton Babich talked about little else. "The more we thought about it," Kathleen told me, "the more we dreaded telling our folks. We'd disgrace them." Nothing in Milt Babich's life showed criminal tendencies. If ever a crime had a social context, this one did—and the context was the rigid morality of the middle class in 1949. Such a crime is almost unimaginable today. One has to reread the Babich story to realize fully what is meant by the phrase "the revolution in morals" of the 1960s and 1970s.

In some such cases, I began concentrating not only on the social context of the crime but also on the mysteries of human behavior. On the night of September 15, 1951, in Ann Arbor, Michigan, a quiet college town, a nurse was walking home alone on a tree-lined street from the hospital where she worked. Three teen-age boys came along in their car and one of them, Bill Morey, got out, stalked her with a heavy rubber mallet in his hand, and, coming up behind her, smashed her skull for no apparent reason. They did not even know her. Two of them were eighteen, and the other seventeen. They had no felony records. They came from respectable families. They were nice-looking boys, well spoken, neat, mannerly. The town was shocked. More than one parent thought, as one told me, "There but for the grace of God goes my own son." Why? Why did they kill? I went to Ann Arbor to try to find out.

Ordinarily I would have talked to the parents of the boys last, but in this case I realized that if the parents, especially the parents of Bill Morey, would not talk to me freely, I had no story; so I went to see Mr. and Mrs. Morey—I might as well find out now.

The Moreys lived in Ypsilanti, Ann Arbor's neighboring town. I went there by bus and walked to their house. Bill Morey lived all his life in the same house on a quiet street shaded by fine old trees. His house was a low rambling cottage, comfortable and lived in, Bill Morey's father had been born in this house.

Mr. and Mrs. Morey were reluctant to talk to me. The whole thing was over, Bill was in prison, they did not want to relive it—but they actually relived it every day, they dated everything in their lives as "before *this* happened" or "after *this* happened," this terrible shattering event, the murder. I told them I was trying to write not a sensational story but a thoroughgoing study for a serious magazine that would try to discover *why* it had happened. They said they themselves did not know why. I talked awhile about my own life, saying that in high school I had done many of the same things Bill Morey had done—drinking, driving fast and recklessly—and I talked about Fran's and my own daughter, approaching adolescence with all its perils.

At length they began responding, Mrs. Morey nodding her head at things I said, volunteering something about Bill—they both still called him that. I said I wanted to find out what kind of boy he really was, not what the newspapers said, and they began to tell me. For an hour and a half. I did not press them on anything and, leaving, I said I'd like to come back tomorrow. I did, and we talked for two hours, and the day after that for four hours, and the following week for more.

But although I spent weeks talking to them, to the families of the other boys, to their schoolteachers, to their friends, and to everybody else I could find who knew them, to their lawyer, to a psychiatrist who thought Bill a psychopathic personality, and to the boys themselves in prison,* I never really answered the question of why—why they had killed. Why?—to a reporter, it is the only question that matters and it is the only question he can never really answer.

An important part of the boys' lives was the world they lived in—Ann Arbor, the quiet, somewhat stuffy college town, and its rowdy neighbor, Ypsilanti, where they themselves lived, a blue-collar town turned upside down by the war, which drew thousands of hillbilly workers to the Ford Motor Company's huge Willow Run bomber plant, hillbillies who after the war went on relief and turned Willow Run into a slum and whose children ran wild and smoked marijuana and drank; Ypsilanti and the automobile with its roaring exhaust became characters in the story. So the Morey story combined crime in its social context and inquiry into the roots of human behavior, an ambitious undertaking. I made a book of a longer version of the Morey story and there I had room to expand the material on the boys' society. It was well reviewed. But it didn't answer "why?"

I did a piece about racial segregation—the web of legal and traditional barriers that kept Negroes† jammed into a Chicago ghetto. This was 1947, before the civil rights movement, long before the Negro revolution; it was not only before the Supreme Court struck down school desegregation but even before it struck down the restrictive real-estate convenant that helped keep housing racially segregated. I wanted to do not an article, crammed with demographers' statistics, but, rather, a story about a man. James Hickman had been a sharecropper in Mississippi. He was deeply religious and deeply devoted to his children. In 1945 Hickman came to Chicago seeking to better his lot. He found a job in a steel mill and began looking for an apartment so he could bring his wife and eight children up from

---

* Morey and one of his confederates were sentenced to life in prison—in Michigan life is not parolable; the third boy was sentenced to twenty-two years to life.
† Instead of "blacks," the word in current usage. I write "Negro" for historical reasons, as does Ralph Ellison.

Mississippi. He looked for months—apartments open to Negroes were desperately scarce. Finally he found a place, an attic room atop a four-story tenement owned by a Negro. The three youngest children slept with Mr. and Mrs. Hickman; the others slept in the other bed. The attic had no electricity, no gas, no heat, no water. But it was shelter. Soon, however, the landlord decided to cut the building up into smaller apartments in order to produce more rent. To do this, he wanted to evict all the present tenants. He and Hickman quarreled, and the landlord said if he couldn't get the tenants out any other way he'd burn the building down. On January 16, 1947, the fire occurred. Four of Hickman's children were killed in the fire. The coroner's jury could find no innocent origin for the fire but no hard evidence of arson.

Hickman was convinced that the landlord had burned the building. He sat alone and spoke to the dead children. He bought a .32-caliber automatic pistol. He shot the landlord dead. He was indicted for murder. An organizer for the Socialist Workers party, two Chicago labor leaders, and two civil liberties lawyers formed the Hickman Defense Committee. After the first trial ended in a hung jury, the defense committee brought pressure to bear on the Chicago political machinery and reached an agreement with the state's attorney, and the judge found Hickman guilty of manslaughter and sentenced him to two years on probation.

In preparing to do the piece, I read Gunnar Myrdal's *An American Dilemma* and other books, but only for my own background information—I wrote the piece almost entirely from interviews, especially interviews with Hickman and his wife and with the landlord's relatives. I simply told the story of Hickman's and the landlord's lives and their world—the world below.

I fear that in describing all these stories here so briefly and so baldly, I have robbed them of their humanity. And that I may have seemed to reduce human suffering to journalistic techniques. If this is so, I am sorry. While I was doing the work, while I was listening to these people and writing about them, I felt quite otherwise, and I like to think I helped the reader feel some of what they felt.

Russell Lynes of *Harper's* asked Ben Shahn, the artist, to do some drawings to illustrate the Hickman story. Ben and I talked in the quiet paneled library at *Harper's.* He was a big burly man with the kindest eyes I ever saw. He asked what Hickman and his family looked like and I described them; he asked about the tenement and I drew a sketch for him. (*I,* drawing sketches for Ben Shahn!) We became friends and collaborators. Soon I did another piece for *Harper's,* one about the Mecca Building in Chicago, once a fancy apartment house on the South Side, now a vast slum, and about the lives of some of the two thousand–odd Negroes who lived there in misery, and Ben came to Chicago to see it and illustrate the story, wonderful drawings. He and his wife and Fran and I took to spending weekends in each other's homes. When I visited New York, Ben would take me on walking tours of the Lower East Side slums where he had grown up; and when he came to Chicago I would take him on walking tours of the Negro ghetto and the white criminal slums, where dwelt the people I wrote about. He believed that the human eye can really see nothing unless it is traveling slower than five miles per hour. I had known this intuitively all along—I never made notes on the appearance and atmosphere of a neighborhood from a car but always on foot. I like to think I saw things as he did.

I had known little about Ben's work but now I went to see all his pictures I could find. I came to love his slab-faced men, his savage portrayals of the persecutors of Sacco and Vanzetti, his passionate pictures suffused with liberal idealism. He had what most of us lack—a vision of life. His was a tragic vision. Yet he was a very funny man. He was fond of saying that Michelangelo, up on a scaffold painting the Sistine Chapel, hollered down to the pope, "What color you want the ceiling, boss?" Once at the height of the Senator Joe McCarthy madness an FBI agent came to see him, for he was considered by the McCarthyites a radical. The FBI man tendered his identification. Ben, instead of glancing at it perfunctorily and handing it back as most of us do, held on to it and gazed at it long and carefully, several times glancing up from it to stare at the agent's face. Finally he shook his head and said, "That ain't you." The agent protested. Ben just kept repeating it and also saying, "A nice-looking fella like you, you shouldn't let them make you carry a picture like that around. That ain't you." The agent retreated in disarray. Ben told me that once as a child he had come home from school late, and when he knocked on his apartment door, his mother had called, "Who's there?" and he had said, "It's me," and she had called, "That ain't you." He had been terrified. Later, on a day when Ben had received word that he had won some high international honor, his small son asked him to tie his shoe, and Ben said, "Not today, son, not today." Ben thought the most romantic experience of his life was a visit to the villa of a wealthy South American friend where, when he went to bed, he found that his hostess had sprinkled perfume on his pillow. During the years of America's prosperity in the 1950s, he and I thought to collaborate on a book about poverty in Appalachia; one of the regrets of my career is that we never did it. He once told me that I should write only about things I deeply loved or hated; it was, he said, the way he painted.

The Hickman story affected Ben powerfully and it influenced his work. Later, in a book, *The Shape of Content,* he traced the origins of one of his most powerful paintings, *Allegory,* to the Hickman story. It was a picture of a great red beast, part lion, part wolf, standing over the huddled figures of its child victims. Ben wrote that when Russell Lynes of *Harper's* first asked him to make the Hickman drawings, he had assembled visual material, then discarded it, for he felt the universal implications of the event transcended the immediate crime. He tried an abstract approach and discarded that too. He finally returned to "the small family contacts, to the familiar experiences of all of us, to the furniture, the clothes, the look of ordinary people." This had been my own approach. (I always made notes on the things in a man's apartment while interviewing him.) Of all the symbols he developed in his preliminary Hickman drawings, Ben used only one—a highly stylized wreath of the tongues of flame with which he crowned the Hickman house. When he finished his *Harper's* drawings, he could not get the story out of his mind. It had awakened memories—the tenement where he lived as a child had burned. The lionlike head, its mane derived from the tongues of flame over the Hickman house, became the painting *Allegory.* He tried to imbue that great red beast with all the terror he had ever felt about fire, and under its body he placed the figures of the four dead children, "which, to me, hold the sense of all the helpless and the innocent." Thenceforward, Ben repeatedly used the beast's fire-ringed head in his work. He gave Fran and me a rendering of it;

under it he lettered in Aramaic, "Where there is a pen there is no sword; where there is a sword there is no pen."

3.

The *Post*'s normal length for a piece was eighteen and a half pages, about five thousand words. So was most magazines'. This was good discipline for a writer—it forced you to write tightly, without an unneeded word. But some stories simply could not be forced into that straitjacket. Stuart Rose and Ben Hibbs knew it and occasionally would give me eight thousand or ten thousand words and print the piece as a "special double-length feature," or give me even more space and print it as a series of articles. (The Morey story ran as a four-part.) A few other magazines did the same.

As I have said, today there may be editors like that but I don't know them. Like television "news," printed articles have gotten shorter and shorter. Instant info. Recently I proposed an op-ed page newspaper piece comparing U.S. policy after the fall of Somoza with our policy in the Dominican Republic after the fall of Trujillo. (I had been U.S. ambassador there then.) *The New York Times* editor said it absolutely must not exceed 1,000 words. I asked for a double-part space. No. I wrote about 5,000 in rough draft, cut it radically down to 1,120, and submitted it; he turned it down—too long and not very good. He was right that it was no good—it couldn't be done in 1,000 words or anything like it. I sent it, rewritten at 4,500 words and pretty good, to *The Washington Post*. The editor liked it but regretfully turned it down: His absolute limit was 3,000. I do not blame these editors; they are following publishers' dictates. But under their rules they never would have published my Centralia story, at 18,000 words. They never would have published John Hersey's "Hiroshima"—to make room for *it*, the editor of *The New Yorker* threw everything else out of that issue. I am not arguing that my little piece on the Dominican Republic and Nicaragua was worth as much space as Centralia or Hiroshima. I am only arguing that an editor is supposed to have the freedom, and the judgment, to edit. His present course may make him extinct—if one has a computer to count words, who needs an editor?

Each of the stories I have presented so far dealt with a particular criminal case. Gradually, under the guidance of Stuart Rose, I began writing for the *Post* long series of pieces not on criminal cases as such but about subject areas—a series on abortion, another on divorce, another on school desegregation, a series on Joliet-Stateville Penitentiary in Illinois and one on the riot at the maximum-security prison in Jackson, Michigan, as well as a long series on Columbus State Hospital in Ohio and the care of the mentally ill, another long series on television, and another on criminal justice and why it sometimes goes wrong. These stories ran as serials in the *Post,* sometimes as many as seven installments. These were not midwestern stories, they were national stories. On abortion, I did most of my legwork in Los Angeles. On divorce, I did the legwork in Las Vegas and New York, in Los Angeles and Beverly Hills and Long Beach, California, as well as in Chicago, Toledo, and Brownstown, Indiana, attending court, talking to divorce lawyers, divorce judges, marriage counselors, law professors, and couples that were going through divorce.

My writing was changing in another way. Earlier, in the pieces about crimes, almost my entire effort had gone into packing into the story every single fact I had space for and, to a great extent, letting the facts speak for themselves. Now, in the desegregation and divorce stories, not only was I permitting myself to draw conclusions, but also my pieces were more consciously *written,* were not simply agglutinations of facts. In the divorce piece, for example, I wrote, "But he moved out and she sued him for divorce; and indeed the story is repeated so often that after a few days in divorce court you would think that every little ranch house in the suburbs is a little nest of hate." I even quoted the wonderful passage from E. M. Forster that ends, "May Love be equal to the task." I don't know why my work was changing. Perhaps it was the confidence that comes with experience—I'd been writing for a good many years by now. And perhaps I was now able to spend enough time on each story to feel, when I started writing, that I had become an expert on the subject, enough time too to allow me to reflect upon the facts—and to shape the language.

In publishing some of these stories, the *Post* showed considerable courage. At the time I wrote the abortion story, abortion was a far different issue from what it is today. Abortion was entirely secret and illegal, a crime in every state except to save the mother's life. Moreover, it was something never mentioned in polite society; the newspapers still called it "illegal surgery," not abortion. Once again I was proud that the *Post,* a family magazine, dared publish anything about it at all. (I saw other examples of editorial courage—in a story for *McCall's* I wrote a picture of the bloody butchering inside the Chicago stockyards; a major meat-packer threatened to pull his advertising out of *McCall's* if the magazine published it; Otis Wiese, the editor, defied him and published it as I had written it.) On abortion, I concluded that support was growing for medically therapeutic abortion, that it was growing less rapidly for abortions for socioeconomic reasons, but that in general the trend seemed to be toward more permissive laws. Neither I nor anybody else had any idea the trend would move so fast as to bring us to where we are today.

When the *Post* editors asked me to do a story on what had happened since the Supreme Court school desegregation decision two years earlier in 1954, they did not know exactly what they wanted but felt sure there was a story in it for them. I spent about two weeks floating around the Deep South looking for the story. South Carolina, Georgia, Alabama, Mississippi—it was all new territory to me, and eventually the South itself became the central character in my story. Like many northerners, I had tended to think of the South as monolithic, had not realized how much state differed from state, South Carolina from Mississippi, how great were differences even within one state—raw Birmingham had little in common with graceful Montgomery. But in the region as a whole, what struck me most forcibly was that I, a northern liberal, had never fully comprehended the breadth and depth of southern resistance to desegregation. The resistance's principal instrument was the Citizens' Councils, called White Citizens' Councils in the northern press. This, I thought, was the story—the councils, their leaders, and the South itself. Whether I could get the story was a different question. Southern segregationists were at that time suspicious of, if not downright hostile to, northern reporters, who, they thought, had used them ill. I managed. In the end I cast up accounts on the Citizens' Councils. I thought that at that time the councils were losing momentum and the Ku Klux Klan gaining. I thought anti-Semitism was on the rise and free speech on the decline. Labor unions were being hurt, for while their national organizations supported desegregation, most of their southern members opposed it. Negroes were leaving the Deep South. I thought violence might replace peaceable resistance and Birmingham was the most dangerous city. (Both opinions later proved correct.) I raised the question whether the Supreme Court's Fabian approach to desegregation had been a mistake, allowing resistance time to organize. Three revolutions, I thought, might in time, by altering the situation of Negroes, swallow up the whole issue—urbanization, industrialization, and farm mechanization. (I also thought that in the long run the only solution to the problem was miscegenation but I did not say so.)

The *Post* editors liked the series but thought it left the impression that desegregation could never be accomplished anywhere, so I did a fifth installment on successful desegregation in the border states and failure in Chicago (still, in the 1980s, probably the most segregated city in the nation). This was a national, not a regional, problem.

After the series was published, J. J. Simmons, a moderate council leader, called me up from Mississippi and told me, "They're tearin' down all the statues of Robert E. Lee down here and erectin' statues to John Bartlow Martin." I told him that had not been my purpose but I was glad he thought the piece fair. He came up to visit Fran and me and spent a night with us. (Fran had some American Civil Liberties Union literature lying on her desk in the kitchen; she quickly hid it.) We got along fine with Simmons, and both he and I thought it important, in those difficult days, to maintain some sort of North-South dialogue, even if only between him and me. Later the *Post* series was published as a book, *The Deep South Says Never,* and Arthur Schlesinger, Jr., contributed a generous foreword to it. Still later, at the 1960 Democratic national convention, southern delegates arrived wearing lapel buttons reading simply NEVER.

A series I did for the *Post* on the Jackson prison riot, as well as other pieces about other prisons, convinced me that big maximum-security prisons—still the heart of the American prison system—make no sense. Jackson Prison in Michigan blew up in riot in 1952, one of a wave of riots that swept the country like a contagion, as prison riots do. In a certain way, the Jackson prison riot resembled the Centralia mine disaster. Over the years, investigation after investigation had been warning that Jackson was some day going to explode. But nobody had done anything about it. The investigations had warned that all the ingredients of trouble were there—it was too big, too overcrowded, and its convicts were too diverse. Big—it was the biggest prison in America, with 6,569 inmates. Overcrowded— because Michigan's state mental hospital and its reformatory and its only other prison were overcrowded, Michigan had for years been using Jackson as a dumping ground, until by the time of the riot no cells could be found for more than 100 inmates, and they were sleeping on cots in the halls; and overcrowding means idle convicts with no prison jobs, and that means trouble. Diverse population— young first offenders thrown in with hardened criminals and psychotic killers: Jackson had everything, including 547 lifers (*Michigan* lifers, nonparolable), but also 307 men who could just as well have gone to the county jail, including 35 convicted of nonsupport, and it had 859 sex offenders and 126 sexual psychopaths. Jackson had no psychiatrist. But it had between 1,000 and 2,000 prisoners who should have been in mental institutions, not prison. Jackson was almost totally unmanageable—and everybody had known it for years.

I concluded that Jackson had not worked under the old system of iron discipline in the 1930s, not when discipline relaxed and the convicts ran it, nor when prison industry expanded, nor when "individual treatment" became fashionable. Perhaps it was time to conclude that Jackson wouldn't work under any dispensation. And the same could be said of most other American prisons.

This suggested, I thought, that prison itself is at fault. Its purpose is to protect society. But it doesn't. The most remarkable fact about the Jackson riot and the others in 1952 was that none of the inmates tried to escape. They simply wanted to vent their fury against their condition. Just so, the Negro rioters in the city streets of America in the 1960s did not attack whites; they wrecked their own slums. A riot never occurs in a prison honor camp. A few men walk away from one. But they never show the terrible tension and hatred they showed at Jackson. The pressures built up by prisons themselves cause prison riots. Parole boards know that a prisoner who adjusts well to prison life will not necessarily behave himself in free society. Did not this suggest that we were really teaching men to adjust to prison, not to the free world? That we were prisonizing them, not rehabilitating them? And 95 % of them return to live among us. Most of those go back to prison for new crimes. Prison controversy tends to polarize around whether convicts should be "coddled" or "cuffed." This, I thought, missed the point. We had known for years that we should separate the prisoners who could be rehabilitated from those who could not, should help those "curable" find their way back. But we didn't do it. We were manufacturing habitual criminals then turning them loose on ourselves.

One afternoon at Jackson a middle-aged inmate told me, "I got what I deserve. But the punishment never ends. This abnormal life, this regulated life, the dull, deadly, corroding monotony—you can't expect anything good to accrue from such a life. Of course we know this is no hotel, it's a prison. . . . [But] here there is no hope, nothing. Without hope you're a zombie, a living dead man. They come to life when there is a riot somewhere else. Then there is feverish excitement. I never saw such an outpouring of hatred as I saw in the riot. The hate in here would sicken a pig. Hate begets hate, violence begets violence. Here all you hear is lock up, lock up, lock up, day after day, year after year in this cold gray world, you lose touch with the decent men, no one ever says 'please' or 'thank you'—" He broke off, a red-faced Irishman, a devout Catholic, and looked upward, saying, "If God spares me I'll never come back."

"But," I wrote, "they do."

I expanded the Jackson series into a book on prison reform, *Break Down the Walls,* visiting other prisons and studying what we know about the roots of criminality, especially the "psychopathic personality." I became convinced that prisons were being run according to a myth, the myth of rehabilitation. Rehabilitation, I thought, was all but impossible inside a maximum-security prison. I concluded further that prisons as we know them should be abolished. That was a long-term aim. We could not rehabilitate a man until we knew what made him a criminal. To find out we needed research into the roots of criminality. When we knew how to rehabilitate him we would not put him into prison to do it. In the meantime, until that distant day, we should institute certain reforms, including separating hardened criminals from the others, razing or breaking up such monstrosities as Jackson, building numerous prison camps and farms and a few medium-security prisons plus institutions for the criminally insane, letting about half of all inmates out of prison (to prison farms and camps, parole), putting the few truly dangerous ones into a few small maximum-security institutions, revising the inequitable criminal code, and abolishing the death penalty. Ballantine published the book and *Harper's* published a brief summary of it under the apt title "Prison: The Enemy of Society."

But all this noble crusading had little effect. Nearly thirty years later, Attica prison in New York and a number of other prisons blew up in riot for roughly the same reasons that Jackson had blown up. So, in 1981, did Jackson itself. And we are still building big new maximum-security prisons.

Having used Jackson Prison as a way to write about convicts and prison reform, I wanted to use a state hospital to write about the mentally ill and their care. Looking for a hospital that was neither snakepit nor showplace, I visited several and fastened on Columbus State Hospital and did a six-part *Post* series. For five weeks I lived there day and night.* (One night Fran tried to call me and the switchboard operator told her, "He's on a locked ward.")

There were in the United States some 750,000 persons in mental hospitals. One of every 12 children born today would spend some part of his life there. Mental illness was America's number one health problem.

Columbus State was in many ways like all the other state hospitals in America—big, overcrowded, short of doctors and attendants. And full of human suffering. There were only 10 doctors who were actually seeing to the day-to-day psychiatric care of the 2,700 patients—and not one of them was a full-fledged certified psychiatrist. Attendants, mostly farmers and laborers, were so scarce that frequently at night one attendant had to try to handle three wards alone, a block-long labyrinth of rooms and corridors and locked doors with 250 patients. Day after day after day, I prowled the cav-

---

* I should make it clear that I did not, here or ever, masquerade as an inmate, as some reporters do. I consider that melodramatic, phony, and useless. A reporter masquerading as a convict, for example, does not really feel like one, because, unlike the real thing, he knows he can leave anytime he wants to. All he gains is a melodramatic line in his story that he "lived like a convict." He did not. I simply lived at Columbus State to get the feel of the place and because it was convenient.

vernous old high-ceilinged wards, usually with a doctor, sometimes alone. Psychotic patients wandered about aimlessly, dim figures moving silently in dim passageways, some fixed rigid in grotesque trance, some screaming in terror. Some of us think, "It's OK—they're crazy, they're happy, they don't know anything's wrong with them." But this is simply not so. They are most assuredly not happy—they live in agony, in a private hell; and they *do* know that something is terribly wrong with them. At first, the wards seemed forbidding to me, chilling, unfathomable. Later, after I had come to know the doctors and understand what they were trying to do, after I had talked to the patients and studied the histories of their broken lives, the lives for them unbearable, I realized that this place, far from frightening, was for the patients a place of peace. Sometimes the old words are best—we no longer call such a hospital an asylum but that is, really, what it is: an asylum, a refuge.

I presented cases to illustrate each of the major diagnoses of psychoses and patients to illustrate the treatments they received. Only a handful were receiving psychotherapy, 117 were on electroshock. The tranquilizing drugs such as Thorazine and Serpasil were new at that time, and on them patients became more manageable and less violent, the drugs were eliminating psychosurgery and reducing electroshock. They had originally been called miracle drugs, but by the time I was there some of the early enthusiasm had abated, and the medical director told me, "The new drugs are not a cure-all." And, speaking of one schizophrenic patient, "We know darn well a pill isn't going to change her into a normal girl. We'll hope to get her out someday, but we'll never make her well."

Later, after visiting other hospitals and doctors, I made a book of all this, a book about the care of the mentally ill in America in the mid-twentieth century. Dr. Daniel Blain, medical director of the American Psychiatric Association, wrote a generous introduction for it. Ben Shahn made a marvelous dust jacket, and Harper published it under my title, *The Pane of Glass*. (A schizophrenic once said to a psychiatrist, "There is a pane of glass between me and mankind.") Though it was flawed, I thought it the best book I'd yet written. What surprises me upon rereading is the sympathy it evokes not for the patients but for the doctors, whereas in writing about prisons, I had evoked sympathy for the prisoners, not their keepers.

In the book, I wrote of the need for more support for both public and private mental institutions—some patients at Columbus who might have benefited from the new drugs were denied them because the state did not provide enough money—and above all the need for more money for research—we simply didn't know enough about schizophrenia. While I was still editing the book, a stranger telephoned me long distance early one Sunday morning and said she had read my stories in the *Post* and wondered if I knew of any worthwhile psychiatric research projects she might support financially—she was, I believe, the wife or widow of a wealthy Texan. I told her about two projects, and she contributed a good deal of money to them. I dedicated *The Pane of Glass* to her.

The *Post* editors asked me to do a series on television but, as with the Deep South, didn't know exactly what they wanted. As before, I floated around in the field for a while, then proposed a series that would raise these questions: Why is so much of television so bad? Why is some so good? How do programs get on the air? Why do they go off? Who is responsible—who decides what comes into your living room? Can television be improved? How?

I knew almost nothing about television. I began my work by arising one day at 5:30 A.M., breakfasting hastily, and, sitting down in front of our television set, turned it to Channel 5, stared at the screen with its ellipse containing a figure 5 and the words "NBC WNBQ Chicago," watched the screen blink, and heard a voice say, "Good morning, we welcome you to another day of outstanding television programs." Outside it was barely light. I had chosen the day and the channel wholly at random. I stayed seated in front of the set, watching unremittingly, commercials and all, until Channel 5 went off the air twenty hours later. Like many of my friends, I myself seldom watched television, considering it uninteresting, tasteless, and a waste of time. Until that day, however, I had not fully realized how uninteresting, how tasteless, and what a waste of time television was. No one, of course, watches twenty hours of television straight. Nonetheless, this was what one television station, affiliated with a leading network in a big city, sent out over the airwaves, which were owned by the people, that day.

I did legwork in Hollywood, Chicago, Washington, and New

York—spoke to local broadcasters, network executives, advertising agencies, news broadcasters, film producers and directors, members of Congress, Newt Minow (the Federal Communications Commission's new reform-minded chairman), and people who operated the life-or-death oracle called the Nielsen ratings. I was with Walter Cronkite in the CBS news room in New York—the real one, not the one you see on the evening news—when the Bay of Pigs invasion story broke. I was having breakfast with Frank Stanton, president of CBS, in his private dining room atop the CBS building in New York the morning the United States was shooting a man into the air in a missile, an early preparation for later space shots, live on all networks, and Stanton, watching intently, said, "We'll do more and more of this. . . . All entertainment goes in cycles. Fatigue sets in—audience fatigue. But there's no fatigue for this," nodding toward the screen.

I concentrated my study of a network on CBS, reporting on its economics and its bureaucracy, on what kind of people its executives were, on why *Playhouse 90*, one of the highest-quality series of television drama ever, went off the air. (Stanton told me, "Because the audience turned its back on it. The fatigue factor. Television wears out ideas and men faster than anything." Because, said some of the people who had made *Playhouse 90*, CBS decided it was easier, cheaper, safer, more popular, and more profitable to present junk.) What all networks and stations and what all advertisers were interested in was "cost per thou"—how many dollars it cost an advertiser to reach one-thousand viewers. The bigger the audience, the lower the cost. Network TV was first of all a business. It was a tough business, like the auto-making business. Theater people sometimes did uneconomic things because they wanted to or thought they ought to. Publishers still published poetry. There was little room for such sentiments in television.

I reached several conclusions. Television people seemed vaguely uneasy. They had always deeply feared—and held in contempt—the viewing public. Now they had begun to fear that people would simply quit watching. They wished that programs were better but felt there was little they could do about it—they must make profits. Anyway, nobody knew in what ways people wanted television improved. The people themselves could not know. If one hundred years ago you had asked people how they wanted lighting improved, they would have asked for a longer wick or better kerosene. Nobody would have asked for an incandescent bulb. How could TV be improved? Some people looked hopefully to pay television, to public television, to UHF stations, hoping their high-quality presentations would force the commercial networks to upgrade their programming. Some people thought the government ought to establish its own network much as the Tennessee Valley Authority had been established as a yardstick by which to measure utility rates. But not much of this has come to pass in the quarter century since I wrote this series. To date, nobody has invented that incandescent bulb.

Over the years I had seen criminal justice go wrong many times—innocent men convicted, guilty men convicted but convicted wrongfully, guilty men set free. I decided to do a series on why and how criminal justice sometimes goes wrong, and the *Post* approved.

For a long time I had been interested in civil liberties, the citizens' defenses embodied in the Bill of Rights in the Constitution. I suppose I was drawn to this by my sympathy for the guy who never had a chance. By now Fran had gone on the Illinois board of the American Civil Liberties Union, and I became somewhat involved. In doing preliminary legwork for my *Post* series, I saw that justice sometimes went wrong because of an overzealous prosecutor, incompetent defense counsel, misidentification by eyewitnesses. Sometimes it went wrong because of procedural matters: illegal detention, coerced confession, no right to counsel, self-incrimination, illegal search and seizure—things that laymen term "mere technicalities" but things that lie at the heart of the Bill of Rights and so at the heart of freedom in our democratic system. I wanted to find criminal cases illustrating each of those problems. And cases scattered around the country, for injustice knew no geography.

In San Antonio, Texas, I found the case of Álvaro Alcorta, who, while a Mexican migrant farm worker of twenty-seven, had married a beautiful girl of fifteen. She neglected their children, became a B-girl in a bar, and taxi drivers told Alcorta she was prostituting herself. She took a young Mexican as her lover. Alcorta, crazed with jealousy, came upon them together one night by chance and stabbed her to death. At his murder trial he had a fumbling elderly lawyer who presented a weak defense. The overzealous young prosecutor, eager to run up a record of death penalties, suppressed all evidence of her love affair, and her lover testified falsely—with the prosecutor's knowledge. Alcorta was sentenced to electrocution. But another lawyer intervened, and the U.S. Supreme Court overturned the conviction—during the arguments the justices took the hide off the prosecutor—and in the end Alcorta was sentenced not to death but to a term of years that would make him eligible for parole in one more year. The lawyer who saved his life, Fred Semaan, told me, "It was hard. I was groping. And all for a 'Meskin.' That's what they call 'em. Everybody said, 'Why the hell do that for a damn Meskin?' Everybody's attitude—that was the damndest thing about the case." And "They damn near got away with it. And if they can do that to a poor Mexican like Alcorta, and someday they decide to get you or me, they can do it."*

An expensive Chicago criminal lawyer in another case told me the night his client was aquitted of murdering his former wife, though many Chicagoans still considered him guilty, "He might have been convicted, but he was lucky—he had money. The terrible thing about it is, what do you do if you don't have money?"

In my series, I used another half-dozen cases to show why justice went wrong. In Georgia, a happy-go-lucky ne'er-do-well with a minor criminal record was accused of murdering a small-town grocer in a stickup; the grocer's wife identified him positively, and he was sentenced to the electric chair; the Georgia Supreme Court affirmed the verdict and the U.S. Supreme Court refused review. But before he could be executed another man confessed the murder and was sentenced to life, and the man on death row was set free. Lay-

---

* One night Semaan's investigator took me down into the West Side Mexican slums and parked, and we sat watching the young men and women promenading along the shadowy sidewalk in front of the bars. Presently he signaled to the leader of a little band of street musicians, and they played for us a new song that was on all the jukeboxes, a sad song, *El Corrido de Alcorta:*

> *Alavaro Alcorta mató,*
> *Y es necesario un castigo;*
> *Pero hay que ser de razón*
> *Y comprender los motivos*

> (Alavro Alcorta killed,
> and a punishment is necessary;
> But one must be reasonable
> And understand the motives)

I bought a recording and took it home to Highland Park.

men tend to consider "circumstantial" evidence—physical evidence—less reliable than eyewitness testimony, but actually criminal justice probably goes astray more often because of mistaken eyewitness identification than for any other single reason. (At a murder inquest while I was working on this series, a witness, asked to point out the man who was suspected of the murder and whom the witness said he had seen near the scene of the crime, pointed straight at me. A funny feeling.)

Two cases, one in North Dakota and one in Chicago, illustrated the issue of coerced confession. In Chicago, a young man, Emil Reck, was beaten mercilessly by the police for several days until, vomiting blood, he confessed a murder, and he was sentenced to 199 years in prison. An ACLU lawyer (and friend of ours) appealed the case to the U.S. Supreme Court, which reversed the conviction because the confession had been coerced, and he was freed. In North Dakota, the sheriff took two Indians suspected of murdering a girl out to the countryside, where a hostile crowd gathered, and somebody brought a wrecking truck and they chained one prisoner's arm to a fence post and his other arm to the wrecking truck winch— "They were going to stretch him," a witness said. Not surprisingly he confessed, pleaded guilty, and was sentenced to thirty years. The Supreme Court of North Dakota upset the conviction—"The acts that took place at the Big Flat schoolhouse are a reversion to mediaeval methods condemned ages ago." The rack was used in medieval times to torture prisoners. On it almost anybody would confess to almost anything. No confession obtained by torture can be trusted. In sixteenth-century England, men protesting the inquisitorial methods of the Star Chamber and the ecclesiastical courts advanced the idea that "no man is bound to accuse himself." From this derives the clause embedded in the Fifth Amendment of the U.S. Constitution—"No person ... shall be compelled in any criminal case to be a witness against himself." Only the Fifth Amendment saved the Indian in North Dakota—that and the fact that his ordeal took place in front of witnesses, whereas most police torture is done in secret.

In this series, the case that meant the most to me was the case of John Simon, I suppose because I myself became involved.

I received a fan letter from a *Post* reader in Pittsburgh, an almost illiterate letter saying that her son John Simon had been imprisoned eighteen years ago even though he was innocent. They all say that, of course, but one thing in her letter caught my attention: She said he had had no lawyer. Through Fran and her Illinois ACLU board, I asked the ACLU in Pittsburgh to look into the case. It refused, but a young lawyer there, Martin Lubow, was interested. I went to Pittsburgh, and Lubow and I investigated the case together.

Eighteen years earlier, between April 30 and May 28, 1942, in the wooded hills overlooking the West End of Pittsburgh, a series of five women and two little girls were assaulted by a robber usually wearing a blue hood over his face. He grappled with them; sometimes he used a club; he took most of the women's purses and raped or tried to rape the two little girls. All these crimes were fumbling, clumsy. The newspaper outcry was enormous. Mothers escorted their children home from school armed with clubs, citizens held a mass meeting and threatened to "take the law into their own hands," as newspapers say. The police superintendent promised the mothers that the man would be caught. Sure enough, a man was caught, and quickly, on June 2—John Simon. Just seventeen days later he began serving a prison sentence of twenty to forty years.

Lubow and I began by checking court papers, talking to John Simon in prison, and talking to his mother. Even that preliminary check convinced me we had a story. The court papers showed Simon had not had a lawyer. They showed that one of the crimes of which he was convicted had never occurred, statutory rape: A police inspector testified that the child's own doctor said she had not been raped. John Simon was feebleminded. He had been eighteen or nineteen years old at the time. He had no father, his mother was a scrubwoman and she had not been present at his trial. (So disorganized had his life been that it was not even certain when he was born.) He had little schooling. His IQ tested between 55 and 61. He had been in juvenile court several times.

He had been convicted almost entirely on the eyewitness testimony of the victims (though the attacker usually had worn a hood) and on the report of a court-appointed psychiatrist or psychologist. We would have to try to find and interview those long-ago eyewitnesses and get the doctor's report. I asked the *Post* editors if they would pay expenses and pay Lubow for his time. They would.

To find the eyewitnesses, we hired a skip-trace agency, a private detective agency. Awaiting their report, I interviewed the policemen I could find who had been involved. Simon had told us the police had beaten him and had planted a hood in his pocket, an unlikely story, and had told him he could see his mother, as he begged, if he would sign a confession, so he did. The police, of course, denied beating him, and indeed they probably had not needed to, but they did hold him four days. During that time nobody told him he had a right to remain silent, to have a lawyer, to telephone his mother, to be arraigned before a magistrate. The police brought the seven victims in and asked them if, as eyewitnesses, they could identify him. Only one did positively, so far as we could learn, though the impression at the time was that all did.

The skip-trace agency found most of the eyewitnesses. One told me, when I asked about the lineup at which Simon was identified, "I said I wasn't too sure. The other woman said, "Yes, that's him exactly." and I was pretty young—seventeen or eighteen—and when the others pointed to him, I guess I did too." In court she testified that when the attacker tried to force her over backward, he failed because she was "a lot taller" than he. She was five feet two or three; John Simon was five feet six. She told me, however, she did not doubt his guilt.

Another of the victims did. She told me she was certain he was not the man. "He was by himself in a room, and all the women came." (Standard police procedure is, of course, to put the suspect in a lineup with other men and oblige the witness to pick him out, not to put him in a room alone.) "They said, 'This is the man.' I said, 'No it isn't. The man who grabbed me was bigger, older, taller, sharp-featured.' One of the others said at first she was not sure, but then she went along with the others. They were out to get somebody." The charge against Simon was dropped in her case. The skip-trace agency also located a man who had grappled with the attacker unmasked and he told me he had not been taken to the lineup—a fact that had always puzzled him.

Mrs. Simon told me that she had tried to hire a lawyer, John J. McGrath. When he asked if she had any money, she said she would cash a one-thousand-dollar life insurance policy. She took the policy to him, she said. To me, McGrath denied that he had been John Simon's lawyer at the time of the trial and insisted that he had not talked to John Simon or Mrs. Simon before the trial, though oddly he said he had been in the courtroom at the trial "as a spectator . . . out of curiosity." He did, however, later represent Simon at a clemency hearing. Who, then, I asked, got the insurance money? He said he didn't know. I pursued it, however, and found that the Monumental Life Insurance Company of Baltimore had in its files a check made out to the order of McGrath for $108.76, the cash surrender value of the policy. The check was endorsed by John J. McGrath and was dated July 7, 1942—shortly after Simon was sentenced. Apparently it came too late. (At a legal proceeding ten years later, both Mrs. Simon and John Simon testified they had not tried to get a lawyer before the trial, and Mrs. Simon testified she had not employed McGrath until after John was in prison. But of course they were then trying to get John out on the ground that he had had no lawyer.)

Awaiting trial, Simon had been examined by a psychologist or psychiatrist from the Behavior Clinic of the Allegheny County Criminal Court. The clinic's report was confidential, to be seen only by the judge and prosecutor, but we got a copy. It said that Simon was "potentially dangerous," would repeat his crimes, and should be locked up for a "prolonged or indefinite" period in a place like the Huntington School for Defective Delinquents. In jail, Simon had waived arraignment and presentment to the grand jury, though he told me he did not know he had, and when they took him to court only twelve days after he was put in jail, he did not know, he told me, that it was his trial. The judge, William H. McNaugher, was by the time I got into the case president judge of the court of common pleas, one of the most respected judges in western Pennsylvania, a Republican and a Presbyterian elder; he had been serving his twelfth year on the bench when John Simon came before him. The courtroom had been crowded that day with witnesses and victims, spectators and press. The trial lasted perhaps a half hour. Somebody asked Simon if he pleaded guilty and he said yes and the man said, "Sign right here," and Simon did. The transcript showed that no attorney for Simon was present nor was Simon advised that he had a right to one. The prosecutor told him he had signed pleas of guilty to six charges and asked if he understood. He said, "Yes, but I only had five," and denied guilt in one case. A police inspector thought it must be a certain case and the prosecutor said, "Well then, we will leave that out," but it turned out that the one Simon denied was another, and so the prosecutor dismissed that one, though its victim was the only one who had positively identified Simon in the police lineup. From first to last the case was shot through with the incomprehension of a feebleminded youth, with the haste and sloppiness of the machinery of criminal justice. No victim identified John Simon in court. The judge pronounced sentences including a sentence for the statutory rape that had not occurred. No single sentence was longer than five to ten years but the judge made the sentences consecutive; they added up to twenty to forty years in prison. At a later hearing, Judge McNaugher said Simon was "entitled to a correction" of the sentence for the rape that never had occurred—he changed the conviction from rape to attempted rape, thus cutting six months to a year off Simon's long sentence.

I interviewed Judge McNaugher. He told me he had made the sentence so severe because of the Behavior Clinic report. "I was left with nothing else but to give him a life sentence for the protection of society—of course, subject to change, as all sentences are. And I'd do the same today." He said he could not have sentenced Simon to the Huntington School. The penitentiary where he sent him had no program for reeducation of mental defectives.

There matters stood when Martin Lubow and I got into the case eighteen years later, in 1959, eighteen years that John Simon had spent in prison. That Simon was guilty of at least some of the crimes seems pretty sure. But even assuming guilt, the way he was convicted raised serious questions about the process of criminal justice. Even a guilty American is not to be imprisoned except through the just processes of the law. How we convict matters more than whether we convict. Due process is society's fundamental protection because it is the individual's only protection. Due process is more important than the incarceration of individuals, however dangerous.

John Simon was held by the police for four days. During that time he confessed, thus providing virtually the only evidence against him. The police may not have beaten him, but a confession seems dubious when it is obtained from a suggestible feebleminded youth during four days of questioning. The eyewitness identification too seems questionable. The other damning evidence came from the Behavior Clinic examination. There Simon was induced to incriminate himself. No one else was present. No one may know what happened at the proceeding. The psychiatrist or psychologist—not the victims or the police—became Simon's chief accuser. Yet he did not confront Simon in open court, was not under oath, and Simon had no chance to cross-examine him. It was this opinion—and it was only an opinion—that sent Simon to the penitentiary. All this smacks of the Star Chamber—gives too much power to one who works in secret, when the accused is surrounded by no safeguards at all. Nor was John Simon surrounded in open court by the safeguards offered by a lawyer. Several defenses were possible. Nobody made one on his behalf. And the proceedings were, to say the least, lacking in exactitude.

Eventually, however, we got John Simon out of prison. Lubow filed a petition for a writ of habeas corpus on the ground that Simon had had no lawyer. Judge McNaugher denied the petition. The constitutional right to counsel had not yet been established by the U.S. Supreme Court. We decided to try to establish it. Lubow appealed to the Superior and then to the Supreme Court of Pennsylvania. Both courts upheld Judge McNaugher, though both split. Meanwhile, a similar case was going up to the U.S. Supreme Court from Florida, *Gideon* v. *Wainwright,* and in 1963 the Court decided it for the defendant, establishing the right to counsel. The U.S. Supreme Court had refused to take the Simon case direct from the Pennsylvania courts, though Justice William O. Douglas had been of the opinion that it should, so Lubow started over, moving into the federal chain of courts. A federal district judge, following the landmark *Gideon* ruling, granted the petition for habeas corpus but kept Simon in prison until the Pittsburgh district attorney could try him again. After negotiation with Lubow, the DA recommended to the judge that at his new trial Simon be placed on probation. He was set free June 22, 1964, almost exactly twenty-two years after he went to prison.

The Supreme Court has held that the police may not obtain a confession while holding a man illegally, even though they did not mistreat him—what is called illegal detention. The landmark case is *Mallory* v. *United States.*

Andrew Mallory was charged with rape in Washington, D.C. He had been arrested the day after the crime betweeen 2 and 2:30 P.M. At police headquarters, he at first denied guilt. At 4 P.M. he agreed to take a lie detector test. During it he confessed. At 10 P.M. the police tried to reach a U.S. commissioner—a magistrate—to arraign him. They failed. Next morning they brought him before a commissioner. At the trial, the confession was introduced as evidence. He was sentenced to death. He appealed.

The U.S. circuit court of appeals affirmed the conviction but Judge David Bazelon wrote a dissent that soon became, in effect, the Supreme Court decision overturning the conviction. The Supreme Court applied one of the Federal Rules of Criminal Procedure, which provided that a federal officer making an arrest must arraign the prisoner before a commissioner "without unnecessary delay."* Andrew Mallory, the Court held, had not been arraigned "without unnecessary delay," nor while being questioned had he been advised of his rights to counsel, to preliminary examination, and to stand mute. The Court unanimously reversed the conviction and ordered Mallory tried again. But the district attorney dropped the case because the only evidence was the confession. Mallory was set free.

After making his mark on legal history, Andrew Mallory was arrested in Philadelphia and convicted on charges of burglary and aggravated assault. More than once civil libertarians have been chagrined when defendants for whom they won freedom have committed new crimes. I myself had misgivings about whether John Simon was still dangerous when we got him out of prison. None of that, of course, invalidates the constitutional rights of the accused.

---

*The purpose of the rule had been spelled out in 1948 by the Supreme Court in the famous *McNabb* case—"The awful instruments of the criminal law cannot be entrusted to a single functionary. The complicated process of criminal justice is therefore divided into different parts." Now the Court wrote in the *Mallory* decision: "The scheme for initiating a Federal prosecution is plainly defined. The police may not arrest upon mere suspicion but only on 'probable cause.' The next step in the proceeding is to arraign the arrested person before a judicial officer as quickly as possible so that he may be advised of his rights and so that the issue of probable cause may be properly determined. The arrested person may, of course, be 'booked' by the police. But he is not to be taken to police headquarters in order to carry out a process of inquiry that lends itself, even if not so designed, to eliciting damaging statements to support the arrest and ultimately his guilt."

The *Mallory* case blew up a storm—police, prosecutors, and conservative legislators cried that courts were "handcuffing the police," and civil libertarians replied equally shrilly. Congress investigated, and support arose for the notion that hoodlums and subversives "should be made to talk." In my conclusions I wrote:

> The fundamental importance of the Bill of Rights must not be lost sight of in fleeting uproar over subversives and Teamsters. To deny a hoodlum the right to "take the Fifth" is to start down the road that leads to Emil Reck's vomiting blood on the stationhouse floor. To hoot at "Fifth Amendment Communists" is to start down the road that leads to the prisoner on the wrecker's rack on the North Dakota plain. Undeniably the police today are impaled cruelly on the horns of a dilemma by courts that say they may not interrogate and by a public that cries for a solution of crimes by any means. But it is no remedy to permit the police to enforce the law by breaking it.

Today, what is astonishing about that series on criminal justice is that it was published at all. It was published, remember, not in *The New Republic* but *The Saturday Evening Post,* a journal not noted for liberal crusading. Yet the overarching idea of the series was to uphold the rights of the accused. As I write today, in the 1980s, the climate in the country being what it is, with cries of "law and order" abroad in the land, and with the Congress and the attorney general and the president and sometimes even members of the Supreme Court itself climbing aboard, it is almost inconceivable that such a series of articles could be published anywhere. Yet they were published during the Eisenhower years, with Senator Joe McCarthy barely behind us and his poison still infecting the body politic. Apparently there were antibodies against it. Today, in the 1980s, liberal antibodies seem absent or at least scarce.

4.

Out of these stories and many more, almost without my willing it, a theme was developing—our society does not always work as well as it ought. The Centralia mine disaster; the boy who killed his playmate; Murl Daniels, who was electrocuted; James Hickman, who killed his slum landlord; prisons; criminal justice—through all those pieces ran the theme of society's stresses, its failures, its downright wrongdoing.

And in some, such as the Daniels and Morey stories, another theme: What are the roots of human behavior, especially human misbehavior? Indeed, all this could be subsumed under the heading "The Psychopathy of People and Their Society." I don't think I ever stated these themes explicitly, but they were there. Crime-in-context had expanded into a rather dark vision of society.

5.

Writing about politics was more cheerful. Those years, the years when I was working the Chicago streets and slums, its courts and city hall, for the big slicks, were the great years of the Chicago Democratic political machine, the machine lush and wicked, smooth and powerful. In the 1920s, the Republican machine had run Chicago, but at the bottom of the Depression, the Democrats elected one of their own, Anton Cermak, mayor in 1931, the 1932 Roosevelt earthquake destroyed the Republicans, and by 1936 most of their good precinct captains had switched to the Democratic party, and the Democratic machine, led by Mayor Ed Kelly, was on its way to becoming in the 1940s and 1950s, my time, the most powerful political organization in America.*

The machine covered every one of Chicago's fifty wards but its greatest strength lay in the river wards, the slums across the Chicago River from the city's shining false lakefront. On various stories I spent a good deal of time there, especially in the Hull House district centered on Halsted Street and Blue Island Avenue across the river—a region of garbage-strewn alleys and sagging tenements, truck docks and cheap saloons. The first waves of immigrants to wash over the Hull House district had been Germans and Irish. Then the Italians poured in, and the Germans and Irish moved westward. Then came the Negroes, and now the Mexicans. As each

---

*Mayor Cermak was assassinated in Miami at the side of Franklin D. Roosevelt. Officials believed the assassin, a crazed anarchist, had intended to shoot Roosevelt and had hit Cermak by mistake. But the Chicago whisper I heard when I reached Chicago a few years later was that the Syndicate had sent a gunman to kill Cermak because of some obscure short circuit in Chicago's notorious crime-politics switchboard.

of these peoples came here, their children went wrong, but when they moved west their later children did not, leading one sociologist to suggest that the neighborhood itself was delinquent, that it taught its children crime as other children are taught to eat with a spoon. (The trouble with this theory is that all children learn to eat with a spoon but not all the children raised here went wrong— Supreme Court Justice Arthur Goldberg, Admiral Hyman G. Rickover, William S. Paley of CBS, and Benny Goodman, among others, didn't.)

The Democratic machine controlled the election machinery, of course, and in the old days of paper ballots its poll watchers and judges could tie the pencil in the voting booth on a string too short to reach the Republican column; counting ballots, they could spoil a ballot by marking it wrongly with a bit of pencil lead concealed under a fingernail. When voting machines appeared, they could set the counting dial on the back of the machine to arrange the needed Democratic majority before the machine ever reached the polling place from storage. When computer punch-cards came in, they could while counting alter a ballot by punching a nail-hole in it. Tales abounded of ballots dumped in the river, of votes cast by dead men or by voters registered from vacant lots. No doubt mostly true. The Republicans, of course, were equally perfidious years earlier when they were in control. This is Chicago. I enjoyed it hugely. And as a matter of fact, the Democratic machine, with all its money and with more than enough city and county jobs to put a precinct captain and at least one assistant on the public payroll for every one of the city's precincts—such a machine had little need of chicanery to win. On election day the precinct captains delivered the vote. A vote—this was the payoff their constituents made to the captains, who had been doing favors for them yearlong. The rest of us forget that politicians, from precinct captains to presidents, think of nothing else, all their waking hours every day for 365 days a year, but politics.

Becoming a precinct captain was one of the few ladders a slum boy could climb up from the depths. A politician was respected. He had power. He was a white-collar man. Indoor work. He might get rich. And the entire party machine—the mayor, the ward committeemen, the aldermen—rested at bottom on the precinct captain. He was likely to be an intelligent if uneducated man, industrious, a longtime resident of his ward. One whom I knew wore a sports shirt and slacks and spoke in breezy, side-of-the-mouth tones. His leader was the ward committeeman, who wore a diamond ring and expensive suit and drove a Cadillac, a powerhouse, member of the Cook County Democratic Central Committee, which decided who would run not only for mayor but for governor, senator, and president. Ward headquarters was only a dingy abandoned storefront with a single naked light bulb dangling over the ward secretary's desk, but it was not only a hangout for the precinct captains but also a power center where at least once a week the committeeman held court and received the supplications of the citizens whom the captains brought in. A friend of mine, an idealistic young man fresh out of law school, thought to do his bit for the democratic system by entering ward politics, despite its noxious reputation, and he walked into his ward headquarters and so announced. The ward secretary, head bent over a voters' list, looked up at him suspiciously and asked, "Who sent ya?" "What do you mean, who sent me?" "Your precinct captain send ya?" "Nobody sent me." The ward secretary said, "We don't want nobody nobody sent," and went back to his list. (The young man, Abner Mikva, later became a congressman and is now a judge on the U.S. court of appeals for the District of Columbia.) Most good precinct captains did nothing but politics lifelong, for they were rewarded with good jobs on the city or county payroll. The chief bailiff of the Cook County municipal court, for example, Al Horan, a ward committeeman, the second most powerful man in the Democratic machine, had four hundred deputy bailiffs—four hundred patronage jobs. He gave them to his precinct captains. To hold so good a job a captain had to bring in about three hundred fifty votes. How did he do it? One of them once told me, "You have to canvass the precinct. When new people move in, you make sure they change their address so they're qualified to vote. You call on them, leave your card; if we can be of any service in the future, don't hesitate. You help them renew their driver's license, pay their real estate taxes, pay their parking and speeding tickets. They're working men, they got no time to go to court. You take them to different hospitals. Who wants a letter to a state institution? There's so many things you can do personally." Trivial? Of course. But votes won that way can help decide who is president of the United States.

A precinct captain could do other favors for his relatives or close friends. He could get a man a job driving a city garbage truck, or fixing street lights. He could intercede quietly with the Parole Board on behalf of a convict in Stateville Penitentiary. He could get a man on the Chicago police force. This was supposed to be a civil-service appointment but if no civil-service examination had been held recently and the eligibility list was exhausted, anybody could be appointed temporarily. Some "temps" held their jobs for years, political patronage.

"And of course," a politician told me, "the West Side wards are your crime centers. So the most important thing the precinct captain does there is help out when someone gets in trouble with the police. Here you get into the twilight zone. The precinct captain tries first to induce the police not to file charges or to file a lesser charge. If that doesn't work, he goes to the courts, talks to the deputy bailiff and has him talk to the judge. A deputy bailiff is merely supposed to keep order in the court. But he can be the fixer."

Sometimes the fix can go pretty far. I did a piece about a Chicago policeman who, off duty, went on a drunken spree and killed two lads, one Mexican and one Italian, and wounded another Mexican in the Hull House slum. One of the policeman's brothers, a precinct captain and a deputy bailiff, had put him on the police force and then got him a choice assignment to the state's attorney's police. (The brother was a precinct captain in the ward of Al Horan, who was a close ally of the state's attorney.) The Chicago Crime Commission got a tip the case would be fixed, and sure enough, the grand jury refused to indict. But the commission and the *Sun-Times* got the case reopened and a special prosecutor appointed, and despite efforts to intimidate or bribe the key state witness, the policeman was sentenced to life imprisonment.

All this was Chicago politics. But there was more.

In years to come, Mayor Richard J. Daley of Chicago became a national figure. The election that set him on that road took place in 1955, when he was first elected mayor, and I did a series on it for the *Post*. In the state senate, Dick Daley had been Governor Adlai Stevenson's floor leader. Ward committeeman of the Eleventh Ward, a South Side Irish and East European ward near the Stockyards, he had become the powerful Democratic county chairman when Jacob M. Arvey moved up to national committeeman. Now in 1955 the Democratic Central Committee slated him for mayor. Thus they were trying to dump the incumbent Democrat, Mayor Martin H. Kennelly. Kennelly, however, declared he would run for reelection. So there would be a Democratic primary fight, a rarity.

Martin Kennelly was an honest businessman, not a machine politician. The Democratic machine was nothing if not flexible, and a few years earlier when outcry had arisen about bossism, its leader, Jack Arvey, had persuaded Mayor Ed Kelly to step down and had slated Martin Kennelly for mayor. Jack Arvey had been a founder of the machine and was at that time its mastermind. A lawyer, a small bald man with a quick grin but a viselike mind, a man of great courtesy who could suddenly become hard as steel when crossed, Arvey had grown up in the Twenty-fourth Ward on the West Side, where Jews had moved a generation earlier to escape the Hull House ghetto. Arvey had made the Twenty-fourth Ward the most powerful Democratic ward in Chicago—Adlai Stevenson carried it by 25,000 against Eisenhower (and so could have any other Democrat, something I understood if Stevenson did not.) It surprised many people to learn, as I did when I came to know him well, that Arvey himself was far more than a machine politician; he was, by conviction, a fiercely partisan fighting liberal. As mayor, Martin Kennelly had run neither the machine nor the city but had made himself a ceremonial figure. His predecessor, Ed Kelly, the machine boss, had said, "If you don't run the machine, it'll run you." Since Kennelly chose to reign but not rule, he created a power vacuum, and in Chicago what fills a power vacuum is the criminal Syndicate; during Kennelly's reign the Syndicate took over six of the city's fifty wards, I've been told, and it drove the Democratic state chairman out of office and into hiding by sending him in the mail a little black coffin. By 1955, the machine had had enough of Mayor Kennelly and so slated Daley. And it faced more trouble that year. A young Alderman, Robert Merriam, intellectual, liberal, son of a well-known university professor, wanted to run for mayor. He had led the little bloc of reform aldermen in the city council who opposed the Democratic machine. He himself was a Democrat but he had told me if the Democrats would not slate him for mayor, he would run as a Republican. This he now did.

All this was the most formidable challenge to the Chicago Democratic machine in its twenty-four years. For weeks, starting in the slush and snow of February, I spent my days interviewing candidates and their workers in their headquarters, in city hall and the county building, in law offices and hotels, spent my evenings at their little ward meetings.

Mayor Kennelly's strategists rented a large Loop office, filled it with publicity men, a speakers' bureau, all the paraphernalia of campaigning. They attacked "the bosses." They used television as never before—"Television is our precinct captain." Every newspaper supported Kennelly. Their attacks on Daley and the machine were merciless. On television and in the papers, Kennelly was doing fine. But not in the wards, I knew.

Dick Daley, being a machine politician, inspired precinct captains. Yet good-government groups could hardly object to him—he had never been touched by scandal. (Nor was he ever.) Labor liked him. He already had twenty-eight years' experience in politics and government. He was an Irish Catholic and he was running in the largest Catholic archdiocese in the country. He never stopped campaigning. He was a thoroughgoing professional politician and looked the part—chunky body, ruddy complexion, wide-set blue eyes, dark hard-finished suits, black polished shoes. He was almost overpoweringly Irish. He was affable, smart, quick thinking. He too was by conviction a strong liberal. Around reporters, he seemed on guard. He had a wide-eyed way of talking in public about the sanctity of the American home; cynical politicians were surprised to learn that he truly believed such homilies.

The goods of Daley's political trade were his humble boyhood, his wide personal acquaintance, his loyalty to his friends. Campaigning, he lost no opportunity to proclaim that he had seven children and still lived at 3536 South Lowe Avenue, where he was born. He used the English language cruelly. Once in a speech when he meant to say "St. Lawrence Seaway," he said "St. Lawrence seaweed." Introducing an a cappella choir, he called it the "Acapulco Choir." (He is reported to have said, "We look forward to the future with nostalgia," but I never heard that.)

Daley denied it to me but his basic strategy against Kennelly seemed to be to lie low. Instead of making high-visibility appearances, he was working on the ward organization, the committeemen and precinct captains—taking care of the good ones, getting rid of the weak ones. The machine was closing ranks. It invited back to the fold a traitorous Negro leader. It asked a liberal congressman, Sid Yates, who had never been close to its bosom, to help Daley. It asked Senator Paul Douglas and former governor Stevenson to come out for Daley. The machine showed its might the last week of the campaign—filled the downtown Opera House with four thousand party workers, and Jack Arvey warmed up the crowd, and when Daley came down the aisle surrounded by aides and body-guards, the crowd arose and cheered, and the men close to the aisle stretched out their arms to him and screamed, "Dick! Dick!" and the pit band struck up "Chicago, Chicago, that toddlin' town" and "Happy Days Are Here Again." Happy days! They were ready for it, after the limp years of Martin Kennelly. Daley in his speech defended the machine, said, "Good politics is good government," and, scarcely mentioning issues, drew around him the mantle of the party and the common man and his beloved city. (He really did love it.) One night that week I went with him to a ward meeting, and in a bar across the street a precinct captain in a yellow shirt told me in the detached way of a surgeon facing a minor operation, "I run a precinct here, and Kennelly's going to get killed." He did, citywide—on election day, Daley got 369,362 votes to Kennelly's 266,946—a plurality of 102,416.

Next, in the general election, Daley had to run against Bob Merriam, whom the Republicans nominated and whom all the newspapers endorsed. Merriam campaigned hard. His attacks became increasingly shrill. I thought he had fallen into the hands of bad advisers. His advertising agency prepared television commercials showing not only traffic jams and uncollected garbage but also the bodies of hoodlums in the trunks of cars, which seemed to have little to do with Daley. Merriam referred often to "the Morrison Hotel politburo," which seemed to me a rather McCarthyesque attempt to attack both the machine's Morrison Hotel headquarters and the national Democratic party's supposed softness on communism.

One of Daley's aldermen said on television that Daley had seven children and they were all his own. (Merriam had been married twice, so had his wife, and two of their three children were his wife's by her first marriage.) In Catholic neighborhoods, Daley's workers said, "You don't want a divorced Protestant for mayor, do you?" A leaflet distributed in Negro wards in Merriam's behalf said that Daley was anti-Negro. In Jewish neighborhoods, Daley workers passed the word that Merriam was anti-Semitic; in other neighborhoods they said he was a Jew.

I spent the last Sunday of the campaign in the famous Twenty-fourth Ward, riding around with the ward committeeman in his big red convertible, watching him check on his precinct captains making their final canvass. Election day, Daley won—708,222 votes, to Merriam's 581,555. Claiming victory, Daley said, "As mayor of Chicago, I shall embrace charity, love, mercy, and walk humbly with my God." He was reelected mayor every four years until he died twenty-one years later, in 1976. Though he became a national figure, he never changed, remained the same man I knew in that 1955 campaign. He was, almost surely, the best mayor Chicago ever had (but he had two flaws—he had an ineradicable blind spot for Negroes and, like most authoritarians, when he died, he left no successor). That 1955 election convinced me that reformers may turn out no better than what they seek to reform and that politics is best left to the professional politicians, and this piece and others on Chicago politics and on the state legislature in Springfield reminded me—by then I was a liberal partisan Democrat—that all virtue did not reside in the Democratic party nor all wickedness in the Republican party, that all probity did not reside downstate nor all villainy in Chicago, and that many legislators and other public officials were better than their constituents thought, that they were at least as good as their constituents deserved, that the best got too little credit, and that not enough of the worst ones got caught.

SIX

PROFESSIONAL

1.

What I have said thus far about my writing probably makes it sound a good deal more orderly and carefully planned than it was. I was doing legwork and writing all the time without any plan at all, simply taking up whatever subjects I could find or came to hand. To make a living, a freelance writer must above all keep busy. While working on a story, I always tried to look ahead to what story I would do next. Often I started on a new story the day after I finished one. Thus from time to time I took targets of opportunity—a story that presented itself in the papers, one that I ran across, or one that I had had in mind for some time.

I did a couple of *Post* stories about cases my detective friend from the fact detective days, Emil Smicklas, and his squad were working on, stories that illuminated the jungle that Chicago criminals and detectives alike inhabit. Night after night I rode the squad car with Smicklas and his two partners, cruising the West Side criminal slums, watching them stop a man on the street, search him, and put him in the squad car and take him to the dingy downtown police headquarters. I listened while Emil talked to his stool pigeons on the street. I spent days with Emil in his home. He thought of himself as

a "professional policeman." His hobbies were policeman's paraphernalia, especially wiretaps—he had his whole house wired. He
loved tape recorders, invisible ink, fingerprints. But he knew that
most cases are solved through information from stool pigeons. Over
the years, Emil and I became friends, and he helped me with my
legwork and, as I became involved in Chicago Democratic politics, I
was able to help him with promotions, and he ended up a captain,
the highest operating rank in the department. Once, when in her
teens our daughter decided to run away to New York, I called Emil,
and he and his squad intercepted her at the airport.

I put together a collection of six crime pieces from *Harper's* and
the slicks for a book, *Butcher's Dozen*. I first took it to Alfred Knopf
but he was in the hospital with an ankle broken from skiing and referred me to his wife, Blanche, who, the publisher of Camus and
Sartre and Brazilian novelists, could not make head or tail of my
project. I then took it to the Harper book publishing house, where
Simon Michael Bessie and Joan Kahn accepted it. *Butcher's Dozen*
was the first of several books of mine that Harper published. Ours
was a good publisher-author relationship. Nevertheless, I have often
thought that if I had it to do over, I would never have left Knopf.
Knopf always said, "We publish authors, not books," but that sometimes makes trouble too. Ivan von Auw of the Ober agency never
thought it was necessarily in an author's interest to stay with one
publisher; each particular book should find its best publisher. This,
too, has disadvantages. I have had several publishers, and our relationship was always good at first, but inevitably trouble came, and I
about concluded that although an author and his publisher are
bound together, they are, in a sense, natural enemies.

At that time, most people in the United States probably would
have dimly recognized the name of Nathan Leopold. Thirty years
earlier, Leopold, together with Richard Loeb, had been convicted of
senselessly kidnapping and murdering a child in Chicago they chose
at random—a "thrill murder," the newspapers called it—and they
had been sentenced to life for murder plus ninety-nine years for
kidnapping. But few Americans probably thought of Leopold as
someone still alive. He was, however. I wanted to do a piece about

what happens to an intelligent man during thirty years in prison. I drove down to Stateville Penitentiary, with its high massive wall, and told him so. He listened to me without expression. Then in his precise pedantic voice, he said he wanted to consult his lawyers, his brother, other advisers. He did, and we reached agreement—the story would concentrate on his life in prison, not his crime, and he would have manuscript approval. Agreement wasn't easy—his advisers were men of substance in Chicago. And I had a special problem—some of them were friends of ours who belonged to the Jewish community in Highland Park. We saw them at dinner parties, some were involved in Fran's ACLU or in liberal Democratic affairs (as by then was I), some had grown up with Leopold himself, and their parents had been friends of his parents. At the time of this crime, the 1920s, the wealthy Jewish community of Chicago, leading merchants and philanthropists, had lived near the University of Chicago on Chicago's South Side. They belonged to the same clubs, supported the same charities, and contributed largely to the city's cultural and intellectual life. Their homes were mansions. Later most of these families had moved to Highland Park and Glencoe, where we knew them. I'm sure none welcomed my news that I was doing the piece—those memories were painful. But not one objected or tried to dissuade me. Indeed, they helped me re-create that long-ago milieu. And after the *Post* published the series, an elderly neighbor of ours who had known Leopold's parents told me it was the first fair and understanding story she had ever read about him.

Born to wealth, small and sickly as a boy, precocious, with a phenomenal IQ, Leopold had entered the University of Chicago at fifteen and by the time he was arrested at nineteen he had studied fourteen different languages, including Vulgar Latin, Sanskrit, and two Italic languages called Oscan and Umbrian that have not been used since the destruction of Pompeii.

Most of my story was an account of Leopold's thirty years in prison. As I piled up the details, it became a story of human endeavor and human endurance, in places moving; for whatever one thinks of Nathan Leopold's rather cold, forbidding character or of his terrible crime, he was a human being, and he had to survive in prison, not an easy thing—brutal guards, dehumanized convicts, deadly deadly *deadly* monotony. And always the struggle to submerge himself in the vast mass of inmates, something he, being the famous Nathan Leopold, could never do. Over the years he went through several periods, some lasting months, some years, when he strove to accomplish something—studied semantics and languages, rebuilt the prison library after it was wrecked in a riot, helped other convicts get paroles by helping them find jobs on the outside, even establishing, with Richard Loeb, a correspondence school for other inmates both here and in other prisons. But when Loeb was killed in prison by another convict, Leopold lost interest in everything. He was just doing time. He was becoming an old con.

Finally in 1944 he was assigned to the prison X-ray laboratory. The war was on, and the United States was losing more men in the Pacific to malaria than to the Japanese, and Army doctors wanted to test new drugs on human volunteers. Leopold took the lead in getting inmate volunteers. He told me candidly, "I wanted to do my part [in the war]. And here was a chance to do myself some good; I knew nobody was going to hate cons for this, and there might be a reward." Sure enough, in 1947 Governor Green directed the Parole Board to review the cases of all the malaria volunteers. Some were paroled immediately; others, including Leopold, ineligible for parole, were told to petition for executive clemency. Finally in 1949, Governor Stevenson commuted Leopold's ninety-nine-year sentence to eighty-five years, making him eligible for parole in January 1953—three and a half more years.

The Stevenson Parole Board might well have paroled Leopold. But Stevenson ran for president, and Governor William G. Stratton was elected to replace him, and Stratton appointed a highly political board. It postponed the Leopold case until May, 1965—he would not even see the board again for twelve more years. Many people believed that the decision was a political one, though to me the governor denied it.*

Leopold applied for a rehearing again and again. He thought he'd be dead in twelve years. That was where things stood when, in 1954, I wrote my story. Finally the board granted a rehearing on February 5, 1958. At his request, I went down to Stateville and testified for him. I emphasized that neither the coroner nor the trial judge had

---

*No wonder convicts follow politics more closely than most of us—their freedom, indeed their lives, many hang on an election result.

found evidence that the murdered boy had been sexually molested, as was widely believed, and that Leopold himself during all those years in prison had received not a single guard's citation for any sort of homosexual activity. I recommended parole. The board paroled him. Later a newspaperman told me that it was my testimony that had won the parole—it got the board off the hook of paroling a "sex criminal." Leopold went to Puerto Rico to work in an X-ray clinic run by a religious order. Soon he married. Then he died. Few men have lived lives like his.

2.

A freelance has to go where the story is that some editor wants. Otis Wiese of *McCall's* sent me to Washington to cover the treason trial of Axis Sally, an American woman who had spent World War II in Germany making radio broadcasts for Hitler beamed at American troops. *Harper's* sent me to Labrador to do a piece about the opening of the iron ore field there. Herbert Mayes, a creative editor who liked to think of stories he wanted in *Cosmopolitan* and then match them to unlikely authors, called me to New York to do a piece about *South Pacific,* the most successful musical play till then produced. I asked Mayes what kind of piece he wanted. He said, "I want *your* piece." I knew next to nothing about the theater.

I read *Tales of the South Pacific,* by James A. Michener, and *South Pacific,* the musical play that Oscar Hammerstein II had adapted from it for the stage, then I went to see the show. I took notes all the way through it. Later I saw the show several more times, but what I used in my *Cosmopolitan* piece came from that first look. I have always believed in the technique of "the first look." A reporter can see a thing, anything, for the first time but once. A young newspaper reporter will for the first time race to follow a fire truck to a neighborhood alley, watch while the firemen raise a ladder to the top of a telephone pole and rescue a cat. This first look of his will be vivid, clear, all-inclusive, brilliantly lit as on the morning of creation, and he can write that kind of piece about it. But forever after, when the same thing occurs, he will simply write, "Firemen today rescued a cat on a telephone pole in the alley behind the 3000 block of Westover Street." Or he will write nothing at all. I myself could never repeat my description of the first electrocution I witnessed. I have never visited a steel mill; I wanted to save my first look for the time I needed it.

In any event I loved the first *South Pacific* performance I ever saw, thought it dramatic, exciting, even in places magical. I must have communicated some of this in the Ober office, for Dorothy Olding said, "We're going to have a very stagestruck young author on our hands."

The play's central plot deals with the romance between a wholesome young American girl who is a naval ensign in World War II, played by Mary Martin, and a worldly French planter in the South Pacific twice her age, played by Ezio Pinza. (You see? Firemen rescued cat. Period.)

Oscar Hammerstein II, the author, and Richard Rodgers, the composer, were trying out a new play in Boston, and I spent several days with them there, learning how they had done *South Pacific*. Among American theatrical producers at that time, Rodgers and Hammerstein ranked at the top, and their earlier show *Oklahoma* had helped transform the American musical play. In their hotel rooms in Boston they discoursed to me on this as well as on *South Pacific*, and by going with them to see their new show and afterward listening to them criticize it I learned a good deal about casting and guiding a play to Broadway. I found them both careful, hardworking craftsmen. Back in New York I interviewed almost everybody connected with *South Pacific*, from Ezio Pinza and Mary Martin down to stagehands. In talking to them, I was struck again by their no-nonsense professionalism. Pinza was the premier basso of the Metropolitan Opera. When Rodgers first offered the female lead to Miss Martin, he told me, "She was scared to death. She didn't want to get out there and be made a fool of by a Metropolitan Opera star. She has no illusions about her singing." She had never met Pinza and had heard him only on the radio. They took her to one of Pinza's concerts. She told me, "I'd never been to a concert before. The thing I couldn't get over was, here was just this man and a piano and a bare stage. The audience was still coming in. To watch this man wait and wait and wait until you could hear a pin drop, then just start to sing—I was floored." When I saw her, she still seemed as astonished as a schoolgirl and this similarity between the leads' roles in *South Pacific* and their offstage personalities may have contrib-

uted to the believability of *South Pacific*. One night, having removed
her makeup and changed into street clothes, she emerged from her
dressing room with her husband, Richard Halliday, and walked
down the quiet, dimly lighted corridor. As she passed Pinza's dressing room, she called out, "Good night, Ezio," and he called, "Good
night, beautiful." My own silliest behavior occurred the first night I
went backstage. I encountered Miss Martin's husband and, recog-
nizing him, I introduced myself as I was accustomed to doing: "My
name is Martin, M-a-r-t-i-n," spelling it for him, who was married
to a Miss M-a-r-t-i-n. When I had finished the legwork on *South Pacific* and the time had come to go home and write the piece, I was
sorry, an unusual circumstance; I had become involved with the
story and with the people. I suppose I was indeed stagestruck. It was
not that I was bedazzled by glamour but that the people involved
made so much sense. They were just workmen, as I was myself. Yet
down to earth as they were, what they made was magic. I found this
fascinating. I even wondered if some day I myself might not make
that magic. It was no longer mysterious.

Herbert Mayes of *Cosmopolitan* sent me next to Norway to do a
story on Kirsten Flagstad, the Metropolitan Opera's Wagnerian so-
prano who was being picketed in America by people who believed
she had been a Nazi or a Nazi collaborator during the German occupation of Norway in World War II. Mayes wanted me to find out
if it was true. Fran and Cindy and I went to Europe aboard the
Nieuw Amsterdam—what a marvelous way to travel!—and came
back aboard the *Queen Elizabeth,* a stuffy bore. I spent several weeks
on the life of Madame Flagstad, studying court documents and
talking not so much to her musical associates as to her personal
friends and neighbors and to business associates of her husband. I
concluded that Madame Flagstad's husband had indeed collaborated with the Nazis, that he had made a great deal of wartime
money from it, and that, a rabid anti-Communist himself, he had to
some extent sympathized with them, but that Madame Flagstad
herself had not been directly involved. She was never charged in
Norway with collaboration with the Nazis. She seemed to have remained almost indifferent to wartime events, even when the Germans sent the young man next door to a concentration camp. She

was almost completely apolitical, her whole world was her music (and herself and money).

3.

I wrote a few—and only a few—fragile off-trail pieces that, unlike criminal cases or big subject areas, were not "given," did not exist until I concocted them. A few and only a few—they were too risky for a freelance. But they were pieces I wanted to do. A self-indulgence.

Up in Michigan one summer, the teen-age son of our friends Earl and Hilma Numinen got lost in the big woods, and I joined the sheriff's posse that searched for him for three days before he found his way out. When I proposed a piece on it, Fred Allen of *Harper's* was dubious and advised me not to try it unless I could make it a work of art. I wrote it anyway, and Fred liked it and published it.

One year at spring vacation time when Cindy was in fourth grade, Fran and I took her on a trip by car to follow the trail Abraham Lincoln's family followed in coming to Illinois. We started at the Cumberland Gap and headed northwest across Kentucky to Springfield, Illinois, stopping at Lincoln's birthplace and at other quiet places where his family had lived. We rummaged through ancient courthouse records, finding a land title written in blood on a sheepskin. Fran's maternal forebears had come from Kentucky and we were doing research into their lives too. This was indeed a high-risk piece, one that had to be lyric, almost poetic; it was successful, Jack Alexander of the *Post* thought, because it was so evocative of Midwest history and rural life.

One of the last pieces I did for the *Post* was a sort of valedictory on Chicago (though I did not think of it that way at the time). It was quite unlike any other story I had ever done. It was a lighthearted, nostalgic piece about my experience of Chicago and the history of its reputation. The idea for it came when Ben and Bernarda Shahn came to town and Fran and I took them to lunch at Henrici's, an old ornate Loop restaurant near city hall favored by politicians and, in earlier times, celebrated gangsters. I found the Shahns immensely cheered. For in recent years they had heard that Chicago had mended its roaring, wicked ways and assumed a dull respectability, but the previous night Roger Touhy, an important gangster in the beer wars of the 1920s, had been shot dead on the steps of his sister's home. The noon editions were filled with gory photographs of Touhy's body, expert opinions on the prospects for a renewal of gang warfare, and fond reminiscences of the good old days when bodies had been dropping all over town. A newspaperman had asked the police commissioner if he thought hoodlums had killed Touhy for something he had done in the 1920s, and the commissioner had responded as he always did, "There are no hoodlums in Chicago." (A friend of mine wondered if Touhy had been done in by a committee of bank presidents.) Bernarda Shahn thought "There are no hoodlums in Chicago" ought to be set to music. Somehow Touhy's demise rejuvenated her and Ben, and Bernarda, a gentle little lady, said, "Thank heavens, there'll always be a Chicago." So I did my piece about what kind of place I had found it and I called it "To Chicago with Love."

As I had grown up in Indiana and become a reporter, I wrote, Chicago had come to be for me the place where the Big Story happened. Even Indiana's John Dillinger made it to Chicago to get assassinated. In my piece now, I recounted how I had come to Chicago in 1938 to write and how foolishly I had loved it—with my passion for the poor, I had even loved its slums, acres and acres of them, all mine; with my yearning for excitement, I had loved the speeding traffic on the Outer Drive and the roaring elevated trains on the El, Randolph Street in the theatrical district with blazing lights, the French restaurants and Syndicate gambling joints on the Near North Side. Each person in a saloon eyed everybody else warily, each wondering if all the others were gangsters, and it seemed to be part of the code not to touch or talk to strangers, though you might drink beside one for hours, lest a false move, as in a grade-B movie, trigger violence. I took to carrying my money loose in my pocket; no wallets for me any longer. (In Indiana, men squeezed pennies from tightly zippered wallets, called pocketbooks.) And always there was the wondrous lake, the limitless inland sea.

It was all rather innocent foolishness, I acknowledged in my piece. By now the El no longer seemed romantic to me, just an obsolete nuisance; the slums were not picturesque, just appalling; Randolph Street and Rush Street were not glamorous, just tinsel cheap; gangsterism not exciting, just dreary and dangerous. But this change was in me, not the city.

By now I had developed a tour of Chicago that I took visiting eastern friends on. Most Chicagoans took visitors to lovely upper Michigan Avenue, yacht harbors, the Art Institute. But those were places where Chicagoans spent holidays. I took visitors on a different tour, to places where the millions lived and worked and where over the years I had done my legwork, and in the piece I described the tour—down clangorous Western Avenue thick with trucks and lined with the two-flats of workingmen, the Twenty-fourth Ward birthplace of the Democratic machine, the factories on the southwest side, the house of my detective friend Emil Smicklas up Blue Island Avenue to Halsted Street, the Hull House district, where old Greeks wearing hats sat drinking coffee in the windows of little coffee shops, where Mexicans drank liquor and fought in tough saloons, where Gypsies encamped in tenements; to Maxwell Street close by, with open-air stalls selling used clothing and kosher hot dogs, little doorways leading into tiny hole-in-the-wall shops that years later I remembered when I visited the *medina* in Fez, in Morocco. I took Ben Shahn on a walking tour near Hull House, and he showed me the Star of David carved in stone over a doorway, now so eroded I had missed it, a relic of the poor Jews. I then took my visitors south to the Negro ghetto—and I told them I thought that in not many years Chicago would be an all-Negro city ringed by sullen white suburbs.

Chicago's boosters, I wrote, would probably think I did Chicago's reputation no good by my tour. Chicago's defenders had always been numerous and sensitive. Rudyard Kipling once wrote after visiting Chicago, "It is inhabited by savages." Chicago was outraged, as it was at A. J. Liebling's *New Yorker* pieces on Chicago entitled "Second City." When Billy Graham said that Chicago's reputation was "the worst in the world," Mayor Daley was deeply wounded, and he invited the Reverend Dr. Graham to accompany him on a tour of the city to view its glories.

Chicago's defenders usually made two points: that Chicago's reputation for wickedness was born during Prohibition, and that it was a reputation undeserved today. They were, I thought, wrong on both points. I adduced historical evidence: When Father Marquette arrived on the site of Chicago, he found a bootlegger selling liquor to the Indians, and the writer Lloyd Lewis discovered that the census that admitted Illinois to the Union was crooked, and time and again in the nineteenth century preachers and other reformers led crusades to cleanse Chicago (in one parade through the tenderloin a float was emblazoned somewhat enigmatically, THE CUBS MUST CUT OUT CIGARETTES, MURPHY SAYS). I went on to relate twentieth-century history, including the St. Valentine's Day Massacre and press conferences held by Al Capone. Then I presented evidence that Chicago in recent years, during the benign reign of Mayor Kennelly, still had been run by a corrupt alliance of politicians, police, Syndicate big shots, union leaders, and businessmen. I added a few private anecdotes of my own: Recently the wife of a wealthy friend of ours, attempting to organize a mothers' committee at her child's private school, had insisted to another mother that she participate, until the woman told her gently it would be inappropriate—her true name was not the one she was known by at school, for her husband was one of the most feared leaders of the Syndicate. And when the daughter of another Syndicate leader planned a birthday party and the mothers of some of the invited guests expressed misgivings, they were assured by the hostess that the children would be perfectly safe, for they would be picked up in a bulletproof car.

Nonetheless, during the dozen years before 1959, Chicago's leaders, throughout Mayor Kennelly's reign and Mayor Daley's rule, pretended that crime and corruption and the Syndicate did not exist. The city seemed to be rebuilding—superhighways sliced through slums, the St. Lawrence Seaway opened, new industries arose, high new apartment buildings sprang up along the lakefront, high new office buildings sprang up in the Loop, planners and editorialists proclaimed the rebirth of the central city. Mayor Daley hailed it. He toured it. He announced that suburbanites were returning. Did minor scandal erupt in city government? Mayor Daley moved on it swiftly. Thus, I wrote, for a dozen dreary years Chicago dwelt in an atmosphere of virtue, and prosperity, and progress.

Then in 1959 the roof fell in. It began in the fall. A Chicago police lieutenant was found touring Europe with Tony Accardo, the head of the Syndicate. Hearts lifted a little, faith was renewed. But the police commissioner announced there was no Syndicate in Chicago, and the lieutenant was suspended for associating with a gangster. (It was reported that the Syndicate suspended Accardo for associating with a policeman.) Then Roger Touhy was assassinated, the historic occasion that so delighted Ben and Bernarda Shahn. And a few weeks later a young burglar said that he had stolen merchandise to the order of policemen and that while he was at work they had acted as his lookouts, helped him carry the merchandise out of stores, and hauled it away in squad cars. (The policemen were indicted, but the indictments were dismissed.) The police scandals spread. The press was in full cry. Civic leaders held emergency meetings. The mayor returned from Florida. The police commissioner became the goat and resigned. The state legislature met in emergency session. It was all like old times.

The mayor appointed a new police commissioner, a California criminologist, and he went on television and appealed to the people to support him tangibly by desisting from carrying five- or ten-dollar bills clipped to their drivers' licenses, an old Chicago custom to ensure against arrest if stopped for speeding. Chicagoans enjoyed it all immensely. I heard a joke: The Outer Drive was "the last outpost of collective bargaining." Another: A speeding motorist, stopped by a cop, asked, "What is it—a pinch or a stickup?" The new superintendent said he didn't want his policemen working as part-time bartenders; the bartenders' union passed a resolution barring members from working as part-time policemen. Policemen in district stations, mindful of the merchandise their brethren had stolen, took to answering the stationhouse phone, "Good morning, Polk Brothers." Polk Brothers was a big discount house.

Why, I wondered, was Chicago's spirit so indestructible? I thought it best epitomized a few years earlier when, during a scandal over horsemeat—gangsters and others had conspired to sell horsemeat for hamburger—Fran's butcher asked her, "How do you want your hamburger—win, place, or show?"

Chicago, I wrote, was a friendly town. During World War II, it had been every serviceman's favorite. It was a tolerant town. People approved aldermen's wearing three-hundred-dollar suits (an outrageous price then). Congressional investigators said sixty-four Chicago disc jockeys accepted bribes, a claim that no other city could make (Los Angeles had only twenty-three). Chicago, remember, housed the only major-league baseball team that ever threw a World Series (so far as is known, a true Chicagoan would add darkly). Crime was played up heavily in all Chicago papers. A visitor told me, "This is your sport. This is your baseball."

Chicago was an openhanded, openhearted, young, and foolish town, I thought. Chicagoans believed that everything was fixed. And many things were—a man I knew who opened an office in Chicago encountered one frustration after another in getting routine services connected until friends told him whom to get in touch with. "It is universal," he said in awe. "You have to be able to say 'Joe sent me' everywhere." This society ran on clout, on influence. Europeans called Chicago the most American city, perhaps for the very reason that it ran on clout, and so indeed did America. But Chicago did it best. A word to a judge's bailiff that the accused is a ward leader's friend, a phone call to an alderman if you want an alley vacated, the five-dollar bill clipped to the driver's license—this is clout. If Chicago hadn't existed, America would have had to invent it.

What kind of place was it to live in? Terrible, I thought—cruel winters, stifling summer heat, broken streets in spring, hopeless rush-hour traffic jams, and at times small dead fish came out of kitchen faucets. The Stock Yards stank, the streets were filthy, restaurants were overcrowded, many people were afraid to go on the streets at night. On Lake Shore Drive, life in Chicago was lovely—for the few. For the millions, life in Chicago was toil and ugliness, if not squalor and privation.

As for me, I wrote, I lived in a suburb and wouldn't have Chicago if you gave it to me—but always, away from home, said if asked, "I'm from Chicago." I shared Fran's feelings. She was born there, and she often said, "I never think of Chicago any more till I drive down the Outer Drive and see all those tall buildings and see how pretty the lake is, and then I feel excited and wonder why I stayed away so long. I don't ever feel strange there; I always feel at home. I think it's the people. The people of Chicago are wonderful."

"They are," I wrote. "These big cities are, really, monuments to human endurance. People will put up with anything; they can survive anything. Chicago is quite possibly the worst place to live in the United States—except maybe New York."

4.

The 1950s were not only the golden years of the big slick magazines, they were also the golden years of serious television, the years of *Studio One* and *Playhouse 90*, and I began to get involved. (I wrote my *Post* series on TV later, in the 1960s. By then, television was destroying the magazines and was somehow managing almost to destroy itself.) John Houseman, then a theater and film producer, later an actor, had wanted to make a movie of my Centralia mine disaster story ever since it was published. Now he saw his chance to do it for television: He would produce it as one show in his series for CBS-TV, *The Seven Lively Arts*, calling journalism one of the arts. Fran and I spent a long weekend with John and Joan Houseman at their spectacular house at High Tor up the Hudson from New York, John and I planning the Centralia show. John looked the part of and indeed was one of America's most distinguished theater people, a remarkably talented man who had produced the Negro *Macbeth* and other plays for the Federal Theater during the New Deal's efforts through WPA to help the theater in the Depression, the original Martian star-wars fantasy on radio (with Orson Welles) that scared everybody in America to death, *Lute Song* for the commercial theater, Gertrude Stein's *Four Saints in Three Acts*, a number of big films including *Julius Caesar*, *Lust for Life*, and *The Bad and the Beautiful*; and he had made both a reputation for taste among serious critics as well as a good deal of money (though never so much money as later when, after himself starring in *The Paper Chase*, he made TV commercials selling cooking oil and a stock brokerage's services, a development of his career in his seventies and eighties that pleased and amused [and profited] him vastly.)

For the Centralia TV show, he was getting Loring Mandel to write the television play and George Roy Hill to direct it. Off and on in coming months I worked on the script with John and George Roy Hill. Hill was a kinetic, creative man who laughed easily and was fun to work with. I had never before worked on a dramatic script, and thought it fascinating. Loring Mandel had written a good one; I think Hill and I improved it. The script was extremely faithful to my original story. One particularly effective sequence showed the bureaucracy endlessly shuffling and stamping and filing and ignoring the mine inspectors' reports warning that the mine was dangerous. The show went into rehearsal in January of 1958, as I recall it, and the cast included two of the finest actors of our time, Maureen Stapleton and Jason Robards. Miss Stapleton played the widow of the coal miner, Joe Bryant. Jason Robards, who can do anything, from *The Night They Raided Minsky's* to *Long Day's Journey into Night*, did not appear on camera in Centralia—the script employed a device, a voice-over or narrator who represented me, the journalist, explaining the story, and Robards did the voice-over. I attended rehearsals, first in a big bare rehearsal hall at CBS, then, shortly before air time, in a small uptown movie house converted into a television studio. Here the set had been built—our underground mine tunnel, the living room of the miner's widow with the "heir-room" photographs of her dead husband and son, the office of the state Department of Mines and Minerals. During rehearsals, I made a number of suggestions to George Roy Hill, one, for example, that when the newspaper reporters try to interview Governor Green they not behave, as they were, like a bunch of raucous characters out of *The Front Page* but that, rather, they be serious and subdued—after all, 111 men had just died. Only the day before air time, I believe, a high executive at CBS, watching a rehearsal on a monitor at CBS headquarters, telephoned Houseman and told him he would have to make a change. In the script, among my own conclusions that Jason Robards was reading as voice-over, was a sentence saying that the system that runs our lives does not always work well. The CBS executive thought "system" sounded vaguely "communistic"; it would have to go. John told me to try to find a substitute. I came up with "the machinery that runs our lives," which was, I think, an improvement. And it satisfied the CBS man.

In the studio during rehearsals, I sat in the darkened little control booth with Hill and John Houseman, and I was fascinated as I saw how a TV show was directed, Hill watching a monitor for each camera and ordering "take one" or "take two," and his assistant flipping a switch to put camera one or camera two on the air. Hill wanted me to play myself on camera, interviewing Maureen Stapleton, the miner's widow, and so I too rehearsed, pretending to be a reporter making notes while she talked. She told me she was afraid she'd forget her lines, and so I copied them onto my reporter's notebook, placed so she could read them. John Houseman smiled; he knew she wouldn't forget. The show went on the air live on Sunday afternoon, January 26, 1958. I nearly blew the whole thing. During rehearsals, as Hill took breaks between scenes, I had grown accustomed to taking my time strolling from the control booth to the stage and onto the set to "interview" Miss Stapleton. When the show actually went on the air, I left the control booth on cue but I had forgotten that Hill would cut immediately to my scene, and I had to race downstairs and onto the set, barely getting into a chair facing Miss Stapleton before the camera took us. During rehearsals, like many fine actors, Miss Stapleton had held herself back, not giving all she had; but now on air live, she did, and it was the emotional climax of the show. Needless to say, she did not forget her lines.

The show went beautifully. After it, John and Joan Houseman took Fran and me to a party at the home of the actress Viveca Lindfors, a big party filled with show people, and Marilyn Monroe was expected but didn't show up (as usual, I'm told). The Housemans and we had a fine time, congratulating each other and being congratulated by the others. Late that night Fran and I took a plane to Chicago. We arrived in a blizzard but it didn't matter, I had parked our Jeep at the airport, and we drove home in the blizzard, and I remember shouting to her, "This is the greatest night of my life." Not publishing a book, not publishing a magazine piece, not winning a prize is nearly so exciting as seeing something you wrote come alive on a screen (or I suppose on a stage), and I still cherish that night.

Another television adaptation of a piece of mine turned out less happily. CBS had decided to do a dramatization of my book about the care of the mentally ill, *The Pane of Glass,* and I went to New York to advise during rehearsals. Elaine May was the star, one of the patients, and she wanted to throw a schizophrenic fit and tear up the set; she walked out on rehearsal, and one of my assignments was to seek her out and take her to dinner and persuade her to come back and not tear up the set. I did not think the television play very good nor did I find the people involved so congenial as those in the Centralia TV show. It was shown on the network on April 21, 1960. Almost at the last minute the producer tried to take my name off the screen credits, which he could not do under my contract. At the time

I didn't understand why. Later I did: He developed the script into a stage play, though he didn't own the stage rights to my work, and it appeared in an off-Broadway house. Ivan von Auw and I went to see it, and Ivan put the producer and the author of the stage play on notice, but the show folded anyway. During those years several television plays appeared on my home screen that seemed to contain material lifted from *Post* stories of mine without permission or pay, but I never did anything about it, I was too busy writing to clutter up my life with litigation.

Having produced *Executive Suite* for Metro-Goldwyn-Mayer, a movie about the power struggles in the board of directors of a big corporation, John Houseman wanted to make a movie for MGM about big labor and he wanted me to write it with him. I told him I knew nothing about writing a movie; he said it didn't matter, I wouldn't have to write the screenplay, only research and write a "screen treatment," and he would work with me on that. MGM would pay me. First, research: I started with my own writings that touched on labor—Centralia, stories about the Pennsylvania coal miners and the Upper Michigan copper miners, the Muncie autoworkers. I was surprised to find I already knew a fair amount about labor. I read books on it and in Chicago did fresh legwork—interviewed labor lawyers, politicians with labor support, and local labor leaders like Carl Shier, a friend of mine and a left-wing activist shop steward in the UAW. I began to see glimmerings of a story line and characters. After six weeks' work, Fran and I went to California.

We stayed with John Houseman and his wife Joan in their beach house at Malibu, only a few yards from the glorious ocean's edge. Early every morning—everybody in the motion picture industry went to work early, and most worked late—John and I would drive to the MGM lot and in his office talk out the story. I had the union background in mind and the main character too—a young iron miner from the Upper Peninsula of Michigan who goes to Chicago to organize production line workers for one of the big new CIO unions. John devised the plot, brought the hero into conflict with an elderly labor leader named Bannon, introduced female characters, invented scenes. We named the movie *Bannon*. We usually ate lunch at the MGM commissary. Once Fran came down and was taken on a tour of MGM's famous back lot, with its fake villages and castles and rivers. John and Joan took us to a cocktail party or two at Malibu and once to the Garden of Allah, the sad hotel on Sunset Boulevard where F. Scott Fitzgerald had lived toward the end.

Back home, I set to work to write the screen treatment. A treatment is simply a narrative—it might be only twenty-five pages, it might be five hundred; I think mine was some five hundred—that contains background, develops characters, describes scenes, and moves plot. I was, for the first time, doing something like writing a novel. To feel comfortable doing it, I made it as much like my regular magazine writing as possible—made a card outline of all my research and of the sizable manuscript that John and I and his young associate Judd Kinberg had produced, then made a writing outline, then wrote and rewrote the rough draft. John Houseman liked the treatment and so did Dore Schary, production head at MGM, and John began planning how to cast it. But when the project reached the high corporate officers of MGM in New York, they vetoed it: They were afraid it would get MGM into trouble with the unions MGM itself dealt with. Years later John Houseman told me that the abandonment of *Bannon* was one of the greatest regrets of his life.

5.

As time passed, it is probably clear by now, I came to write almost exclusively for the *Post*. And increasingly long series on big national issues, sometimes spending a year on one. Stuart Rose and Harold Ober once estimated that no more than fifty people in the country were successfully doing what I was doing for a living—full-time freelance heavy fact writing. What I was writing ended up, without my intending it, as a panorama of our times in America and our problems.

Nevertheless, to me they were always "stories," never "articles." The distinction was important. To my somewhat fuzzy way of thinking, an article was a collection of facts about a given subject, likely to be abstract, and almost certain to be pontifical. But a story was about people, some people in a time and place and what happened to them. Even when I did a long series about a subject for the *Post*, it was always in my mind "the divorce story" or the "criminal justice story," as it had been "the Centralia story," not "the mine safety article"; "the Daniels story," not "the capital punishment story." The individual man, the woman, the child—that was what mattered to a storyteller.

Everything I worked on was potentially libelous, and I was acutely aware that I was writing for the biggest magazines; I could not afford even a nonlibelous mistake. Increasingly I submitted my manuscripts to my sources, asking them to point out factual errors (but reserving my right to my conclusions), and took to rechecking every fact in a piece after I had finished it. Only once in my writing career did I make a factual mistake—at least one that was called to my attention. In my series on the Deep South, I quoted Senator Herman Talmadge of Georgia as saying in a public speech that the "Supreme Court refuses to recognize that it cannot by a mandate shrink the size of a Negro's skull, which is one-eighth of an inch thicker than a white man's." Senator Talmadge protested that he had not said it, the Citizens' Councils' theoretician had. I asked that man; he acknowledged it. I had found the quotation in a Birmingham newspaper. In rechecking my manuscript, I had sent the quote to the newspaper, as I sent other quotes to their sources. I received no reply to this query. That should have made me suspicious but I let it pass and published the quote. I was wrong. The *Post* apologized to Senator Talmadge. It was one of the few times I ever printed a newspaper quotation without corroboration.

The *Post* began emblazoning the titles of my stories on the cover and promoting them heavily with newspaper ads proclaiming me "One of America's Great Reporters." Heady stuff. The association of American magazine publishers established a group of prestigious awards, the Benjamin Franklin Awards, for magazine nonfiction, and I won one in each of four years until, as magazines declined, the awards ceased. They were presented at an annual dinner in New York attended by all the magazine editors and publishers, and Fran and I went, together with Ben Hibbs and the other *Post* editors, a gala occasion. Once when Theodore H. White and Robert Bendiner (one of the most underrated writers of our times) and I were all receiving awards, White remarked that he never saw three more unlikely-looking winners—everybody else at the dinner looked more distinguished than we. Once during these years, Ben Hibbs sent me a proof of a new masthead. Without consulting me, he had added Stewart Alsop and me to the list of contributing editors. I declined, preferring to remain freelance, and with help from Harold Ober succeeded in extricating myself without offending Ben Hibbs.

My friends in Highland Park, most of whom took the daily 8:10 to Chicago, considered my work risky, writing about crime. A few times I thought to be careful. I did not consider one *Post* story entirely safe, a story about a Chicago murderer and politicians who were trying to intimidate state witnesses; some of the fixers were dangerous, and I took care to interview one of them only in his lawyer's Loop office and to interview the state's key witness in my parked car on a street with his police bodyguard watching. The only time in my career that I was actually threatened was while I was doing legwork on the Centralia story; two mining officials waited on me at my hotel in a coal town and told me to drop the story and get out of town. One of them had a reputation as a bad man with a knife. Later that day I tried to continue my interviewing, but my sources had dried up. I got out of town. But I did not drop the story.

Whenever I met a criminal to get information, I made sure a detective knew I was meeting him. I got a good deal of fan mail from readers of the *Post;* I usually answered it on stationery without my home address. For years we kept our telephone number unlisted. Once a man called me up from St. Louis, said he'd read a crime story of mine, and said he had some information I'd be interested in. Ordinarily I would not respond to such a call, but I thought that if he already knew my telephone number, he knew a good deal about me and I'd better find out who he was. I told him I'd meet him in the Loop, in a bar off the main lobby of the Palmer House, a conspicuous place. I took Fran with me and found a chair for her in the lobby near the bar and told her that if I came out and turned right she would know everything was all right, but if I turned left she should call my detective friend, Emil Smicklas, at headquarters. The man arrived, we talked, he had some information that he thought might lead him to a lot of money and wanted my help in using it, I turned him down and walked out alone and turned right, and Fran followed me out. One night, while doing a *Post* series on the Illinois legislature, I accompanied a representative who was also a Chicago ward committeeman to his ward headquarters in the Hull House slum to watch him doing favors for his constituents, as he did every Thursday night. When he took me to the railroad station to go home, I was surprised to see he was wearing a revolver. I made a date to meet him again the following Thursday at his headquarters. But something came up that morning, I had to break the date. That night when he left his headquarters and drove to his home, three men kidnapped him. He was never seen again, presumed murdered. I did a *Post* story on an infamous gang of gunmen led by the Shelton brothers who for years had controlled gambling and other rackets all over downstate Illinois and had been involved in the violent deaths of at least thirty-five people; the Chicago Syndicate had recently moved in on them, killing two of the Shelton brothers and breaking the power of the sole survivor. I went to see the survivor, Earl, at his farm. When I rang the bell, he came to the door with a shotgun. I told him what I was doing. He said nothing. I asked if I could come in and talk to him. He said, "I've got to go slop the hogs." I said I'd go with him and we went to the barnyard. He was a big hulk of a man. Finished, he picked up his shotgun and walked back to the house. I went along. He let me follow him inside. He showed me around his house; he was proud of it, so new and so neat. He said, "Let's go downstairs," and led the way to the basement bar, got a couple of cold beers out of the cooler, and sat down. He looked at me and said, "I'd do anything I could to stop you from writing that story." "Do anything"—one did not take that lightly when it came from a Shelton, especially, perhaps, a Shelton with a shotgun. I told him there was no way to stop it, I was not alone, other *Post* reporters and writers were also working on the story, I was just covering this end of it, and whether I wrote it or not, there was going to be a story in the *Post*. I couldn't tell whether he believed me. But I got him started talking about his house, his farm, his brothers, his mother who lived down the road. I got the story. A local guitar player had composed a country ballad about the murder of his brother Carl and made a recording of it, and Earl played it for me to show me in what high esteem Carl had been held by folks around there and he gave me the record. I have it yet, a prized possession.

Doing legwork on the Sheltons, I had asked Emil Smicklas what he knew about them, and he said he knew only that the Chicago Syndicate had offered a reward of ten thousand dollars for any of the Sheltons dead or alive and he knew a gunman who had tried to collect it. He had been Smicklas's stool pigeon on a case I'd written about, and Smicklas arranged for me to meet him alone on a certain street corner on the Near North Side. I drove there at the appointed time and saw a man who seemed to fit the description. He was reading a newspaper. He didn't look up, or at least I didn't think he did. Puzzled, I drove around the block and came back. He was gone. I paused. In that moment, he was at the front door of my car, getting in. I never saw him approach. I asked where he wanted to go to talk. He said, "Just drive around." So I drove around, all afternoon, and he talked about the Sheltons and about the Syndicate. And about his own trade—he was a lifelong professional criminal. Explaining this, he pointed to a young woman walking down the sidewalk and said, "What do *you* see? A pretty girl. But *I* see she's got an envelope under her arm and I recognize the envelope—it's her boss's money, and she's taking it to the bank. See what I mean?"

He was a loner, would have nothing to do with organized crime. Indeed, he preyed on organized crime—with a submachine gun, he led several other gunmen in holding up Syndicate handbooks, about as dangerous a trade as is imaginable, and when I was with him, both the police and the Syndicate were looking for him. His viewpoint was that of the professional criminal. The world simply did not look the same to him as it looks to the rest of us. I decided to do a piece about him for the *Post* and then a book—the autobiography of a professional criminal. And he became a friend of sorts. Fran and I had him out to our house for Sunday dinner several times, sometimes for the weekend. He was about forty-five though he looked younger and he was always neatly dressed in sport jacket and slacks. Women, I suppose, would have considered him just short of handsome. He laughed easily, squinting as he did so. He was soft spoken and well spoken, well mannered, clean-cut, and extremely funny. Fran enjoyed him, and he was nice to Cindy. He had one drink with us before dinner, no more. After Sunday dinner, he would sit all afternoon in the living room talking of his criminal career. For a time he had been a confidence man—though his principal trades were burglary and armed robbery—and he enjoyed explaining how his confidence games relied on the foolish sentimentality or the secret dishonesty of "straight" people. He seemed lonely and glad for a chance to spend a weekend in a suburb with us. I trusted him and he came to trust me. (Most people did.) Once Fran's mother came to visit while he was there and she took Fran out into the kitchen and asked if this was somebody Fran herself "found attractive." (It was her Victorian way of asking if Fran was having an affair.) Fran explained. Her mother disapproved vehemently—a criminal in the house wasn't safe! (Actually, the only conceivable danger was if somebody who wanted to hurt him did so while I was with him. I was the last person that he himself would have harmed.) Once he told Fran he wanted to buy a Christmas present for his nine-year-old niece and asked if a heart-shaped ring would be appropriate—"Would she like it?" Fran said, "She'd love it." His story that she liked best was how he'd held up a roadhouse that kept a fierce watchdog: He tossed it a frankfurter loaded with strychnine.

Though I probably came to know him as well as anybody on earth knew him, I was sure I did not understand him completely. When he was in our house, we felt he was one of us. But as he left to go back to his own world, we realized that instead of having pulled him into our orbit, he had pulled us into his.

I was impressed by what he had accomplished in his chosen field, crime, and by what he might have accomplished in another. He possessed charm, intelligence, physical courage, human warmth, a quick intuitive insight into people—and none of the qualities most people associate with lifelong criminality. Why did he choose crime? I do not know. In his background were none of the usual elements of criminality—slum life, broken home, poverty, truancy, bad luck, bad heredity. Even the label of psychopath did not fit him.

For two weeks straight, he and I sat together at my desk while he talked and I took down on my typewriter verbatim his life story, occasionally asking questions to clear things up. We ended with a rough draft of about five hundred pages. I edited it, arranging the material on chronological lines, breaking it into chapters, eliminating repetition, tightening, inserting footnotes and bracketed explanations. But it was not an "as told to" book; it was his own story in his own language, a picaresque tale of his wanderings, his girls, his crimes.

Harper thought the book a potential best-seller, but it sold only about ten thousand copies, I believe. It suffered from a bad title, *My Life in Crime*, as did other books of mine. The Ober agency sold the paperback and foreign rights. Before publication, on the day I received galley proofs, I telephoned him to invite him out to the house to read proof with me. Somebody in his rooming house answered and said somewhat hesitantly, "Oh, that fella. He's dead. They found him dead in bed last week." I called Emil Smicklas. He knew nothing about it. I could not believe he had died a natural death and so I looked up the coroner's inquest. Sure enough, he had died in his sleep of a heart attack. Since his was an old Chicago family, it owned a grave site in one of the most respectable cemeteries in Chicago, and he was buried there.

Today as I go through my appointment books of those years, I am astonished at my energy and single-minded, almost relentless devotion to my work. I was out of town more than I was home. Often I would return home on a Saturday from a trip doing legwork, repack my suitcase, and leave on Sunday on another trip. I carried a briefcase stuffed with railroad and airline timetables. In New York, I scheduled appointments every hour (except for two hours for lunch). At home, writing, I kept regular office hours and I often ate lunch at my desk. Sometimes I would finish writing one story in the morning and begin another in the afternoon. I have always thought I managed to make a success of freelance writing not because of any talent but because I worked hard. I almost never took a day off, except in the summer in Upper Michigan—we bought a camp at Three Lakes but even there I took work with me. It is perhaps a measure of my later tendency to relax this discipline—or perhaps grow a little more sure of myself—that when I was in my room working, our first child, Cindy, was not allowed there; when our second, Dan, came along, he was allowed to come in and crawl under my desk and sit there so long as he remained quiet; and the third, Fred, was allowed to climb up on my lap and pretend to help me write.

In the midst of all of this writing, something happened that changed the direction of my life: I met Governor Adlai E. Stevenson.

PART THREE

PRESIDENTIAL POLITICS

SEVEN

CAMPAIGNING WITH ADLAI STEVENSON

1.

Adlai Stevenson did not win the 1952 presidential election, he lost it to General Dwight D. Eisenhower, but in losing he won the admiration of millions of people who responded to graceful speeches and to ideas and he aroused an excitement and a fervor that no presidential candidate save the Kennedy brothers (and, God help us, Reagan) has aroused since. I became involved in Stevenson's 1952 campaign by chance alone.

As I have said, in Upper Michigan I had met John Voelker, the writer and district attorney; he had suggested I look up a friend in his old Chicago law firm, Raymond Friend; Raymond in turn had introduced me to one of his partners, Louis A. Kohn. That had been four or five years ago; since then, Lou Kohn and I, and our wives, had become close friends. In 1948, Lou Kohn had helped get Adlai Stevenson nominated for governor. In his campaign, Stevenson had used my Centralia story, denouncing Governor Green for failing to save the coal miners' lives, but I never had met Stevenson. Now early in 1952, Lou Kohn wanted me to edit a book of the speeches Stevenson had been making as governor, which, he said, were extraordinarily thoughtful and eloquent. I presumed he hoped to use the book in Stevenson's forthcoming campaign for reelection as governor. But suddenly that winter people began talking about Stevenson's running for president—they wondered if President Truman could be reelected (and soon he declared he would not run). I interested Jack Fischer of Harper in the book—a collection of speeches with a long biographical introduction by me. Our daughter Cindy's birthday was February 5, a Tuesday, and on the preceding Sunday Fran and I took her down to the Chicago Loop for dinner and afterward to Lou Kohn's apartment—Governor Stevenson's birthday was the same day as Cindy's, and Cindy and he cut the cake together. After that Stevenson and I talked about the book of speeches. Stevenson was more interested in a different book. He said it was a shame that so few people were interested in state government and he proposed that after he was reelected governor I come to Springfield and spend six months or a year sitting inside his administration and finding out how things worked then write a book about it. This sounded interesting, and I told him it might also make a series for the *Post*. Meanwhile I'd go through his speech texts with both books in mind.

My first impression of Stevenson was one of a thoroughly engaging man. His forehead ran almost to the back of his head, his features were uneven—a big irregularly shaped nose, high unruly eyebrows that gave him a quizzical expression, eyes of the bluest blue and large, staring out at the world perpetually perplexed. His was an intelligent and a striking face. He laughed easily, smoked often. He continually made self-deprecating remarks, often funny. He grumbled about the burdens of office and his own weariness. Always he pretended not to be a politician but, rather, an amateur good-government man surrounded by politicians who probably wanted to do him in. He pretended astonishment and bewilderment at the presidential boom. In his presence, at that time, friends and advisers did not mention the presidential boom—like anxious relatives hovering at the bedside of a patient they know is stricken with a fatal disease but who doesn't know it himself.

I consulted Francis Nipp. He was dubious about the book—feared that if I became too closely identified with Stevenson, I would compromise my position as an independent freelance. I wanted to go ahead anyway. The Stevenson speech file was huge;

Francis agreed to help research it. In New York, I found my friends in the publishing world agog about Stevenson. They thought him a liberal in the Roosevelt-Truman tradition. Actually, he was not so liberal, was a man who favored balanced budgets, feared federal executive power, looked with favor on business, deplored what he considered labor's excesses. Elected governor, he had simply gone down to Springfield as a buttoned-down-collar reformer from Lake Forest out to cleanse the cesspool of Illinois politics. His reputation for liberalism rested on his veto of the Broyles bill, a McCarthyesque bill designed to ferret out Communist sympathies, on his deposition in behalf of Alger Hiss's reputation, and on his support for Truman's Korean policy. Nevertheless he was emerging as the champion of liberals and intellectuals in the Democratic party. That week in New York, at lunch at the Algonquin and in editors' homes, everyone wanted to know about Stevenson, and something like a holiday mood prevailed. Even Fred Allen had two drinks before lunch, and Fran told him she'd rather have him, Allen, for president than anybody; he stood up straight, bowed, and asked her to dinner. Fran and I went to see Ethel Merman in *Call Me Madam,* a musical play about a Washington society leader and politician, a play that spawned what became one of the most effective campaign songs in American political history, "I Like Ike." Another of its songs contained the line "If you're feeling presidential." We all were. Eric Larrabee made a cardboard button six inches across on which he lettered, MADLY FOR ADLAI, and Fran wore it going home on the *Twentieth Century.* It was an exciting time. I don't think any of us, I least of all, fully realized how serious a commitment we were making.

As the Stevenson boom grew, Harper bade me hasten—another publisher had commissioned a book on Stevenson. I went to Springfield and spent a week with Stevenson and his young staff and cabinet. Francis Nipp had researched Stevenson's speeches, and he and I made an outline of the book. By then Harper and I had decided to expand my "biographical introduction" and to print the speech texts as an appendix. (Eventually we dropped the speech texts entirely and the book became simply a brief biography rather like a *New Yorker* profile.) Hastened by the rival biography, I wrote the rough draft in about two weeks. As I finished it, Stevenson issued a statement on April 16 that most people thought took him out of contention for nomination. I didn't believe it. During the rest of the spring I tried to get definitive word from his staff or the Democratic party that he would be drafted and would accept, as I believed. Nobody could give it. So Harper stalled on my book manuscript.

I gave my manuscript to Stevenson to check for factual errors but he had no time and asked his sister, Elizabeth Ives, called Buffie, to read it, and I went over it with her. Later I came to know Mrs. Ives well. She was a strange woman, at times outgoing and charming, at times as difficult as one can be. She was not a well-educated woman nor one with wide political experience. To this reading she brought principally an almost single-minded adoration toward her mother and father and brother, plus a temperament that saw no blemishes but only joy and success in their lives. Our meeting was not easy but we got through it without too many scars. Scars were things Buffie Ives bore well anyway, if indeed she suffered them.

2.

Ever since Dan was born, Fran and I had been thinking of buying a bigger house, preferably on the northeast side of Highland Park, a "better" section and closer to the schools. Fran had found one she wanted to show me; I took one look at it and knew I wanted it. It was an old, high, narrow, Victorian white frame house with eleven-foot ceilings and a marble fireplace and ornate gingerbread on the roof line, set on a wooded ravine lot nearly an acre in extent. It had been built a year after the Chicago fire in 1871 by a contractor who was burned out and bought a big farm out here in the country; this was his version of a Chicago townhouse. His granddaughter still owned it and, a spinster, lived in it alone. We bought it. We live in it yet, more than thirty years later.

We moved into it on June 26, 1952. The trouble with a big old house is that, if you don't maintain it, it looks like a rooming house. Ours did. It was what was then called "an old clunk," today "a charming historic Victorian." We began rejuvenating and restoring it.* And in the midst of this, our house guests arrived to attend the

---

*State and federal government agencies have recently asked us to consider letting them declare it a historic landmark; we have declined.

Democratic National Convention in Chicago—Eric Larrabee of *Harper's* and his wife Eleanor, Ben Shahn and his wife Bernarda and two of their children. And during the week other New York writers and artists came out from the convention for drinks and dinner. Fran kept cooking turkeys, and we ate at a long roughhewn table we found in the basement. Bernarda Shahn said she loved old houses—"They're so solidly built,"—and Ben said, "Yes, Bernarda, that's why they're putting a new foundation in." Ben said he saw no need to build a new kitchen—he would simply paint a mural on the walls depicting kitchen cupboards, new sink, automatic dishwasher, even a Negro maid, then we could all go to a restaurant for dinner.

We went down to the convention every day. The first day, I was on the floor just below the podium when the chairman introduced Governor Stevenson for what is ordinarily a perfunctory governor's welcoming speech; the delegates broke into applause so long and loud—"WE WANT STEVENSON!"—that he had difficulty getting started. His speech was incandescent; in the supercharged atmosphere of this convention and in the national atmosphere of foreboding as Senator Joe McCarthy stalked the land and clouds of bigotry descended, this speech bespoke freedom of thought and belief: "Here [in Illinois] there are no barriers, no defenses, to ideas and to aspiration. We want none; we want no shackles on the mind or the spirit, no rigid patterns of thought, and no iron conformity. . . . As a Democrat perhaps you will permit me to remind you that until four years ago the people of Illinois had chosen but three Democratic governors in a hundred years. One was John Peter Altgeld, whom the great Illinois poet Vachel Lindsay called the Eagle Forgotten—he was an immigrant; one was Edward F. Dunne, whose parents came here from the old sod of Ireland; and the last was Henry Horner, but one generation removed from Germany. John Peter Altgeld, my friends, was a Protestant, Governor Dunne was a Catholic, Henry Horner was a Jew. And that, my friends, is the American story, written by the Democratic party here on the prairies of Illinois." His speech broke up the convention. It was one of the most thrilling political moments of my life.

What was happening was that the diverse old Democratic coalition held together by Roosevelt and Truman was rearranging itself, and it could rearrange itself only around Stevenson. This was one of the last of the old-fashioned conventions, with power brokers and bitter floor fights. It was also the first television convention, and some evenings we watched it at the dining room table on television. We did when, past midnight, Stevenson was nominated, Ben Shahn keeping a tally of votes on a sheet of typing paper, and while Stevenson delivered his acceptance speech—which I did not much like though it became famous—Ben turned his tally sheet over and sketched a caricature of Stevenson. It, along with other sketches he made that week, hangs now on our wall.

Stevenson's press secretary called and asked me to go to Springfield and help him. I went on August 21.* I had been there only a few days when I discovered I was less interested in the press operation than in what was going on at the Elks Club.

The campaign had rented space in the local Elks Club building for the writers who had come to Springfield to write Stevenson's speeches. Stevenson wanted them out of sight—he liked to think he wrote all his speeches himself, and they were obliged to call themselves speech researchers. Only once or twice all fall did "the Elks" see Stevenson himself. Now and then Carl McGowan, his trusted chief of staff, would visit the Elks and tell them what Stevenson was thinking about and wanted to say. Sometimes they themselves decided the themes, even the policies. Carl usually edited the speeches before giving them to Stevenson. Some Stevenson delivered almost as he received them, some he himself edited. Carl McGowan always accompanied Stevenson on his road trips. One or two Elks went along on each one. I joined the Elks Club writers.

The principal Elks, those who stayed throughout and wrote most of the speeches, were David Bell, thirty-three, tall, blond, affable, who had been a member of President Truman's White House staff for five years and who assigned speeches to us; W. Willard Wirtz, about forty, a member of Governor Stevenson's administration, a man in whom Stevenson had great confidence and who usually encouraged Stevenson to do what Stevenson wanted to do, a man who later became Stevenson's law partner and still later secretary of labor in the Kennedy and Johnson cabinets; Robert Tufts, thirty-

*A full account of Stevenson's 1952 presidential campaign appears in the first volume of the biography I wrote, *The Life of Adlai E. Stevenson.* The first volume is titled *Adlai Stevenson of Illinois.*

six, tough-minded and clear-minded, a professor of economics at Oberlin College who, as a former member of George F. Kennan's policy planning staff, wrote Stevenson's foreign policy speeches; and Arthur M. Schlesinger, Jr., gay, funny, articulate, brilliant, an Americans for Democratic Action leader, professor of history at Harvard, biographer of Andrew Jackson and Franklin D. Roosevelt, Pulitzer Prize winner, rapidly becoming at thirty-four a leading American intellectual. Other writers contributed drafts to the Elks, including John Kenneth Galbraith, the towering—in physique and reputation—Harvard economist, Jack Fischer and Bernard De Voto of *Harper's,* and Archibald MacLeish, the poet. Stevenson was an extraordinary candidate who burst like a meteor across the political firmament and galvanized such writers. Thus, suddenly, a whole new cast of characters came into my life. And many of them stayed there: Thirty years later some are among my closest friends. It was for me a new world.

Never before had I written a speech. From my work on the Stevenson book that spring, I knew something about Adlai Stevenson's speaking style, I could tell when something sounded Stevensonian or didn't. But I knew nothing whatsoever about speech structure. And I knew little about the issues of this campaign. In my writing, I simply had not handled issues as such—had written stories about people that raised such issues as segregated housing and prison reform, but I had rarely handled the issues frontally.*

Nor did I know the politics of the issues. Furthermore, as a writer I had never collaborated with another writer, for freelance writing is the loneliest trade; but speechwriting is more often than not collegial.

Some of the Elks were mainly interested in the quality of the prose in a speech draft. Others, like Arthur Schlesinger and Dave Bell, possessed highly developed political instincts and were interested in a speech's political effectiveness. I began by worrying about the prose and soon learned to worry more about the politics. I had never before thought of politics this way. I had, of course, never before allied myself with any politician. Indeed, I had always shared most reporters' skepticism or even suspicion of all politicians. At

---

* Later I did write articles that attacked these issues frontally, not simply through a set of characters. Indeed, it may have been my experience in the 1952 Stevenson campaign that impelled me to change my approach.

first I was almost shocked to hear Arthur Schlesinger and Dave Bell talking about people as voting blocs—Jews, Catholics, Negroes, farmers; I had thought that was the language of political hacks in ward headquarters. I came to see that in a diverse pluralistic democracy like ours, a politician can approach his electorate in no other way. (Stevenson himself intensely disliked doing it, and two of his worst speeches of the campaign were to union labor in Detroit and to Negroes in Harlem.)

But for me, the biggest wrench of all in joining the Elks was the complete reversal of my own situation. All my life, I had been a reporter, on the outside looking in. Now suddenly I was on the inside looking out. I was not reporting what the public man said; I was putting the words in his mouth. I was not reporting policy nuances; I was making them. All my life, reporters had been my colleagues and friends; now of a sudden they were the enemy, to be avoided.

Arthur Schlesinger considered Stevenson far too conservative, even antilabor and anti-Truman, and most of the other Elks agreed. I soon found myself joining their efforts to make Stevenson sound more liberal than he was. Liberalism seemed to come almost automatically to me. I've often wondered about the sources of it. An underdog feeling in childhood perhaps; and certainly the authors I read in high school, such as Dos Passos, must have had an influence, and so did my high school Communist friend. And surely important was what President Roosevelt did for my family, and my own standing in line at a factory gate during the Depression. Later, when I covered a strike for the *Times,* I was instinctively on the strikers' side. Not long after Fran and I were married, we visited her uncle Lowell Lathrop on his farm in Wisconsin. When younger he had been an active leader of the Progressive party, and he had been the head of the local Rural Electrification Administration office in FDR's time, and one evening he stood with me on a hill beside his barn and pointed down to the Kickapoo Valley, the farmhouses a string of lights up and down the valley, and he said, *"That's* what Roosevelt and the REA did for us." His wife told Fran, "If it hadn't been for President Roosevelt, people would be driving past today and say, 'That's the old Lathrop place.'" When Lowell Lathrop died, florists in the county ran out of flowers, and a hundred mourners couldn't get into the church, and REA provided loudspeakers for them. Things like these go into forming liberalism; it is not a program but a state of mind. In my own serious magazine writing, I wrote almost instinctively about life's losers—men in prison, the Centralia coal miners, James Hickman whose children were burned to death.

The underdog, *los de abajo*, those from below—the purest I ever heard it given voice was about this time when I was doing a piece for the *Post* on copper mining in the Upper Peninsula of Michigan, not far from where we spend summers. This had been Michigan's first boom country. But now only a half-dozen copper mines were still operating, deep underground mines, far deeper and hotter than the iron mines. I spent an evening in a workingmen's bar with a union organizer, Gene Saari, and two of his friends. Drinking beer at a round table, Saari and a younger man were complaining loudly about working conditions in the mine and saying that young men were refusing to go underground, preferred safer, cleaner, better-paying jobs in city factories. An older man, Finnish like Saari, spoke up. He had been sitting without saying much, smiling a little, picking at the label on his beer bottle. Facing me, he began slowly: "You asked why we do this kind of work if we don't like it. Well, I'll tell you why. You can work awhile and sit down awhile. You don't punch a clock. You're all by yourself all day. You're your own boss in a way. I started in the mine in 1922. Two dollars and seventy cents a day. I worked one year, and I decided to go to the city to improve my status. So I went to Detroit; an auto company paid me five dollars a day. I operated what they call a reamer on connecting rods. Standing up all day. That assembly line moving. Wearisome toil. My quitting time was four o'clock. One day I shut down two minutes before four. The foreman came running over. 'What's the trouble?' he said. 'Trouble? No trouble, quitting time.' He looked at his watch. 'Well, I don't mind half a minute, but two minutes is too much.' Well, it was September, and I started thinking of bird season, and I thought, 'Detroit, the hell with you and your five dollars a day.' I quit and came back in the mine."

He took a drink of his beer. Both Saari and the young man were listening with respect. He went on, "You want to hear some more of this life history? I was twenty years old. I stayed here till 1926, working in lumber camps and mines on and off. Then I decided to see what Butte, Montana, was like. So I grabbed up a armload of freight cars and I landed in Butte, Montana, with fifteen cents. That same night I saw a white man running down the street with a Chinaman shooting at him with a forty-five. And I thought, 'This is the town for me.' I went to work in the Belmont Mine about which the only thing they could brag about was that they had just installed a big electric hoist. It was the hottest mine on The Hill. I hired out as a miner. They paid four seventy-five then. But in the fall of the year I'd heard about the Coeur d'Alene district of Idaho and so I went down to Idaho and I hired on as a miner there at the Sunshine Mine. And at the Sunshine Mine I learned something more about mining. I learned to work the glory hole. The bottom. Going straight down. And I also learned about the IWW [Industrial Workers of the World]. I carried a red [IWW] card. Which you had to do. There was no choice. I had signed up in Butte." He laughed. "In Butte also I got my rustler's card. Do you know what a rustler's card was? In order to apply for a job in Butte, Montana, in 1927 you had to have what is known as a rustler's card. You went to the Anaconda offices on Main Street to apply for one and they put you through a third degree—your political opinions and affiliations, background, and if they found that you met their requirements they issued you a rus-tler's card. It entitled you to apply in any mine in Butte, Montana, for a job as a mucker or a miner. One of the prime questions I re-member—and I'll remember till I die—was: What is your opinion of unions and organized labor? And I told him that my experience with unions and organized labor was a sad one. What did I mean by that? I meant by that I wanted to get that rustler's card," he said, grinning sardonically. "Also, in Butte, Montana, I decided to be-come a Democrat because the cheapest place to eat was a little beanery and they had a big sign in their window that said: IF YOU DON'T EAT HERE I'LL VOTE FOR HOOVER. And he did a land-office business. I'll be back in a minute." And he got up, a long-waisted man in a T-shirt, with powerful arms, and walked around the bar to the men's room. While he was gone, Saari said, "He doesn't hold any office in the union now but he could have about any office he wants. He doesn't want one. Thinks it might hurt the union. Because of his background. The name I introduced him by isn't his real name. When he gets up to talk in the union meeting, they all listen. They've got more respect for him than for anybody else."

He came back and sat down and continued: "Do you know Coeur d'Alene? Wallace, Mullen, Bunker, and Kellogg sets down between two mountain ranges, down at the bottom of a V, you might say. Well, after a while I wanted to see what was on the other side of that western mountain range. So I went to Spokane, Washington, and I got off at the union depot and went across to skid row. And do you know what paid my fare? That red card. The IWW card. Without it you couldn't travel." Saari looked at him in surprise. He said, "That's right, Gene. West of Minnesota you couldn't ride a freight train without it. They asked you, 'What are you ridin' on?' and if you didn't have it you got off. That was the way I was inducted into democracy," he added. "Well, on skid row I looked around out there in Spokane, Washington. They were all strikes on, 1927, '28. Wheatfields and all over. Wheatfields was burning." Saari looked perplexed. "Burning, Gene. They set 'em afire. The big struggle was on. There was a big battle down in San Francisco. I didn't look for a job. I was looking for a fight. I was a soldier and I was on the front line. I went to Bellingham, Washington, where the coal mines are and—well, we wound up in a lot of trouble." He paused. "Well, anyhow, I came back here. Why? I was born and raised in the Copper Country. And I thought the fight should be extended this way. I started thinking of '12 and '13." (In 1913, the miners, led by the head of the Western Federation of Miners, an affiliate of the IWW, struck. It was Upper Michigan's bloodiest strike. It lasted nearly a year. The strike leader was mobbed. Riots began; the militia came. People went hungry. On Christmas Eve, strikers' families were gathered in a hall for a children's party, and somebody falsely cried, "Fire!" and in the crush to escape more than seventy people were killed, most of them children.) "I knew what my aim was going to be here—the struggle. Suppose your old man left home and didn't come home for three days. Like mine did during the 1913 strike. He left our house to go to the store and the vigilantes got after him and he skied across country and holed up in Quincy. He was from Finland, came here before 1900 and worked for Copper Range. I was born in 1904. I was nine years old at the time of the strike. The first day of the strike a big Austrian came up to me in Painesdale and said, 'What are you?' I said, 'I'm a union.' I had on a Western Federation of Miners button. Nine years old." He laughed. "Well, anyhow, I came back here late in 1928 and I was broke. I went to work for the Copper Range. Mining. I stuck it out. Speaking unions. In 1928 I got fired. They didn't want me anymore. You see, after the 1912 and 1913 strike my old man was on the blacklist. He had to work at the White Pine, forty-two miles from where we lived, came home every two weeks to see the family. My old man died in 1941. He was seventy-one, seventy-two. He pooped out in 1921. He was played out, couldn't make it anymore. There were five of us kids— two sisters and three brothers. I'm the baby. Only two of the brothers are living. The sisters died of polio. One of my brothers is a clerk in the post office in Detroit. I'll explain that too. In 1924 he was held up and robbed of the U.S. mail and his skull was fractured and he was left blind on the side of the road. One of the brothers also is a polio victim, crippled. He's at home in Painesdale."

He drank his beer slowly. Others had gathered around. Nobody else said anything except Saari, who said, "Jesus." The older man said, "Where was I? Oh yes, I was working for Copper Range in the Champion Mine about 1928. I'd been on the blacklist anyway because my old man was. I got fired. What happened next? Well, I don't know if I should tell you."

Saari said quickly, "Don't tell him. It's better not. Just leave a gap." He turned to me. "There's a gap from 1930 to 1943. I know about it. Just leave a gap."

He said, "I'd just as soon tell him."

I said it was up to him. Saari said it was better to keep still.

He shrugged. "I came back here in 1943 to the Copper Range. Mining. I was more or less restricted; I was confined to the boundaries of the county," he said sardonically. "I was injured a few months ago, a rock burst. Ruptured the sciatic nerve. You want see my scars again?" His face was seamed and leathery. He wore gold-rimmed glasses and a little baseball player's cap. "And in conclusion, gentlemen, all I can do is quote Joe Hill just before the firing squad executed him in prison: 'Don't mourn for me, you're the guy.'"

Saari waved for more beer. He said, "I never heard your story before. It's some story. Now listen. I'm going to get you into a discussion right here and now. I'm—"

"It's hard to do," the older man said. "I had to learn to keep my mouth shut."

"—when I came to this country in 1939—"

"I was still day shift," grinning at a secret joke.

"—the problem has not changed fundamentally from then. Failure to put through the subsidy and conservation program will be the most costly error ever made. During the war"—the Korean War was on—"America is consuming more copper than she is producing. I've got all the figures. I love these people in the Michigan copper district. But I'm concerned about the basic problem. It's a problem greater than these goddamn trade unions and companies. Every pound of copper in the United States of America must be extracted. And if we don't put in a subsidy for our own marginal mines and stop paying a subsidy to Chilean mines, we're going to become dependent on Chile and Rhodesia for our copper. But Calumet and Hecla"—the big mining company here—"will have copper for eighty years—if the government does what it ought to do. If not, we'll lose it for the economy of our nation and the prosperity of our people. The Korean War—"

Saari was pounding the table and shouting. The young miner was saying to him intensely, "We know where the copper is and we can get it out of there if they give us the kind of living we ought to have." But the older man had stopped listening and was trying to talk to me about the novels of John Dos Passos, which he admired. Saari, noticing he wasn't listening, said directly to him, "This isn't an ordinary trade union problem. This is a problem in the unorthodox economies of this area. What are we going to do about it?"

The older man said, as though reciting a lesson, "Through education and consolidation of our forces, progressively through the increasing understanding of trade union problems, we will win through to our goal."

Saari said, "Quit it."

He said quietly, "My interests lie with the downtrodden people. I'm a Finlander. But my interests lie just as deeply with the Austrian or the Croatian. I know what happened here in '12 and '13. You see a man riding a horse and slapping a miner across the face with a billy club that long, you know. I'm here for a cause."

Saari, distracted in spite of himself, asked, "What is the cause?"

"Humanity."

"What is the answer to humanity?"

"I don't know."

"What is the answer?"

He said, smiling a little lopsidedly, "I haven't quite put my finger on it."

Adlai Stevenson of Lake Forest, Illinois—surely a strange spokesman for revolutionaries like that. And yet, in my confused head at the Elks Club in 1952, he was. Liberalism, the labor union cause, racial segregation, injustice, the underdog—at the Elks Club, all this was unsystematic, was emotion, instinct, feeling for people. In college I had not learned to think rigorously or systematically. I had never worked out a liberal credo, had never needed to. Now suddenly I had to. What I brought to liberalism and to the Elks Club was, in addition to writing, a life's experience and instincts. With the tutelage of Arthur Schlesinger and Dave Bell and the others, I managed to translate this into a system of liberalism that could be applied to political campaign speeches. One cannot be the biographer of Jackson and Roosevelt as Schlesinger was, one cannot work in the Truman White House as Dave Bell had, without working out a rational system of liberalism. No more could I spend that fall in the Elks Club without doing it.

Preparing to write a speech, I read the speeches written by the other Elks. From Bob Tufts I learned a good deal about foreign policy, which I had never thought much about. And I had a memorable lunch alone with Senator Hubert Humphrey. We Elks were struggling with a speech about foreign trade and aid, and I knew little about it, and I mentioned it to Hubert Humphrey; at the lunch table he delivered for me a speech he himself often gave on his idea of exporting surplus food to other countries. This was the principal origin, in Hubert Humphrey's head, of what later became the Food-for-Peace Act, PL 480, which began as a way of getting rid of U.S. farmers' surplus crops and ended as a U.S. foreign policy instrument and a way to feed the hungry world. I conceived an admiration and affection for Hubert Humphrey that I never lost, and in later years, we became collaborators in politics. Indeed, that fall nearly all the Democratic heroes became my heroes. Two or three years later, I was in New York, walking up Forty-fourth Street from the Algonquin Hotel, when a car double-parked and a woman got out and walked across the sidewalk to the Harvard Club. It was Eleanor Roosevelt. Without thinking, I stopped and stood at attention and took off my hat and held it over my heart, something I have done only that one time. Seeing her drew together so many threads for me—Brookside Avenue in the Depression, Franklin Roosevelt, my own mother and father, unions and liberalism, my writing about the disadvantaged, Adlai Stevenson's doomed 1952 campaign.

That September at the Elks Club, the Stevenson candidacy seemed anything but doomed. We thought we had the best of it on all the issues. Eisenhower was not turning out to be, as the song had it, "good on a mike." A scandal almost blew Richard Nixon, running with him, off the ticket. We Elks worked and ate and slept together. We talked of almost nothing but the campaign. Few things are so all-consuming as a presidential campaign. Now and then we telephoned our wives at home to ask not only about the children but about how the campaign was going in our home states.

We put nearly all major speeches through at least six drafts. Sometimes we would sit around the big worktable and mark up a draft together; sometimes Dave Bell would assign rewrite to one of us alone. Arthur Schlesinger and I developed a way of writing a rough draft together—he would write the substantive center of the speech while I would write the pleasantries and setup at the beginning and the rising rhetoric at the end; then we would trade drafts and mark them up, then put them together. In talking, we Elks poked fun at Eisenhower, and at Stevenson too, for we were having a good time. But underneath we were deadly serious about the campaign. We regarded Senator Joe McCarthy as a sinister force in American life. We came to despise Eisenhower because he refused to renounce McCarthy's support. We came to think his election would be a national disaster. We hated Nixon and his hatchetwork. The other side of all this was that we became fiercely loyal to Stevenson even though he sometimes disappointed us. We were more partisan than he. Before long I ceased to wonder even privately how I, an "objective reporter," could feel so partisan.

Where Truman was able to ad-lib at whistlestops, where FDR was able simply to go out to the rear platform and wave to the crowd with his cigarette holder—where others could win crowds that way, Stevenson insisted on a full text and a different one for each whistlestop speech. He was ill at ease without one, and he grew bored repeating the same speech. But this made endless trouble—he rarely had time to familiarize himself with each text, newspapermen riding the train, being lazy, didn't like it for they had to write their stories several times a day, and we Elks were obliged to produce ten or eleven different speeches for a single day of campaigning instead of concentrating on the big speeches that, being nationally televised, reached millions of voters, not a few hundred.

The first trip Dave Bell sent me on with Stevenson was to Indiana and Kentucky. I had written the speeches since I knew the area, and on the trip I worked with Stevenson rewriting them and went with him while he delivered them. In Indianapolis I took my mother and father aboard his plane and introduced them to him. At Paducah our motorcade took us to Vice-President Alben Barkley's country home and we ate a leisurely picnic lunch on the lawn. Eight years later, in the fiery furnace of John F. Kennedy's nonstop campaign for the presidency, such a leisurely lunch would have been unthinkable.

Back in Springfield, I reported on the trip to the other Elks. I thought we were on the wrong track with our courthouse speeches. A courthouse speech could not be the lyrical graceful speech Stevenson liked, nor a serious substantive speech, nor a rousing rally speech to a partisan audience (a courthouse crowd contains people passing by, at least half Republicans). Rather, it should be partisan enough to arouse Democrats but not so partisan as to offend Republicans; it must be an "image" speech, creating an impression of the candidate, not an "issue" speech, and if it must contain an issue that issue must be presented bluntly, in black and white; above all it must be simple. Furthermore, I thought we needed to know more in advance about the occasions we were writing speeches for. Too often our speeches were inappropriate. And I wished we could become involved in scheduling. This appeared impossible—the schedulers decided where Stevenson would go on an almost purely political basis, with little regard to what he might say when he got there. As I traveled increasingly with Stevenson, I became convinced that scheduling is the heart of any campaign. Only scheduling brings together the candidate, the issues, and the audience. It involves, or should involve, the highest political strategy. Is it wise to maximize your Democratic vote or should you fight for the Republican and independent vote (with the risk of stirring people up to vote against you when they might stay home)? What kind of audience is your candidate best with and whom does he need most—students, labor, businessman, suburbanites? And if the writers decide he needs to deliver a foreign policy speech the day after tomorrow, the schedulers should change his schedule to give him a thoughtful indoor sitdown audience, not a state fair grandstand; and if the writers decide he should switch to the attack, the schedulers should provide hot partisan crowds. Television was a major problem. Stevenson used it poorly, and so did our schedulers, sometimes buying TV time to broadcast a partisan speech to a rally of screaming machine Democrats—when at least half the people watching in their homes were Republicans. We never solved these problems. I resolved that if I ever again became involved in a campaign I was going to try to bring scheduling and speechwriting together.

I wrote a speech for a Democratic-Farmer-Labor party rally in St. Paul, putting into it material from my long-ago memo on the Midwest for *Life* about the terrible times on upper Midwest farms during the Depression—"When FDR took office in 1933, the farmers of the Northwest were burning their wheat in their stoves because they couldn't sell it for the price of coal. The land lay barren, just gray-black dirt, and thistles blew across it, and farm wives canned the green thistles to have something to eat." That came almost verbatim out of my *Life* memo. It became something of a model for later rollicking rally speeches. I enjoyed writing them more than any others, and Stevenson seemed to enjoy delivering them, but afterward he seemed apologetic about them—no doubt some of his personal friends in Republican Lake Forest chided him. I went with him on a long southern trip and a long west-coast trip, and virtually all the Elks and I went with him on his train on a final grand eastern tour. Whistlestopping homeward from New York to Chicago, I stayed up all Friday night working on the next night's Chicago Stadium speech, the last of the campaign. So did others. Carl McGowan put the drafts together.

That Saturday night, Fran met me at the Conrad Hilton, and after dinner, the motorcade led by a torchlight parade headed slowly west on Madison Street. No crowds—I was worried. We were riding with

Lou and Mary Jane Kohn. A crowd was massed around the stadium, and Democratic ward committeemen were trying to drive the precinct captains up to the topmost gallery but their feet hurt. The stadium was vast and it was packed. The Chicago machine had done its job. Fran and I found standing room with the working press just below the platform. The speech was broadcast on nationwide television. The crowd was hot, it had come to laugh and boo and cheer, and Stevenson was delivering the speech well. But he had started slowly, as he often did, and as he approached the ending, he was running out of TV time. He reached the ending I had written:

I see an America where no man fears to think as he pleases or say what he thinks.

I see an America where slums and tenements have vanished and children are raised in decency and self-respect.

I see an America where men and women have leisure from toil—leisure to cultivate the resources of the spirit.

I see an America where no man is another's master—where no man's mind is dark with fear.

I see an America at peace with the world.

I see an America as the horizon of human hopes.

This is our design for the American cathedral, and we shall build it brick by brick and stone by stone, patiently, bravely, and prayerfully. . . .

He had reached that litany almost at the end of his TV time, and he knew it, and when the audience tried to break in with applause at every line, he held up his hand to stop them. At the end the crowd took the roof off. Some had tears in their eyes. And when he finished, the press arose and applauded him, something rare. Next morning's *New York Times* carried his "I see an America" litany on page 1. I liked to think that the opening welcoming speech to the convention, with its Altgeld-Dunne-Horner litany, and the closing stadium speech, with its America litany, framed the lofty elegance and idealism of the campaign.

Fran and I took Dave and Mary Bell and Arthur Schlesinger and Bob Tufts home with us. One the way I asked Fran how we were doing. She said, "I think you're doing fine most places. Of course, you're not going to carry Illinois." Dave said, "If we lose Illinois, we lose the election." Arthur called his wife in Cambridge, and she said

Stevenson was doing find although of course he would lose Massachusetts. Arthur went home next day and at the airport in New York encountered Max Lerner, who said that everything looked great for Stevenson except of course he would lose New York.

We spent the weekend at our house in Highland Park then on Tuesday, election day, aboard Stevenson's plane in Springfield, devised a pool among those aboard, including Stevenson himself, each of us contributing five dollars and writing down the number of electoral votes he thought Stevenson would get. He needed 266 votes to win. Arthur Schlesinger's guess had been 325, Bob Tufts's about 450, Stevenson's own 325 or 350, mine about 400. Fran did her own figuring and came up with Stevenson losing. I told her she couldn't put down a losing figure, so she put down the bare minimum he needed to win. All the rest of us thought he was going to win. Nonetheless, on the plane we were quiet and subdued. In Springfield as the polls were closing, we Elks at dinner listened to early returns. They did not sound good. When industrial Democratic Bridgeport, Connecticut, came in wrong, Dave Bell said, "That's bad—we'd better go," and we went to the ballroom of the Leland Hotel where an election headquarters had been set up, crowded but quiet as state after state came in for Eisenhower. Here and there we saw glimmerings of hope, as when a flurry of Stevenson votes came in from Minnesota, and we told each other, "Just wait till we hear from Ohio," or "Michigan and Illinois"; before the night was over we were saying, "Just wait till we hear from California." John L. Lewis stalked around the ballroom, scowling and alone.

About 10 P.M. we went to the Governor's Mansion. Stevenson was working in his ground-floor office, working I suppose, on his concession speech. About fifty of his friends and close staff were upstairs in the living rooms, sitting quietly. Fran and I sat at a little end table that had a radio on it. Stevenson's sister, Buffie Ives, asked me how it looked. I told her very bad. By 10:30 the Republican national chairman claimed victory. Stevenson wanted to concede at once but the Democratic national chairman dissuaded him—premature concession might imperil Democratic senatorial and congressional candidates. By midnight, however, the Eisenhower sweep was clear, and at 12:40 A.M. Stevenson went to the Leland ballroom and before TV cameras delivered his concession speech.

We Elks, thinking he would want to be alone with his family and personal friends, started to leave, but as we did, he came back from the Leland and asked, "Where's everybody going?" And "Come on upstairs and have a drink; let's celebrate my defeat." We went, and he told a butler to bring in the champagne. His Lake Forest friends were there. Most of them had voted for Eisenhower, and one woman was wearing a big diamond Eisenhower pin. One told him, "Governor, you educated the country with your great campaign," and he said, "But a lot of people flunked the course." The champagne came, and Stevenson offered Fran the first glass. She had won the electoral vote pool; drinking the champagne, she gave the pool money to Stevenson and told him it was an early contribution for the 1956 campaign fund. "I take it shamelessly," he said, putting it in his pocket. After a time we left.

Fran and I went home to Maple Avenue. A carpenter was working in our house and when we arrived he said, "Yah, yah, we beatcha." I should have told him to leave immediately (and in a few days did—he was not only a rude Republican carpenter but an incompetent one). For a week Fran and I moped around the house, lost. The campaign was over; suddenly there was nothing to talk about. The newspapers and television were full of Eisenhower's landslide. I felt a stranger in my own country. You put so much of yourself into such a campaign. I could not help it—I did not want to stay in this country. On the Tuesday after the election, Fran and I went to Cuba and spent two weeks in the sun on the beach at Varadero, healing. What do to? Well, I would go back to writing for the magazines. But after this campaign, nothing would ever be the same again.

EIGHT

THE LONGEST CAMPAIGN

1.

Reentering the world of magazine writing was not so easy as I had imagined. I had an assignment for *McCall's,* and I went to Cleveland to do the legwork, but after a few days I realized I couldn't do it, couldn't stop thinking about the campaign, had no heart for this story, and I went home. It was the only time I ever did that. I felt ill. I had not realized fully how emotionally involved I'd been in the Stevenson campaign. My doctor, Sylvan Robertson, an internist but one psychoanalytically oriented, suggested that my malaise might be due to guilty feelings that I was to blame for Stevenson's defeat and suggested I write something about the campaign to get it out of my system. I was not conscious of such feelings and anyway knew enough about politics to know that the results would have been the same had I never been involved. I also knew enough about magazines to know they would not be interested in such a piece. But I took his advice and wrote a five-hundred-page memorandum on the campaign. I added to it my files along with all the speech drafts, itineraries, and research matter from the Elks Club, a Stevenson archive. Years later, when I came to write Stevenson's biography, I was glad I had it, and I did feel better after writing it.

Many serious newspapers and magazines will not take back a writer who takes a leave of absence to work for a political candidate; they fear he has lost his objectivity. Stuart Rose and the others at the *Post*, though most of them were Republicans, welcomed me back after the Stevenson campaign. So did other editors. And I found that I could understand some stories the better for having been in the Stevenson campaign. It was the *Post*'s confidence in me—and Harold Ober's—that helped me forget the Stevenson loss and restored my confidence in myself as a writer.

2.

But I kept in touch with Adlai Stevenson and I did some work for him. Hundreds of organizations wanted him to speak to them or, if he could not, to send them a message of encouragement, and he paid me to write the messages. I worked closely with Bill Blair, who was his partner in his small new law firm, along with Bill Wirtz and Newt Minow. Fran helped him too—she went down to the Loop every Thursday for the American Civil Liberties Union board meeting at lunch in the YMCA cafeteria and after it she worked in Stevenson's law office as a volunteer, drafting answers to some of his mail. In drafting messages and letters, Fran and I learned to imitate Stevenson's eloquent and rather arch style, and he once told Fran, "You sound more like me than I do." Sometimes at the end of the day on Thursday, she drove him home, occasionally bringing him to our house for a drink en route. On the ACLU board, Fran usually voted with the moderates, with neither the purist constitutionalists nor the leftists who saw a civil liberties issue in every liberal cause. When she tells people now that she was at the ACLU in the 1950s, the time when Senator Joe McCarthy was riding high, they are greatly impressed, but actually at the time we thought little about it.* Once when the ACLU held a fund-raiser in Chicago, it wanted Stevenson to speak; Fran asked him, and he said he would if I'd write the speech. I did. I also drafted other speeches for him, especially during the 1954 congressional campaign, and that election

---

* I proposed a series to the *Post* that would show McCarthy in action at some of his famous hearings. Stuart Rose and Ben Hibbs approved, but someone in higher authority, no doubt at the corporate level, vetoed it, the only time the *Post* refused to let me do a political piece on what I have to believe were political grounds.

night we watched election returns with him in his house in Libertyville, Illinois. It was a happy occasion, for the election was a triumph
for Democrats—and for Stevenson too. Since 1952 he had made a
reputation as a world statesman and he was the acknowledged
leader of the Democratic party. When in 1955 it became clear, at
least to me, that he was going to run for president again in 1956, I
did a piece about him for the *Post*—how he lived in his country
house at Libertyville, what he'd been doing since 1952, his prospects
for 1956. It was a nice affectionate piece yet a highly political one,
and I was greatly pleased when the *Post* published it as I wrote it.

That fall, 1955, Fran's father died at eighty-nine. For Fran, his
death was hard. He was a patriarchal figure. Fran's mother and
brother brought his body back from Colorado, where her parents
had retired, and we buried him in Elmhurst, Illinois. He actually
had three funeral services—a religious one, a Masonic one, and a
military one, which seemed a little excessive. He had risen to the
rank of lieutenant in the Spanish-American War and during World
War I, I believe, he was elevated to captain, although he was not in
that war, and so when he died he held the rank of captain. Many
years later Fran was checking on something about his grave site,
and the man at the cemetery said, "Oh yes, Colonel Smethurst." He
was the only man I ever knew who was promoted posthumously, a
triple promotion at that.

That year I quit smoking cigarettes. The cigarette–lung cancer
linkage was just surfacing. I had smoked since high school; quitting
was no fun. After seven months Sylvan Robertson told me, "There
are some things worse than lung cancer, and one of them is your
disposition when you're not smoking." He was an excellent doctor. I
have always thought quitting smoking gave me ulcers. Perhaps,
however, it was the stress of the work I'd been doing, or some sort of
midlife crisis—I was forty. Dr. Robertson diagnosed gastric ulcer
and put me in Highland Park Hospital early in 1956. It was the beginning of an ulcerated existence I led, off and on, for some fifteen
years—restricted diet, in and out of bed, in and out of hospitals. It
did not, however, seriously interfere with my work. During the 1956
Stevenson campaign, traveling almost constantly, I carried a
thermos of milk, which airline stewardesses suspected contained
martinis. How I wished it had.

3.

In earlier presidential election years, preconvention maneuvering had been largely behind the scenes and indeed the actual nominee was usually chosen at the convention behind the scenes. This year, 1956, was the beginning of the system of primary election contests that increasingly, at each four-year interval, have so overwhelmed our political system. In 1956 it was clear that if Stevenson wanted the nomination again, he would have to fight for it in the primaries —Senator Estes Kefauver of Tennessee was running against him.

While I was still in the hospital, Bill Wirtz, Stevenson's law partner, had come to see me and said that when I got out they wanted me to go to work writing Stevenson's speeches. I agreed. I joined the staff on March 20 and I stayed until the election in November, with only, as I recall it, a single two-day holiday. For me, as for Stevenson, it was the longest campaign.

Stevenson was running in four contested primaries that spring and his name was on the ballot in a number of others, but as things turned out the most important were the contests with Kefauver in Minnesota, Florida, and California.* He had assembled a small staff. This time for a campaign manager he picked not an amateur, as in 1952, but a thoroughgoing professional, Jim Finnegan, leader of the Democratic organization in Philadelphia, a congenial funny man whom I liked enormously. When Stevenson was not present, Finnegan called him "my tiger." But face to face with Stevenson, Finnegan was so in awe of him that he hesitated to give him the advice he needed.

To do research Stevenson brought in John Brademas, who had been a Rhodes Scholar and who was running for Congress in Indiana (he didn't win that year but eventually he did and became Democratic whip in the House, one of the ablest men in Congress). Helping him was Ken Hechler, a scholarly young man also later elected to Congress. The writers were three—Bill Wirtz and I and Harry Ashmore, a southern editor of great charm who loved to tell yarns, and who later went to the Center for the Study of Democratic

---

* A full account of the 1956 campaign appears in the biography I wrote, *The Life of Adlai E. Stevenson,* Volume 2: *Adlai Stevenson and the World.*

Institutions in California. From time to time Arthur Schlesinger or Ken Galbraith or someone else sent in a draft for a major speech.

The day I joined the staff, Stevenson lost the Minnesota primary. He had been supposed to win Minnesota big, for he had the support of Senator Hubert Humphrey and Governor Orville Freeman, the leaders of the Democratic-Farmer-Labor party, then at the peak of its power. But Kefauver fooled everybody. Seizing the underdog position, he made "the bosses" the issue, and he won big.

For Stevenson, Minnesota was a disaster, and that night Finnegan and the rest of us discussed whether Stevenson should withdraw from the entire campaign. What was most dangerous to him was that Minnesota might start an unstoppable Kefauver bandwagon in California. And already Stevenson was not doing well in California—he had gotten in trouble on civil rights. Following the U.S. Supreme court decision ordering school desegregation, Stevenson recently had been making statements on civil rights that sounded to Negroes like "gradualism"—they could have their rights, but gradually. This hurt him badly with California Negroes and liberals, his strongest supporters there.

We decided that Stevenson must go to California at once and "put out the Kefauver fire" with a television speech from Los Angeles and San Francisco. Stevenson agreed. He wanted the speech to avoid substantive issues, to attack Kefauver, and to be angry and aggressive in tone. I wondered if this could be "the new Stevenson" some people had been clamoring for. Wirtz, Ashmore, and I each wrote a draft. We spent most of one day working together on the passage on civil rights. Stevenson would have to move left on civil rights in California. At the same time, he could not forget that what he said there would be read in segregationist Florida, where he was also running in the primary. It was the most dangerous issue of all, the one that could derail Stevenson's candidacy. But it also could rescue him if he could convince the Democrats that he alone could unite the party. We went over our civil rights passage with Stevenson word by word. He took our full drafts and put them together. He asked me to go to California with him. He, Finnegan, Bill Blair (his law partner and right-hand man), Roger Tubby, (his press secretary), and I went the next day, March 28. Aloft, Blair told me to sit beside

Stevenson. Stevenson spent an interminable time going through his briefcase, reading memoranda, handing some to me. I became impatient. Finally he asked what he should talk about at a rally and a labor meeting that night in Los Angeles after his television speech. I said, the same thing—attack Kefauver. He asked what he should say when he arrived at Los Angeles airport. The same thing, I said. What should he talk about on TV from San Francisco tomorrow night? Repeat the Los Angeles speech, I said. He balked. I suggested labor, Social Security, or foreign policy. The minute I mentioned foreign policy he seized it and talked about it the rest of the way to Los Angeles, but in the end decided he would not have time to do it justice, he would have to resign himself to repeating the Los Angeles speech.

That speech went well. So did his other meetings afterward. To me, before going to bed, he balked again at repeating the TV speech in San Francisco and, in the morning, I rewrote it, strengthening a passage on labor because I'd been told that San Francisco labor leaders were lukewarm. When I gave it to Stevenson on the plane to San Francisco, he demanded, "Why do I have to give them all this crap about labor?" and irritably hacked up the labor passage. He kept saying he'd never finish before reaching San Francisco and he didn't. He was angry with himself for having spent so much time on the speech and at the rest of us for not having it ready in final form. At the San Francisco airport he was mobbed, and, during a wild motorcade into town, started trying to rewrite the speech's desegregation passage; I begged him not to in these circumstances, and he finally desisted. But at the hotel he closed his bedroom door to work on the speech. He was running late, and the speech was getting long, and Blair and I were marking optional cuts that would keep him within his TV time. Two Negro leaders were waiting for him in the parlor. Stevenson finished only five minutes before time to leave for the TV studio and the Negroes barely had a chance to shake his hand as he brushed past them. And he was in trouble with Negroes here. So often I saw him seclude himself to work on a speech when he should have been talking to local leaders. The speech turned out to be one of his best TV performances ever.

Next morning on the plane back to Chicago he talked to me for two hours about what he ought to do and say and about an all-purpose whistlestop speech that he had been demanding, it seemed, forever. He never got it, it can't be written. And he showed me a memo from an eastern friend who asked hard questions about foreign policy—admission of Peking China to the UN, arms for Israel, the impossibility of reunifying Germany. Looking out the window at the barefaced Rockies, he mused that perhaps he should tell the people the truth about these questions—"I'm sure it would be the end of me as a politician, but I think it would make my reputation as a prophet."

Nonetheless, when we had been home a while, it seemed to us that, if Stevenson had not entirely put out the Kefauver fire in California, he had certainly damped it down. And some of us thought the Minnesota defeat might have been the best thing that happened to Stevenson. He had been the front runner for so long, and had been so widely acclaimed as a world statesman after 1952, and had so immersed himself in lofty issues, that it had seemed impossible that a lanky man in a coonskin cap like Kefauver could beat him. Now during his two-day trip to California he had suddenly seemed not the visionary philosopher-statesman but a hard-hitting candidate in a primary fighting for life. Not since his 1948 campaign for governor against Green had he sounded that way. Some of his Lake Forest friends didn't like it and thought he was demeaning himself. But after Minnesota he had no choice—Kefauver had pulled him off the pedestal and he had to fight on the ground.

The campaign was disorganized. We writers were putting too much energy into polishing the big prestigious speeches in the East, where Stevenson was entered in no contested primaries, and not enough into the day-to-day political stuff for Florida and Oregon and California, where he was. We had not even divided up the states. Now we did. I took California. Nobody from our headquarters was out there. I went there alone on April 26 and I stayed till the primary on June 5. California, everybody agreed, was the key to the nomination.

I began by meeting with Stevenson's California supporters, including state attorney general Pat Brown,* Fred Dutton, Don Bradley, and Alan Cranston. Then I did the kind of legwork I'd always

* Edmund G. Brown, soon elected governor, as, later, with his son, Edmund G. (Jerry) Brown, Jr.

done—interviewed people of all sorts to find out what was on their minds. I worked especially closely with Don Bradley, Democratic organization man in San Francisco, and Jack Abbott, his friend who knew issues. Together we worked out Stevenson's schedule and decided what issues he should discuss at each stop. Thus, for the first time in a campaign, I was able to bring scheduling and issues together.

And I did something else. Since I alone was writing nearly all of Stevenson's California speeches, as many as sixteen whistlestops a day, I obviously could not provide a full text for each one. He would have to speak extemporaneously. But I knew he'd balk if he had no paper in front of him. So I developed a technique of preparing briefing sheets for him on each stop—a page or two on the nature of the occasion, the setting, the size of the expected crowd, its composition (whether farmers, laborers, Negroes, aircraft industry workers, Democrats, general public), indoors or outdoors, who would introduce him, where he would be standing, which issues he should raise and which avoid, which local candidates or local leaders he should mention and which avoid, and a few lines on the locale so he could identify with the audience. If the issue to be discussed was a new one or a dangerous one in California, I provided language designed to handle it. If it was an old issue, I simply copied out enough material from earlier speeches to remind him. To gather material for this, I talked not only with Bradley and Abbott in San Francisco and Fred Dutton in Los Angeles but also with local people of all sorts. All this required hard political decisions; by now I had learned not always to trust local advice, to keep in mind not other people's interests but only the interests of my own candidate.

When Stevenson came to California the night of May 1, I met him and told him what was up. At first, he was dubious about the briefing sheet system but agreed to try it. (Like many of us, he was dubious about anything when it was first proposed.) Next day in San Francisco he had twelve stops between 9:45 A.M. and midnight. We handed him my briefing sheets one by one, just before each stop, and Stevenson took them and read them then scribbled notes on the back of them, making the pages his own, and he used them, speaking, in effect, extemporaneously from notes. The crowds loved it. The newspapers wrote of "the new Stevenson" who enjoyed hand-shaking and whistlestopping. It was one of the best days of whistle-stopping of his life.

He was all over California for nearly two weeks. My editorial advance, as the briefing sheets came to be called, helped keep him on the track; he never arrived at a speech without knowing what to expect and what was expected of him. In years to come, I used this system with other candidates, and I believe others adopted it.

One of Stevenson's most difficult appearances was before the Ministerial Alliance in Oakland, a Negro group where Stevenson was in trouble. It had originally been planned as a closed meeting, with Stevenson submitting to questioning. I opposed that. I didn't like the question-and-answer formula, if the meeting was closed the press would try all the harder to find out what was said, and an unfriendly minister might leak a distorted paraphrase. Bradley and the others finally agreed to open the meeting but insisted that Stevenson make a brief statement, then take questions. As I saw it, my job was to write a statement that would anticipate all questions so none would be asked. By doing legwork, I ascertained what questions were likely then I drafted a statement to answer them. Stevenson resisted the project strongly—didn't see why he had to say all over again what he thought about civil rights. We persuaded him he must. The meeting started badly—the room was small and dark and crowded and no lectern had been provided, and Stevenson, near-sighted, could not read his text and had to speak sitting down. Manfully, he read my draft word for word. When he finished, the chairman asked, "Any questions?" No one spoke up, Stevenson left. It had worked.

Until then, national Democrats had been afraid to attack President Eisenhower. For a major speech in San Francisco, I wrote for Stevenson what I think was the first speech attacking the president frontally, attacking him both for his policies and for playing golf at times of national crisis, picturing him as an amiable man but not a serious president. I did not take up the issue of Eisenhower's health, though it was on everybody's mind—he had suffered a heart attack and a serious intestinal disorder. Later I came to the conclusion that we should have raised the health issue from the start. But we did not.

The rest of the primary campaign was frantic. Stevenson won easily in Oregon. He squeaked through in Florida. And he won California big, overwhelming Kefauver with 1,139,964 votes to 680,722—he got 62 percent of the vote, far more than anybody on his own staff had expected.

After the convention nominated Stevenson, I moved to Washington with him and his expanded staff. The writers were Wirtz, Arthur Schlesinger, and I full-time, Bob Tufts and others part-time. Jim Finnegan remained campaign manager. It was odd. When we met with Stevenson, often Finnegan, the professional politician, took the lofty idealistic position, while Arthur Schlesinger and I found ourselves urging a hard-nosed political view. But early on we all agreed that the only way Stevenson could beat Eisenhower was by campaigning as he had in the California primary—whistle-stopping hard in pockets of discontent in a largely complacent country, maximizing his support among workingmen, Negroes, coal miners, and others. California had, however, made Stevenson overconfident. He wanted to make foreign policy his major issue—we told him there were no votes in it—and to make eloquent speeches on grand themes, as in 1952. The conflict was never really resolved.

The 1952 campaign had been exciting fun but 1956 was just hard work. I traveled with Stevenson some, especially in the Midwest and California, but I spent more time in Washington. When President Eisenhower began to campaign about mid-September, I realized we were going to lose. Nevertheless, we ran a good campaign. Indeed, I have always thought it a better campaign than 1952, though most of Stevenson's friends and idolaters thought not. It was, really, two campaigns. It was, inevitably, an attack campaign—Eisenhower was the incumbent. And it was a programmatic affirmative campaign. In sober specific speeches, and in long position papers, we set forth affirmative programs that went far beyond the New Deal–Fair Deal, that dealt not just with food and clothing and shelter but with issues affecting the quality of American life—better education, better medical care, the defense of civil rights and civil liberties, the problems of children and of the elderly. In doing this Stevenson laid the groundwork, really, for President Kennedy's New Frontier and President Johnson's Great Society. And he made two national security proposals that the Republicans loudly denounced but that soon became Republican policy—stopping nuclear testing and ending the military draft.

Toward the end, Polish Communist leaders defied the Kremlin, and the Hungarian revolt began, and Israel invaded the Sinai Peninsula. Some of us regretted having persuaded Stevenson to avoid foreign policy—he had laid no groundwork to attack this collapse of the administration's foreign policy. At the very end, on election eve, he made his worst mistake—predicted, on national television from Boston, that Eisenhower would not live out his next term if reelected.

Back in Chicago, Fran and I listened to the returns in the Blackstone Hotel with Stevenson and the others. It became clear early that Stevenson was losing badly. Scotty Reston of *The New York Times* telephoned Jim Finnegan and asked if Stevenson wouldn't concede now. Jim said, "I'll have to ask my advisers," and turned to Fran and asked her opinion. She shook her head, and Jim told Reston, "The answer is no." I set to work on a concession statement. Ben Hibbs of the *Post* told me later he hoped Stevenson would run every four years because he so enjoyed his graceful concession statements. It turned out that Stevenson lost by a bigger margin than in 1952, carrying only seven states, every one but Missouri from the old Confederacy. Eisenhower received 57.7 percent of the votes. I think that Suez and Hungary turned an Eisenhower victory into a landslide—when the country gets in trouble, the people rally round the president, even though he may be the one that got it in trouble. Afterward, Arthur Schlesinger, Seymour Harris, and I edited a book of Stevenson's 1956 speeches and position papers, published under the title *The New America,* which had been his campaign slogan.

NINE

THE KENNEDY BROTHERS
AND JIMMY HOFFA

1.

I had had much more influence on the 1956 campaign than on the
1952. Now, I thought, I was through with politics. I went back to
full-time magazine writing. As things turned out, I was by no means
through with politics, but my way back into it was quite by chance.
This is how it was charted:

Stuart Rose had an idea. The Senate Rackets Committee had
been investigating Jimmy Hoffa and his Teamsters union for more
than two years. When it held a public hearing, the newspapers carried scrappy reports. But, Stuart said, nobody had ever put the
whole story together, and he suggested I do. It took nearly a year
and ended as a seven-part series, the longest yet.

Robert F. Kennedy was chief counsel of the Senate Rackets
Committee. I knew him—he had been aboard Stevenson's 1956
campaign plane for a time, seeking, with his brother Jack in mind as
a candidate in 1960, to learn how to run a presidential campaign.
(He told me later he had learned how *not* to run one.) I went to
Washington. I was there off and on during the next six or eight
months, for as the Rackets Committee investigation dragged on so
did my legwork, and I came to know something of Washington—the

cluttered frantic offices of the Rackets Committee in the Old Senate Office Building, the splendid gilded Senate Caucus Room where the Army-McCarthy hearings had been held, the shabby little Carroll Arms Hotel across the street where senators' staff aides ate lunch and where I usually stayed; dinner at the Metropolitan Club and at a French restaurant in Georgetown, parties in narrow three-story brick houses crowded close together on Georgetown's old narrow streets; Bobby Kennedy's opulent estate, Hickory Hill, out in McLean, Virginia, rolling hill country dotted with white rail fences and old trees, a gracious antebellum house with high ceilings, crystal chandeliers, white woodwork, marble fireplace, candlelit dining room.

I liked Bobby Kennedy from the start. Though born to wealth and power, he had about him not a trace of superiority or affectation. He was young, only thirty-two. He was handsome, slender, standing five feet ten and weighing about 150 pounds. He had a boyish grin. His trademark was a lock of dark-blond hair falling over his forehead; it blew in the wind as he drove his big convertible. He drove fast and skillfully. He had hard, direct blue eyes. His white, even teeth protruded slightly. He was tanned. He had a high-pitched, nasal voice. He spoke with a flat Boston accent. His expression in repose was sober; his quick flashing smile was infectious. He thought fast, his memory was remarkable. He wore narrow-shouldered dark blue suits, button-down collars, narrow neckties. At his desk he worked in his shirt sleeves, sleeves rolled up. Often, discussing committee strategy in his office, he and his administrative assistant, Kenneth O'Donnell, passed a football back and forth— both had played football at Harvard. He moved fast, handling his body well, like an athlete. He ran upstairs and downstairs. He scheduled himself remorselessly, and he drove his staff just as hard. Staffers conversed with him freely, as equals, but when he wanted something done he could be curt.

On this story, I probably spent more time with Bobby Kennedy than with any one else. Sometimes I spent all day talking to him in his office, with a sandwich sent in at noon. I watched him at the hearings. Many times he took me home for dinner with his wife Ethel and their six children, and on weekends I played touch football with them (not very well) and went swimming with Bobby in his pool (not very well). A number of times when he came to Chicago on an investigation, sometimes accompanied by one or two of his investigators, they stayed at our house with Fran and me, and one night there he, before setting out with his men to try to dig up an ex-convict's body in a cornfield near Joliet, had dinner with us in Highland Park and he played cops and robbers all over the house with Dan and Fred. At that time Fran was betting on horses, and once while Bobby was at our house, the laundryman came to collect her two-dollar bet and she had to ask me for the money in front of Bobby, and, knowing he was investigating Syndicate gambling, she said "I owe the laundryman two dollars." Understanding, I gave it to her and said nothing. Bobby never knew.

When at the end of a day at his office on Capitol Hill he went home to Hickory Hill, his children and dogs swarmed all over him; he loved it. Watching, I thought that this was a Bobby Kennedy nobody knew who only saw him boring in on hostile gangsters at the hearings. It was during these years as counsel for the Rackets Committee that he acquired a reputation for being "ruthless." I did not think him ruthless—thought him hard driving, tenacious, aggressive, competitive, suspicious, abstemious, a man with a single-minded purpose, for his struggle to get Hoffa had become for Bobby Kennedy a holy crusade. He considered Hoffa the most dangerous man in the United States; something had to be done about him. In later years, I came to know another side of him—compassion, a deep concern for the disadvantaged, the poor, and especially Negroes, an abiding devotion to justice, a passionate interest in young people, a spontaneous warmth and affection, a brooding, almost tragic sense of life. Perhaps, in later years, after the Rackets Committee had ended its investigations and he had gone on to other things, just as in those years I discovered these qualities in him, so did he discover them in himself.

I had no way of knowing it at the time, of course, but meeting Bobby Kennedy on this story changed my life (and Fran's and our children's), just as had my first meeting with Adlai Stevenson. It was the beginning of my long association with Bobby Kennedy and his brothers, Jack and Ted. I wrote speeches for them and advised them throughout two of their presidential campaigns, advised them during other campaigns, and became a member of President Kennedy's administration. It all began with the Bobby Kennedy–Jimmy Hoffa story for the *Post* in 1958–1959.

I talked to some of the senators on the committee—John F. Kennedy, John L. McClellan (the chairman), and the leading Republican, Barry M. Goldwater, whom I approached with some trepidation because of his conservative reputation but whom I found to be an amusing, engaging man. I spent more time with Senator Kennedy than any of the others, seeing him alone in his office, at breakfast in a New York hotel, at dinner in Washington with his wife Jacqueline. When alone, he and I talked politics almost entirely. He was getting ready to run for president in 1960. The primaries would start in a little more than a year. He knew I had worked for Stevenson in two campaigns, and he wanted to know what kind of campaign staff he would need, what I thought of various issues such as the worldwide population explosion (I thought it important but voteless; he disagreed), and, though himself a Harvard overseer, he wanted to know how he could get "wired into" the academic world of policy ideas and position papers, as Stevenson was. Jack Kennedy struck me as an extremely attractive and extremely intelligent young man. He presented a lighthearted funny exterior, sometimes almost frivolous, but inwardly he was deadly serious and he had an astonishing fund of information about all manner of subjects, such as France's problems in Algeria and the number of Nigerian exchange students in the United States. He was tall and strikingly handsome, his mind was lightning fast and compelling, and he seemed much more tightly focused, both on issues and on his own ambitions, than Stevenson ever had. And he seemed to welcome challenges, not be burdened by them. Many people whom I ran into in Washington that winter and spring were already committed to Kennedy and were proselytizing for him, including some, like Hy Raskin, who had served Stevenson. I myself did not quite put Kennedy down in my mind the way Walter Lippmann had once described Roosevelt—a very nice young man who would very much like to be president—but I was not sure at first that he was presidential material. He was so young.

I spent a good deal of time with several members of Bobby Kennedy's staff. O'Donnell, Bobby's administrative assistant, was a tough, small, wiry young Boston Irishman who later became chief executive officer on Senator Kennedy's campaign plane in 1960 and still later President Kennedy's appointments secretary in the White House. Walt Sheridan was a former FBI man and one of Bobby's best investigators, another slight, taut young man. Nearly all of Bobby's investigators were in their late twenties and early thirties, and they lacked the tolerance of human weakness that big-city detectives like Emil Smicklas acquire. They condemned wrongdoing unequivocally, they had the moral certitude, the fervor, and the lust for a better world that go with youth, and sometimes I thought there was something a little chilling about their certitude and zeal. Pierre Salinger was somewhat different. A tolerant, self-indulgent, cheerful, cigar-smoking fat man, he had been a newspaperman and magazine writer. I had known Pierre ever since the 1956 Democratic primary in California. While I was resident there, alone and swamped with too many speeches to write, Salinger had sought me out and offered to help. I welcomed him. At that time he was the San Francisco correspondent of *Collier's* magazine. The editor of *Collier's* came to San Francisco, and Pierre brought him around to see me, and he wanted me to do a series of articles for *Collier's* on the Teamsters union. (At that time the investigation of the Teamsters had not yet begun.) I told him I couldn't undertake it till after the presidential election; he said he couldn't wait; I suggested he get Pierre Salinger to do it, and he did. At about the time Pierre finished his story, *Collier's* folded. The Rackets Committee was just beginning. Pierre took his material to Bobby Kennedy, and Bobby hired him as an investigator. By the time I went to work on the story, Pierre was acting, really, as the committee's—and Bobby's—press secretary, not only putting out press releases but also drafting the committee's reports, summarizing the testimony and stating its conclusions. Later, of course, Pierre became Senator Kennedy's press secretary in the 1960 presidential campaign and, still later, President Kennedy's press secretary in the White House. The Rackets Committee investigation changed quite a few lives.

It was one of the biggest investigations in recent American history, perhaps the biggest since those of Teapot Dome in the 1920s and banking and securities in the 1930s. Those investigations exposed wrongdoing by big business. The McClellan Committee alone went after big labor, especially the Teamsters. It also investigated eleven other unions as well as the Mafia and the Chicago Syndicate, but it concentrated on the Teamsters because the Teamsters, the biggest union in America, with more than a million and a half members, controlled truck transportation and so possessed the awesome power to stop the United States in its tracks. And its president, Jimmy Hoffa, in Bobby Kennedy's view, was evil and was in league with the worst criminal elements of the United States.

If Bobby Kennedy and his committee were half of my story, obviously the second half was Jimmy Hoffa and his union. I had first brushed up against the ponderous bulk of the Teamsters union as a kid reporter on the Indianapolis *Times.* During a truck strike, I was sent to interview the president of the Teamsters, whose national headquarters was then in Indianapolis. Dan Tobin, an old man who had been president since 1907, had an office with a door that was locked and steel-barred, like a prison cell, and I had to stand in the corridor outside it and shout my questions at him, and, sitting at a little desk, he yelled the answers at me, usually "No" or "No comment" or "Go to hell." I got nothing out of him. No reporter ever got much out of the Teamsters. Jimmy Hoffa was no exception. When I set to work on my story for the *Post,* he was seeing no reporters. He sat in the Teamsters headquarters in Washington facing the Capitol across the park, surrounded by secretaries and aides and assorted characters, and simply refused to see anybody except his own people. After several weeks talking to Bobby Kennedy and his staff and studying committee documents, I was ready to talk to Hoffa. While Hoffa would not talk to other reporters, I thought he might talk to a reporter from *The Saturday Evening Post,* with its prestige, particularly if I could convince him that I offered him a chance to tell his side and would write an unbiased story. But how could I get to him to convince him of that?

I adopted a stratagem. I went home and every day went down to the Chicago advertising office of the *Post* and put in a call for him. This had two advantages. The switchboard operator placed the call and announced that it was the *The Saturday Evening Post* calling and left the *Post* number in Chicago for him to call back. Moreover, this kept my home telephone number, and hence my address, out of Teamsters headquarters, which seemed only prudent in view of the reputation of some of Hoffa's associates. Every morning for a week I placed the call then sat all day in a little cubicle in the *Post* offices, waiting. Finally he called back and agreed to see me in Washington the following Thursday.

I interviewed him for two hours. We were alone (except that I thought, from the way he guided me to a particular chair, that our conversation was probably taped). He looked oddly out of place alone in his sumptuous office. It was so big, he so small. Yet he dominated it by force of personality and by his sense of his own power. He was built like a truck, low to the ground, burly, boxy, hard to knock over. He stood only five feet five and a half inches tall but he weighed 180 pounds. He was muscular, with thick legs, thick wrists, broad heavy shoulders, big feet. He ran up and down stairs. His shoes were scuffed and his pants baggy. His features were rugged and somewhat Indian in cast—straight black hair, high cheekbones. A hint of a sardonic smile often played around his mouth. His eyes were small, bright, green, hard. He had big, hard, calloused hands, stubby fingers. He could flash a quick grin but it was not a boyish grin, it was somewhat lopsided as though he didn't really mean it. He sometimes talked out of the side of his mouth, as Chicagoans do.

I no longer remember what we talked about at that first interview—I probably asked him what he thought of Bobby Kennedy and the committee and how the union worked, anything to convince him I wanted his point of view. And this was easy for me, because I really wanted his point of view. I told him I would need to see him several times again and needed to talk to other Teamster officers, but that even more I needed to talk to the guys on the trucks, men in the locals, and not just heads of locals but organizers and plain truck drivers. I told him I'd go anywhere and visit any locals he wanted me to. For I wanted to understand the union (and again, I really did).

Somewhat to my surprise, he would cooperate. He said he himself tried to stay close to the union membership. "It's a pretty elaborate building here, and you get pretty prominent visitors; you're staying in good hotels—but I think you got to get back where you belong. Back where you come from." He arranged for me to talk to other Teamsters officials in the Washington headquarters and he telephoned the head of a big Chicago local and told him to see me. He would telephone others.

I saw Jimmy Hoffa next in Chicago—spent a week with him at a lakefront hotel while he negotiated a new contract with Midwest truckers. From Chicago he was going to Miami for the annual meeting of the Teamsters executive board. I asked if I could go with him, and he said I could. I met him at Midway Airport at midnight. He arrived accompanied by Joey Glimco, a Chicago man whom newspapers usually identified as an associate of the highest leaders of the Chicago Syndicate. Hoffa and Glimco had been taking a steam bath; Glimco was just there to see him off. Hoffa had an airline ticket for me. I had anticipated this and bought my own. We flew to Florida together, and I spent a week with him at the Eden Roc, one of the gaudy seaside hotels on Miami Beach, and Hoffa introduced me to members of the executive board and told them to talk to me, and they did in bars and hotel rooms. They in no way resembled the caricature of lazy pot-bellied unionists; they were hardheaded, hard-driving men who knew what they wanted and how to get it.

I did other legwork on the Teamsters but I made the story that night I flew from Chicago to Miami with Jimmy Hoffa. On the plane, I sat beside him all the way. He could not escape. We talked all night. there was no telephone, no interruptions (though a stewardess recognized him, which secretly pleased him). I did not ask questions about the various cases the committee had brought against him, for I knew I would simply get the unresponsive answers the committee got. Rather, I was interested in his own life and character and his views on unionism, and by the time the long flight ended at dawn at Miami Airport, I had it. I liked him. He was first and last an underdog—born in Brazil, Indiana, son of a coal prospector who died when Jimmy was seven, taken to Detroit with his brother and two sisters by his mother "looking for some way to keep us alive," seventh-grade school dropout, street boy, grocery warehouse worker—and at the warehouse, because of bad working conditions, he organized a union, took it out on strike, won, and took it into a Teamsters local. The Depression was on. He told me, "The Depression in Detroit—it was knock down, drag out, starving people; it was murder, murder." He went to work for the union full-time, organizing, day and night. "We'd go out, hit the docks, talk to drivers, put up picket lines, conduct strikes, hold meetings day and night, convince people to join the union." They moved in on over-the-road drivers; they followed trucks to terminals and told dock workers there not to unload hot cargoes. "In the early days every strike was a fight. We used to sleep out in cars on the picket line. Detroit was the open-shop capital of America. Every time you'd go near a place to organize it you'd get picked up and put in jail. The police beat you on the head with night clubs. It was a mess. We fought everybody on the streets, mounted police, tear gas, I got in a lot of fights, got my head broke, got banged around. My brother got shot. We had a business agent killed by a strikebreaker." Once Hoffa was arrested eighteen times in one day. His police record did not show his picket line arrests; it showed only that between 1937 and 1946 he was arrested sixteen times, not counting traffic charges. Not one of his arrests was for an offense unconnected with his union activities. He had three convictions, none serious. He became president of Local 299 in Detroit. That became and it remained his power base. From there he clawed his way upward to the Teamsters presidency, using along the way rough tactics and men who did not scruple about force.

He was a far different man from Dave Beck, his predecessor. Beck was remote, cold, lofty, a "labor statesman"; Hoffa called hundreds of truck drivers by their first names. Beck had traveled with a retinue; Hoffa traveled alone. "His great delight," Hoffa said scornfully, "was to travel to Europe and come back, make a speech about it." Beck took the Fifth before the Rackets Committee; Hoffa did not, he defied it. Hoffa had no interest in sports, had no hobbies. Ideas did not interest him. Neither did political issues that did not directly affect labor. "I got no time," He deeply distrusted politicians. He disliked lawyers and public relations men. He was difficult to work for, demanding, curt, impatient of stupid men and old fogies. He ran the union out of his hat. He made snap decisions. He was explosive and unpredictable. What little he said seemed emotion charged. He probably trusted no one. He was a "more and better" unionist—more pay and better working conditions. I asked what labor leader he admired most, and he said without hesitation, "John L. Lewis." What historical figure? "Henry Ford. Then Truman," another underdog. He did not smoke or drink. He was an oddly moralistic man. In the lobby of the Eden Roc in Miami Beach, he and I were watching bellhops and elevator girls parade past in military style as they changed shifts, and Hoffa said, "If I had a hotel union, the first thing I'd do is stop parading people like cattle." He once walked out on a nightclub striptease act. He once forced nightclubs to stop requiring their hatcheck girls to wear uplift brassieres. Hoffa had married a girl he met on a picket line; he showed up for their first date wearing a bloody bandage on his head. By the time I was working on the story, she was forty, a shy tense disturbed woman, perhaps because of her age, perhaps because of the continuing pressures of the investigation. Hoffa treated her gently, with real affection. He was protective of her, and once when Bobby Kennedy considered Hoffa's answers on the witness stand evasive and threatened to call Hoffa's wife as a witness, Hoffa quickly said it wasn't necessary, he'd answer, and he did.

He and his wife had a modest house in Detroit. They rarely went out. Weekends they visited her sister or went to the house of one of his organizers or went to a lake where they owned a cottage. Saturday nights they watched television. Hoffa was interested in nothing but work—the union. And, in Bobby Kennedy's view, enriching himself. Kennedy, of course, suspected that Hoffa was not nearly so devoted to the welfare of the rank-and-file truck drivers as Hoffa claimed. He suspected Hoffa of making sweetheart contracts—contracts with employers, in return for kickbacks, that gave the drivers less than their due. This enraged Hoffa. Kennedy also suspected that Hoffa was anti-Negro, another lie, Hoffa said.

Although the backgrounds of Bobby Kennedy and Jimmy Hoffa could hardly have been more different, I was struck by certain similarities between them. Both were aggressive, competitive, hard driving, somewhat authoritarian, suspicious, temperate, at times congenial and at other times curt. Both were physical men who wanted to keep their bodies in shape—both did push-ups. Both spent their leisure time with their business associates; despite their wealth and power, both eschewed frivolity or indulgence and both seemed oblivious of their surroundings. Both were serious men and, in their own ways, dedicated.

The committee ended its work after three years. I drew some conclusions. It had produced a strong demand for reform labor legislation, and a bill eventually passed. The new law did little to shift the fundamental balance of power between big business and big labor, restricted picketing somewhat, probably drove a few crooks out of unions and made it harder for them to loot union treasuries (though that is still going on), and tried to improve union democracy but accomplished little. As a result of the committee's investigations, the AFL-CIO expelled the Teamsters and another union and put three more on probation. On the whole, I felt that the committee staff had performed an investigation task of greater difficulty with great skill. Bobby Kennedy and the senators conducted the hearings in a responsible way and with a high regard for accuracy. On the other hand, the committee did browbeat some Fifth Amendment witnesses mercilessly, forcing them to take the Fifth over and over again. Some lawyers felt the committee strayed far from legislative purposes. It produced damaging evidence against Hoffa and showed that his financial deals were, to say the least, odd. It never proved in the legal sense that he took a dime of union money or that he accepted an employer's payoff to sell out the workers—but it came close to proving both. The committee was unable to find the hoard of cash it believed he possessed. And it proved his affinity not only for ex-convicts but also for important Syndicate leaders. But it did not get him—he was acquitted in two criminal trials growing out of the investigation.

When I finished the story I offered to show it to both Bobby Kennedy and Jimmy Hoffa. Hoffa didn't want to see it, he didn't care what I wrote, they never do. Bobby and I spent the better part of a day going over it, not an easy negotiation—he was as tenacious with me as with the witnesses. He kept saying, "But you know he's a crook—why don't you just say so?" Fran, who was present, told him—a lawyer—"But Bobby, you know there are libel laws in this country." What bothered him most, I think, was my view that there were similarities between him and Hoffa. He never had thought of it and he simply refused to believe it.

My series was published as a paperback book by Fawcett under the execrable title *Jimmy Hoffa's Hot.* (I disliked the title so much that I never listed it along with my other books till now.) Bobby Kennedy went on to prepare for his brother Jack's run for president. Eventually Jimmy Hoffa went to a federal prison, though not on a charge directly connected with the committee's investigation. Released, he was no longer president of the Teamsters, and after a time he disappeared, apparently kidnapped and killed.

2.

The campaign for president began that spring of 1960. Senators John F. Kennedy and Hubert H. Humphrey were contesting the primaries. I considered this unfortunate, since I liked and admired both. Stevenson had not entered. But he would not declare himself out. Kennedy had made overtures to him to take himself out (and once may have offered to name him Secretary of State if he would). I myself advised Stevenson to do so, and so did Bill Blair and Newt Minow. I told Stevenson I did not think he could be nominated, and even if he were, he might lose to Richard Nixon, who seemed certain of the Republican nomination, and losing to Nixon would break his heart. But Eleanor Roosevelt and Agnes Meyer, wife of the owner of *The Washington Post,* and various other Stevenson idolators kept urging him to keep himself available, and that was what he was doing, right into the Los Angeles convention.

Bobby Kennedy asked me to join his brother's campaign staff. He said he had not wanted to mention it until after the Hoffa story was done but now he could, would I write speeches for and advise Jack? I told him I couldn't—I was for his brother's nomination, I thought Stevenson should take himself out and thus get out of Jack's way, but I had been with Stevenson a long time and I could not support another candidate so long as Stevenson remained obdurate. Bobby understood; all the Kennedys understood loyalty. I told him I would go to work for his brother the day after the convention nominated him, which I predicted would happen. In June, I saw Bobby again, and after that did a draft of an acceptance speech for his brother and also a memorandum proposing that I do editorial advance for him as I had during Stevenson's 1956 California primary race.

3.

During those years, the 1950s, my ulcers had not responded to medication and diet, and in 1956 Dr. Robertson, thinking they might be of psychosomatic origin, had referred me to Dr. Maxwell Gitelson, a Chicago psychoanalyst, and I had entered into analysis with him that lasted an hour a day three days a week for four years. Some people who have gone through analysis have found it the most rewarding experience of their lives. I found it painful and, as a way of getting through a midlife crisis, extremely helpful. But one's analysis is, really, of no more interest to anybody else than one's surgery.

Several years earlier, Fran's mother had come to us from Colorado. We took her to a Chicago hospital, but nothing could be done for her, so we put her in a nursing home in Highland Park, and it may have been analysis that enabled me to pick her up and carry her into the nursing home and put her in bed. She, who had not wanted Fran to marry me because I drank and had been divorced, looked up at me from her bed and said, "I wish you were my son." After three years she died. Fran was in Europe with Cindy at the time. I was home, however, and took care of things. Dan and Fred helped me, marching into the front row of the funeral home in their best suits like soldiers. Fran's brother, John, Jr., came from Colorado, and the boys and I helped him as best we could. I needed pallbearers—all her own friends were dead—and called our next-door neighbor, Jerry Goldwach, and he mustered out his company executives and they carried her casket to the grave beside her husband in an Elmhurst cemetery. It was a restricted cemetery. Jerry Goldwach and his pallbearers were Jewish. Only after the funeral did I call Fran in Paris. John, Jr., was not supposed to drink but after the funeral, taking him to the airport to go back to Colorado, I gave him a couple of whiskey miniatures, and he was grateful.

Fran and I were at an age when our friends were dying—Frederick Lewis Allen, Harold Ober, Lou Kohn, Dr. Robertson, and, a little later, my analyst Dr. Gitelson. Aside from that, however, those years, the 1950s, were among the best years of our lives. We were doing a little traveling—Cuba, Mexico, Central America, especially Nicaragua, which reminded me of the Dominican Republic; but for the most part we were living the suburban good life in our old Victorian house on Maple Avenue in Highland Park. (We had bought it in 1952, as I have said, and we live in it yet, and love it.) We saw our Highland Park friends at dinner parties and garden parties. Francis and Mary Ellen Nipp often came out for weekends. We had become

close friends of several people we had met in the Stevenson campaigns, especially Marshall and Doris Holleb of Chicago. So many
people you meet in a campaign become your permanent friends. A
campaign is a watershed in your life and later you tend to date
everything by whether it happened before or after a certain campaign. In the summer we sat on the screened back porch I had built
low to the ground overlooking the lawn sloping down to the ravine,
drinking martinis and cooking steaks on a charcoal grill. If you rode
the Northwestern Railroad train to Chicago on a Sunday afternoon,
you would see a little plume of smoke arising from every backyard
along the tracks, and I fear we were no exception to the convention.
Sometimes we had a lobster race—put a big kettle of water to boil
on the charcoal grill and set live lobsters on the porch floor and
prodded them to scramble toward the grill, and the first to get there
was privileged to be the first boiled. Dan and Fred loved it and soon
were big enough to pull the wooden plugs out of the lobsters' claws.
And big enough to play softball in our backyard. Fred was big
enough too to argue with me—"That's not three strikes, it's only
two." Fred was our risk-taker. As a little boy he got into more scary
adventures than anybody. Most of them were not funny, though he
thought they were. One fall day he lay down in the gutter of the
street in front of our house and covered himself with leaves, and a
man who drove around the corner and almost ran over him got
trembling out of his car and told Fred over and over, "Don't you
ever do that again." Even when he had been tiny and still in a crib,
trouble: One night Fran was wakened by a peculiar grinding sound
and went into his room and found that he had broken his baby bottle and was chewing the broken glass. A constant joy. But he was. So
was Dan. Fred, the youngest of our three, was highly competitive,
pedaling his tricycle furiously to try to keep up with Dan on a bicy-
cle on their way to school. Dan was not competitive, was quieter,
gentler. Cindy was bright but she was not doing well in Highland
Park High School, a big public school, and we feared she soon
would sink without a trace. And so I called on my friends in politics
and publishing to write letters recommending her to private boarding schools—in those days, admission to boarding school and college was difficult, and a father would do anything short of murder to
get his child in—and I took her to visit several schools in New

England. She wore a long drab coat with a fake-fur collar, and at her interviews with the school people, she somehow managed to look like a drowned mouse. And to mumble. None of the sparkling Cindy that Fran and I knew and loved came through. She was admitted nowhere. So she went back to Highland Park High, and only after many rescue operations did she graduate in 1960. And again I went with her through the whole miserable business of taking her to visit schools, and she was finally admitted to Sarah Lawrence College.

During those years, Fran and I played nickel-dime-quarter poker with the neighbors and we went to the track, to the horse races at Arlington Park. My greatest day at the races came when I, after diligent study of Moe Annenberg's *Daily Racing Form,* picked a long shot named A Dragon Killer, bet him five dollars across the board, sat down to watch, decided he was sure to win, went back and bet him again across the board and also to win, bet also two dollars our maid had given me to bet for her, then went down to the rail to watch; and as they came down the stretch A Dragon Killer was far back, but I yelled, "Wake up, A Dragon Killer," and he woke up and ran around all the other horses and won going away. I never kept accounts but I'm sure I lost far more at the races than I won. Fran did rather well, both at the track and betting through a bookie in Highwood, the next town north of Highland Park, filled with taverns and handbooks controlled by the Syndicates. Fran had a system. She bet on horses whose names she liked. She bet on Painted Porch because she had just painted our porch (as her mother had painted hers for our marriage). She bet on Yukon Jake because Yukon Jake is the hero of a takeoff on a Robert W. Service poem about the Arctic that we recite at camp in Upper Michigan. And others—all were long shots; all won. Word got out around Highwood that Mrs. Martin must have an inside pipeline to the mysterious "they" who fixed the races, and the laundryman and others respectfully solicited her picks.

Summers Fran and I often took the boys to the Lake Michigan beach a block and a half from our house, in front of the house of Lawrence and Viola Stein. This friendship went back to the time we first moved to Highland Park and I published my book on Indiana. Mrs. Stein's daughter was Ruth Nath, one of the owners of the

Chestnut Court bookshop in Highland Park. Mrs. Stein's other daughter, Louise Steele, was about our age and married to John Steele, chief of the Washington bureau of *Time,* and they became good friends. Louise visited her parents, the Steins, for part of every summer, and with her, Fran and I took our boys and her children down to the beach to cook hot dogs and drink martinis and watch the kids swim, long golden afternoons, usually ending with dinner at the Steins' house or ours. John Steele would come out from Washington and at neighborhood parties he and I would talk national politics. We sometimes stayed with the Steeles in Washington; I was staying with them when President Kennedy was assassinated. In 1956 John Steele had wanted to go to work as Adlai Stevenson's press secretary, for he was an admirer of Stevenson, and I had brought them together, and Stevenson wanted him, but *Time* would not guarantee to give him back his job after the campaign, so he had been obliged to turn it down.

Every summer we spent a month or six weeks at the camp we had bought at Three Lakes in the Upper Peninsula of Michigan. I taught the boys to fish, as I had Cindy, and took them to other lakes to sleep in a tent for a night or two. When they were small, I put them in a pack on my back and carried them up to a high rock bluff from which we could see all three of the lakes and the woods and highway spread out below. In 1956 we bought a Jeep, enabling us to go farther into the woods to remote lakes, and we took the boys on day-long Jeep rides, looking for animals and stopping alongside a logging road in the woods to cook lunch. But Three Lakes was changing. The highline came in, and while electricity made life easier, it also changed the camp's atmosphere from the kerosene lamp days. We put in gas space heaters, and that destroyed the fireplace, made it purely ornamental, not essential. We even put in a telephone. But there was worse. When we first had come here to Three Lakes, there had been few camps on our lake, you seldom saw another boat, and it was quiet. Now a nightclub opened up, traffic on the highway became terrible, a cluster of trailers sprang up behind our place, the shoreline was almost completely ringed by camps, and water-skiers despoiled the lake. Fran and I began looking for a piece of land farther out in the woods. We studied maps and the platbook, checked titles at the courthouse, and went by Jeep into the woods to look at property. We started out looking for only a 40-acre tract on a lake. We came close to buying several. But there was something wrong with all. I knew, however, of a lake far out in the woods north of the highway, Smith Lake, extremely remote, no road to it, only a wretched logging road reaching within a mile of it, virgin land in the wilderness. I checked the title and found that there were three owners on Smith Lake, all loggers. I felt pretty sure two of them wouldn't sell—I knew them—and even if the third one would, his was a big piece of property, a quarter section—160 acres plus a narrow strip along the far shore, too much for us. It looked discouraging. But one day I took Fran to Smith Lake, parking the Jeep and walking through the woods the rough last mile to the lake by compass, took her up on a high granite bluff with a mighty hemlock grove sixty feet above the glistening water, and I told her, "Someday we're going to have a camp here." She thought I was crazy. But, as we shall see, one day we did.

Several times during those years my mother and father came to visit us up at Three Lakes, he with great enthusiasm. Anything he did, he did with great, even boisterous, enthusiasm. These last years of theirs had been good years. He had sold the old house on Brookside Avenue and built her the lannon stone house on Kessler Boulevard up on the North Side she'd always wanted. His health was good, he took her on auto trips, they traveled abroad, they visited us more often than ever before, he and I came to terms as I came to like and understand him, and he took pride in articles and books I published and in my association with Stevenson and Kennedy. My father loved to fish and had taught me to fish as a boy. He had never before fished north of Indiana, I think, until he came to us in Upper Michigan. His first fishing rule was, as we began, to put one finger to his lips, and whisper loudly, *"Shhh—don't say anything—you'll scare the fish,"* meanwhile himself stomping on the boat bottom heedless. He was essentially a live-bait fisherman but in the 1920s he had taken up casting artificial baits for bass. It was new in Indiana, it was the latest, and he, the quintessential consumer, always had to have the latest. His method of casting was to stand up in the boat— which is unsafe—to draw back his arm full-length, and then, spinning his whole body half around, to heave the bait, a wooden plug with three wicked treble-hooks, toward shore not overhead but side-arm, which is not only inaccurate but downright dangerous to anybody else in the boat—I always had to duck. I don't think he had any idea where the bait was going. Hunting, he was not a very good shot, and fishing, he was not a very good fisherman, but he was a good sportsman if only because he loved it. By this time I had graduated to split bamboo casting rods but he still used his old, long, bent steel rod, tubular steel at that. The reel was tied to it with a string, the reel-seat being broken. The reel—that was his pride. I believe when he originally acquired it he was under the impression that it was a fly reel, but it was not, was only a bizarre casting reel. It was six or eight inches in diameter and its spool was less than an inch wide. On a rod, it looked as ungainly as a windmill, and it worked not nearly so smoothly. It was called a Winona reel, after Winona Lake in Indiana. In the 1920s my father used to take my mother and me up to Winona Lake for a week or two in a rented house. The Winona Lake colony was led by an evangelist, I forget whether Billy Sunday or E. Howard Cadle. My father took a contract to build sewers for it. But when the work was done, the Depression came on, and the reverend evangelist's flock could not pay my father, so under Indiana law, he took instead a number of vacant lots. I believe he let them go for taxes in the Depression. About all he salvaged as a souvenir was the Winona reel. By the 1950s it had broken down time and again, but he had fixed it up with wire and an assortment of wing nuts, square nuts, bolts, and string. He was proud of it. It was special. And proud of how he'd fixed it. No one else had a reel quite like it. Indeed, I never saw another Winona. One day up in Michigan I took him fishing, as he had taken me as a boy, and we went to a lake out in the woods that was full of bass and walleye pike. I rowed him to a cove I knew was good and told him to go ahead. He stood up, rocking the boat, drew back, stretched his arm, let fly with a mightly whoosh, I ducked, and the Winona reel flew apart, it showered us with wing nuts, square nuts, bolts, wire, pieces of reel. He stood there, astounded. I could not help it: I laughed. He turned to me. He was grinning sheepishly. He said, "I'll be demmed." He never really swore unless he was angry. He couldn't believe the Winona had failed him. I asked if he wanted to go home. "No," he said, "you go ahead and fish. I'll see what I can do," and he laid down his old rod and began poking around in the bottom of the boat looking for parts, though some of them had flown into the water. That night at camp he sat up late at the kitchen table, poking through little boxes of nuts and bolts to find something that would save the Winona, a single long white hair floating above the bald top of his head. I watched him and loved him.

That June of 1960, my father and mother and my aunt Verl visited us in Highland Park for Cindy's graduation from high school. He had not been feeling well, most unusual for him, and when he reluctantly told me his symptoms, I thought he might have a heart condition. With difficulty, I persuaded him to see Dr. Sunoll Blumenthal, who had taken over Sylvan Robertson's practice and was now my doctor, and Dr. Blumenthal told him he had had a heart episode and strongly urged him to go into the hospital for further tests and treatment. He refused. I tried to persuade him. He was adamant. I knew what was in his mind—prolonged hospitalization, perhaps even a nursing home. Can you imagine that big strong man in a nursing home? Next morning he got up early as usual, dressed, ate a big breakfast, and in that big booming voice of his called upstairs, "Anybody going to Indianapolis?" My mother and Aunt Verl came down and away they went, he no doubt driving seventy as always. They made it.

Fran and I went up to our camp at Three Lakes the Fourth of July weekend. At dawn four days later somebody knocked on our screen door, an unheard-of thing. Our best friend, Earl Numinen, was standing at the door, his face as gray as the presunrise dawn, and he said, "John, your dad died last night."

Several times in recent years I had brought my father up to Michigan in October partridge hunting, and he and Earl had become good friends. Why not—not only was Earl a construction engineer and my father a contractor but they were both great human beings. Several times my father told me, "I like that Earl Numinen." It was about as high a compliment as he ever paid anyone. We took my father hunting on the terrible logging roads, and when in the Jeep we would come to a mudhole, he could not believe we were going to try to go through it, no vehicle could, and when we had ground our way through successfully he would look back at it, still in disbelief.

He became enthusiastic about partridge hunting and discarded his old double-barreled shotgun and bought a new automatic. An automatic is really not the best gun for partridge but it was the latest so my father bought it. After he died I gave it to Earl.

That dawn I wakened the children and told them their grandfather had died—they had loved him—and I went to town with Earl and from his house called my mother, who had called Earl, and asked her what had happened. She said that in the middle of the night he had half-raised himself on the bed and had looked at her and had said, "Poor dearie." He always called her dearie. Then he had lain down dead of a heart attack. In the bed they always slept in and that I was born in. I told her we'd be down. We drove the six hundred miles that day, I mindful all the way of something my father once had said: "More demmed fools get killed goin' to funerals"—grief stricken, they become heedless. My uncle Paul, my father's brother and my favorite relative, was there. As a young man Uncle Paul had played semipro baseball and now he had retired to Arizona. He told us how one day he had gone out to watch the Chicago Cubs in spring training in Arizona and how, after watching awhile, being then past seventy, he had gotten up and strolled to home plate, picked up a bat, gestured to the pitcher to throw, and hit a home run, then strolled over to the bleachers on the other side. Everybody thought he was a big-league scout and from then on he didn't have to pay to get into spring training. That story, and others he told, were about all that made that week bearable.

After the funeral, Fran and I stayed on a bit, helping Mother with the estate, and although she wanted to move into an apartment at once, I insisted that she stay in the house on Kessler Boulevard for at least one year, and I did some figuring to show her she could afford it and told her we'd help her if she couldn't. She stayed in her house on Kessler until she died ten years later.*

The day in 1960 my father was buried, the Democratic National Convention began in Los Angeles, and three days later it nominated John F. Kennedy for president. The Kennedys sent Richard N. Goodwin, a young writer and issues man on Kennedy's staff, to

* Her sister, my aunt Verl, to whom I had always been close—I was her only living relative—died ten years after that, in 1980. During their last years, Fran and I had helped take care of her parents and my mother and my aunt. A melancholy task.

Highland Park to talk to me. (Goodwin had made his reputation as counsel to a congressional committee investigating TV game-show shenanigans.) We went over the issues and positions Kennedy intended to stress. Kennedy wanted to try my editorial advance system on his whistlestop trip down the Central Valley of California, coming up in ten days. I would go at once.

TEN

JFK

1.

So, though it was not clear then, a period of my life ended, the period that encompassed Chicago crime and Adlai Stevenson.

I went immediately to Philadelphia, told Ben Hibbs and Stuart Rose I was going to work for Kennedy, and went to California. I spent a week there, doing legwork and writing briefing sheets for Kennedy's whistlestop tour, and went to Detroit and did the same thing for his swing through Michigan the next week. On Labor Day, I stood in the crowd in Cadillac Square, watching Kennedy speak, as I had watched Stevenson speak, and I was struck by how much more forceful, even aggressive, Kennedy was. He seemed to assume this labor crowd was with him, and if it wasn't he would convert it, and he did, to cheers.

I went with him through the Michigan whistlestops and stayed with him aboard his plane the next two days through the Northwest then on to California and the whistlestops down the Central Valley, five-minute speeches delivered from the back platform of a train, and before each one I gave him my briefing sheet. He liked it and wanted me to continue throughout the campaign. I couldn't do the sheets all myself, so I taught a young journalist, Joseph Kraft, and another man to do them.

* * *

I had joined John F. Kennedy with some misgivings. After all, he was a totally different man from Stevenson, and I had admired Stevenson so long. Transferring political loyalty is not easy. And Stevenson had seemed a statesman. Kennedy was so young. I had never followed a leader younger than I. At the start of the campaign, Theodore Sorensen once wrote, people thought of Kennedy as wealthy, inexperienced, young, and Catholic; while his Catholicism did not bother me, the other things did. By the end of the California trip, however, I knew I had my candidate, a candidate for president I believed in.

He never wavered, never took his eye off the ball. He was out to win. And he was out to convince a complacent nation that its peace was precarious and its prosperity false. He stuffed even his whistle-stops with facts—the average wage of female laundry workers in the five biggest cities, how many more classrooms and how many more jobs the country would need in the next ten years, per capita income figures in Libya. He began such recitations by saying, "I am not satisfied when . . ." He ended each by saying, "I think we can do better." And over and over and always he declared, "It's time to get this country moving again."

Sometimes watching Kennedy speak, I felt a twinge of nostalgia for Stevenson's graceful prose, his choked uncertain utterance, his convoluted, almost tortured sentences that sought out the truth, all the qualities that endeared him to his followers. It takes nothing away from Stevenson to say that Kennedy was being far more effective in rallying the country to him. Kennedy differed from Stevenson, not only in his youth and personality, but in his approach to issues, a hard pragmatic decisive approach quite unlike Stevenson's thoughtful discursive expositions. Kennedy spent far less time preparing speeches and far more time talking to local politicians. He repeated the same speech over and over and over. He gestured forcefully, almost seemed to seize the audience physically, and threw himself wholly into every speech and upon every audience. His speeches did not soar and capture the imagination as had Stevenson's 1952 speeches, but they got his message across—that he was young, vigorous, and could get this country moving again.

In writing a Stevenson speech, as I have suggested, you put your

emphasis on good writing. For Kennedy, you put it on political effect. Nevertheless, when I first went aboard the Kennedy plane, Ted
Sorensen, telling me how to write a Kennedy speech, said, "A Kennedy speech has to have class," and he was right, it did, and some of
the most eloquent campaign prose in our time came from Kennedy,
particularly in some of the endings that were almost parables, in
what he said about his Catholicism, in the parallelisms he devised.
But when he spoke on foreign affairs, he did not seem burdened or
tentative, as Stevenson sometimes had; rather, he seemed to know
exactly where we should go and how we could get there. Clearly he
cared little whether people admired his speeches as oratory, cared a
great deal about whether his speeches made people want to follow
him, to vote for him. Once that fall, introducing Kennedy at a rally,
Stevenson said, "Do you remember that in classical times when
Cicero had finished speaking, the people said, 'How well he
spoke'—but when Demosthenes had finished speaking, the people
said, 'Let us march.' " It was so apt it stung.

The campaign raised no single big decisive issue. It set forth no
new proposal except the Peace Corps. Kennedy's religion dominated until he squelched it at Houston. Such issues as Castro and
the missile gap rose and fell. (I became involved in working on the
Castro issue since I knew something about the Caribbean area,
especially Cuba and the Dominican Republic.) He had almost unbelievable appeal to young people, and when he motorcaded at a
college campus, they stopped his car, yelling and screaming and
jumping up and down, beside themselves. But he appealed too to
others less demonstrative—workingmen, suburbanites, Negroes,
even farmers. People began saying, "That young fella's got something." He had a regional strategy—concentrated on the seven biggest states, especially doubtful ones, plus most of New England and
the South. But he was above all, as few are, a national politician. His
great causes—America's future, America's prestige, America's
peril—these were national causes. He spoke thus even at the whistlestops, a candidate for the whole nation swooping down on some
little farm town for a brief bright moment.

I was the only one aboard the plane who had also been with Stevenson. The Kennedy people played with a hard ball. Ted Sorensen,
sitting right outside the door to Senator Kennedy's private cabin,

was the keeper of the portals—nobody got in to see Kennedy unless Sorensen approved. Just so, Kenny O'Donnell, with his jutting Irish jaw, stood at the foot of the stairs while the plane was boarding, and nobody went aboard unless O'Donnell approved. It was a no-nonsense campaign, work to be done, no time wasted on people's feelings. Arthur Schlesinger wanted to come aboard and help, and called me, and I spoke to Ted Sorensen, but Sorensen said no— Arthur was a good writer but he was identified with the liberal ADA and why should Kennedy take on the burden of being criticized as the captive of the ADA, as Stevenson had been? It was a hardboiled political decision. Sorensen was a quiet, solid, abstemious man. He had been with Kennedy so long that they communicated almost by shorthand. When the plane came to a stop for a brief airport speech, Kennedy, on his way out to speak, would pause beside Sorensen, and Sorensen would look up at him and utter a sentence or two, suggesting a speech theme, and Kennedy would think, nod, remember, and go out and deliver it. Dick Goodwin was brilliant and he became my friend but at that time he was terribly young, only twenty-eight, and he was somewhat abrasive and heedless of others; once sitting beside me in the window seat, he sprang up to go talk to Kennedy and in his haste actually stepped on my stomach. Ted Sorensen wrote, rewrote, or reviewed every speech. In delivering a speech, Kennedy almost never followed the prepared text. Stevenson's texts always had read better than they sounded. Kennedy's always sounded better than they read—reading some of them later, I wondered why the applause. It was, of course, Kennedy's own personality, his conviction, his purposefulness, his mastery, the confidence and enthusiasm he inspired, inspired as few candidates if any since Roosevelt have. When the campaign began, Kennedy was an underdog. His opponent, Nixon, was better known, was considered more experienced in government, was certainly more experienced in national campaigns and national television, while the Democrats were divided, Kennedy's nomination had soured the South, his choice of Lyndon Johnson for vice-president had soured the North, Stevenson diehards were unreconciled, and the nation's newspaper editors and publishers were against Kennedy (but the reporters covering the campaign were for him). And this underdog, by the sheer force of his campaigning, did turn it around.

* * *

It would be tedious to relate my travels across the country during that 1960 fall campaign. About half the time I was out ahead of Kennedy doing editorial advance, about half with him aboard his plane. He was far easier to work with than Stevenson—he never complained, never lost patience, never became short-tempered, was far more accessible. He took advice more readily, made decisions faster. He wasted no time. He used his staff well. He did not hold large staff meetings, believing that nothing ever gets decided by a committee, only by two men talking to each other—or by one man alone.

As time passes, all campaigns tend to blur into one another, but I retain a few scattered impressions of the 1960 campaign. Early one morning in Kennedy's hotel suite in St. Louis, while his aide Dave Powers was rousing him as usual by asking him, "What do you suppose Nixon's doing while you're lying there in bed?" I waited in the living room with Jacqueline Kennedy. When Kennedy came out, he greeted us briefly, and she started to say something, but he went into another room, where a delegation of men—I have the impression they were from India—was waiting, and the door closed behind him. She stood staring at it. She looked absolutely alone and lost. I never felt sorrier for anyone. She was terrified by campaigning, helpless in its inexorable pull. Several years later, at Bobby's house in McLean, after both he and her husband had been assassinated, I saw her again like that, that same vulnerable look on her face. To millions of Americans, she was in those years a great lady, a glamorous creature; to me she was a frightened child.

Once in Kennedy's hotel in Baltimore I needed to see him about a coming speech, and Kenny O'Donnell told me to go ahead, but when I went into his bedroom I found him stretched out flat on his bed, his face grimacing in pain from his back, his eyes glazed, even a Kennedy utterly exhausted by the cruelties of campaigning, and I left him alone.

One day near the end of the campaign, on the plane as we were approaching Chicago, Kennedy called me into his cabin. He showed me a copy of the current *Saturday Evening Post* and it contained my piece "To Chicago with Love," and he said, "What are you trying to do—lose Illinois?" He was kidding—he had read the story and enjoyed it. But of course it did contain material on Chicago's corrupt crime-politics alliance, and the Chicago newspapers were making a brief uproar over it, and Mayor Daley had told a press conference, "I think John must have come through Chicago with blinders on." He knew I was with Kennedy. I sent Mayor Daley a letter saying, as I recall it, that I was sorry if the piece had discomfited him, I had written it in fun out of my great affection for his great city of Chicago, and, furthermore, in this campaign we had the candidates and the issues and we were going to win. The mayor had his floor leader in the City Council read the letter into the record. On that trip Otto Kerner, running for governor, came aboard and wanted to advise Kennedy on his Illinois speeches, and Kennedy told him to talk to me. When he had finished, I went into Kennedy's cabin, told him what Kerner had advised, and told him I thought it all wrong. He said, "OK, then forget it." On that trip we made a swing across the far southern counties of Illinois, and at the first main stop, Southern Illinois University, Kenndy was introduced by state representative Paul Powell, an old boodler whom I had known in the legislature, and Powell outdid himself. He told at great length the famous story of Kennedy's heroism when, in the Pacific during World War II, the torpedo boat he commanded, PT-109, had been cut in half by a Japanese destroyer, and Kennedy had heroically rescued his men. Powell, embellishing the tale, described how Kennedy the young hero had tied a rope not around only one of his injured seamen and towed him to safety, as the story usually related, but had tied the rope to half of the shattered hulk of the torpedo boat itself, containing his entire crew, and, putting the other end of the rope in his teeth, had dragged all hands to safety on an island through mile after mile of mountainous seas—"and he swum and he swum and he swum," Powell cried hoarsely, chopping the air with his arms in swimming motions. His introduction was far longer than Kennedy's speech. And to a college audience. After the speech, as we got back in the motorcade, Kennedy called me over and told me to persuade Powell to soft-pedal it the rest of the day. A delicate mission—Paul Powell was a formidable figure; but I managed, and we survived the day.

On election night, Fran and I were in Hyannis Port, up all night—it was one of the closest elections in history. Kennedy won by less than 120,000 out of nearly 69 million votes cast. He carried

Illinois by only 8,858. He lost California, lost Indiana, Wisconsin, and Ohio; he barely won Michigan. He was a minority president—had got less than half the total votes cast.

In a sense, I grew up politically in Kennedy's 1960 campaign. Stevenson in 1952, as he had while governor, had maintained a certain amateur attitude toward politics. Kennedy never had it at all. From him and his staff and his campaign strategy, I learned hard politics. And this was backed up by what I had learned writing about politics. For almost the first time I began thinking of myself as, if not a professional politician, at least no longer an amateur.

2.

That winter, while I was going back to write for the *Post*, the Kennedy administration was being formed. Arthur Schlesinger went on the White House Staff as a sort of cultural attaché, with the title special assistant to the president. Other friends of mine were going on the president's staff, Ted Sorenson to head it and Kenny O'Donnell, Pierre Salinger, Fred Dutton, Dick Goodwin. Bobby Kennedy was attorney general. Stevenson's entire law firm joined the new administration, Stevenson as ambassador to the UN, Bill Wirtz as undersecretary of labor (later secretary), Bill Blair as ambassador to Denmark, Newt Minow as chairman of the Federal Communications Commission. And so many more people I knew were ambassadors, aides to Bobby at Justice, officials at State and other places (Dave Bell was budget director, Ken Galbraith ambassador to India). Never before had I known so many important people in an administration. It was an aspect of political campaigning to which I had given no thought.

Fran and I were invited to the Kennedy inauguration. Numerous parties preceded it; we watched amused as others played the game of the "A Party" and "B Party"—a man will sacrifice his closest friend in order to himself get to the "A Party," the one behind guarded doors, where will be found all the political figures that count. We were staying with John and Louise Steele. They and we had been invited to the party at the house of Kay Graham, daughter of Agnes Meyer and now the wife of *The Washington Post*'s publisher, the most prestigious party of all, held the night before the inaugural.

That night a blizzard paralyzed Washington and, since John had to meet his boss, Henry Luce, at the airport, Louise essayed to drive Fran and me to the Kay Graham party. For what seemed hours we struggled through blinding driving snow and mounting drifts, traffic askew all over the streets, cars abandoned; and at last we drew up in front of what looked like an abandoned library. Not a track crossed the snow. The house was dark. "My God," Louise gasped, "I've brought you to her mother's house. Agnes Meyer's." We spent the rest of the evening in our finery getting back to Louise's house, where we had several drinks.

Inauguration day was clear but bitter cold, with an icy wind, and rather than sit out in the open at the Capitol to witness the swearing-in and hear the president's speech, Fran and I went to the chambers of Judge Bazelon* in the Federal Courthouse not far from the Capitol and, with a party of his friends, watched President Kennedy's inaugural speech on television: "Let every nation know, whether it wishes us well or ill, that we shall pay any price, bear any burden, meet any hardship, support any friend, oppose any foe to assure the survival and the success of liberty," and, after setting forth in soaring prose the tasks ahead, "All this will not be finished in the first one hundred days. Nor will it be finished in the first one thousand days, nor in the life of this administration, nor even perhaps in our lifetime on this planet. But let us begin."

That night we went to the Inaugural Ball at the Washington Armory and next day to a brunch at the home of Phil Stern, a Democratic publicist whom we had known in the two Stevenson campaigns. All the old Stevenson people who were going into the Kennedy administration were there, a gala time. George Ball shocked me a little by saying, "Well, I always thought if Stevenson won, I'd be undersecretary of state for economic affairs, and now I am anyway." He and Stevenson and others left to go to the White House to be sworn in. In a day or two Fran and I went home. How I wished my father, a lifelong Democrat, could have lived a few months longer to see John F. Kennedy elected president.

---

* David Bazelon, originally from Chicago, a judge on the U.S. court of appeals for the District of Columbia, was one of America's most distinguished jurists, a champion of the rights of the accused, often mentioned for appointment to the Supreme Court. We had become friends while I was writing my series on criminal justice.

3.

The firm that handled public relations for Puerto Rico invited Fran and me to visit Puerto Rico for a week or ten days, expenses paid, in the hope that I would find something to write about but placing me under no obligation to do so. I checked with the *Post* then went. I found no story for the *Post* but this did not seem to bother our hosts—they were playing for the long haul, and indeed in years to come I did do some writing about Puerto Rico.

We were about to leave when I suggested to Fran that on our way home we visit the Dominican Republic. I had never been back since Barbara and I had been there the winter of 1937–1938 (twenty-three years ago—was it possible?). I had always wanted to go, for I had liked the Dominican Republic and its people better than any other in the Caribbean, but, since I had published my anti-Trujillo piece, I had not thought it entirely safe. Trujillo had had the author of an anti-Trujillo book kidnapped in New York and murdered in the Dominican Republic. Now, however, I thought it might be safe because of my connections with the Kennedy administration.

Knowing that, since I entered the republic as a journalist, our hotel room would probably be searched, I wrote letters to Ted Sorensen and Arthur Schlesinger in the White House, giving them our detailed itinerary and telling them when to expect us back, and I left carbons in my briefcase in the hotel room. Trujillo's secret police and their informers were everywhere. And now that events seemed to be closing in on him, his iron rule tightened. Last August the United States had joined the other members of the Organization of American States in imposing economic and diplomatic sanctions on Trujillo; we had no ambassador there now, and our economic sanctions were hurting Trujillo.

Fran and I spent a week there, ostentatiously visiting tourist sites and, more quietly, talking to a wide scattering of Dominicans about the dictatorship. The country, especially the capital, seemed unnaturally tense. When we got home, I wrote a memo on Trujillo, the republic, the effects of the sanctions, and the likelihood of subversion directed, organized, or inspired by Castro, and I sent it to Arthur Schlesinger in the White House.

* * *

Several times that spring while in Washington doing legwork for the *Post,* I saw friends in the administration, and one evening Arthur Schlesinger startled me by asking, "How'd you like to be ambassador to Switzerland?"

I told him I didn't know anything about being an ambassador nor did I know anything about Switzerland, though I had the impression it was a rather dull place. He asked, "How about Morocco?" but it turned out that the king of Morocco still cut off the hands of thieves, not a pleasant prospect. Arthur said, however, that it was not easy to find capable people to staff the new administration and that I ought to think about it.

It was, as I have said, something I never had thought of during the three presidential campaigns I had worked in. But Washington was always a lovely city, never lovelier than that first spring of the Kennedy administration, for it was suffused with an atmosphere of youth, of vigor, of hope. The man who made it so was the new young president. And my friends were now at his side, dealing every day with high policy, at the very center of power in the most powerful nation on earth. But here was I, applying to television executives for information about their grubby businesses and peddling it to the *Post.* But there was more than that wrong. Recently I had done a four-part *Post* series on changes wrought in the Midwest since World War II. It was a good enough story. But it troubled me. I was repeating myself. Was doing all over again what I had done so long ago in Muncie for *Harper's.* It was getting too easy, too expectable. I have always worked best when I worked against a resistance, writing something new, something hard. And recently too I had written a piece for *Look* about a young man in New Jersey who had given ample warning that there was something wrong with him but had got no help from his schools and a state hospital and had killed. It was a good story, and *Look* loved it. But I knew I was repeating myself. I was restless, wondering if I ought not to change course, try something new, take a risk.

Three New Frontiersmen asked me to write a speech that spring—Bobby Kennedy, Newt Minow, and Bill Blair, the last off to Denmark as ambassador. I did. Of the three speeches, Newt Minow's had the most impact. It was his first speech as chairman of the FCC to the National Association of Broadcasters, the powerful organization of broadcasters. It was for Newt an important speech, perhaps the most important he would ever make, for he intended to try to reform television and the FCC alone had the power to do it. At that same time, I was starting to write my series on TV for the *Post,* and I began that series by describing the day I had put in watching Channel 5 for twenty hours straight, concluding that it had presented "a vast wasteland of junk." Now in writing Minow's speech I suggested he say to the broadcasters, "I invite you to sit down in front of your television set when your station goes on the air and stay there . . . and keep your eyes glued to that set until the station goes off. I can assure you that you will observe a vast wasteland of junk." In editing the speech himself, Newt had the wit to cut "of junk." He delivered the speech in May 1961, in the old Wardman Park Hotel. Riding there with President Kennedy, he told the president that what he intended to say was pretty tough on the broadcasters, and the president told him to go ahead. He stunned the broadcasters. More, he became something of a symbol of the newness and boldness of the Kennedy administration. And the phrase "vast wasteland" made his reputation and clings to him yet. As for me, in writing my *Post* series, I stuck to my lead on my twenty-hour day but I was obliged to change the ending of the passage, offering "vast wasteland" not as my own summary of what I had seen but, instead, writing, "This is what Newton N. Minow, the beleaguered new chairman of the Federal Communications Commission, has called a "vast wasteland." I had approached in my work a conflict of interest. It didn't bother me.*

The newspaper headline on May 31 that year, 1961, said that Generalissimo Trujillo, dictator of the Dominican Republic, had been assassinated, and all of a sudden, having a drink with Fran on the back porch, I asked, "How would you like to be the wife of the ambassador to the Dominican Republic?" I had not previously thought much about what Arthur had said about my becoming an ambassador. But the Dominican Republic and its people—if, after

---

* To say that I originated the "vast wasteland" phrase takes nothing away from Newt Minow. This sort of thing happens all the time. Louis McHenry Howe put ". . . the only thing we have to fear is fear itself" into Franklin D. Roosevelt's first inaugural; Dick Goodwin named President Johnson's "Great Society"; Ernesto Betancourt coined President Kennedy's "Alliance for Progress" and passed it on to Goodwin via Karl Meyer. It is the business of holders of high public office to broker ideas to the public; Newt Minow had the wit to recognize a good phrase and the courage to throw it in the teeth of the broadcasters and thus show the public the need for reform.

Trujillo's thirty-one years of bloody tyranny, now under President Kennedy's Alliance for Progress I could help establish freedom and democracy there: That was worth trying.

I called Arthur. He was enthusiastic and said he would see what he could do. Almost immediately it became clear that nothing would happen soon. The first question to be decided by the administration was whether to send any U.S. ambassador at all—the Organization of American States economic and diplomatic sanctions against the Republic were still in force. The OAS was preparing to send a delegation there to investigate conditions and determine whether to lift the sanctions. Reports were coming out of the Republic that Trujillo's secret police and his heirs were making a bloodbath to avenge his assassination. Arthur thought I might go down with the OAS commission, but Bobby Kennedy thought I should stay clear of it. Arthur persevered, however—at lunch with President Kennedy and Ambassador Stevenson at the UN, he asked Stevenson if he didn't think I'd be a good choice for ambassador to the Dominican Republic. To Arthur's surprise, Stevenson raised his eyebrows and said something like "John? I don't know. I'd have to think about it." I hasten to add, however, that subsequently Stevenson did write a letter to Secretary of State Dean Rusk, recommending me for the job.

But now things dragged, and early in August Fran and the boys and I went up to our Michigan place at Three Lakes. Toward the end of the day on September 1, a Friday, when we came out of the woods in the Jeep, Earl Numinen and Maurice Ball at Michigamme told me President Kennedy had been trying to call me all over town and wanted me to call back. By the time I got my call through, President Kennedy had left Washington for the long Labor Day weekend, and I talked instead to his brother-in-law, Stephen Smith. He said the president wanted me to come to Washington at once about the Dominican Republic.

There, I saw Bobby Kennedy, increasingly involved in foreign affairs since the Bay of Pigs, and Steve Smith, running a "crisis center" in the State Department because President Kennedy was impatient with the Department. They told me that at a meeting on August 28 the State Department had asked President Kennedy for some policy decisions on the Dominican Republic. The central question was: Should we urge the OAS to lift its sanctions against the Republic? This, in effect, would mean that, with Trujillo himself gone, we accepted his heirs as rulers of the Republic. President Kennedy felt he lacked sufficient facts to base policy on. He wanted me to go to the Republic, investigate, and report to him. I asked when he wanted me to go. Steve Smith said, "Yesterday." He gave me a huge file of cables to study. The cables were classified, and of course I had no security clearance and no time to get one, but Steve told me, "You've got a Smith clearance—take them."

I was in the Dominican Republic three weeks. I did my work in the capital and in the second city, Santiago, and I did what I had always done in magazine legwork—talked to people of all sorts: businessmen, workingmen, doctors and lawyers, widows whose husbands had been murdered by the secret police only days ago, militant university students, a frightened Negro dock worker who wanted to organize a labor union, Trujillo's puppet president, cabinet officers, the boss of Trujillo's old political party—the only party he allowed—and leaders of the powerful but enlightened oligarchy in Santiago. I talked to leaders of the government, to Army officers cradling submachine guns in their arms, to leaders of the underground opposition parties.

José G. Fandino, a chubby young State Department career officer, bilingual, born and educated in the United States but of Cuban and Puerto Rican inheritance, went with me everywhere to interpret. Shapshots of that mission remain in my mind—

—inching forward in a car on a narrow downtown street with our political officer and a CIA man through a mob of thousands of demonstrators, the mob pressing against our car so that it could not move, banging on it, screaming, their faces contorted with rage, till the tanks came;

—from a balcony overlooking a plaza by the sea, watching delegations of the opposition bold enough to come to hear a civic leader speak, demanding that the OAS keep the sanctions on till the last Trujillos left;

—trying to talk to a young Marxist, evasive, smiling, rigid, clearly under Communist party discipline, impossible to communicate with;

—talking to a young lawyer who wanted to form a political party; neither Trujillista nor Marxist but ignorant of politics, he asked me for copies of the U.S. constitution and political party platforms, and when I suggested he get them at the library, he looked at me as though I'd lost my mind—didn't I know Trujillo hadn't allowed such subversive literature into the Republic?

—dinner on the terrace at his villa by the sea with the handsome young dandy Ramfis Trujillo, son of the murdered dictator and his heir apparent, listening to him talk about the future of this shattered republic, the difficulty the OAS sanctions caused the national economy (which to a considerable extent meant his private economy), the danger of communism, the restlessness of his own military, his contempt for the opposition, the difficulty of his own position and his desire to "retire" after he had ensured "stability," the magic phrase. (I began to think we might be able to negotiate him out of power);

—and being driven by men of the underground by a circuitous route to a little house where I met the wife of a young oligarch, Yale educated, in whose tile factory two of Trujillo's assassins had hidden; he was still in prison, his wife unable to see him. She told me Ramfis Trujillo was making a great show of "democratizing the country," but "nothing is changed. There's been thirty-one years of murder. People now don't want any more Trujillo. There's a feeling that if you don't help us, we'll let anyone else do it. But we don't want to. We go to vacations in the United States, we send our children there to school, not to Czechoslovakia. Those sanctions—please don't lift them."

Everybody said the same thing, even businessmen whose businesses were badly hurt by the sanctions, everybody that is except Ramfis Trujillo.

During these three weeks I seemed extraordinarily sensitive to the sights, the sounds, the mood of this island, sensitive as I had been in the early years of my magazine work—sensitive to the clank of the tank treads on the capital streets, to the sinister whine of the Volkswagens used by the secret police, to the awful stillness of the city by night, its deserted streets and shuttered restaurants, all waiting for God knew what. These, and the bewilderment on the faces of everybody, a disoriented people, made impressions still fresh twenty-five years later. One evening I sat on the little balcony outside my hotel room, gazing out at the sudden black tropical night where lay the sea, and I asked Joe Fandino what life was like for an ambassador in a small country, and he said, "Why, an ambassador is just like a king." King in a doomed country.

Back in Washington, I wrote a hundred-page report to President Kennedy. I thought the Republic was a sick, destroyed nation, to be viewed as one ravaged by a thirty-year war. I thought Ramfis was beginning to like the feeling of power; his puppet president Balaguer's "democratization" was window dressing. The military and Trujillo right, not the Communist left, was the danger to Dominican democracy. The democratic center, the opposition, was divided, its young leaders patriotic but childlike and of doubtful ability to govern, and I saw none we could wholeheartedly support. There was, really, no political structure; Trujillo had permitted none and bequeathed none. Now we faced the critical question of the OAS sanctions. We must adopt a policy.

Three choices were open, all bad.

First, we could do nothing. Dominicans kept saying, "If you don't help us, we'll kill each other," and one might be tempted to reply, "Go ahead," but we could not. Doing nothing was, really, a policy, for it would create a vacuum, and what filled the vacuum might or might not be in our own interests.

Second, support the Ramfis Trujillo regime—work with it, vote to lift the sanctions, and send an ambassador. That would, in my view, be wrong; we would be turning our backs on the people.

Third, try to help establish a broad-based provisional government until free elections could be held with OAS help; negotiate Ramfis out of his economic power at once by buying him out and later negotiate him out of the country; force Trujillo's brothers to leave the Republic immediately; disband the secret police, end the terror; establish political freedom, break the power of Trujillo's own party; help the Republic borrow money to get the economy moving; and lift sanctions gradually. It amounted to negotiating the Trujillos out if possible or, if that was not possible, throwing them out. I recommended sending a high-level negotiator immediately and sending the fleet to the horizon to back him up.

I gave the report to the Department but I also sent a copy direct to President Kennedy. Upon learning this, George Ball's assistant was highly indignant—I should have gone through channels; what did I mean, going around Undersecretary Ball; he should have approved the report before it went to the president. George himself did not appear bothered when I saw him.

We were to see President Kennedy on Thursday, October 5, almost exactly five weeks after he had telephoned me in Michigamme. The political risks facing President Kennedy were grave. If he supported a Trujillo restoration, he would make mockery of all the brave words about democracy in the Alliance for Progress. But if he tried to help establish a democracy, and if it failed, that might result in "another Castro in the Caribbean." And so might doing nothing. Thinking of domestic politics, the worst thing that could happen to him would be a Communist takeover, the next worst a Trujillo restoration. The best was a successful democracy—but that last was by far the hardest. It was, however, the policy I advocated.

In the morning several high Department officials and I met in George Ball's office, a big suite on the seventh floor of the State Department, the power center of American foreign policy. Some of the others thought my recommendations too risky, I argued for them, and, in the car going to the White House, George said to me, "Look, John, we don't want to get in a row in front of the president," and I said I didn't want to get into a row but he and the president knew what I favored and I would argue for it if necessary.

At the White House, we were joined by others, including, as I recall it, Secretary Rusk; Undersecretary Ball; Undersecretary George McGhee; then Assistant Secretary for Latin America Robert Woodward; Wymberley Coerr of State; the director or a deputy director of the CIA; Teodoro Moscoso and Arturo Morales-Carrión of the Alliance for Progress; McGeorge Bundy, the president's national security adviser; and Arthur Schlesinger and Dick Goodwin of his staff. In the West Wing we waited in the Fish Room, where in FDR's time, Arthur had told me, Harry Hopkins, Ben Cohen, Robert Sherwood, and Adolf Berle had worked on the Four Freedoms speech. Soon, bidden, we went across the corridor into the Cabinet Room, large and white and quiet, with sunlight streaming in through high windows overlooking the Rose Garden, and we ranged ourselves around the long gleaming six-sided cabinet table. Presently Dave Powers, President Kennedy's personal aide, a constant companion and confidant, came in from the Oval Office and said, "Gentlemen, the president," and we all rose and President

Kennedy came in, not striding but moving as if he knew where he was going, to the center of the table; and as he sat, gesturing to us to be seated, he said to me across the table, "I've been reading your novel, John." He had it with him, my long memo; a speed reader, he had read it at lunch. He began by saying the alternatives didn't look attractive, and one by one the others joined in, and often he interjected questions; he was clearly in command of the subject. He asked how we could negotiate the Trujillos out. George Ball and George McGhee had worked out a plan for the Trujillos to deed their vast holdings to the Republic in return for money we would help the Republic raise. I thought it was going my way. It was—in the end the president adopted approximately the recommendations I had made and told George McGhee to go to the Republic the same day. As I was leaving, he said, "Thanks, John." I went home to Highland Park that afternoon. Seeing President Kennedy made you feel good all the rest of the day and for several days thereafter. There *was* hope. If ever a man was a leader, John F. Kennedy was. President Roosevelt must have been like that. They say that every man in his whole life has his president, and only one. Mine was President Kennedy (as Roosevelt had been my father's).

I told Fran about my trip and told her I had decided I wanted that embassy. She said, "I've never been married to a king before." I explained that my recommendations meant we wouldn't send any ambassador to the Republic soon.

That fall and early winter I talked to my friends in the Department and the White House. McGhee and Ramfis Trujillo reached agreement in principle at their first meeting, and Trujillo's brothers left the country. But the political parties could not get together, sporadic rioting began, a general began to emerge as a strongman, and the Trujillo brothers returned. We made it clear we would not recognize the regime or lift sanctions, they defied, us, and we sent the fleet to the horizon; and the brothers left again and this time Ramfis left too, taking his father's body with him. The day we sent the fleet is the only time in our recent history, so far as I can recall, when we threw our weight, including the threat of force, solidly against a rightist dictatorship.

But events stalled. I waited at home, pacing the floor. A presidential appointment—most of us read in the paper that the president has appointed So-and-so to Such-and-such, and we nod and think, "Of course—the president needed a man for that job and he looked around and found the best one for it." Reality is otherwise. In appointive politics, as in elective politics, nearly always the man seeks the job, not the other way around. A man who wants an appointment campaigns for it, but quietly, inside the administration. And in many ways appointive politics is more difficult, more mysterious, and more cruel than elective politics. Few people in government, sometimes not even the president, know all about how decisions finally get made. In a sense, government is the perfect reflection of life itself, vast, fumbling, capricious, sometimes benign, more often malevolent, always inscrutable. Finally George Ball told me the Department had a candidate of its own for ambassador, a career officer, but George had an interesting ambassadorship to offer me instead, Tanganyika, newly independent (and now called Tanzania). I said I wanted the Dominican embassy and I would come to Washington.

There, he was quite discouraging. At breakfast next day, I talked to Newt Minow. He said I should go see Bobby Kennedy—earlier Newt had told Bobby I wanted the embassy badly, and Bobby, looking surprised, had said, "But John knows he can have any job in this administration he wants." I went to Bobby's office. I told his secretary, Angie Novello, whom I knew well from the Rackets Committee days, that I had to see him right now, on a personal matter. She said he was booked solidly but she'd squeeze me in somehow. She did, and I told him, "I've never asked you for anything in my life, Bobby, but I want the ambassadorship to the Dominican Republic and they're about to give it to the Department's candidate." He looked at me a long time. Then he said, "I'll speak to my brother." I left.

And waited again, this time in Washington in the apartment of a friend, Congressman Sidney Yates of Chicago. After six days, the crusty old deputy undersecretary of state for administration called: I was being appointed and should report to his office to start the paperwork.

This, and official briefings, took forever. I paid courtesy calls on my two Illinois senators: Paul Douglas, my old Democratic friend, who of course was delighted, and Everett Dirksen, a Republican leader of the Old Guard, anathema to liberal Democrats, who could not have treated me more courteously. Fran and Dan and Fred came to Washington. She went to several briefings for ambassadors' wives but the most useful advice was given to her by Senator Douglas: "Foreign Service wives are terrible. Be on guard against them. Never meet them on their own ground—government, appointments, promotions, that sort of thing. Always keep them off balance—talk to them about books, art, things they don't know anything about."

After the Senate confirmed me, George McGhee swore me in, and I paid my courtesy call on President Kennedy. He had said publicly, "The Dominican people and their leaders confront a great and seldom given opportunity: the construction of a democratic society on the ruins of tyranny. It is a noble task, but it is not an easy one. We wish them well, and we assure them of our desire to assist them in their efforts." Now alone with me he said, "This one isn't going to be easy," and we talked a little about the Republic's problems. He said he intended to send Vice-President Johnson down about mid-April and "we don't want any riots." He asked if I'd seen Jacqueline's tour of the White House on television the other night; I hadn't, and he described it: "She was terrific." He talked a little about rumors around Washington that he himself was a skirt chaser—"You've heard them; they always do that." Twice he said, "Let me know direct if there's anything you want," and, seeing me to the door when I left, "If you blow this, you'd better not come home."

Fran and the boys and I took a plane to New York, spent the evening with Adlai Stevenson in his embassy residence, and next morning, March 4, 1962, took a plane from New York to the capital of the Dominican Republic, its rightful name now restored, Santo Domingo. As we flew high over the sandy islets and reefs of the Bahamas, I was thinking of the strange chain of circumstances that had led me here. Entirely by chance, many years ago in 1937 with Barbara, I had come to the Dominican Republic and en route home I had met a detective story writer, and that had led me to Chicago. Then the chain of chance led through John Voelker, the Upper Michigan writer, to his friend in a big Chicago law firm, and thence to Lou Kohn, who had introduced me to Adlai Stevenson. Because of the Stevenson campaigns and because of my writing about Hoffa, I had met the Kennedys. Because of that, I had joined the Kennedy presidential campaign. And by chance, not long after President

Kennedy had been inaugurated and I had begun thinking about joining his administration, Trujillo had been assassinated. And so now to the embassy. It was all chance, blind chance.

I thought of other trips I had made, traveling the United States and writing about it, finding much that was wrong and trying to make it better and never doubting it could be made better, and so into politics with zest and hope and dreams, traveling the nation with Adlai Stevenson and John F. Kennedy. In a sense, I was going to the Dominican Republic to test the dream, going with the same zest and zeal and hope. President Kennedy, I thought, must dream and hope for the world what I dreamed for the Republic. I remembered President Kennedy's speech to the Latin American ambassadors setting forth his Alliance for Progress, and his inaugural address presaging it: "To those peoples in the huts and villages of half the globe struggling to break the bonds of mass misery, we pledge our best efforts to help them help themselves, for whatever period is required, not because the Communists may be doing it, not because we seek their votes, but because it is right. If a free society cannot help the many who are poor, it cannot save the few who are rich."

Well, now I would try it. Now I really was on the other side—was no longer a journalist, was in government; was not on the outside looking in, was on the inside looking out; was not writing about policy but making it. This was, I thought, the end of a part of my life. And the beginning of a new part. I told myself that if it didn't work out, I could always go back to writing heavy fact for magazines, anyway I would after this was over (or would I?). The plane crossed the northern coast of the Republic and began letting down but not too steeply—we had yet to cross over the central mountain range, dun brown below, a narrow trail winding back from the coast into the mountains; then in a few minutes we swept in low over the Caribbean, turned, and landed at Aeropuerto Punto Caucedo, the Santo Domingo airport, concrete blazing blinding white in the sun. Fred, nine and round-faced and solemn in his best blue suit, led us off the plane and down the stairs, then Dan grinning and not quite eleven, then Fran smiling and pretty in a flowered dress, then I, carrying incongruously a heavy overcoat in the hot tropical sun.

PART FOUR

WATERSHED

ELEVEN

AMBASSADOR TO THE DOMINICAN REPUBLIC

1.

Four days after I arrived in Santo Domingo, anti-American mobs took to the streets. They burned my car, they stoned our consulate, and they invaded the Dominican-American school and were finally driven away by soldiers with submachine guns, while Dan and Fred watched from an upstairs classroom window. In the midst of this, I ceremoniously presented my credentials as ambassador to the Council of State at the National Palace.

After President Kennedy sent the fleet, we had helped patch together a provisional Council of State to govern for a year and hold free elections. The seven members of the council were a lawyer, two heart specialists, a businessman, a priest, and two assassins, the only two survivors of the twenty-odd men who had assassinated Trujillo.* Only one or two of the seven councillors had had any experience in politics and government.

* During the 1970s, in the United States, some U.S. government officials and the press indicated that we, the United States, had assassinated or assisted or procured the assassination of Trujillo, and an author who interviewed President Lyndon Johnson quoted him as saying, "We killed Trujillo." President Johnson probably believed it. I don't. As ambassador I read many classified documents written by Americans and Dominicans who had investigated the assassination; Antonio Imbert Barreras, one of the two surviving assassins, told me its story in great detail; I talked about it with many other Dominicans and later I studied the transcript of testimony before the Church Com-

215

The president of the council and of the Republic was Rafael F. Bonnelly, a lawyer, fifty-eight years old, light-brown-skinned, with graying hair, soft brown liquid eyes, a kind smile, and a fast skillful lawyer's mind. He was a sentimental man, and often when Dan and Fred walked past his house on their way to school he stopped them to talk and to give them Indian arrowheads. In a normal situation, an ambassador requests an appointment with a chief of state formally, through the Foreign Office. But this was not a normal situation, and if I wanted to see President Bonnelly, I did not call on him at the palace, I simply walked down the street to his house. Thus we avoided the public impression that the United States was exerting undue influence on the Dominican government. Bonnelly was no revolutionary—he was tied by birth and marriage to the landed oligarchy. Nor was he a demagogue or a charismatic popular leader. Early on when I saw him privately, I told him, "I've never been an ambassador before." He said, "That's all right, I've never been a president before." He was an effective one.

2.

We, the United States, had three major policy objectives: to help keep the shaky council in power for its year, to help it hold free elections, and to persuade the losers to accept the winner's victory.

To promote that policy, my jobs were two—to work with the Council of State and to work with the twenty-six political parties that had sprung up since Trujillo.*

As to the council, I had to adjust U.S. policy to help it (e.g., per-

---

mittee of the U.S. Senate. I lived with this for several years. In all that mass of evidence there is none that the U.S. government or any of its agents perpetrated, assisted, or procured the assassination of Trujillo. During the spring when he was killed, many plots were afoot in the Dominican Republic to kill him, and evidence indicates that the special group that passed on CIA covert actions did authorize the CIA to smuggle several guns into the Republic, but these guns were never passed on to any of the numerous dissident groups. Moreover, the men who actually killed Trujillo had no need of U.S. guns—they had access to the guns of the Dominican Army, for one of the plotters was head of the armed forces, drawn into the plot by Luís Amiama Tío, the other surviving assassin. But to my mind the best evidence that we did not kill Trujillo is that President Kennedy never told me we did. He sent me to the Republic on a fact-finding mission shortly after Trujillo's death, he sent me as his ambassador, he knew me well, he confided many things in me, and never, either in our meetings with other U.S. government officials or in our private meetings alone, did he so much as indicate that we were involved in Trujillo's assassination.

* As ambassador, I spent nearly all my time working on Dominican politics. A full account of that appears in my book *Overtaken by Events.*

suade the Kennedy administration to amend its worldwide sugar quota bill); to suggest programs to the council, such as public works programs to soak up unemployment, financed by loans from us; to suggest when to placate the military by cracking down on the extremist left. I worked on our Agency for International Development program with the council and our AID officers, devising AID programs to provide schoolbooks, school uniforms, and housing for the poor as well as money for big AID projects; and I lobbied with Washington ceaselessly for money for the council—in its one year, I believe, we gave or loaned the Republic more money than we had sent Trujillo in his thirty-one years as dictator. We supported the council publicly and privately. I not only made public speeches praising it but also in private talks in receptions at the embassy residence I made our aims clear to the nervous military inherited from Trujillo and to leaders of the church, oligarchy, business middle class, press, and political parties.

When people began to call the council a do-nothing government, we devised a program of reforms, including agrarian reform, and I urged it on the council. But President Bonnelly told me he didn't have the votes to pass it. Probing, I discovered which of the seven councillors was blocking it. By chance, Pierre Salinger, my old friend, now President Kennedy's press secretary, came to the Republic on vacation. I gave a reception for him, briefed him in advance, and during it he took the balky councillor aside and told him President Kennedy was greatly interested in the council's progress, particularly agrarian reform. The council passed it. Thus agrarian reform came to the Dominican Republic.

The military was the real danger to the council. Under Trujillo, the military had had absolute power; now they wanted it back (under the guise of anticommunism). Scarcely a week passed that rumors did not sweep the capital that the military was plotting a coup. Then I would call my three military attachés and my political and CIA chiefs to the embassy residence and send them around the city to talk to military men and politicians, while I hurried to see the councillors of state and President Bonnelly, all of us up half the night. I lost no chance to make it clear to the Dominican military that we supported the civilian council—Fran and I gave receptions for them at the residence, and when they seemed restive, we would bring in the aircraft carrier *Boxer,* it would anchor offshore, and Fran and I would take the Council of State and the military high command aboard for lunch with full honors for President Bonnelly and the other councillors. It reminded the military that our fleet was never far over the horizon. President Kennedy authorized me directly to tell the military, "The United States would find it extremely difficult to recognize and almost impossible to assist any regime which took power by force or threats of force." A Dominican colonel, after several drinks at an embassy reception, sneered at me, "You and your little bow tie—we'll show you and your democracy." One of his civilian rightist friends told my political officer what he and the military would do to "all these Communists": "You know why there are no Protestants in Spain? Because we boiled them all in oil." Nice group.

My second job was to work with the twenty-six political parties ranging from extremist left to extremist right. To the leaders of all I insisted on elections on schedule, encouraged them to participate fully, and discouraged extremism. We could live with any of them, at least any that had a chance of winning. My political officers helped handle them. The favored party represented the middle class; the underdog was the Revolutionary party, led by Juan Bosch, with mass support among *campesinos* and the urban workers and poor. As for the far left, it was split into four parties, and some of its leaders received training, guns, and money from Moscow, Prague, and Havana. Taken together these leftists extremist parties could not have cast fifty thousand votes. But with their constant agitation they kept the Dominican military nervous and kept the Council of State off balance, they tried to disrupt elections, they generated anti-Americanism, and they paid unemployed young men fifty cents a day to riot at our embassy. Our CIA arranged counterriots. (As disorder increased, embassy people urged me to travel with a bodyguard. I declined. Those days were different from today.)

Soon I found myself urging the Council of State to deport some Communist leaders and to harass others as Emil Smicklas and his Chicago robbery squad did. It was illegal detention, perhaps even police brutality, an invasion of constitutional rights previously denounced by the ACLU and me. Now, trying to save a tottering democratic government, I found myself favoring it.

Trujillo had trained the Dominican police, when faced with rioters, only to shoot to kill. Now the council forbade this. So they stood by helpless. Home briefly for consultation, I told President Kennedy at a meeting in the Cabinet Room that the council was losing control of the capital streets; so far I couldn't get an AID public safety mission to train the Dominican police, and I didn't see why we couldn't get a couple of cops from Chief Parker's Mexican Squad— W. H. Parker was chief of police in Los Angeles. The president turned to Ralph Dungan, who handled Latin America for him, and said, "Ask Bobby if he can get him some help." Shortly, two excellent Spanish-speaking Los Angeles detectives arrived in Santo Domingo, and in a few weeks the council rewon the streets.

Intervention, all this? Of course. But the Dominicans, except for the left and right extremists, welcomed it, or at least recognized the need for it.

Everything we did, we did under President Kennedy's Alliance for Progress. This was crucial, both atmospherically and materially, for the Alliance provided both ideals and practical objectives understood throughout the Republic and the hemisphere. One of the seven councillors told me that while he was in Trujillo's prison, "One thing gave me hope—someone smuggled in a translation of President Kennedy's speech about the Alianza. At last the United States was going to pay some attention to Latin America." President Kennedy is indeed the only president since FDR to really care about Latin America. And to this day, in thatch-roofed huts in the Republic, families tend small shrines to President Kennedy.

3.

Fran and the boys and I lived in the embassy residence, a big blocky stucco structure that resembled a library and stood on spacious grounds, royal palms plumed on high, in a garden an enormous tree like a banyan tree sending limbs and roots down into the ground, a swimming pool, an acacia festooned with great split-leaf philodendron vines, the whole sloping down to the little chancery, a cramped building where the embassy staffers had their offices and the code clerks their equipment. The residence was well suited for official functions but unadorned and bleak; Fran put up pictures we had brought and a revolving show of paintings by Dominican artists.

Fran and I frequently gave "receptions," or cocktail parties, for 250 or 300 guests—the Dominican government, Dominican military, foreign diplomatic corps, American business community. Had a stranger dropped in, he would have thought it nothing more than a party. Actually, we were working. I always had my senior staff attend, and before the guests arrived we would meet in my study and divide up the guests—who would talk to whom, what we were trying to find out, whom we were trying to influence.

I did most of my work in my little study at the residence, not in my office at the chancery—talked privately with Dominicans, wrote cables. I also wrote, about every six weeks, a summary of the situation for the State Department and for the White House, where it was read by Ralph Dungan and Arthur Schlesinger and, sometimes, President Kennedy. I believe they sometimes passed the summaries along to Senator J. William Fulbright, chairman of the Foreign Relations Committee. In all this, I was, really, doing what I had done for *The Saturday Evening Post:* doing legwork and presenting facts and conclusions. But now I was writing for a smaller audience than the *Post's:* the president and the secretary of state and their aides.

Our mission contained about 200 people (plus some 160 Peace Corps volunteers) and I was responsible for everything all of them said or did—the political and economic and administrative officers and the three military attachés of the embassy proper, the CIA, the consulate, the Agency for International Development, the U.S. Information Service, and the Military Assistance and Advisory Group. Some of my Foreign Service career officers were terrible— one was fond of saying of all Dominicans, "If we go home, they'd all climb back up in the trees." On the other hand some were first-rate. Harry Schlaudeman, for example, head of the political section, was one of the best Foreign Service officers I ever knew. He was imaginative, analytical, precise, yet he had kept a young man's passion. He was an activist and a student of Marxism-Leninism and of Dominican history. (More recently, now an ambassador himself, he has been our envoy negotiating with the Nicaraguan Sandinista government.) Schlaudeman wrote well. Though I had little time to improve the staff's prose, I did ban from our cables two words then fashionable in the State Department, "viable" and "counterproductive." As chief of mission, I had to sign all outgoing cables and I wouldn't sign gibberish.

The functions of the CIA station chief were two—collecting information and conducting covert operations. Some ambassadors wanted nothing to do with the CIA, holding that CIA men were all a bunch of dirty spies; they could do as they pleased as long as the ambassador didn't know about it. But I wanted to know everything the CIA was doing—I had to in the supercharged Dominican political atmosphere. My first CIA station chief was fine; he reminded me of Emil Smicklas. But he was replaced by an older man who, near retirement, played it safe. Any station chief when he sent a piece of information to Washington was required to rate it on a sliding scale as to probable truth and as to the past reliability of its source. This man rated everything right in the middle, may be true, source may be reliable, when I knew better; I protested and won only after carrying my protest to the White House.

I strove to get the Peace Corps to do practical down-to-earth things close to the people but it was hard—too many of them had studied philosophy in college, not enough carpentry and plumbing in vocational school. Nonetheless, the Dominicans understood immediately their young eager faces and their eagerness to help.

AID presented awful problems and I never really got hold of it. When I saw the hovels in the slums and the men without work, I wanted to plunge in with massive work-relief and housing programs—a New Deal. But it wouldn't work and even if it did it would simply accelerate the rush to the cities. I managed to do a few things—stopped AID from building expensive concrete houses that the people refused to use, established a school for diesel mechanics—the Dominican educational system produced thousands of poets and philosophers but few mechanics—helped establish an agricultural school, got money to build little farm-to-market roads to help the *campesinos* get their coffee and cacao down out of the mountains. Some of these projects still flourish, more than twenty years later. But there was never enough time, or enough peace, really to do it right.

I fear I slighted the other ambassadors in the Republic, though I liked several of them; I simply had no time, and many of them were in a different business from mine. Some played golf most of the time, some were promoting trade, few if any involved themselves in Dominican affairs as we did. Their receptions were almost purely social. Nonetheless, I learned to respect one thing by which they set great store: protocol. The diplomatic corps had to attend certain Dominican public functions, and had it not been for protocol, confusion would surely have reigned when we entered—there might even have been unseemly scrambling for front-row (or back-row) seats—but with the Dominican chief of protocol assigning each of us his rightful place according to his seniority in the corps, all went smoothly; we looked as though we knew what we were doing, which set a good example for the common folk.

I fear I slighted too the American community. My predecessors had belonged to the country club and their personal friends had been U.S. businessmen; I spent my time with Dominicans. Some U.S. businessmen understood. But others, I fear, did not, such as some at La Romana sugar plantation, the biggest U.S. enterprise in the Republic, with several thousand workers (its overseers rode horseback through the canefields and wore pith helmets). And once I had trouble with the United Fruit Company. Striking workers shut off the lights and water at its headquarters town in the interior, the strike sounded nasty, and to make sure that the company's property and employees were in no danger I interceded with President Bonnelly and several other Dominican officials and labor leaders and sent my own staff officers there to check. For several days and nights I followed it closely. But in the United States, the president of United Fruit wrote to Secretary Rusk, complaining that American lives and property were gravely endangered and I had done little or nothing about it; a local fruit company representative called on me to show me the letter. Angered, I told him step by step what I had done; he apologized; I told him I wanted his president to apologize to Secretary Rusk; he said he himself intended to go to President Bonnelly; I told him to go ahead if he wished but I had been assured his people and property were in no danger at present, and if he ever had reason to think they were he would do better to come to me than to Secretary Rusk, who was too far away to do much about it. Rusk reassured the company. In the end, through my political intervention, the strike was settled.

My relations with the U.S. community probably hit rock bottom on the Fourth of July in 1962. In the past, they had become accustomed to coming to the embassy on the Fourth for a day-long champagne celebration. And the embassy staff always had come too. I decided otherwise—such a celebration would seem almost obscene in the midst of Dominican privation. Instead, I arranged to have several hundred Dominican orphans brought in buses to the embassy to swim in the pool, eat hot dogs, drink Coke, and be entertained. Many embassy staffers and members of the U.S. community bitterly resented it. The Dominican kids loved it. (I also asked Louis Armstrong, the great jazz musician who celebrated his own birthday on the Fourth of July, to bring his band down and give a public concert for young people in Independence Park. He agreed enthusiastically and would charge only traveling expenses and minimum union wage. But I could not get the six thousand dollars out of the State Department.)

As a former journalist, I had good relations with most U.S. reporters. No U.S. paper or wire service kept a man full-time in the Republic. Instead, they all flocked there when something went spectacularly wrong. For this reason, lacking background, they sometimes got things a little out of focus. Few of them spoke Spanish, and so they had to rely on Dominican sources who spoke English—mostly upper-class Dominicans. Furthermore, they could not know fully what we, the U.S. government, were up to because I would not tell them. I never lied to a reporter. But several times, during crises, when their questions pressed too hard on policy, I had to simply say, "I'm sorry, no more questions." The task of a U.S. reporter abroad is hard. He is a reporter but he is also an American, and sometimes that makes him uncomfortable. I understood the problem. But I could never forget that I was now firmly seated on the opposite side of the table from the press, and *that* made *me* uncomfortable.

Every morning Fran and I were awakened by the military band at police headquarters across the street playing "The monkey wraps his tail around the flagpole," then the stirring Dominican national anthem. Listening, we drank our morning coffee on the upstairs porch outside our bedroom. Before going to bed at night we had a drink there too, talking about what this country could be if we could only get it to work. We had Dominican friends, but our life was in a sense a lonely one, I could never open my mouth without speaking for President Kennedy. And so I could never relax and speak freely with Dominicans. Nor could Fran.

My mother and my aunt Verl came down to visit. How I wished my father could have lived to come. Our daughter Cindy came down, met a young Englishman who worked for Shell, Anthony Campbell, and dropped out of Sarah Lawrence and was married in the embassy garden. Fran and I managed to spend some time with Dan and Fred. I sometimes swam with them in the pool before lunch, and on official trips to the interior I was able to steal a half day to take them fishing or hunting. On a Sunday evening, I sometimes took Fran and the boys down to Columbus Park beside the great gray cathedral to sit on a stone bench with Dominicans and listen to the band concert and watch young couples promenade. Many times at dusk, during the lull between embassy activity and the evening's reception, Fran and I drove out the highway by the sea to the place where Trujillo had been assassinated: scrubby palms and a rusty wire fence, a fading monument erected in honor of the deed, the sun setting fast over the purple sea beyond the palms. I do not know why we did it; now it seems a little macabre.

I wanted to do some legwork of my own to find out what ordinary Dominicans were thinking and to tell them what we were up to, and so I made a series of trips into the interior, taking Fran and Dan and Fred. We went to towns that had never before seen an ambassador. I was whistlestopping, campaigning to promote Dominican-American relations and our policies. At each provincial capital I called on the governor and other provincial officials, inviting them to tell me their problems, then, in the evening, held a town meeting to which everybody was invited, several hundred people in the government hall or a thatch-roofed restaurant. I made a short speech then invited questions. They asked about slums, housing, jobs, the broken highway to the capital, squatters, exploration for oil, agrarian reform, no electricity, no drinking water. Later I took their complaints to President Bonnelly or our AID director, and now and then was able to get something done. Sometimes the crowd listened in friendly spirit; sometimes some of them sneered openly. Often heavily armed soldiers guarded the meeting. One morning in a provincial capital while Fran and I and the boys were with the governor, I heard the noise of a crowd in the street outside shouting,

"Yankees go home," and Dan and Fred stood in the window and called back, *"Viva los Domincanos,"* and high school kids in the crowd laughed, it seemed good-natured, but it made the governor nervous; and sure enough, when we came to leave, the crowd turned ugly; by now it was no longer just kids, it was grown men, some carrying sticks and rocks. A police line formed to cordon it off. Our car was at the curb. Just as we scrambled into it, the crowd broke the police line, beat on the car with their fists, shoved it, threw things at it, and two peach stones whizzed into the front seat where our boys were. That evening at our hotel, by prearrangement, the local leaders of political parties came to see me, including the leftist party that had organized the demonstration. (Its handbills had taken the standard Communist line on issues those kids knew nothing about.) Its two young leaders didn't know much either—they told me they wanted U.S. financial help to carry out social reform in the Republic but "it must come without interference—we are very nationalistic." I asked what kind of help. "Economic aid in the form of developing ways of eliminating unemployment," one said. I asked for specifics. They had none. Then I asked them what the hell they thought they were doing throwing rocks at my kids. They grinned foolishly. I told them that anyone teaching teen-age children to go into the streets and throw rocks at other children was doing his country no service. They were untroubled. They seemed brainless, posing as intellectuals but only mouthing canned slogans and speeches. One of their slogans was "Culture or death." I could not talk to them.

On one of these trips, in the arid southwest, the poorest section of the Republic, out in the country on a road so deep with dust we were in danger of getting stuck, we came suddenly upon a foreign plantation with a thick, lush grove of banana trees. Irrigation. The water had come from the Yaque del Sur River. We forded it and came to the village of Vicente Noble—mud huts set stark on a dusty plain, women in black with cans lined up at a trickle of water from a rusty pipe; nothing green, nothing growing, the whole place a gray, baked plain, gray earth, gray dust, gray and silent people. "Every night one third of mankind goes to bed hungry"—I'd always heard it; now I was seeing it. These people scarcely gazed up at us, imprisoned by the heat, the grayness, the dust, the hunger, as inert and dull-eyed as patients in a mental hospital. Here, I thought, was our opportunity:

to change this place. Dig wells, even dam the river. Put water on the land. If you did, you could grow anything, including healthy people. I resolved to do it. When I got back to the capital I talked to President Bonnelly about it; he would work with us. I got help from our Peace Corps and AID. But the project got lost in the Dominican bureaucracy; our Peace Corps did little; local people wouldn't work on the wells without pay, why bother, their wives had always carried water in cans from the river. The project failed.

I tried a different approach. The Dominican government had proposed to build a dam on a big river in the Cibao Valley up north near Santiago. They needed money from us. But the Cibao was already the richest part of the Republic, lush and green; dams there would benefit chiefly the oligarchy that owned the land; and development there would only lure Dominicans from elsewhere to the Cibao, already overpopulated. Rather, I thought, we should dam the Yaque del sur in the southwest desert near Vicente Noble—dam it not only for irrigation but also for hydroelectric power. For in all our travels in the interior I had become keenly aware of the need for electricity, and I envisioned a vast electrification program like Roosevelt's Rural Electrification Administration. That, together with irrigation, could truly change the lives of the *campesinos*. I set to work, talking first to Bonnelly and the Council of State, then, after the election, to the new president; writing and cabling to the State Department; talking to AID in Santo Domingo and Washington. And I realized that we, the United States, possessed precisely the agency that could make it work. The TVA. If we could transform the Dominican Republic as the Tennessee Valley Authority had transformed the Middle South of the United States, we would have gone a long way toward making President Kennedy's dream of an Alliance for Progress come true. Finally I got some money from AID and got a commitment out of the TVA chairman to himself bring technicians down to undertake preliminary studies on September 28, 1963.

Something else came out of our whistlestop trips. During them, Fran had been shocked by what she learned about the health of infants in the interior. Babies were dying simply because their mothers knew nothing about hygiene and nutrition. Fran decided to establish a baby clinic in Higüey, a small remote provincial capital with no public medical facilities. Fran called on the bishop there, on the governor and mayor and city councilmen, on the local police and military commanders, on the doctors and on the wives of leading citizens. To all she explained she wanted to help them set up a clinic that they themselves could run, not an American clinic but a Dominican clinic. In a muddy square behind the market, two Peace Corps boys poured a slab of concrete, the Dominican Army gave her a big tent, people in town gave lumber to make tables and chairs. A friend of ours from Highland Park, visiting, gave her five hundred dollars to buy medicines. The wife of a staffer made brightly colored signs like WASH YOUR HANDS BEFORE EATING to hang in the tent clinic. Five local doctors agreed to donate one afternoon a week of their time. So did ten or twelve Higüey housewives. Fran taught them to keep a card index recording each baby's length, weight, age, condition, treatment. Since this was a "well-baby" clinic, it would treat only babies with minor ailments. The key was the card-indexed weight chart.

When the clinic opened, the papal nuncio came from the capital to bless it, and it was christened, in Spanish, "The Little Clinic of Higüey." Thirty or forty mothers came on the first day; soon more than sixty were coming each day, mothers and often fathers bringing their babies on horseback or carrying them miles afoot, waiting patiently for hours to see the doctor. Medicines ran short; doctors or volunteers didn't show up; when it rained the Little Clinic flooded; once the tent blew down. Fran persevered. The Little Clinic became a passion for her. Something, at least, that one North American could do to help these people. She badgered CARE, the Peace Corps, the minister of health, politicians and fund-raisers for help; friends of ours in Highland Park sent contributions and set up a tax-exempt foundation there to receive funds. When Fran explained the clinic to Lloyd Cutler, a Washington lawyer who came down on a business trip with Edgar Kaiser, the industrialist, he said he represented an organization of pharmaceutical firms—soon they sent so many drugs they filled the embassy residence.

Fran saw everything—babies with swollen bellies and copper-colored hair and skin shredding off tiny legs, all signs of malnutrition; babies with acute and often fatal diarrhea; babies so tiny that when she unwrapped the scrap of torn bath towel in which they were swaddled she found little sticks of hands and feet that resembled more a bag of chicken bones than a human life. Almost without exception it was disease resulting from the mothers' ignorance—not contagion, not neglect, not lack of concern, but simple ignorance. Indeed, concern was strong in the mothers, and in the fathers too. Once Fran weighed a baby and found it had gained two ounces in the week since it had been there; the mother watched tensely during the weighing and then, in a burst of emotion, snatched up the baby off the scale and smothered Fran in her embrace.

Going to Higüey once or twice a week, staying in the miserable hotel there or in the Peace Corps house, Fran learned, I think, more about daily Dominican life than any of us. And she learned the real difficulties of improving things—poor Dominicans saw her simply as the nice North American lady with the big basket of goodies; provincial officials thought they might hurt their political fortunes by cooperating with the Yankees; local doctors saw their private practice and their siesta hour threatened; some of our own embassy staff looked upon this as the meddlesome pet charity of the ambassador's wife whom, God save them, they must indulge. She was, in fact, attempting the most difficult venture of all—a joint enterprise between North Americans and Dominicans, a sort of Alliance for Progress in miniature, with all its promise and difficulties. Her hardest task was to make clear the idea of self-help. Dominicans understood well the idea of charitable works and government largess. Trujillo had taught them. But he did not teach them self-help and community projects. No wonder—those are potentially revolutionary weapons. Fran learned too that Dominicans were unwilling to accept responsibility. Worse, she discovered, when the card index languished, that it languished because the white-uniformed housewife volunteers were as illiterate as their patients' mothers. They couldn't keep a card index because they didn't know the alphabet. Fran kept trying. Once a big black-skinned mother told her, "You have come down from your white heaven to help us." This idea of charity was, of course, exactly what she sought to oppose by teaching Dominicans to help themselves.*

* In later years, having seen what Fran could do with the Little Clinic of Higüey, which cost almost no money, I was struck with wonderment when I read from time to time that the U.S. government or some multilateral bank had allocated millions of

4.

Every now and then, a young reporter new to Washington, bemused by instant satellite communications and computers and other high-technology miracles, "discovers" that "old-fashioned" diplomacy is no longer of use. In the nineteenth century, the story usually goes, when it took weeks for an ambassador's dispatches to reach Washington by boat mail, an ambassador had considerable freedom of movement and, so, considerable personal influence. But today, so it runs, he is on a tight hot-line tether, and personal diplomacy is outmoded. I don't believe a word of it. True, the U.S. ambassador to Moscow can scarcely open a window in the embassy without instructions from Washington, but most of our ambassadors have considerable leeway (which is one reason it's more fun to be an ambassador to a place like Santo Domingo than to Moscow). Even the ambassador to Moscow's effectiveness depends in part upon his personal relationship with the Soviet leaders. In smaller places, everything may depend on it. Several times, upon my personal relationship with President Bonnelly depended the Dominican Republic's fragile experiment in democracy. Nor can anyone convince me that my own whistlestopping and Fran's clinic at Higüey did not in some small way advance the interests of the United States. Nor

---

dollars for a "small project" loan to some underdeveloped country for a health facility. And, having seen the crowds of mothers with their children in the tent at Higüey while the big fancy maternity hospital in Santo Domingo stood almost empty, its expensive infant incubators, gifts from the United States, dusty and unused, I was saddened by such big showy medical projects launched in poor countries by well-intentioned people of rich countries. So much more could be done modestly, it seemed to me. I was heartened to find agreement when I came across an article in *Foreign Affairs* by no less an authority than Dr. Lewis Thomas, M.D., chancellor of the Memorial Sloan-Kettering Cancer Center in New York. Dr. Thomas said that our own complex expensive system of medical care was designed primarily to cope with the medical concerns of people middle-aged or older, focusing on such diseases as cancer, heart disease, and stroke; whereas what is killing children in the Third World is diarrheal disease caused by contaminated water and faulty hygiene, especially dangerous to children fed inadequate or ignorantly chosen food, and, beyond infant and childhood mortality, parasitic disease. Replicating our own system, including, say, Sloan-Kettering, Massachusetts General Hospital, and a top-drawer U.S. medical school, would not benefit, might even harm, the people living in city slums or rural parts of poor countries. Instead (as Lewis Thomas has recently said), what they needed were plumbers and sanitary engineers, nutritionists and hygienists, antibiotics and vaccines, and, above all, nurses to run the program and a distribution system to bring it to everyone, probably through some equivalent of our old-fashioned local boards of health. Not high technology, just basic public health. What the people of poor countries want is not a comfortable old age but a better chance at life itself.

my cables and six-week summaries; for one of the really important things an ambassador can do is influence the policy of his own government toward the country he is accredited to. Especially can he do this if he has a personal relationship with the president, members of Congress, and the press. Above all the president.

When I went to Washington for consultations, I took with me a long list of the Republic's problems and a shopping list of things I wanted from the State Department and AID, then, with the other principals, met in the Cabinet Room with President Kennedy. I summarized the policy we intended to pursue from now till next February 27, when the Council of State was due to leave office and the new elected president to take over. President Kennedy asked questions incisively. Wasn't there a danger that so many political parties and so complicated an election law might produce a splintering election, with no one able to govern? How clearly could Radio Havana be heard in the Republic? Should we jam it? Was our military advisory group any good? Did I want more? What about coastal patrol boats? What about counterinsurgency training? What about the Social Christians—any hope there? What was the chance of Juan Bosch's party—Partido Revolucionario Dominicano (PRD)—winning? I answered his questions as rapidly and crisply as I could; I knew he was impatient with discursive replies, it was one thing about Stevenson that put him off.

I shocked the State Department by telling him Juan Bosch's proletarian PRD was now about even with the middle-class party. I said the Dominican military was getting more restless, and he told me carefully how far I could go in stopping a military coup. As the meeting broke up and he headed back to the Oval Office, he stopped for a moment with me and said, "I saw you last night," and then, "Good luck—and let me know if you need anything."

The previous night I had attended the annual White House correspondents' dinner, and President Kennedy, in top form, had done a takeoff on himself, one of the funniest speeches I ever heard. At that time, Washington was gay and hopeful. I was staying with the Arthur Schlesingers in their little rented house in Georgetown. Bobby Kennedy, I discovered, like me felt he had wasted a good deal of his time in college and had not received a good education, and so now he had organized what came to be called the Hickory

Hill Seminar, gatherings of cabinet members and other New Frontiersmen in Bobby's house, Hickory Hill, or another of their homes, to listen to a lecture by whatever leading intellectual was visiting Washington and to ask him questions. Arthur arranged the programs. One night while I was there the seminar met at Arthur's house, and the speaker was Sir Alfred Ayer, a visiting British philosopher (a logical positivist, Arthur helpfully informs me); and when he had finished, Bobby's wife, Ethel, an extremely devout Catholic, who was sitting up front with me, said she thought she had understood him to say he didn't believe in God and she wondered if this was possible. From the back of the room Bobby called out, "Shut up, Ethel." It brought down the house. And may have saved the positivist.

President Kennedy was planning to entertain all the Nobel Prize winners from the Western Hemisphere at the White House and he had to make a few remarks, so Arthur and I produced a draft, writing a line that went, "I think this is the most extraordinary collection of talent, of human knowledge, that has ever been gathered together at the White House." Delivering it, the president added "with the possible exception of when Thomas Jefferson dined alone." It was the Kennedy touch.

5.

On December 20, 1962, the Dominican people voted freely for a president for the first time in thirty-eight years. It was a day everyone had dreaded, a day everyone had predicted would result in riots, gunfights, God knows what. It passed calmly, cleaner than most elections in Chicago. The vote was huge. Juan Bosch and his PRD won by a landslide. Now we had a rarity in the Caribbean, a freely elected government of the non-Communist left. Could it endure? Could Bosch make his peaceful revolution? Could we help him? Would he let us?

Juan Bosch was a short-story writer and, by Dominican standards, an intellectual, a man of striking appearance, high cheekbones and curly snow-white hair and bright blue eyes. Even before he was inaugurated, he got in trouble. When a draft of his new Dominican constitution was published, President Bonnelly and other councillors took me aside at a private party to denounce it—said it was "a Communist Constitution," did not protect private property, legalized concubinage and made divorce easy, did not guarantee civil liberties, did not consecrate the Vatican Concordat. This was the first outcry of the propertied class against Bosch and his revolution, real venom. Bosch went on the radio with a long foolish rambling speech, viciously—and pointlessly—attacking the Council of State and the business middle class. The reaction of the power structure was almost instantaneous. Important Dominican and U.S. businessmen thought him anti-American; press and politicians attacked the draft Constitution; churchmen thought their worst fears confirmed; the military stirred—the Air Force commander told my attaché that Bosch was "at least" beholden to Communists and that "it's easier now than later." My commercial attaché was flooded with phone calls; business came to a standstill.

Vice-President Johnson would lead the U.S. delegation to Bosch's inauguration. The day before he was to arrive, the CIA told me that U.S. immigration authorities had stopped two Communist terrorists from leaving New York for Santo Domingo. An American businessman who was always messing around in Dominican politics was demanding to know what our attitude would be if the Communist Bosch was overthrown before he could be inaugurated. A plot was afoot to assassinate President Romulo Betancourt of Venezuela, who was also coming to the inauguration. I wondered if we really should bring Vice-President Johnson into this mess.

We did, with the *Boxer* offshore and its helicopters flying air cover over him, and all went well. In the middle of the festivities, Dan's burro threw him, breaking his arm, and a Dominican doctor set it and cast it, but I wanted it X-rayed next day by a U.S. doctor aboard the *Boxer;* and I had to tell Vice-President Johnson about it, saying that unfortunately it meant that my wife could not accompany his wife to the Dominican School for the Blind next morning, as scheduled. Instantly the vice-president said, "Why don't you let me take the boy, and his mother too, up to Washington with me Thursday? They can take better care of him at Bethesda [Naval Hospital] than here." He said it absolutely spontaneously, purely a human gesture. Ever since, when people ask what I think of Lyndon Johnson, I think first of Dan's arm. Johnson saved it—it was broken near the growth center at the elbow, and if it had not been reset properly it would not have grown.

6.

I never developed the close comfortable relationship with President Bosch that I had had with President Bonnelly. One might have expected otherwise—after all, Bonnelly was quite conservative and he belonged to the oligarchy, while Bosch, was, like me, a writer, a liberal, and the accepted spokesman for the underdog. Bosch had spent twenty-five years in the underworld of Caribbean exile politics, which ill equips a man to govern. His was a dark and conspiratorial mind. To him, everything had to be a plot. He was brilliant and intuitive, but unstable and reckless. He was moody and unpredictable, arrogant and vain and streaked with martyrdom. As a child, he told me, he had become anti-American and now he was determined to pursue a course independent of the United States.

I sometimes thought I judged him too harshly. He was a wandering writer and teacher. It was unfair to compare him to the only other presidents I had known—to Kennedy, born to wealth and influence in Massachusetts, to Bonnelly, nourished in the Santiago oligarchy. At times I felt deep sympathy for Bosch. Both his mother and father died shortly after he took office as president. When his father died, I went impulsively to his house and told him I wanted to offer my sympathy. His face showed surprise, then set tight. He motioned me to a chair, and we sat down, and I told him my own father had died only two years before, I thought I knew something of how he must feel, and it might help him if he remembered that his father had lived to see him elected president, and so had his mother—he had made them very proud, and that was all a son could do. He said nothing for a moment, nothing at all. Then he asked, "How is Mrs. Martin?" Fine, I said. "And the boys?" We sat another moment, then I got up and said I did not want to keep him longer. Standing, he asked, "May I embrace you?" He was a strange man.

Personality aside, Bosch faced grave problems. The awful history of the Republic gave him little democratic tradition to build on. The economy was a mess. Politically, he was caught between the left and right. He owed political debts to the left. On the right, he was unalterably opposed by much of the oligarchy and the rising business middle class; he was viewed with grave suspicion by elements of the armed forces and the Church. In short, most of the real power structure of the Republic was arrayed against him. His overwhelming six hundred thousand votes (60%) meant everything on election day—but between elections they meant nothing, an inert mass. But his single greatest handicap was that he had almost no one to help him run his government. His election had been truly revolutionary: It had brought to power a whole class of people who had never before entered the mainstream of Dominican national life—the *campesino,* the small shopkeeper in the roadside store, the workingman, the poor. I knew a governor swept into power with Bosch who could not sign his name, a mayor who had never before worn shoes. True, it was time these people took their rightful place in Dominican life, but the fact remained that they were unqualified to govern.

The foreign aid policies of our own U.S. government had suddenly become restrictive. AID had no money. The World Bank was talking big projects but they were years away. Meanwhile, where was Bosch's revolution? What about unemployment, high as ever? When would he launch programs for the poor?

Justice William O. Douglas of the U.S. Supreme Court came down to the Republic, drawn, I suppose, by Bosch's reputation and opportunity. Justice Douglas was one of those rare men whom I had long admired from afar and, upon meeting, found even better than I had expected—not only courageous and liberal but also warm, sensitive, and very funny. At lunch and dinner, I told him about the Republic's problems. Believing we should promote education in democracy after Trujillo, Justice Douglas thought he might establish an institute here and bring in such lecturers as Robert Oppenheimer and Rexford Tugwell. Or send promising young Dominicans to Princeton for a few weeks' intensive training in government. The foundation of his friend Albert Parvin would commit its resources to the Dominican Republic this year, and he was open to suggestions.

I thought that Bosch could not spare any promising young Dominicans, not even for a few weeks' training. (Ralph Dungan and I had already discussed it.) As for lecturers, at first I had had the same idea but soon had realized that such a project was hopelessly too sophisticated. What was needed was to reach and teach the Dominican people themselves simply and directly. I had thought of a way: by television. The idea had developed out of my larger idea of rural electrification and the damming of the Yaque River. And out of

AID's experiences with education and the diesel and agricultural schools. Over television, we could teach the people not only about democracy, we could teach them mechanics, carpentry, plumbing; we could even teach them to read.

Justice Douglas was enthusiastic. He thought he could get American manufacturers to contribute the TV sets. I would ask President Bosch to give us time on the government television station and to permit us to put a television set in every town hall or in every abandoned local headquarters of Trujillo's old party.

For a holiday, Fran and the boys and I took Douglas to the mountains. We arrived at Constanza as dark dropped fast over the high valley. The bartender in the deserted hotel confided to me that local leftists were plotting guerrilla activity; they had been here last week, whispering together, and after they left he had picked up bits of paper on which they had scribbled battle plans. At dinner Justice Douglas and I amused ourselves by whispering conspiratorially and scribbling on scraps of paper in Spanish, Justice Douglas adding a few words in Persian. Next morning at dawn we crossed the backbone of the Central Mountain Range, ten thousand feet, I driving my Jeep, Douglas sitting beside me, the cold wind blowing his white hair.

I got Bosch's cooperation with our TV project, and in ensuing months Justice Douglas sent technicians down and they began taping a hundred programs to teach the Dominican people to read and write. Local teachers would have to be found, lesson books written. It was a formidable project. By late summer the first tapes were finished and the television sets were promised. We thought we could reclaim the generation Trujillo had wasted.

Bosch had begun badly; it got worse. The splintered political parties issued an anti-Bosch manifesto, uneasy businessmen muttered about communism, lines of unemployed people formed each morning at the Palace gate. Bosch tried to counterattack—senseless attacks on red-baiters and the defunct Council of State. I tried to help him quietly—offered several public gestures to demonstrate his ties to the United States, including lunch aboard a flagship of our Atlantic Fleet, coastal patrol boats, private mediation with the editor of the leading opposition newspaper, support if he would restrict travel to Cuba, a dinner party for him and suspicious businessmen. Bosch accepted all this.

But at the same time he almost went to war with Haiti. I tried to restrain him, urged him to take his complaint against Haiti (which was legitimate) to the OAS. His military commanders suspected he wanted to destroy their forces in a Haitian adventure. In the end, Bosch did not get OAS help, he realized his armed forces were incapable of invading Haiti, and he himself felt defeated and betrayed and alone.

Harry Shlaudeman told me Bosch was losing his own political party supporters. Wherever I went, I myself heard poor people saying, "Juan Bosch is good for nothing." And my AID director told me quite casually, "Moscoso and Betancourt and Harriman have agreed that Bosch is gone and so hands off." I thought I too had noticed a certain reserve in Washington. Hal Hendrix of the *Miami News* wrote a series of articles attacking Bosch hard, and me too— the specter of communism. Other U.S. reporters were attacking. These correspondents would come to the Republic, talk to the Dominicans who spoke English and who were mostly businessmen opposed to Bosch, be told that he was a Communist or was handing the country over to Communists, would file their stories to their papers in the United States, and there the stories would be published in English then translated into Spanish and sent down to the Republic and printed in the Dominican newspapers—and the same businessmen who had inspired them in the first place would show them to the military and say "You see? Even the impartial United States press considers Juan Bosch dangerous and soft on communism." (No doubt most of the U.S. journalists believed what they wrote. I considered the Hendrix articles a vicious hatchet job, however, and told Hendrix so.) These stories also fed the fires in Washington. Congressman Armistead Selden of Alabama, chairman of the House Subcommittee on Inter-American Affairs, made a speech on the House floor denouncing "the advancing communist offensive of subversive penetration in the Dominican Republic." Bosch publicly denounced Congressman Selden. Senator Hubert Humphrey on the Senate floor defended Bosch. The lines were hardening. It was early June; Bosch's first hundred days were over. He had squandered them. I went to Washington to try to save him.

Coming into Kennedy Airport in New York was breathtaking: It was so big, so organized, everything worked, the young businessmen hurrying through the corridors exuded confidence; everyone knew what he was doing and how to do it. This was power, these educated, trained, competent people. This was a great nation. The poor Republic.

In Washington, I went all out to rally support for Bosch. I explained the Dominican political situation. Soon Bosch would have to move left, might even expropriate land without compensation. This would alarm the United States. To make it unnecessary, I wanted us to help him now. I asked for a $15 million loan for agricultural development; Moscoso of AID thought my AID director hadn't made a good case for it. The assistant secretary of state for Latin America, Ed Martin, denied there'd been a change in the Department's attitude toward Bosch and said if Bosch wanted financial help he'd have to come up with sensible projects, and he'd better not expropriate land without compensation as he'd threatened. I went over to the Pentagon, trying to get Bosch's patrol boats. I asked Abram Chayes, the Department's legal counselor, to work out an acceptable method of land expropriation. John Steele of *Time* arranged a dinner with fifteen or twenty leading writers and editors.

On Capitol Hill, I appeared in executive session before Senator Wayne Morse's Latin American subcommittee and Congressman Selden's House subcommittee. At lunch privately, Senator Humphrey told me Bosch couldn't expropriate U.S. land and he'd better give Dominican landowners fifty-year bonds. Congressman Selden received me courteously and sympathetically, and I tried to disabuse him of some of Hal Hendrix's notions, while he tried to disabuse me of any notion that he didn't want Bosch to succeed.

Over the Fourth of July weekend, I went to our camp in Upper Michigan. As soon as I saw the pine and lakes and deep blue sky, I knew they still held me. One day Earl Numinen and I walked in to Smith Lake, far out in the woods to the north, where I still hoped to buy land. And evenings sitting alone in front of the fire, I thought the long thoughts that always seemed to come in Michigan. It is still the most healing place on earth for me. Years ago I had first come here to fish, or thought I had, but as time passed I was less interested in fishing, more in merely being in the woods, driving the Jeep or walking, watching for deer and coyote, partridge and bear. Once I had seen a timber wolf.

I stopped briefly in Highland Park, and when I tried to explain Dominican politics to our friends there, they simply looked bewildered. And went back to small talk—their children's summer camp, the racetrack, the musical season at Ravinia, golf and travel, whose daughter got into what college—the people and things they had made their place among. To me, thinking of Juan Bosch and Dominican democracy, my friends' lives seemed empty. But were they really? Living was nothing but personal relationship, private relationship. While I had been writing professionally, I had thought writing was what mattered—trying to help improve an American society that did not always work so well as it should. And I had felt that way too in the political campaigns. Then toward the end of that period I'd thought that those things mattered less than personal life, private life and inner life. Now in the Republic and in Washington I was involved with large public issues; I thought they were what mattered. Were they? It was an unsettling trip. Well, howsoever all that might be, the Michigan woods abided.

Back in Washington I wanted to be photographed with President Kennedy and have the photograph published in the Republic, and to return there with a public statement using President Kennedy's name and reiterating our firm support for Bosch. But I did not want to put President Kennedy out on a limb unless I was sure the Communists could indeed be contained, and so I asked for help in training an effective antisubversive force for Bosch—and, as a double check, I wanted a greatly stepped-up CIA covert operation of our own, one capable, if necessary, of keeping several people inside and outside the Bosch government under close surveillance.

When I saw President Kennedy in the Oval Office, accompanied by Ed Martin and Ralph Dungan, I told him about our Dominican problems, including Washington's cooling off on Bosch. We were gambling, I said, in supporting Bosch, but the alternatives were worse—a rightist coup, or a leftist takeover, "another Castro in the Caribbean."

The President listened carefully then asked hard questions. He thought expropriation would create problems no matter how Bosch did it. He approved getting some AID projects ready to go. He liked my talking to members of Congress and the press. Once he got up from his rocking chair and, walking to a blue-green naval painting on the wall, asked if I was coming back to help him in the campaign next year, that is, 1964. I said I was at his disposition. He thought a minute, said, "Maybe you can do more for us holding that place together. Well, we'll see." He approved the statement I proposed to issue. A photographer came in and made the picture I wanted. As I walked out, past the desk of Kenny O'Donnell, the president pointed his finger at me and said loudly, "There he goes—the Earl E. T. Smith of this administration." They roared—Smith had been Eisenhower's ambassador to Cuba when Castro came to power. I was so startled I could only say to him, "What a thing to say," and he grinned and waved, and I left. Going back to Santo Domingo, after seeing him, almost anything seemed possible, even Juan Bosch's success.

But from then on, it was just a hopeless holding operation. The Dominican military, egged on by the businessmen, was hell-bent on exterminating communism. Fran and I gave dinner parties trying to bring Bosch together with the Santiago oligarchy, with Dominican businessmen, and with his own military. Strained parties. His opponents began pretending that the Church was against Bosch; I saw the papal nuncio. I cooked up a new AID program for Bosch; Washington was cool. Even Ralph Dungan was beginning to give thought to what we should do after Bosch fell.

Increasingly Bosch seemed resigned to his own failure. Talking to me he shook his head sadly and said, "There can be no revolution—there is no money." He talked of resigning. Fantastic rumors swept the streets, including one that the Pentagon had broken with me and President Kennedy and was conspiring to overthrow Bosch. We could do little but tell everybody we supported the elected president. Like Bosch, we ourselves were becoming increasingly isolated. In the end, Bosch had the support of only a minuscule Communist party, some of the Santiago oligarchy, and the U.S. embassy, mainly I myself.

On September 20, 1963, businessmen, provoked by Bosch's unwise proposal of another tax and land reform, closed their businesses—a "general strike" against Bosch. Over the weekend violence began in the streets, the military came in, and on Tuesday Bosch sent an aide to take me to a villa where he was hiding out. In a little bedroom with a noisy air conditioner, drinking a Coke, Bosch told me, "There is a *golpe*, a coup. Yes. They are going to kill me or overthrow me. Today."

That night they did: The military overthrew him without bloodshed, despite all our efforts throughout the night. He seemed almost to invite the coup. At dawn I went to the Palace, talked briefly to Bosch, who was confined in his office under military guard, and asked the military to guarantee his physical safety then went back to the residence and called Ed Martin.

In all their history, the Dominican people had enjoyed eleven years of freely elected government. To this total Juan Bosch had been able to add just seven months minus two days. After obtaining the department's approval, I left for Washington, taking my AID director and military group chief with me. Fran and the boys stayed. The day I left was the day the TVA mission had been due to arrive. Police raided the office where we had stored the literacy tapes from Justice Douglas; we rescued them and locked them in my safe. At times in the Republic I had felt that everything in my past life had prepared me for this job—my reporting, my writing, my work in politics. Now all that, along with Bosch, had failed.

7

The military appointed a triumvirate, three unexceptional civilians, to run the government, but the military remained the real power. In Washington I went to work to persuade my government to set its face against the new regime, to refuse to recognize it, and thus, I hoped, to bring it down or at least force it to return to constitutionality. Reaction on Capitol Hill was strong. Senator Humphrey encouraged me. No senator condoned the coup; one demanded that we rescue Bosch from the ship taking him to exile and put him back in the Palace, by force if necessary. In the House, Congressman Selden, while not applauding the coup, said he preferred a dictatorship that sought our friendship to a Communist dictatorship. I testified before House and Senate committees. Most of the press seemed to believe we ought not to recognize the new regime. Sentiment in the Senate was moving that way. The House was less clear. The president would decide.

In the department we drafted policy recommendations for him: as our ultimate objective, a return to constitutional representative democracy; meanwhile, effective government and neither harsh military dictatorship nor Communist growth. What we wanted in exchange for recognition: free political activity for non-Communist parties, restoration of a semblance of constitutionality, a presidential election in one year, and more. We also drafted a public statement for Secretary Rusk.

When we saw President Kennedy, he looked at me and said, "I take it we don't want Bosch back."

"No, Mr. President."

"Why not?"

"Because he isn't a president."

He began discussing the paper point by pont. I said I wanted something in the secretary's statement specifically about nonrecognition. The president didn't want to use the word. Averell Harriman suggested "normalization of relations." The president rewrote the statement, asked what time it was, said, "We've got to get it out right now if we want to catch the bulldog," the early editions of tomorrow morning's papers, and picked up a phone, got no answer, jiggled the receiver impatiently, and still got no answer. Ralph Dungan took the statement and hurried out to release it. It was a tough statement, the kind I'd wanted.

After the meeting broke up, I wished I'd had an opportunity to explain to President Kennedy how Bosch had fallen, and later I asked Ralph Dungan if I could, privately. Dungan said, "If you're worried that the president has lost confidence in you, forget it—he hasn't." I was grateful, but it wasn't that. It was a guilty need to give him an accounting of my failure. I never got the chance.

During the ensuing weeks we struggled with the Dominican regime. We saw President Kennedy frequently. At first we labored urgently. When we went to see the president we sometimes met the officers concerned with Vietnam coming out of the Cabinet Room after meeting with him. But after a time the urgency wore off; other issues, such as Vietnam, claimed his attention; and we were left in the Department to draft new instructions to the chargé. I had a little office on the third floor. We fell back from one position to another, dropping one by one our demands on the Triumvirate. It rebuffed our every move. We were under pressure—we feared a bloody Communist guerrilla rising, we feared the collapse of the Triumvirate and a naked military dictatorship, and we faced pressures from other governments, including Great Britain, to recognize.

Fran and the boys came up to Washington. After a week, they went weeping home to Highland Park. Our house there was rented, as it had been since we went to the Republic, and they stayed with neighbors. I stayed in Washington with the John Steeles. Every day I went down to the antiseptic Department—with its clean desks and locked files it always looked deserted. I came to hate it. It was always cold and wet in Washington that fall.

Bobby Kennedy's wife Ethel called to invite me to a surprise birthday party for Bobby at their home, Hickory Hill, on November 20. The party was big and gay and noisy. Old friends from the campaign were there, Kenny O'Donnell and Steve Smith and others, and while most of the guests danced the twist, we talked about the coming 1964 campaign.

Two months had passed since Bosch was overthrown. Now I had cooked up an elaborate plan to meet secretly with the former president, Bonnelly. It was almost our last plan. On Friday morning, November 22, Bonnelly said he wanted first to consult the Triumvirate. We told him to go ahead. Ethel Kennedy sent my topcoat to the Department—I'd left it at her party. I didn't go out to lunch, was waiting for word from Bonnelly. Restless, I began pacing in the outer office where the typists worked. A young Foreign Service officer came up to me and said, "Mr. Ambassador, the president was shot in Dallas."

That afternoon when the radio said he was dead I called Fran. She knew. She would stay with the kids. I'd be home as soon as I could. Outside my window in the Department, the flags were coming down to half-staff. I wrote a telegram telling the chargé to meet with Bonnelly for me. I left. It was dark, raining hard. At Arthur Schlesinger's house, I found a note on the door: "This is an upset household, forgive us if we'd rather be alone." I went home to the Steeles. We sat. After a while I went up to bed in the attic. Sirens screamed all night. Next day I went as instructed to the White House, walking across Lafayette Park in the rain, seeing the terrible long black limousines pulling up at the portico; and went wet and alone into the East Room where the president's body lay in state with an honor guard. An old man and his wife were ahead of me; I waited till they passed, then went in and stood by the flag-draped casket alone, and said silently to President Kennedy I was sorry and thanked him, as many years ago when Fran's mother died I had silently thanked her for having given me Fran, and felt some vague stirring to ask God to help him and us all, but didn't, then went out of the room, the honor guard changing slowly too.

Downstairs on my way out I saw Clayton Fritchey, my old friend from the second Stevenson campaign, now Stevenson's press secretary at the UN. He was waiting for the Harrimans. They offered me a ride. Mrs. Harriman was crying and, because I was sitting next to her, I held her hand. Harriman asked Fritchey to get Ted Sorensen to work on President Johnson's eulogy for President Kennedy and asked me to work on one that Stevenson would deliver. At the Department, Harriman asked me to go up to his office with him, lonely too, I suppose, and we went and talked a long time, mostly about the Dominican Republic and the Alliance. Harriman felt he should be paying more attention to Latin America, he wanted me to help him think about it when I went back to the Dominican Republic. I told him I didn't think I'd be going back. He said I must, it was my duty, I knew more about it than anybody else, and we should have "rammed you down that bunch's throats" right after the coup.

Leaving, I ran into Ed Martin and said I intended to resign that day. He said I couldn't, President Johnson had asked that no ambassadors resign. I said I'd stay a few days then I'd like to go home for Thanksgiving. I went to Harriman's house in Georgetown and worked with Fritchey on a draft for Stevenson's speech.

Sunday I slept late at the Steeles', and was told of a sudden that the man who assassinated President Kennedy had himself been killed. The television screen was becoming a mirror of our national madness. On Monday the president was buried, and I walked down in the brilliant sun from the Department to Constitution Avenue and watched the procession come slowly past, the awful black and muffled drums. Millions of Americans watched it on television and felt the same agony, the sense that all was lost. I went home to Highland Park. Fran had temporarily retrieved our house. Dan had lettered a sign and put it on my desk: ASK NOT WHAT YOUR COUNTRY CAN DO FOR YOU—ASK WHAT YOU CAN DO FOR YOUR COUNTRY. Dan had decided he wanted to become president. I tried to explain to Fran and Dan and Fred why we were not going back to the Dominican Republic, which they loved. Maybe some day, as private citizens. Right now I wanted to get out of government, to think, to write, to be with them and live privately and quietly. I would go back to Washington, see things through to recognition, then resign and come home. Maybe we would go up to Michigan. But the Dominican Republic, what we had tried to do there for the Dominicans, for our own country, for President Kennedy—that was all over, ended. The world was a different place.

It was hard for them. And Fran thought I should go back to help the Dominicans, and the United States, and our faith in what Stevenson and Kennedy had stood for in the campaigns, for if all who so believed departed, what then? Fran was worried too about the Little Clinic of Higüey. Dreams die hard. And maybe she was right.

On my way back to Washington, I stopped at the Chicago City Hall to pay a courtesy call on Mayor Daley. He too had been President Kennedy's friend and he was as shattered as the rest of us. I asked him if the new president, Lyndon Johnson, would be all right, and he said, "He will if he goes down the line for the program," that is, for President Kennedy's civil rights program. "He won't get his wheat and cotton bill if he doesn't go down the line for the program."

In Washington, President Johnson met privately in Secretary Rusk's office with the half dozen or so of us ambassadors who happened to be in town. Seated, he talked to us quietly, kneading his big hands, talking about himself, his boyhood on a poor Texas farm, now president of the United States.

Two weeks ensued. Guerrillas took to the Dominican hills, and government troops hunted them down. The Republic was polarizing. I told Dungan we could delay recognition no longer. He agreed and so did George Ball and Ed Martin. Ed Martin told me privately that, if I agreed, he also would recommend that the president accept

my resignation before we recognized, so I would not appear to resign in protest against recognition. I agreed. On Saturday he and I
met the press and announced recognition. President Johnson accepted my resignation effective February 15, 1964.

I spent a few days saying goodbye to my friends in the administration, Bobby Kennedy hardest of all. How his face had aged in the
years since I'd known him at the Rackets Committee. Well, whose
hadn't? I stayed only a minute or two, telling him I'd do anything
for him, thanking him, telling him I was going home to write a book.
With that odd tentative half-smile, so little known to strangers, he
said, "Everybody's writing a book," and "All right, John." And
then, "Well, three years is better than nothing."

I took a train home as I had so many times in years past. That
night I could not sleep and dozed, wakened, dozed, wakened, as the
train rolled and pitched and shuddered, stopping a long time beside
a black river near Pittsburgh; and I kept thinking: "Why did they
kill him? Why him?" In the morning the train rolled across the flat
land of Ohio, where I'd been born, and Indiana, where I'd been
raised, that flat endless plain, white houses, red barns, two pheasants
standing in a snowy cornfield, a woodlot, the neat rectangles of
earth scattered complacent. So many years ago, twenty-six years,
just out of college, I had crossed the plain, headed for the Caribbean, suffocated by the flat land, eager for the great world; and had
sailed the Gulf of Mexico and the Carribean, Puerto Rico, Cuba,
and, finally, by pure chance, Santo Domingo. How long ago. Then
the flat fields of Indiana had seemed drab, dispiriting, the blue
Caribbean with flying fish scattering before the prow exciting, mi-
raculous.

Now the Midwest looked different. Here I'd spent most of my
adult life, working, crisscrossing it, talking to its people and writing
about them, I knew it, all of it, knew it in my bones. The scattered
houses, the big town lots, a cord of stovewood in a backyard, here
and there a rivulet, a gully—my father and I used to hunt rabbits on
cold days like this in the gullies, though he always said we'd find
more in the corn and wheat stubble, and he was right but it was less
fun, the gullies were shadowy and mysterious. Now it all looked
comforting, and I needed, the nation needed, comfort. I was going
home.

We got a tall Christmas tree, and Cindy came home from Guatemala with her husband, and my mother and Aunt Verl came up from Indianapolis on the train called the *James Whitcomb Riley*, and after Christmas all of us except my mother and my aunt went up to Michigan. We stayed in our camp at Three Lakes, 25 degrees below zero, and went snowshoeing and rode the toboggan and took a Jeep ride in the woods, seeing a herd of deer black against the snow in a frozen swamp. I had written to the logger who owned the land at Smith Lake, the lake far out in the woods, and he had said it was for sale; now I met him and bought it, about 160 acres, nearly all the shoreline on the big end of Smith Lake in the rough, rocky, uninhabited—and in winter unreachable—country out north. After New Year's the others went home but I stayed alone, dreaming about building a camp at Smith Lake next summer, thinking about the book I wanted to write on my work in the Dominican Republic, at night alone in camp in front of the fire. All my life when hurt or healing, I had wanted to be alone.

TWELVE

LYNDON B. JOHNSON AND ROBERT F. KENNEDY

1.

In the embassy I had dedicated myself wholeheartedly to my work and disdained the trappings of powers. Nevertheless, anybody who leaves high public office and returns to private life has a reentry problem and will, if he is honest, admit he misses some of the perquisites of power. He will not be driven to his office along a tropical boulevard by a chauffeur in a limousine; he will stand in the January slush with the rest of the commuters waiting for the 8:08. At the office no Marine guard will snap to attention when he arrives, all will not rise when he enters. More than one former ambassador has bought a set of official china, bearing the seal of the United States, to use in his private home; but he himself must help his wife scrape the garbage from the plates in the kitchen. In the embassy, he had a sense of history, a sense of serious purpose, of doing something important for his country. On his judgment turned the decision whether to develop the northern valley or the southwest desert; a word from him might topple a government. Looking back, he can see he made mistakes. Reading the morning paper, he cries out to say, "Don't take that road; we almost took it, and it leads to the precipice." Whether he was right or wrong, he cared. He helped make the foreign policy of the United States. What worthwhile can he do now? What—the ultimate question—will he do with the rest of his life?

Actually, there were times during the next four years when I didn't know what I was going to do with the rest of my life. We spent the four years between 1964 and 1968 somewhat adrift, summers up in Michigan, the rest of the year on the east coast at a university or in New York or Washington, often traveling abroad, dragging Dan and Fred to and fro with us.

Of one thing I felt sure: I would not return to writing heavy fact for magazines. I would write—it was all I knew how to do—but not what I formerly had. I could no longer imagine writing a John Simon story, or a Jackson Prison story. Now my interests lay in national politics and in foreign policy. One doesn't go back.

The fact is, I could not have gone back even if I had wanted to. While I'd been away, magazines had fallen on evil times. Television had taken their advertising. When I had written for the *Post,* its issues often had run to more than two hundred fat pages. Now the *Post* had become thin and wizened and had started to lose money, its owners had replaced Ben Hibbs, Stuart Rose, and the others, and the new editors had made changes—tried to jazz it up, to publish sensational exposés. It was no longer a natural market for me. In a few more months the *Post* folded. (Later its name was sold to another publishing company and it resumed publication, but it was an entirely different magazine.)

I had some loose ends to clean up. At the behest of Arthur Schlesinger, I worked in the White House with Bill D. Moyers, President Johnson's young chief of staff, and others, writing a fund-raising book for the Democratic National Convention of 1964. I made several television appearances on foreign affairs. Bits and pieces of Dominican affairs came my way. Fran and I bought a little beach house at Sosúa on the north coast of the Dominican Republic. More importantly, at Bobby Kennedy's request, I helped him set up an oral history project on his brother's presidency, and I interviewed him for it, long sessions in Washington and New York. It was excruciatingly hard work for both of us. He both wanted and feared to have me ask hard questions about his brother, and I felt much the same way, not boring in as I would have in a different sort of interview, but at the same time conscious that I could not escape an obligation to history. We worked all through that spring, a time when he was becoming increasingly estranged from President Johnson, though still in his cabinet. I felt the interviews had been disappointing, even somewhat superficial. But people who since have used them, such as Arthur Schlesinger in writing his biography of Bobby, have told me they are valuable.

Several times during these years I thought to go back into government. Sarge Shriver was expanding the Peace Corps in Brazil to five hundred or seven hundred and asked me to head it. I declined. Several times I thought I wanted another embassy, and the Department once offered me Jamaica, but I declined that too; it didn't sound interesting or important after the Dominican Republic. Once, after I had performed several missions for President Johnson, I saw him alone in his office, and he proposed I come to Washington permanently as a consultant to him and the State Department. I didn't want to do it and made some noncommittal response, and we talked on, then he asked if there was anything else I wanted to say to him. I told him I'd be interested in another embassy but not a sinecure like Jamaica, an important one and one where we had a chance of success. The president said, "You're entitled to it. You've gone everywhere and done everything we asked. I'd like to see you have it,"and he asked where I wanted to go. I told him some place like Venezuela. As I left, he said, "We'll be in touch with you." Bill Moyers pushed the consultant job, saying I'd only nominally be consulting with the State Department, actually I'd be the president's principal speechwriter and one of his principal advisers, and he indicated it might well lead to a very good embassy.

Not until later, after talking to Fran, did I realize how carefully President Johnson had phrased his response. He'd said I deserved an embassy but he hadn't said he'd see that I got one, he'd said he'd like to see me have it. Presumably he never appointed me an ambassador because I declined to join his staff. He punished others more severely for less serious offenses.

Well, if not government, how should I go back to writing? *Reader's Digest* asked me to become its Latin American correspondent. Mike Bessie at Harper had an idea for a book, George Roy

Hill had one for a film. But what I wanted to write, and did write, was a book that was at once an account of my work in the Dominican Republic and a sort of memorial to President Kennedy and his Alliance for Progress. I called it *Overtaken by Events* (one of the few good phrases to come out of the State Department bureaucracy). And I wrote it at the Center for Advanced Studies at Wesleyan University in Middletown, Connecticut.

Fran and Dan and Fred and I lived there for a year and a half. The university gave us a small two-story shingled house converted from an old mill, standing on a high rock ledge above a creek that flowed over a waterfall, a secluded wooded place of winding roads and ravines and hills across the Connecticut River from Middletown and the campus. In addition to the house, I had the rank and salary of a full professor but with no teaching responsibilities unless I chose to give an occasional lecture or seminar, which I did. Only two things were expected of me—to be engaged on a serious piece of work of my own, which I was, writing *Overtaken by Events,* and to have drinks and dinner every Monday night at the center on the campus with the other fellows of the center and its director, Paul Horgan, the writer, and listen to a paper read after dinner by one of the fellows or a Wesleyan faculty member. Paul Horgan was one of the gentlest, most courteous men I ever knew, as well as a good writer, and he presided over the fellows with grace and elegance. Fran and I came to know well a number of the other fellows—Edmund Wilson, the critic, and his wife, Elena; Jean Stafford, the *New Yorker* writer and widow of A. J. Liebling; Sir Herbert Read, the British critic, and his wife. Edmund Wilson usually drank martinis before dinner and wine with dinner and slept through the paper. He was great fun and once, after a young university psychologist had read a dreadful paper on the psychology of mice—he had given mice alcohol experimentally and he seemed to think that rats were the parents of mice—I found in my letter box what purported to be a long complaint by a mother mouse against the professor, especially the difficulty she had in pushing a full bottle of gin across his laboratory in order for him to feed it to her. I guessed its author was Jean Stafford but it turned out to be Edmund Wilson; for several weeks the three of us composed epistles to one another written by mice and rats.

I spent one memorable Monday evening talking to a nuclear physicist who was a protégé of Niels Bohr, and he undertook to explain quantum physics to me, and it all seemed perfectly clear, but next morning I couldn't remember a word he said. On other evenings Fran and I would entertain several of the fellows and Paul Horgan and Victor Butterfield, Wesleyan's president, at dinner, or go to one of their houses for dinner. The atmosphere at the center was what one had always hoped a university atmosphere would be—a civilized community of serious scholars who could be fun. It was a pleasant life, and our millhouse was a good place to work. And I'm sure that by talking to the other fellows about *Overtaken by Events*, and by reading things they suggested, I made it a better book than I would have in Highland Park. I was writing the rough draft at a furious pace, eighty-five pages a day.

We were within easy driving distance of New York and several times took the boys to the theater there, took them too up to Massachusetts and Vermont, New Hampshire and Maine, where we visited my favorite store whence by mail I had bought sporting goods for years, L. L. Bean. Now and then Fran and I went to Washington. Arthur Schlesinger was leaving President Johnson's White House staff to write his book about the Kennedy administration, *A Thousand Days*, and his friends gave him a farewell party, renting a Georgetown bar for a night and putting up funny signs, one of which read, COME AS YOU WERE, and when Arthur stepped onto the dance floor to deliver his farewell speech, a spotlight focused on him and the band played "The Eyes of Texas Are upon You." The hour being late, his speech made little sense but no matter—by then few of us in his audience were making much sense either.

Friends of ours visited us—Harry and Carol Shlaudeman, now back in the Department in Washington, Gustavo Tavares from the Dominican Republic, Dick Goodwin, who had joined the White House staff and was writing speeches for President Johnson. Ben Shahn was lecturing at Harvard, and we went to visit him and Bernarda. We went too to spend long weekends with Dick and Eleanor Rovere at their house in Rhinebeck, New York, on the Hudson. Oddly, Dick and I rarely talked about writing, though we had spent our lives at it, and we knew each other a long time before we discovered that both of us had started out by writing fact detective stories.

Sometimes we talked politics; usually we talked about real estate and money. (Dick once wrote that he had the mind and soul of an accountant; so have I.)

2.

On April 24, 1965, a Saturday, the Dominican Republic blew up in what quickly became civil war. Juan Bosch was in exile in Puerto Rico, but supporters of his, including elements of the armed forces, attacked the Palace, overthrew the Triumvirate government, and passed out arms to the people; General Wessin y Wessin's loyalist tanks and troops began fighting them in the capital's streets. A bloodbath began, perhaps a thousand killed. The following Wednesday, April 28, President Johnson sent the Marines and part of the 82nd Airborne Division, some twenty-one thousand troops, about as many as we then had in Vietnam. That night on national television he said that Americans in the Republic were in danger, Dominican authorities could not protect them, he had sent troops to evacuate them. I was disheartened. I feared that once more we had ranged ourselves on the wrong side—*for* an unpopular regime, *against* the people.

George Ball and Bill Moyers called me at Wesleyan next day and asked me to come to Washington. They sent an Air Force Jet Star for me and I was in Washington on Friday by 6:30 A.M. In the Cabinet Room of the White House I met with President Johnson and the leaders of his administration, including Secretary Rusk and Secretary McNamara, Undersecretary Ball, the head of CIA, and the chairman of the Joint Chiefs of Staff. Until now, U.S. troops were under orders not to join Wessin's loyalist troops in aggressive action against the rebels but only to establish an international zone under an OAS resolution to protect embassies and foreign citizens. Reporting from the embassy was confused. General Wessin's loyalist forces might collapse today. If that happened, would we order U.S. troops to shoot Dominican rebels? Secretary Rusk said he wanted to point out to the president that sending troops into combat in a foreign capital was a very serious business. I said quickly, "Yes, Mr. President, that's the last thing we want to happen." President Johnson looked across the table at me with his hooded eyes and said, "No it isn't. The last thing we want is another Castro in the Caribbean." He foresaw two dangers—very soon we would see a Communist-dominated government in the Dominican Republic, or we would find ourselves alone with our troops in the Republic without any support in the hemisphere. He didn't want either one. He told Rusk and Ball to get to work with the OAS, told McNamara and the Joint Chiefs to get ready to do whatever might have to be done, and told me to go to the Republic at once and open up contact with the rebels—Ambassador W. Tapley Bennett, a conservative career officer who had replaced me, had few contacts among Bosch people—help the papal nuncio get a cease-fire (as the OAS had requested), and find out what the facts were and report to him. Already the press was criticizing him for having sent troops, President Johnson said, and he was willing to work for peace through the OAS or anybody else but he did not intend "to sit here with my hands tied and let Castro take that island. What can we do in Vietnam if we can't clean up the Dominican Republic?"

I went to Santo Domingo immediately on a Jet Star, taking Harry Shlaudeman as my aide. Santo Domingo was all shot up, parts of it burning, the Palace a wreck in no-man's land, gunfire heavy and close to our blacked-out embassy. Seeing thus this city I loved was painful. We got the cease-fire—I persuaded General Wessin, whom I detested and had not seen since the dawn he overthrew Bosch, to walk across the room in his headquarters to the nuncio and sign the cease-fire; then the nuncio and I went into the rebel zone, riding in his car with the gold and white Vatican flag draped over the hood, he in his billowing long white cassock, and persuaded the rebel commander to sign. Come to think of it, I suppose the instruments of U.S. policy, the nuncio and the Marines, were the same as the Spaniards' four hundred years before—subduing and pacifying the natives by using both the cross and the sword.

One night I flew to Puerto Rico to see Juan Bosch. Another night I went to see my friend Antonio Imbert Barreras, Trujillo's assassin and a former member of the Council of State. As we pulled up in front of his house, I was sitting in the front seat beside the driver with two young Marines in the back seat, and one of my young guards let his finger slip on the safety of his rifle and let off a string of shots behind my right ear. I dived for the floor, knowing Imbert's bodyguards would be hidden behind the hedge a few feet away, and began calling out to them not to shoot, it was an accident, I was Ambassador Martin, and waited, expecting them to open up with their machine guns. They did not; they were well trained and they knew me. Had they been any other Dominican troops they'd have killed me.

Often I telephoned President Johnson, once about 3:30 A.M.; he was running this operation like a desk officer. Shlaudeman and I talked to many Dominicans, and I became convinced that political leadership of the rebellion had passed to Communists and other extremists and I said so at a press conference, thereby putting my reputation as a fact finder and a liberal on the line.

The danger to the United States was that we would range our own troops against the rebels; we needed a third force. Tony Imbert undertook to form a provisional government, and I wrote his inaugural speech, and he led Dominican troops in an assault. At my suggestion, we interposed our troops between his force and the rebels and kept the peace. Imbert's government prospered briefly; but liberals in the U.S. press attacked President Johnson for installing an assassin as his proxy, and Undersecretary of State Tom Mann, McGeorge Bundy, and Undersecretary of Defense Cyrus Vance came down and cut the ground out from under Imbert and tried to install a president of more liberal coloration.

I went back to Washington on May 18 and next day met with President Johnson and the other principals—Vice-President Humphrey, Secretaries Rusk and McNamara, and others. President Johnson felt himself at bay, pressed hard by liberal journalists, many of them my friends. His eyes were almost slits. He went around the table and polled us one by one on whether we favored Imbert or the tame liberal. He would brook no equivocation, no suggestion that this was not a matter of either-or; and if one of us balked—as I did—he read aloud a transcript of a recording he had made of a long telephone conversation we had had with him from Santo Domingo, when he had asked our views on the same question. He told us that no American president since George Washington had been subpoenaed by the Congress but that he might be, and if he was he would take all of us with him and the transcript as well. After the meeting had been going on more than three hours, it began to relax simply because of the passage of time, and some of us caught ourselves forgetting we were addressing the president of the

United States, he seemed more like a county board chairman running a courthouse meeting on a sewer bond issue. Throughout, President Johnson kept needling the State Department, and Secretary Rusk did not like it and he did not smile. When the president did this, Vice-President Humphrey would nudge me, sitting beside him, and wink at me. Then the president would turn to Secretary McNamara and, calling him Bob, say something comradely. All this—pressure and camaraderie—was President Johnson's way of getting what he called a consensus. He operated so differently from President Kennedy. President Kennedy's meetings rarely lasted more than an hour, usually less, he never allowed any doubt that he was President, he never used pressure, if he was displeased he simply disposed of the question by hardening his voice, he never descended to our level. I remembered Bobby Kennedy's telling me once that President Johnson despoiled everything he touched by his crudity, his ignorance, his refusal to learn. And yet this was the same man who had saved our son Dan's broken arm.

Life and *Reader's Digest* asked me to write a piece about our intervention, and I did. I spent a good deal of time, with the president's encouragement, talking to reporters and editorial writers. Some had been criticizing me for supporting our intervention. Several, however, defended me, Jack Fischer of *Harper's* writing that if John Bartlow Martin said there were Communists in the rebel movement, there were Communists in the rebel movement. Some of my liberal friends, like Arthur Schlesinger, refrained from public criticism but plainly thought me wrong. (Averell Harriman had loyally gone to South America to explain and defend President Johnson's intervention but Arthur refused to do the same in Central America.) Over the years, vice-President Humphrey and I had manned the barricades together in many a liberal cause, and I explained to him what we'd been doing in the Dominican Republic, especially the Imbert gambit. He shook his head and said, "And now I've got a delegation of neo-Nazi politicians from West Germany waiting for me. You sure get mixed up with some funny people if you hang around long enough." One day Fran and I had lunch at Kay Graham's house with her and Adlai Stevenson, come down from the United Nations where, bewildered, he had been trying to explain our intervention. He and I had a swim in the pool before lunch—Fran said

we made a spectacular pair, he so fat, I so thin, which said something about the ways we had been spending our time—and after
lunch Stevenson and I went to another room to talk. For an hour or
more. At the UN, despite our liberal friends' criticism, he had
loyally if uncomprehendingly defended our intervention, and now
he asked me what the hell we'd been up to. I explained it, and he
seemed satisfied. He also asked me to come to New York to talk to
him about a major writing project he had in mind. I got the impression he wanted me to help him write his autobiography. I never saw
him again; he died a few weeks later.

With considerable difficulty, we persuaded the OAS to join our
peace-keeping efforts. Eventually Ellsworth Bunker, our ambassador to the OAS, aided by Shlaudeman, managed to install a provisional president who would hold free elections. He did, and since
then the Dominican Republic has held five more free elections at
scheduled intervals. These days, when I think of my Dominican experiences, including my efforts to help Juan Bosch succeed as president, I tend to think of them as a failure. But actually, through all
the twenty-four years that have passed from the assassination of
Trujillo to this writing, except for the brief civil war in 1965, the
Dominican people have lived in peace and freedom, the longest period of peace and freedom in all Dominican history. Our military
intervention turned out far better than we had any right to expect.

3.

"Intervention"* has become a dirty word. It is used somewhat in-
discriminately. For the United States, intervention has usually taken
two forms—trying to influence and even control the internal politics
of a smaller country by political means and, usually after that has
failed, by military means. (In recent years, perhaps emulating the
Soviets, we have tried a third method—using a proxy native military
force. This has not led to happy results to date in Nicaragua any
more than it did in Vietnam.)

We have intervened most frequently in Central America and the
Caribbean. Usually our intervention there has been a corollary of
our global policy (and our presidents' domestic political con-

---

*Talleyrand once said, "Non-intervention is a political and metaphysical term and
means about the same as intervention."

cerns)—we intervened in the Caribbean basin under Theodore Roosevelt and Woodrow Wilson in the name of "antikaiserism"; we intervened there under Presidents Kennedy and Johnson and Reagan in the name of "anticommunism." Debate about military intervention is usually sharp and clear, debate about peaceful political intervention more muffled and confused.

We are bound by international law not to intervene in the domestic politics of other sovereign nations. But we do, constantly (and so do other powers, and not only the Soviet Union). Whether we ought to is the subject of intense quiet debate among our policy makers. Viewpoints change. Early in his career, in 1923, Sumner Welles, who later became undersecretary of state, while he was our chief representative to the Dominican Republic brought together the quarreling Dominican political party leaders and virtually dictated a settlement that resulted in a peaceful election and returned the Republic to constitutional rule after years of dictatorship and U.S. military occupation; and later as our man in Havana he virtually engineered one dictator's overthrow and ended by supporting another, Fulgencio Batista. Yet in his later years, as undersecretary, Welles came to oppose any intervention whatsoever, he explicity forbade U.S. representatives to offer any advice on a domestic political question even if asked, and he went so far shortly before Pearl Harbor as to declare that the United States should not intervene in any Latin American country even though its government was under the influence of the Axis, as Peron's clearly was.

As ambassador to the Dominican Republic, I myself had felt that if we did not support the provisional government and influence the contending opposition parties, the provisional government would likely fall, elections could not be held, and democracy would fail— the democracy that we and all Dominican elements except the extreme left and the extreme right were trying to build. In this policy we succeeded, but only through heavy political intervention. Arguments against intervention were many and powerful—that Dominicans must do it for themselves, that if we continually propped up the provisional government it would never learn to govern, and that after the election no government elected only because of our stabilizing influence could by itself succeed.

As it turned out, Bosch, once elected, refused our help until it was too late; whether he might have succeeded with it we shall never know. After his fall, I was not there, but I have the impression that we pursued a hands-off policy, that we did not intervene politically, and that the pro-Bosch rebellion resulted, obliging President Johnson to intervene militarily. Again we shall never know whether our political intervention would have averted the rebellion.

It may be unfortunate but it is true that we do not yet live in a world of enforceable world order, where individual nations are willing to subordinate their own interests to the good of all. We live, instead, in a world of nation-states. In this world, the big powers, especially the United States and the Soviet Union, each has its sphere of influence. We do not declare war on the Soviet Union because it imposes its will forcibly upon its near neighbor Afghanistan; the Soviet Union does not declare war on us because we send some twenty thousand troops to Santo Domigo. This may be far from ideal. But it is a fact of international life today. This being so, the wisest course for us would seem to be to exert political influence in order to avoid using military force; for as the world stands we will always intervene to the extent necessary in our own sphere of influence to protect American lives, property, and other vital interests. What is a "vital interest"? Anything we say it is—that is, anything we would go to war to protect, above all any clear and generally agreed threat to our own national security (the Russian missiles in Cuba were deemed so in 1962).

(To my mind, none of this by any means excuses such harebrained adventures as our invasion of Grenada or our recent dangerous assaults on Nicaragua. Indeed, all this is to denounce those military interventions, for they were undertaken while we ignored or rejected political settlements that might have made the last resort to force unnecessary.)

Even activist political intervention is by no means universally favored. Often it will take us deep into the internal affairs of other countries. It casts us in the unwanted role of judge and court of last resort, it sometimes involves matters beyond our strength or wisdom, and it is certainly not a policy popular among my liberal friends. Nevertheless, in the present state of the world, I see no other course, at least in this hemisphere.

* * *

But intenvention, of itself, is only a part of a wider question: America's place in the world. Perhaps there too we can learn some lessons from our Dominican experience.

In our times, when a dictator falls, he seems to be followed by, first, political chaos and then by an extremist regime, often anti-American—Batista was followed by Castro, the shah of Iran by the ayatollah, Somoza by the Sandinistas.

But Trujillo was followed by democracy. How so? We, the United States, had a good deal to do with it.

When Trujillo fell, as we have seen, President Kennedy sent the fleet to throw the Trujillo dynasty out of the Republic. Then he sent me to support strongly and openly the shaky Council of State for a year, to help it hold free elections, and to support the elected president. True, Dominican democracy stumbled—President Bosch was overthrown. But after we stopped the brief civil war, a new president was freely elected and since then, as I have said, democracy has prevailed for nearly a quarter century.

As we all know, democracy in that part of the world is fragile. Even in Chile, with a long tradition of peaceful civilian government, the military overthrew as a Communist Allende. And to be sure Dominican democracy might collapse again the day after tomorrow. But so far it has worked.

If we had followed the same policy in Nicaragua, we might have avoided much trouble. But we did not. Even with the Sandanistas in the field against Somoza, our ambassador supported him at least as publicly and as fervently as I supported the Dominican Council of State. When it became clear that Somoza was going down, President Carter could have sent the fleet to throw him out, as President Kennedy sent the fleet against the Trujillos. But he did not. (I am told President Carter considered doing it but at the last minute he and Secretary of State Vance lost their nerve.) And after the Sandanistas came to power, we could have supported them wholeheartedly, as President Kennedy instructed me to support the council and Bosch. We did not. True, early on President Carter sent them money and a sympathetic ambassador. But soon he cooled off, and in any case he had only a few months left in office and he had to spend them campaigning for reelection. And after that, under President Reagan, we drifted from "cool but correct" relations with the Sandinistas into outright hostility. We did so for ideological reasons, concern about the wider Central American crisis, and fear of "another Castro in the Caribbean."

If we had thrown Somoza out and wholeheartedly helped the Sandinistas, we might have no better friends in the Caribbean than they. Now we have no more bitter enemies.

But all this is true not only in the Caribbean and not only today. Time and again, around the world, and ever since the end of World War II, we have followed the same misguided policy. As after the war the old colonial empires broke up and rebel forces demanded independence, over and over we tried futilely to prop up the status quo. Why?

Every president from Harry Truman on has known that to be in the White House when any country in the world "goes under to communism" is not politically healthy. With his grand inquisitor's cry of "Who Lost China?" Senator Joe McCarthy made it so. Incredibly, McCarthyism has distorted American foreign policy for at least thirty-five years. It has seized George Kennan's sensible and successful containment policy, which was designed for the heart of Europe, and applied it everywhere, to backward agricultural societies anywhere in the world that communism threatens—to, among others, Korea and Vietnam. And has emphasized almost exclusively its military aspects.

After Vietnam, for a time the United States seemed headed back toward a sort of neo-isolationism—"no more Vietnams." Vietnam, it appeared, would be the high-water mark of military containment. But then President Reagan, with his patriotic chest thumping, seemed bent on taking us back toward worldwide containment or even toward a worldwide "rollback" of communism, a policy of driving the Soviets back to the gates of the Kremlin. One of President Reagan's proudest boasts was that during his first term, no country anywhere was "lost to communism."

At this writing, it is uncertain whether we will intervene everywhere. But it seems certain we will continue to intervene at least in the Caribbean basin.

If so, intervene on which side? On the side of the status quo? Or on the side of change?

It may be wiser to support change, even revolutionary change. Revolutions begin because of local repression, poverty, injustice; as they are about to win, communism from afar may take over. We might consider beating communism to it—consider whether, in prerevolutionary countries (like, say, South Korea today), it might not be better and cheaper to "contain" the revolution by joining it before it wins—by throwing out Somozas before they fall, by throwing out the Trujillos and helping the new government.

This is not an easy course. The future may belong to the young students and labor and *campesino* leaders who oppose the dictator, but they are not easy to work with. Immediately after Trujillo fell, there or four of them came to Washington to talk to Bobby Kennedy. He was probably the most radical of the New Frontiersman but even he told his brother, "They're lunatics—we can't work with them." And indeed on my own mission to the Republic a few weeks later, I found them so. Idealistic and patriotic, yes, but also young and wild and reckless; certainly not set in concrete for Russia but equally suspicious of the United States; rudderless and malleable but unstable; more interested in dignity and honor than in ways and means; more given to heroic gestures than to the hard work of governing; hopelessly naïve and wholly inexperienced. I told President Kennedy so, and we turned away from them as from the stable but despicable Trujillo right, and sought the center. After I became ambassador, these young idealists went into Dominican politics, and often I saw them behave in the same lunatic way. They were forever threatening to throw themselves over the cliff. Time and again, even councillors of state threatened to resign, candidates for president to withdraw from the election. Once the Social Christian candidate and his followers had gone armed to another town and, when opponents tried to break up their meeting, had started shooting; and a bystander had been killed. When I pointed out that this was against the law, he struck a dramatic pose and said, "We obey the law of God." Just so, the kids in Nicaragua who ran the Sandinista government declared with equal passion to one of our negotiators they were Marxist revolutionaries and would gladly die rather than have anything to do with us and our democracy. They knew little of either democracy or Marxism. How could they? The president of Nicaragua had as a schoolboy joined the opposition to Somoza, been jailed by Somoza, been released, and gone to risk his life with the Sandinista guerrillas—he went from teen-age dropout to president. Heroic, yes; but qualified for president? Is it possible to really imagine, as President Reagan seemed to, that such a man could rule an efficient "totalitarian" state that functioned smoothly as an arm of an "evil empire"? The Sandinistas would not have known how to do it even if they wanted to. Far easier to imagine them making the same mistakes President Bosch made. It is no accident that *Don Quixote* is a Spanish novel and that it is set in the same lovely part of Spain, Andalusia, that both the Dominicans and Nicaraguans originally came from. (Nicaraguans are more like Dominicans than any others in the Caribbean.)

We cannot expect that it would be easy to work with such revolutionaries. Far easier to work with the dictator. But since most of modern history shows the dictators on the losing side, and since they are unjust, let us work with the people against them. Even at the risk of "another Castro in the Caribbean."

If we look at what followed Batista and the shah and Somoza, and if what happened after Trujillo was indeed unique in our time, then perhaps President Kennedy's policy and my efforts to make it work amounted to more than we thought.

4.

When, on July 14, 1965, Adlai Stevenson died suddenly of a heart attack in England, Fran and I helped with funeral arrangements, then with Newt Minow and other of Stevenson's friends and relatives went to the services in Washington in the National Cathedral (where President Johnson, offering condolences, said to me, "He showed us the way"), and with other Democratic friends went aboard the president's plane, which took Stevenson's body home to Illinois. En route, Arthur Schlesinger told me I should write Stevenson's biography. In Springfield at a wake in the judges' chambers in the Illinois Supreme Court, the talk turned to a memorial for Stevenson, and I told his three sons I hoped they would not merely name an expressway after him but would do something like establish an institute, perhaps at a university, that could train promising young leaders from the Third World, the Third World whose importance Stevenson had been early to realize. Stevenson's sons and his old friends did establish such an institute, and though it was not precisely what I had had in mind, it did bring together scholars and leaders from around the world.

Stevenson's oldest son, Adlai III, was looking for someone to write his father's biography and asked my advice. Adlai hoped to get some money out of the biography for the Stevenson Institute and asked if I thought a writer would share his royalties, perhaps divide them equally. I told him that I myself had never split royalties but that in these circumstances, to help the institute and because of my feeling for his father, I probably would. I recommended several writers. They didn't work out. After a time Adlai asked me to do it. Fran was against it. She thought it was "going back." She didn't want me to relive the past but to move ahead. She thought Stevenson's family could be difficult. And it would take a long time. But I decided to do it and Doubleday, which was publishing *Overtaken by Events,* agreed to publish it. Being already committed in principle, I agreed to split my royalties equally with Adlai and his two brothers and also to give Adlai, acting for the family, the right to review the manuscript before publication. (If it contained things he objected to and he and I could not agree on changes, the issue would go for binding arbitration to Carl McGowan, Stevenson's former chief of staff and now a U.S. appellate judge in Washington, or, if McGowan was unable or unwilling to serve, to Newt Minow.)

The Life of Adlai E. Stevenson—I thought it would take three years to write. It took ten. I was fifty years old when I started. Your fifties are supposed to be the years when you make the most money and do your most important work. I spent mine writing the biography of Stevenson and I have never regretted it. I've heard it said that some writers who spend so long on a biography become bored with their subject or, worse, come to resent him for taking so much of their lives to write his. Luckily I escaped both infections.

Since my biography of Adlai Stevenson contains a full account of his life, here I will only describe briefly how I researched it and wrote it. Stevenson was a string-saver. He almost literally never threw anything away. Among his papers I found not only longhand first drafts of famous speeches but also Princeton football-game ticket stubs and old dance programs. His archive was enormous. His papers existed, for the most part, in four locations. Most of the papers relating to his governorship, and some early family letters, were at Springfield in the Illinois State Historical Library. Those relating to his ambassadorship to the United Nations were in the State

Department in Washington and in the U.S. Mission to the UN in New York. The rest were at Princeton. In addition, his family and friends had a few of his private papers.

At the outset I persuaded my old friend Francis Nipp to act as research director of my project. He worked at it for two years then gave up, why I never understood. Roxane Eberlein, who had been Stevenson's private secretary and assistant at the United Nations, took over the research. We made Xerox copies of several hundred thousand pages of his papers. We put the copies into several hundred looseleaf binders, each numbered and given a symbol designating whether it contained correspondence, speeches, or whatever. We indexed the copies, making an average of perhaps a thousand 5-by-8-inch cards on each of the sixty-five years of his life, and arranged them chronologically. To fill in the gaps, I interviewed about a hundred people who had been close to him, dictated my interview notes, and indexed them too in binders.

We started out at the beginning of 1966 by renting the house that he had loved in Libertyville. But I realized that if I wanted access to his UN files, many of them classified, I had better get to them right away, while my friends and his were still in power in Washington; so we moved on to Washington and rented a little house in Georgetown. George Ball, still undersecretary of state, arranged for me to have access to all of State's files. I spent the spring researching them and interviewing people who had worked with him there.

I spent that summer back in Illinois interviewing Stevenson's family and friends, especially those in Bloomington, his downstate hometown, for you could never understand Stevenson unless you understood the small town where he grew up. It was there that I discovered that Stevenson's childhood, far from the happy time usually pictured, had been a horror. And from my interviewing in Chicago and Lake Forest I learned that his private life as a Chicago lawyer had been almost equally unhappy.

In the fall we moved to Princeton. By then it was clear that my half of Doubleday's generous royalty advance and research grant would not support me to the book's completion; I needed supplementary income. I could do an occasional magazine piece, not enough. That fall I was given a one-year appointment as visiting fellow in public affairs at the Woodrow Wilson School of Princeton University. After that, Arthur Schlesinger had me appointed visiting professor at the Graduate Center of the City University of New York, where he himself now taught, and I commuted to it one day a week from Princeton to teach a seminar.

The seminar dealt with the limits of American power in foreign policy. Each student was required to write a paper on a single foreign policy crisis, such as the Cuban missile crisis or the Korean War, laying out the policy alternatives among which our policy makers had been obliged to choose and identifying the factors that had limited American power and thus helped force the policy choice. I had been obliged to think about this while writing *Overtaken by Events,* while researching Stevenson's UN work, and while watching those limits operate as an ambassador. Despite all our power, we cannot always do everything we want to do everywhere.

I had been making a number of policy speeches, especially on our Dominican intervention, to universities and the National War College and to several political groups, such as the national Women's Democratic Club in Washington. These speeches cast me in the role of defending President Johnson's Dominican intervention, which I did not mind, since I thought he had had no choice but to intervene. At this time, however, protest was rising against his escalation of the war in Vietnam, and many people tended to link our Dominican intervention with Vietnam. I was careful to explain our Dominican policy but stay clear of the Vietnam War. Nearly all my friends, such as Arthur Schlesinger, opposed that war vigorously. I knew little about it and was slow to pay attention, perhaps because I was preoccupied in 1964 with President Johnson's reelection campaign and in 1965–1967 with the Dominican civil war. By late 1966 or 1967 I was as much opposed as everyone else. Both Stevenson and I had been burned by this—his friends had begged him to resign as ambassador to the UN to protest our involvement in Vietnam, just as my friends had deplored my defense of Johnson's Dominican intervention.

5.

Politics again—in 1964 I helped President Johnson run for reelection. (This was before our Dominican intervention, before Stevenson's death, less than a year after President Kennedy's assassination.) When at his request I went to see President Johnson, he ruminated about politics: "It's going to be Goldwater. He's underrated. He thinks he can take the South, add Indiana and Illinois and Iowa, the conservative Midwest, add New Mexico, Colorado, and the mountain states—and do it. And he might." I told him I'd spent most of my life in the Midwest, and he was right—this year its conservatism would come out as white backlash against Negroes.

He asked, "Is the peace issue important?"

I said, "Very. People are scared to death."

At that time, June of 1964, we were rather lightly involved in Vietnam. President Johnson said, "We need you. You write it and tell me what to say and I'll say it."

He was, in that sense, an easy man to work for—easier than John F. Kennedy, far easier than Adlai Stevenson. As I left, he called, "Get some new ideas, John," as all candidates do, and I said I would, as all writers do.

That fall, I had an office in the Executive Office Building next door to the White House. So did Dick Goodwin and Bill Wirtz, by now secretary of labor but writing speeches in the campaign. In overall charge of speeches was Bill Moyers. I did not travel with President Johnson; I saw him occasionally in the White House but for the most part I worked with the other writers in the White House and I traveled alone to various parts of the country doing editorial advance. For example, I made a swing through Indiana and Illinois, and after talking to politicians and labor and business people and ringing housewives' doorbells, I wrote a memo to the president telling him that people in the Midwest were saying the election was a choice between "a kook and a crook," President Johnson being the crook and his Republican opponent, Barry Goldwater, the kook. (I know this disputes various testimony that staffers dared not bring distasteful news to Johnson, but I never found that true.) Throughout the campaign, we endeavored to picture President Johnson as trying to unite the country, to restore and heal it after President Kennedy's murder, and to picture him as promising peace and, in Vietnam, moderation, while picturing Senator Goldwater as a bloodthirsty mad bomber.* Our advertising agency prepared a tele-

---

*The Pentagon Papers made public several years later indicated that President Johnson was secretly planning to send warplanes and combat troops to Vietnam even at this time, while campaigning as the candidate of military restraint. I can say that, al-

vision commercial showing a little girl plucking a daisy, while a voice-over intoned a countdown, "Ten, nine, eight, seven, six, five, four, three, two, one," whereupon the screen exploded in a mushroom nuclear cloud; and before we were obliged to take the commercial off the air as unfair, the message had come through: Goldwater was the mad bomber. (Goldwater had let slip in a press conference, when asked about ex-President Eisenhower's opinion that our six NATO divisions in Europe could be cut to one, his own view that they "probably"could be cut by "at least one-third" if NATO "commanders" in Europe were given power to fire tactical weapons in an emergency. Even blowing up a bridge can in combat be an emergency. We immediately interpreted this as empowering any second lieutenant in NATO, despite his staff's frantic explanations that he meant the succession of NATO supreme commanders). Another commercial showed a pair of hands tearing up a Social Security card (Goldwater had "ruminated about," as Teddy White puts it, making Social Security voluntary, a silly idea.) President Johnson had decreed that no speech of his could be longer than seven hundred words. With commercials like that to explain complicated issues, who needed long speeches?

Fran came down for election night, and with Clark Clifford and his wife and others we watched returns in Bill Moyers's office. President Johnson won the biggest landslide till then in American history, with 61 percent of the vote. He himself spent election night at his ranch in Texas, and several of us talked to him during the evening, and I did a draft of his victory statement that sounded Stevensonian. He liked it.

For Fran and me, the 1965 inauguration of President Johnson should have been a more satisfactory celebration than that of President Kennedy—the weather was better; we knew our way around official Washington better. We even got to Kay Graham's party. And we happened to arrive at the inaugural ball at the old Wardman Park Hotel just as President Johnson and his party arrived and so found ourselves propelled with them down the roped-off aisle through the crowded ballroom, and saw Dick Daley waving and calling to us from the throng on the wrong side of the ropes. (The

---

though I met frequently with Clark Clifford and Abe Fortas, the president's senior advisers, and although I saw the president occasionally and Moyers, Goodwin, and Wirtz daily, I had no inkling of any such a move and I doubt that my colleagues did either.

president's box itself was full; Adlai Stevenson had entered with us, and Bill Moyers found a seat for him in the president's box; Stevenson had brought the bright beautiful Marietta Tree, who worked with him at the United Nations, and, seeing there was space only for himself, he promptly abandoned her; Fran and I rescued her, found places for her and ourselves in the box of Governor and Mrs. Pat Brown of California. The first rule of the "A Party–B Party" game: Sacrifice your buddy. Loyalty, as I have suggested, was never one of Stevenson's strongest qualities.) All in all, the inaugural was, for us, as joyless as the campaign.

Two years later, in the fall of 1966, out in Illinois, my own senator, Paul H. Douglas, was running for reelection, and during the last weeks of the campaign I went to Chicago to help him. He was an old friend, and that spring in Washington he had let Fred work in his office on Capitol Hill, carrying his briefcase, helping him sign letters, and ushering visiting constituents around. Paul Douglas was, I thought, one of the ablest—and noblest—men in the Senate. But now he was seventy-four years old and a strong young Republican was running against him, Charles H. Percy. At lunch in Washington, when Paul first asked me to help him, I had asked what his position was on Vietnam, and he'd said, "I support the president." I tried to suggest that perhaps he should develop a Douglas position on Vietnam rather than endorse everything President Johnson had said and done. But Paul was adamant—he had supported the policy all along because he thought it right and he was not going to waver now because public opinion was shifting.

His campaign that fall was all uphill. In his headquarters I worked with his son, John, a Washington lawyer close to the Kennedys, and Richard Wade, a young University of Chicago history professor and friend of Arthur Schlesinger. I wrote speeches, as usual, and it also fell to me to appear in public several times on Paul's behalf, including once at an anti–Vietnam War student protest rally, where I had the task of explaining both President Johnson's Dominican intervention and his Vietnam policy, while the students asked questions and a fat girl in a long fuzzy sweater played a guitar and sang protest songs. Election night in Paul's hotel suite I watched the early returns. It was clear we were losing big, and

I thought Paul should concede and end his career gracefully. I went into the bedroom where he and his wife were. He was stretched out on the bed, exhausted—he'd been campaigning on the streets up to the end. I told him what returns we had and advised him to concede. He said he'd have to clear it with Mayor Daley. He called the mayor and spoke to him briefly. When he finished he threw himself on the bed on his back and burst out laughing. I asked what the mayor had said that was so funny. Paul, scarcely able to speak, said, "He doesn't want me to concede yet—he's got some paper wards he wants to hold out," that is, some wards that voted by paper ballot that Daley wanted to hold until he knew how many votes he needed from them to save the county ticket. Paul said, "So after all these years the truth finally comes out."

6

One night that summer up in Michigan, while Earl Numinen and I were taking a sauna, he and I decided to go to Finland. Born there, he had been brought to America when he was nine; now he was nearly fifty-nine but he had never been back. When we left on June 6, 1967, New York was hot and humid, but the minute we stepped off the plane in Helsinki we felt as if we had come home to Upper Michigan—the airport was ringed by pine and the air had the Michigan tang.

The Upper Peninsula of Michigan contains the largest Finnish colony in the United States. The Finns are a lost people. Where they originated, history does not know. Their language resembles no other except Hungarian. Some authorities believe the Finns originated in Mongolia, and I remember that Earl Numinen's father, who lived to a great age, resembled, in his last years, a Mongol. His father, Earl told me, had been a serf in Finland. Earl had always wondered if his father had been the illegitimate son of a nobleman; on this trip he hoped to find out.

We left Helsinki in a rented car and drove to the gentle farmland of south-central Finland whence Earl's people had come. For a week we visited Earl's relatives and childhood friends, a reunion after half a century, and they told us how life had been in Finland during those years. Especially they talked proudly about the Winter War, when tiny Finland had held Russia at bay. Earl uncovered family roots he had forgotten or never known; in old church records he traced out his mother's genealogy but he was unable to untangle his father's (at least so far as I know—after a time he stopped talking about it). He was grandly received by the country folk. Some were landowners, of the class that had held his father in thrall. They served us milk in cut glass, cookies on their best china. On a sloping hillside, we found the ruins of the house where Earl was born; in the dump we found smashed pieces of heavy brown glazed pottery. Earl thought he remembered its pattern from childhood—yes, it was the remains of the kitchen stove. Each of us took a piece, and when Fran and I built the fireplace in our new camp at Smith Lake, I put the shard of pottery into its face.

We left the farming country and spent a glorious day on a boat on the Finnish inland waterway, sitting on the upper deck in the sun, drinking a bottle of gin with lemon and ice; that night we took a sauna at Aulunko, Sibelius's home. We toured a good deal of Finland. But I think what Earl enjoyed most was being invited—the son of a serf—to lunch with the American ambassador. Afterward, on our last night in Helsinki, looking out at the clear blue sky and the blue water of the harbor, Earl said, "This has been a wonderful trip. I'd never have come but for you." Surprised, I asked why not. "Because I didn't think there was anything here I'd care to see. Because I always associated Finland with hunger and want. And being unequal—that was driven into me in school. There was nobody I was equal to." He leaned back, smiling a little. "And now to see Finland so friendly, and the people supposed to be superior treating me as their equals—never in my wildest dreams. Don't you see?"

We went to the Soviet Union for a week—to Leningrad, where we visited the shrines of the Revolution, and then to Moscow. The hotels didn't work, and the police state atmosphere was oppressive—a couple of incidents convinced me we were under the surveillance of the secret police, perhaps because I had been a U.S. government official, perhaps because Earl was Finnish: A Russian girl accosted me on a Leningrad street and gave me her photograph and passport number and asked me to help her escape Russia to find her British boyfriend, and I threw the evidence into a potted plant and a little later returned to find it gone; and in Moscow after we had been in our hotel a few days, the bar we frequented suddenly filled up with good-looking young Finnish girls, students, they said, and in the near-empty dining room the headwaiter seated us next to two of the pretty students and suggested we dance with them once then take them to bed. Trujillo had used such entrapments with visiting American congressmen. But aside from all that, I thought Moscow, with its sweeping streets and onion-shaped domes and yellow walls, exciting, and above all I thought the Russian people admirable—they had accomplished so much with so little; everything was so hard but they did it without complaint. One day, driving about the city with a young U.S. embassy officer, we ran low on gasoline, and our friend pulled into a filling station. It was out of gas; we would have to wait. Presently the tank truck arrived. The driver's helper got out and shoved a small triangular steel platform in front of one front wheel, the driver drove up onto it, and they unloaded gasoline not by pumping but by gravity. One has to be impressed by a people that puts up with such primitive devices and yet finds the resources to send men to the moon.

Earl went back to the States and I went to Italy, picking up a new Mercedes in Germany and stopping overnight in a small hotel in a small German town. There, after supper, I went for a walk but though it was still daylight the streets were deserted, everything closed. I went back to the little hotel. In its bar four or five middle-aged and elderly men were sitting at a table saying nothing, staring into the beers in front of them. The place was dead silent; you could hear the floor creak as the waitress crossed it. Of a sudden the door burst open and in bounded a strapping blond young man in jack-boots and a leather jacket, a motorcycle rider. The men at the table looked up, smiled broadly, asked him for news, bade him sit down, and he straddled a chair and declaimed the news from the outside world. He electrified the room; he was life itself. I suddenly thought I understood at last how Adolf Hitler had come to power in Germany and how the Ku Klux Klan had come to power in Indiana—through the hearts of the men in the small towns who were downtrodden and defeated but above all bored.

To support the Stevenson biography, the Rockefeller Foundation had invited us to its Villa Serbelloni on Lake Como in Italy, a villa to which it invited scholars and men leaving high public office in need of time for decompression. Fran and Fred had arrived a day or two earlier, bringing with them some seventeen footlockers of Stevenson research material. Presently Roxane Eberlein and her sister joined us and we dug in on the Stevenson book. Villa Serbelloni was a huge villa built on a hill overlooking Lake Como by Pliny, whether the elder or the younger I forget. Here we caught a glimpse of the elegant life that Adlai Stevenson had savored both as a young man and in his last years. We had an apartment in an ancient yellow monastery close to the lake. We went up the high hill to have lunch or dinner with the dozen other Fellows. Over us presided John Marshall and his wife, Catherine, an elegant couple who had become expert on the villa and on Italian wine and food, and behind each guest's chair stood a footman. At five o'clock Fran and Fred and I took a thermos of martinis down to the Roman bath at the edge of the lake below our monastery and sat in the bath watching the clouds roll in over the Alps beyond. We discovered that if we caught a minnow in a paper cup and poured a little martini onto him, he stiffened dead instantaneously. The foundation had allowed Fred to accompany us with misgivings—it had never had a child guest, and Fred was only fourteen that summer, they didn't know what he'd do with himself; but he soon allayed their misgivings by defeating John Marshall at chess and playing a piano duet with Otto Luening.

Dan was attending the Putney School in Vermont and that summer he went on a school trip through Scandinavia—they hiked across Lapland at the top of Europe and before the altar of an empty stave church sang, spontaneously and *a cappella,* a Bach chorale. This done, he came to Como, and we all went driving through Spain, and Spain was glorious—the Prado and Goya's blinding *Tres de Mayo,* the great hotels of Madrid and Seville, the awesome plain of La Mancha, a dusty white mountain town jammed with people come to see El Cordobés fight a bull (El Cordobés was a daring young man who looked remarkably like Bobby Kennedy), a picnic with Tad Szulc of *The New York Times* at the little bridge above Madrid where Hemingway had set the climax to *For Whom the Bell Tolls.* (During the Dominican intervention, Tad had written quite critically of President Johnson's policy and of me. Now we put our differences behind us.)

In September, Dan flew back to Putney from Rome, and some weeks later Fred flew to New York alone and went on up to New Hampshire to enroll himself at Exeter. (The Italian police insisted that in the case of a traveler so young they be given the name of someone who would meet him at New York, so we gave them the name of the manager of the Algonquin Hotel, and indeed as it turned out the head bellman at the Algonquin, Earl, a friend for many years, telephoned Exeter for Fred and saw to it that he made the right train and bus connections to New Hampshire.)

Fran and I and Roxane and her sister proposed to leave Italy on a Spanish freighter for the Dominican Republic to spend the winter working on the book in the beach house we'd bought at Sosúa. We were to sail on October 16. Six days before that two young vice-consuls from our embassy in Rome came to Serbelloni with a cable from John Crimmins, our new ambassador to the Dominican Republic, whose appointment I had recommended to President Johnson. Crimmins thought that, because of *Overtaken by Events,* my presence in the Republic now would be politically unsettling and against the interests of the United States. He apparently felt I was hated by both the Dominican right and left; it might not even be safe for me personally. I disagreed with all this and protested by cable to Secretary Rusk. Rusk replied supporting Crimmins. There was, of course, no way the Department could have prevented me from going; on the other hand, one does not like to go somewhere if one's government thinks it against the national interest. I agreed to get off the boat before it reached the Dominican Republic. Aboard a rusty Spanish freighter, the *Ruiseñada,* the voyage took a month. There were ten passengers aboard, counting us four. One was an aging Dominican who, when the Trujillo government fell, had been given his choice of going to prison, where he might find a firing squad, or going abroad as a Dominican consul in Italy. He had found the choice easy. One night I sat up late talking with the ship's first mate, a Spaniard born the year Franco took power and educated in Franco's schools; he was convinced that the United States was at war in Vietnam only because of the influence of "the Jewish bankers." He soon dropped out of our nightly poker game (played in Spanish) when the Dominican consul denounced him, not because of his politics but because he insisted on dealing cards three at a time. At about that point in our voyage, flying fish appeared, for we were crossing the Tropic of Cancer into the third of the world between it and the Tropic of Capricorn; and I dragged a chair to the tiny deck outside our cabin and sat in the sun, holding a clipboard full of Stevenson manuscript and watching the flying fish above the turquoise sea. Our course approximated Columbus's, Roxane informed us after research, and our food was the same greasy chickpea and fish soup served to Columbus's sailors. By now, Roxane had become a member of our family. I was beginning to think about politics again, had written to Bobby Kennedy from Como saying I suspected President Johnson might not be reelectable and suggesting Bobby line up second-choice convention delegates for next year, 1968, for himself. Yet the thought of his running made me uneasy, I had vague stirrings of the fear he might be assassinated.

7.

Every June during these years at eastern universities, Fran and the boys and I went to the Upper Peninsula of Michigan and stayed till Labor Day. Though we didn't think of it this way, we were pioneering—we had bought our remote new land far out in the woods at Smith Lake in 1964 and that summer we set out to explore it. Starting from the logging town of L'Anse on Lake Superior in our Jeep, on one of those great Michigan days, puffs of clouds sailing across a deep blue sky, we needed an hour and a half to drive by logging road to within a mile of Smith Lake, and it took us the rest of the day to carry our tents and boat and outfit the last mile through the woods. We climbed the steep hill to the high granite cliff that I had shown Fran years earlier, rising 60 feet above the lake, covered with a grove of majestic hemlocks. No brush here— only cool shade and a forest floor of leaves and needles. Below the cliff, from water's edge on a narrow bench of land, rose enormous white pines, so tall they soared above the tops of the cliff-borne hemlocks—they must be at least 150 feet tall, and they grow there yet. A beautiful campsite. Here we would build our camp. From here we crossed the bay and found a sand beach. The shores of most lakes hereabouts were either rock or bog; our sand beach was a rarity. Not far from the water's edge, hidden in balsam, stood the ruin of a trapper's shack, the roof gone, the log walls sagging, ferns growing through the rotted floor. This, we decided, we would re-build into a temporary camp. We pitched our tents at the beach be-neath two ancient white pines, and it was past dark when we cooked our dinner. The mosquitoes were not too bad, and we sat awhile on logs in front of the tents, watching the fire die and the stars wheel up. In Chicago, you can scarcely see the stars at all. Here at Smith Lake, the Milky Way looks like a white river, and every star is blaz-ing, and we watched man's satellites slowly tracking across the fir-mament. In the pale afterglow before dark, we heard a mad laughing cry, a loon, no, a pair of loons. So we had loons on our new lake. And after we went to bed in our tents and the fire died, we heard coyotes barking up on our cliff campsite. So we had coyotes too. And a few nights later we heard the commanding howl of a tim-ber wolf.

We stayed several days, mapping our lake and land. Smith Lake lies about 47 degrees north latitude, as does Quebec (and Ulan Bator). The primeval forest in the Upper Peninsula had been white pine; loggers had long ago cut nearly all of it, but Smith Lake was still ringed with it. Smith Lake was shaped like a lopsided hourglass. It was divided into two unequal parts, the west part, ours, much the larger and deeper, the two parts joined by a narrows near the sand beach. On some old maps it is called Cliff Lake, and I like to think that the name got changed when some political hack in the court-house, drawing a map, called to another, "What's this lake, hey?" and his colleague replied, "Cliff Lake," but the draftsman misun-derstood him to say, "Smith Lake."

Fishing, we caught nothing but chub and stunted sunfish and perch. One day fishing, we came upon a deer swimming the nar-rows; we stayed away so as not to disturb him. Game trails were everywhere. On another day I brought out Earl Numinen, the high-way engineer, and he and I laid out a route for a mile of road to our clifftop campsite, climbing steep rock ridges, skirting deep tag alder and cedar swamps. We did not want a good road passable by pas-senger cars—that would encourage curious visitors, and one reason we had come to Smith Lake was to be alone. What we wanted was a Jeep road. On Earl's advice, I went to Herman, a dying Finnish farm hamlet of about eighty people twelve and a half miles from Smith Lake, where the paved road from outside ends, and talked to

Charley Dantes, an elderly man and a remarkable one, well read, once the sheriff, now town leader, Democrat, and when he discovered I had been a friend of Adlai Stevenson, he could not do enough to help us. His son Charley ran a little sawmill at Herman, and at his father's behest he bulldozed our Jeep road to our new campsite.

Originally we had intended to build only a one-room shack at Smith Lake that we could use on weekends, continuing to spend most of the summer at Three Lakes. But Fran had come to dislike Three Lakes, too filled with tourists, and she too had fallen in love with Smith Lake—she wanted to try to live there instead. I told her how hard it would be—hard to build and make comfortable, hard to get to. Equipment, indeed every board and every nail, would have to be carried in by Jeep and by hand. And it would be hard to persuade workmen to come all the way out here. More, it would be lonely living here, with no neighbors for many miles. She wanted to try anyway. We were, however, unwilling to put up with an outhouse and a hand pump. We had started out that way twenty-five years ago at Three Lakes and now we were, as a Hollywood director confronted with Marilyn Monroe's idiosyncrasies told her, "Miss Monroe, I am too old, too rich, and too famous to put up with your temperament." So we decided to try to install conveniences at Smith Lake. But how? There was, of course, no electricity closer than Herman. Instead, we would use bottled gas—propane—for our basic source of power. We would install a thousand-gallon tank (if a truck could bring it in over our terrible Jeep road). We would use gas to cook with, to run a refrigerator, to run a hot-water heater, to light the camp, and, most importantly, to run a generator that in turn would make enough electricity to run an electric water pump—and thus we would have running water in the kitchen and bathroom. This also meant, of course, digging deep enough in this rocky earth to install a septic tank and a drain field. And so on—the project became increasingly formidable. As I made sketches, the camp grew to thirty by thirty feet. It would be built entirely of logs. It would be divided into three main rooms—a big living room, a kitchen, and a bedroom (plus bathroom). There would be an enormous fireplace, or rather three fireplaces, one in each room, with the three separate flues all enclosed in a common chimney, the whole built of some fifty tons of native rock. We would perch the camp amid the hemlock at the very edge of the high cliff overlooking the lake.

The project took four years. Initially Dan and Fred and I, living in tents, rebuilt the crude little one-room trapper's shack at the sand beach ourselves. Then two Finnish log carpenters used it as a temporary camp—lived in it while they built the big camp up on the cliff, built it slowly, painfully, log by chipped and fitted log, a beauty. Dan and Fred and I worked with them, summer-long work. We learned a good deal about carpentry and plumbing, building Smith Lake. Not until 1968 were Fran and I able to use the big camp, and work on its interior and its outbuildings continued for several years. But we succeeded.

It was during these years when we were building at Smith Lake that Dan and Fred passed through that unnoticed transition from the time when I took care of them to the time when they took care of me. It is a subtle shift we all go through. The first year at Smith Lake, they performed only assigned chores—washed dishes, hauled water, made kindling, did what I told them on rebuilding the trapper's shack. In a few years, they were taking initiatives—had learned what needed doing and did it, without being told. It became they who staked out the tent, who rowed the boat, who made the campfire. By the time we had finished building at Smith Lake, they were not only doing the heavy work but were participating in important decisions, such as where to fish on a given day. I do not know precisely at what moment it happened. I only know that one day when we got out of the Jeep at a remote lake in the woods, it was Dan who, without a word shouldered the boat I had carried for so many years, and it was Fred who picked up the pack and oars and tackle box, saying only, "Can you bring the rods, Dad?" I was grateful but never felt older.

8.

Robert F. Kennedy's Indiana primary campaign for the 1968 Democratic presidential nomination was in many ways the climactic event of my life, bringing together writing, politics, and Indiana. Yet it rather sneaked up on me.

We began the year in a rented house in Princeton where I was writing the Stevenson rough draft and commuting once a week to New York to teach my seminar at City University. (After it, I usually went to dinner at the Century Association. I had been admitted to the Century while at Wesleyan and ever since have found it one of the most agreeable places on earth, an ornament of American civilization, as, I believe, Dick Rovere once called it). A search committee looking for a new president of a small college in Illinois approached me; people from Gulf and Western, the conglomerate, told me they were buying the big La Romana sugar plantations in the Dominican Republic and asked me to become their consultant; nothing came of either. (I told the Gulf and Western executives they could either run the plantations the way the former American owner had—authoritarian, colonialist, squeezing out fast every dime of profits even though their cane-cutters were sullen and hostile—or they could plough some of their profits back into workers' schools and housing and look forward to a long future. That ended my consultation.)

All during this period, the presidential politics of 1968 had been moving to the fore. At the end of November, Senator Eugene McCarthy of Minnesota, an opponent of the war in Vietnam, had announced his candidacy against President Johnson in the Democratic primaries in New Hampshire and other states. At the end of January and early February, the North Vietnamese launched the massive Tet offensive. Many people had been urging Bobby Kennedy to announce his own candidacy—as I've said, I myself from Lake Como had suggested the preceding fall that he start rounding up convention delegates. But he had hung back for fear that people would think he was opposing Johnson's reelection not on principle but out of personal animosity.

Bobby Kennedy and Lyndon Johnson had long disliked each other. Even before President Kennedy's assassination, Vice-President Johnson felt that Bobby had usurped his rightful place as number two man in the government. President Johnson believed Bobby had tried in 1960 to deny him the vice-presidential nomination. Bobby considered Lyndon Johnson a liar—"He lies even when he doesn't have to lie," he told me. While I was interviewing Bobby for the oral history project after President Kennedy's assassination, he said, "Four or five matters arose during the period of November 22 [when President Kennedy was killed] and November 27 . . . which made me bitterer, unhappy at least, with Lyndon Johnson." He seemed bothered by the clumsy handling of matters aboard Air Force One as it returned from Dallas and by how rapidly and unfeelingly Lyndon Johnson had moved into the president's office. Bobby went there the day after the assassination—"I wanted to make sure the desk was gotten out of there, and I wanted to make sure all his papers were out." The desk especially seemed to upset him. Johnson had told him at that time, "I need you more than the president needed you." Bobby resented it. In another oral history interview, he told William Manchester, "I said I don't want to discuss it and . . . that it was going to take us a period of time to move out of here, and I think, maybe, can't you wait?" But Johnson said that Secretary Rusk and Secretary McNamara had told him he must move in at once. Soon President Johnson was denouncing Bobby openly to the White House staff, including some who had been closest to the Kennedys. As the presidential politics of 1964 had begun, Bobby had been proposed for vice-president. He told me that spring that the last thing President Johnson wanted was Bobby as vice-president. "I think he's hysterical about how he's going to try to avoid having me." Bobby said that Johnson wanted an "all-American" party, not the Democratic party, and, Bobby said, businessmen and everybody else who had opposed President Kennedy loved it—but he himself didn't like it. I wanted Bobby to become vice-president and suggested that Bobby, with his own constituency, would be different from other vice-presidents. He replied, "I don't think you can have any influence. Lyndon Johnson didn't have any influence." He said Johnson was doing nothing for the Alliance for Progress and not paying proper attention to Panama and Brazil; if Bobby were in the Senate, he could do something about it, but not as vice-president. His running for senator from New York was also being discussed that spring. I said there were a hundred senators. He said, "Yeah, but I'm not just a senator. I'm senator from New York and I'm head of the Kennedy wing of the Democratic party." Finally as the convention neared, President Johnson announced that he would not consider for the vice-presidency any cabinet member or anybody who met regularly with the cabinet. This excluded both Bobby Kennedy and Adlai Stevenson. Bobby told the press, "I am sorry that I had to take so many nice fellows down with me," and soon announced his own candidacy for senator from New York; that fall he was elected.

All this, then, was the background of the Bobby Kennedy–

Lyndon Johnson relationship four years later as the 1968 presidential primaries began. In the New Hampshire primary on March 12, Senator Eugene McCarthy did not win but his supporters justifiably claimed a "moral victory," since his "children's crusade" against the Vietnam War—he had mobilized students at New England colleges and boarding schools—got him 42 percent of the vote to President Johnson's 49 percent. The day New Hampshire voted, Bobby Kennedy called me in Princeton and said he was going to announce his own candidacy on Saturday, asked me to give him a draft of an announcement statement, and said he hoped I could help him in other ways. I drafted the statement and telephoned it to his secretary, Angie Novello, and on March 16 he announced his candidacy for president in the Senate caucus room where he had held the Hoffa hearings so long ago.

Often during the next two weeks I saw Arthur and others interested in Bobby's campaign. Ted Sorensen, who was Bobby's campaign director in Washington, called several times—Bobby was going into the Indiana primary, and he and Ted Sorensen knew I was from Indiana. Such friends from Illinois as Marshall Holleb and Newt Minow called me, asking what they could do to help. I wrote a speech for Bobby for Indiana and one on foreign policy. His announcement generated tremendous excitement, and everywhere he went he attracted huge crowds, especially on college campuses, where students mobbed him, trying to get close enough to touch him. He was the most exciting candidate since his brother had run in 1960. On March 31, President Johnson on national TV stunned the country by announcing he himself would not be a candidate for reelection. He also announced a suspension—later modified to a limitation—of the bombing of North Vietnam. Thus Bobby had lost two of his best issues—the unpopular president and the unpopular war. Three days later, on Wednesday, April 3, at the University in New York as I came out of my seminar, Ted Sorensen called and said Bobby wondered if I could go out to Indiana with him tomorrow. I said yes, went to the Century, called Roxane in Princeton and asked her to pack a briefcase and suitcase and bring them to the Algonquin, got a room at the Algonquin, and early next morning met Bobby and his wife, Ethel, at Washington National Airport.

We had a chartered Electra, a prop-jet plane, crowded with about forty-three press and twenty staff. Bobby's writers aboard were Adam Walinsky and Jeff Greenfield. Walinsky was young, a little abrasive, sure he was right, reminding me of the early Dick Goodwin. Jeff Greenfield, Arthur had told me, was "about eleven years old" (actually, I think twenty-four); he was blond, bright, friendlier than Walinsky. Neither wanted me around, which was natural, of course—permanent staff people are always possessive of a candidate. They had a guitar and played and sang what were, I think, war protest songs. Bobby sometimes said in annoyance, "Where are my writers? Playing the guitar, I suppose." Frank Mankiewicz was aboard as press secretary. Fred Dutton was always at Bobby's side.

Bobby looked fine and relaxed. He was wearing, as usual, a gray plaid suit. He always looked slight, slender, even thin, with a wry grin. But he no longer looked boyish. His hair was turning gray, his face deeply lined. He had aged a great deal since his brother's murder five years ago. He aged even more as this spring campaign wore on. On the plane going to Indiana he came and sat beside me and asked, "Do you think it can be done?" I said I did. He told me about writing speeches for him—said they couldn't be Stevensonian, had to be simpler. He wanted to talk about improving the quality of American life. He suggested I travel the whistle-stops with him for a few days and listen, "to get the rhythm." He wanted me to stay with him on this trip, which included Indiana, Ohio, Louisiana, West Virginia, Kentucky, Michigan, Alaska, and South Dakota. We'd be gone a week. He wanted me to do a foreign policy speech for Thursday for Louisiana State University, a serious substantive speech "for once." He said Walinsky was good but "he's more radical than I am." I proposed a speech about the creative foreign policy of President Truman, rigidity under Eisenhower-Nixon-Dulles, new flexibility and hope under President Kennedy, Johnson's return to Dulles-Nixon rigidity, the need for flexibility now. He said this was fine. I showed him a draft I'd sent him earlier saying the question was whether we would have one nation or two or none. He said he'd liked it and used it but hadn't known where it came from. He especially liked three or four sentences in it, one quoting Adlai Stevenson as saying that self-criticism is the secret weapon of democracy; he now asked me to give those lines to Jeff and have him put them into his speech for today, which was being put on the speech type-writer in the front of the plane. I didn't yet know who Jeff Green-field was so gave it to Walinsky. He couldn't believe Bobby wanted to quote Stevenson and refused to put it in. After the speech Bobby was angry because Walinsky and Greenfield had cut part of his speech without telling him. This campaign promised to be like others I'd been through.

First stop: South Bend, Indiana—a crowd of kids at the airport mobbed him, and he gave his standard speech from the airplane ramp, asking, "Will you give me your hand?" and "Will you ring doorbells?" and "Will you give me your help in this election?" and "If you do, I think we can turn this country around." We motor-caded through the Negro district, kids running alongside his car, to Notre Dame and a packed indoor college crowd, a hot crowd. His jokes were good, he used little of his prepared text, gave them an ad-libbed whistlestop speech, while I made notes on applause break-ins. In the question period after the speech, a student asked what he thought of the draft law. "Unjust and inequitable," he de-clared, to great applause. Then, "And I'll tell you why—we should abolish college deferments." Loud boos, and he waved his arms and cried, "Let me explain," and argued his case that college deferments discriminated against those who could not afford college, and in the end they cheered him. He was nearly always at his best when trying to convince people who disagreed with him.

He left South Bend in a small plane to make another college stop, this one at Muncie. I went with most of the staff in the Electra to In-dianapolis. At the Marott Hotel up on North Meridian Street, I went to Walinsky and Greenfield and proposed dinner. I had learned that in a campaign you always eat and sleep at every oppor-tunity, since opportunities are few. But Walinsky wanted to talk first, and I outlined the foreign policy speech I'd suggested to Bobby, and Walinsky argued against it, saying it was unfair to Presi-dent Johnson and, moreover, he didn't think our foreign policy had been good under President Truman and President Kennedy. A sec-retary came in with a report that Martin Luther King had just been shot. I said we'd better go down to dinner because if it was true we might not get another chance to eat, and we went down to eat and continued our argument—Walinsky was against foreign aid, he thought President Truman and President Kennedy by their loose promises to defend freedom everywhere had got us into the mess we were in now in Vietnam. He was a revisionist and apparently believed that we had started the cold war and that our containment policy was an aggressive act. Some years later, I've been told, Walinsky, like George Leighton of old and others, switched 180 degrees from Democratic liberalism and in 1982, in Ronald Reagan's time, became an important member of the staff of the right-wing Republican, Lew Lehrman, who ran against Mario Cuomo for governor of New York.

Walinsky got a call—Martin Luther King was dead, murdered. Bobby was due to land in Indianapolis at about this time. I said we had to make sure he knew King was dead. He had been scheduled to go to the opening of his Indiana headquarters, then to an outdoor Negro rally. I thought he ought to skip the first and go to the second, announce King was dead, ask them to pray, and then ask them to go home. In a squad car at the curb, I found an Indianapolis police inspector and asked if Bobby should appear at the Negro rally. He said, with a fervor I imagine was rare in him, "I sure hope he does. If he doesn't, there'll be hell to pay. He's the only one can do it." Reports were coming in that Negroes across the country were in revolt. He feared they would riot here. I suggested he call headquarters. He did—Bobby was on his way to the Negro rally. The inspector said he'd go there. Walinsky went with him to be sure Bobby knew. Greenfield and I went to our rooms to draft a statement on King's death for Bobby.

When Bobby and the others came to the hotel, we gathered in his rooms, and Fred Dutton told us what Bobby had said at the Negro rally, and it was so good we threw our drafts away. He had spoken extemporaneously, a short speech, little more than a few words really, eloquent, quoting Aeschylus (something he had learned at a Hickory Hill seminar):

> *In our sleep, pain which cannot*
> *forget falls drop by drop upon the*
> *heart until, in our own despair,*
> *against our will, comes wisdom*
> *through the awful grace of God...*

and going on: "... to tame the savageness of man and to make gentle the life of this world. Let us ... say a prayer for our country and for our people." The Negroes did not riot in Indianapolis. They rioted, however, nearly everywhere else.

Bobby put in a call for Mrs. King, to offer his airplane to go to Memphis to get the body. When the call came in, he asked, "What should I say to her?" Since no one else answered, I said, "Just tell her how you feel. It has to come from you."

While he was talking, we had the television set on. It was showing film clips of King's speeches. Watching, I realized I didn't care about King as much as the young writers. I'd done all my weeping in 1963, when President Kennedy was killed. But now Walinsky and Greenfield were extremely upset, convinced that "some cop" had shot him. The big civil rights march in Washington in 1963, when King had made his "I have a dream" speech at the Lincoln Memorial, had been a high point of their lives. Not of mine. Watching the film clips, I thought King a demagogue, as I always had, and I also remembered that he had not always been worthy of trust, as when he had met privately with Mayor Daley and they had agreed to say nothing publicly about their talk but King, almost immediately on leaving the mayor's office, had told the press everything they'd said.

Bobby came back and we discussed the rest of the schedule. I favored canceling everything till after the funeral. Dutton was reluctant. He thought this would blow over, it wasn't all that big, people forget, life goes on, let's not get excited and cancel everything; and Bobby said, "There are a lot of people who just don't care." He said it flatly, without emotion. I felt the same way, though still favored canceling. The kids thought King's murder would tear the country apart. It turned out they were closer to right than the rest of us. In the end we canceled the rest of the trip except for Cleveland and next day went back to Washington. As our plane came in low we could see smoke rising: Washington was burning. Before our eyes, the American civil rights movement was turning into the Negro revolution. On the ground Bobby and several of us stayed aboard because he wanted to go into the streets of Washington to try to quiet the crowds—"I think I can do something with these people." I told him he couldn't if they were rioting in the streets. Fred Dutton said he couldn't go into the streets without checking with the mayor. I suggested we get more facts and call the mayor. Several went to do it. I argued that going into the streets would look like grandstanding. Reluctantly he went home.

I spent Saturday and Sunday in Washington writing two speeches and went to a meeting at Hickory Hill that lasted from 4 to 10 P.M.—with Bobby, Ted Sorensen, Fred Dutton, Dick Goodwin; two television producers I knew, Charles Guggenheim, from earlier campaigns, and John Frankenheimer, from *Playhouse 90* at CBS; plus people from an advertising agency. The advertising people did most of the talking, much of what they said made little sense, the meeting dragged on, Bobby became impatient, an advertising time buyer said he had "people" out in Indiana, and Bobby, exasperated, said he didn't want those faceless people out there, he wanted *him.* I said everybody should go to Indiana. He agreed. In such a meeting, Bobby would sit and listen for a long time and watch each person who spoke, saying nothing himself, and it was impossible to tell what he thought of what was being said, though usually he looked skeptical or worse, then he would decide. He ran a meeting hard.

The advertising and TV people left, and Bobby, Sorensen, Dutton, Goodwin, and I talked speeches. I gave him my two drafts. They seemed suitable. Bobby said he must start giving substantive speeches, not just motorcading wildly with huge crowds—"I've got to stop looking like Frank Sinatra running for president." I warned against his becoming the candidate of only students and Negroes. He agreed—he had the Negroes in Gary, now he wanted to do something in the Polish backlash suburbs of Gary.

Everybody believed that, of all the primaries, Indiana was the big one—it was the first contest between him and McCarthy and, moreover, everybody in the press was saying it was the big one. Bobby said, "Indiana is the ballgame. This is my West Virginia." In 1960 West Virginia had been the critical primary for his brother in his contest with Hubert Humphrey. He wanted to say this in his speeches. I opposed it. The Indiana primary this year was a three-way race among him, McCarthy, and Indiana's incumbent governor, Roger Branigin. Branigin had a machine that took 2 percent off the state employees' payroll; he had the dominant Pulliam papers in Indianapolis; he was widely considered Johnson's stand-in for Vice-President Humphrey. I thought Branigin might very well win the primary (I didn't say so but at that time thought Bobby's best chance was to come in second, behind Branigin but ahead of McCarthy), and for Bobby to say "Indiana is my West Virginia" risked too much on a doubtful state. Bobby demurred—the press would say it anyway. He argued that the people of Indiana should be reminded that his brother had never forgotten that West Virginia helped him mightily, and after he became president he gave West Virginia all kinds of preferments. I said he could say this privately to politicians but not publicly. Ted Sorensen thought Bobby should say that Indiana can pick a president. I liked this—Indiana's presidential primary had never before been important. He began saying in almost every speech, "Indiana can help choose a president."

Bobby wanted me to go to Indiana and do the same thing for him that I'd done for his brother in California in 1960—editorial advance. I went, for the duration. Soon Fran joined me—she and Marian Schlesinger went to college campuses to speak on Bobby's behalf to little groups of faculty wives whose husbands were bemused by McCarthy. En route to Indianapolis, I stopped over in Chicago to have lunch with Adlai Stevenson III. He was by then state treasurer of Illinois and had been considered for senator or governor but the machine had refused to slate him. I had tried to persuade Adlai not to come out for McCarthy; now I found him leaning toward Hubert Humphrey, who seemed about to announce. He said Daley had called him in recently, told him he himself would stay neutral right down to the convention, and said he didn't see how anybody (meaning Adlai) could do otherwise. Adlai, however, told me he wanted to endorse somebody before Daley did in order to establish a leadership position for himself. But he promised not to endorse anybody before talking to me. In coming weeks, I kept in touch with him but he was independent and soon he did come out for Humphrey—and he did it without telling me in advance, which I didn't like.

In Indianapolis, Fran and I lived with my mother and Aunt Verl in the house on Kessler Boulevard. I worked in the Kennedy headquarters in a loft upstairs over the old Indiana Theater downtown, surely one of the dreariest places in dreary Indianapolis. Milton Gwirtzman and P. J. Mode, two Kennedy staff writers, and Joe Dolan, the scheduler, and I were able to bring together scheduling and editorial advance, able to shape the campaign. Everybody thought the name Bobby unbecoming to a candidate for president, though that was what we had always called him, and they began calling him Robert. This was too much for me; I called him Bob.

I thought that so far in Indiana, Bob had gone to too many universities and had had too many mob scenes with youngsters screaming and tearing his clothes off. For Indiana, this was wrong. I thought that the ordinary Hoosier at home watching TV was sick of scenes of violence in Vietnam, of Negroes rioting in the cities after King was killed, of kids pulling Kennedy's clothes off. Eugene McCarthy, on the other hand, was running a low-keyed soft-spoken campaign, which might be effective by contrast with Bob's. McCarthy was a single-issue candidate—Vietnam—and his main appeal was to students. Bob should be broader-based both as to issues and as to constituency—Johnson had partly neutralized Vietnam for the time being, the Negro revolution was suddenly in full swing, and Bob ought not to compete with McCarthy for students but should also appeal to blue-collar factory workers and many others. So far, Bob was too exciting. The people, I thought, did not want to be excited. This year, 1968, resembled 1952, the year of Stevenson's first campaign, more than 1960, the year Jack Kennedy had won. In 1952 the people had been weary after twenty years of New Deal and two wars; they had turned to Eisenhower for change and calm. In 1960, after eight years of Eisenhower's do-nothingism, they had been willing to follow a new exciting young leader, Jack Kennedy. Not in 1968—once more they wanted change, change from Vietnam and from riots, but change and calm, not a summons to great adventures. So far, I thought, Bob's campaign had had too much razzle-dazzle. The razzle-dazzle had been necessary after New Hampshire, to catch up with McCarthy. But now it was time to cool it, to reassure people, and once in a while make a substantive speech. One way to get away from razzle-dazzle was to identify with Indiana's past greatness by paying quiet visits to the shrines of its heroes, people like Abraham Lincoln and James Whitcomb Riley. Another was to evoke Hoosier nostalgia, and I wanted a railroad whistle-stop trip, and at P. J. Mode's suggestion we picked a train called the *Wabash Cannonball,* a traditional train on the old Wabash railroad recently discontinued. And I wanted to get Bob into some of the red-neck backlash factory cities. All this, of course, meant changing the schedule radically.

Bob was campaigning in other states, coming in and out of Indiana for a day or two. I spent several days promoting these ideas with

Senator Ted Kennedy, Dick Goodwin, Larry O'Brien (who had left the Johnson cabinet to join Bob), and others, working with Joe Dolan to schedule the events I wanted, doing research and editorial advance on the new stops, and writing a memo to Bob on our plans. We worked out a quiet history day in southern Indiana for next Monday, April 22, Bob's next visit to Indiana—the George Rogers Clark and William Henry Harrison memorials at Vincennes, then through several small towns following the Lincoln family's trail through Indiana, then a visit to the grave of Lincoln's mother, Nancy Hanks, in Spencer County down near the Ohio River, actually the Lincoln trip I'd made with Fran and Cindy in 1952 for the *Post*. For Tuesday we scheduled a string of stops in backlash factory cities to the north—Elwood, Marion, Kokomo, and others—and a ride on the *Wabash Cannonball* through northern cities ending with an evening speech at Fort Wayne. I had known every one of those places for many years. By Sunday afternoon we had finished the schedule and the briefing sheets for each stop and I took them to Washington and gave them to Bob at Hickory Hill.

The house filled up—Ted Sorensen, Fred Dutton, Dick Goodwin, George Stevens, others At dinner Bob read my memo about Indiana and I told him about his Monday-Tuesday schedule. He thought he'd be wasting a lot of time at historical markers on Monday and he balked when I suggested he take a couple of his children along on that trip. With Fred Dutton's help, I persuaded him that every Hoosier takes his wife and kids to visit the Lincoln shrines. He did not like Tuesday at all. I explained that the white backlash vote in such factory cities as Kokomo differed from that of the Poles around Gary—it consisted of workers who had come to Indiana from Kentucky and Tennessee to work in war industry and stayed on, red-necks and Klansmen. "Why am I going there then?" he asked. I said, "Because there are a lot of Democratic votes there and you've got to convince them." He asked how. I told him he should change his pitch—should speak strongly against rioting and violence, using his experience as attorney general, but he should not omit a plea too for justice—should say that violence and rioting cannot be tolerated; neither can racial injustice in the big cities be tolerated (big cities far away). Milt Gwirtzman had suggested that he refer to himself as "the former chief law-enforcement officer of the United States" rather than as "former attorney general." Bob nodded, saying, "I can go pretty far in that direction. That doesn't bother me." I also urged him to praise private enterprise in speeches to Rotary clubs; he said he didn't mind and started talking about his Bedford-Stuyvesant project in New York City. As we talked, he seemed to come around to accepting my advice. Dinner finished, he slumped down on a sofa and started reading a speech I'd written for his historical day. He stopped at the first sentence, snorted, read it aloud to everybody, and asked, "What the hell does that mean?" I said it meant just what it said. He went on reading. He didn't like it. We'd already released it to the press—that was unusual but we'd done it because Milt Gwirtzman wanted to mail it out to small papers all over Indiana. He didn't like that either, wanted every statement cleared by Dutton and himself. (It did, however, get widely published.)

He started looking through my briefing sheets, one for each stop he'd make. He read aloud, "Setting," mockingly. He had a wry mocking humor, almost bitter. Nobody said anything. He read on and got interested, he read straight through the Monday historical book without comment. After that the meeting turned back to television, and I went home to the Hay-Adams.

Next morning we flew to Vincennes. I was somewhat surprised to see two or three of his children aboard the plane. At Vincennes, when Bob and his family went into the historic church, his dog Freckles was ahead of him to the altar. Fred Dutton picked him up and handed him to me and we got him out, and Fred or Dick Tuck told a reporter, "This may look like a dog to you but it looks like an embassy to me." Bob walked around several historic shrines in Vincennes, Fred Dutton close by him and I a few feet away, and once or twice Bob said to me, "This is nice," or "It's good, isn't it?" He spoke at lunch to businessmen on private enterprise. Then we motorcaded through a string of little southern Indiana towns like Oolitic, the country my father and I used to hunt rabbits in. I rode in Bob's convertible, he and I and Ethel and the kids and the dog and Dick Goodwin all scrambled together, Fred Dutton lying on the trunk and hanging on for dear life as the motorcade drove fast across the countryside, a police car ahead, the photographers' car behind, then a couple of cars with local politicians and Bob's bodyguard, Bill Barry, then two press buses. At each town the motorcade would stop in the main street and Bob, who had risen to the tonneau of the convertible as we approached town, would climb out onto the trunk and speak. Previously he had been using a bullhorn; I objected that the bullhorn had become a symbol of southern sheriffs during the civil right troubles and of Lyndon Johnson, and a small microphone was substituted. I would hand him the microphone; when he finished he would toss it to me. While he spoke I kept a hand out so he could grab it if the crowds pulled him off the trunk. (Once they did, and when he fell on his face on the street he broke a tooth.) Though the towns were small, the crowds were big. They screamed and tore at him. They were savage. Once or twice we stopped to make a courthouse steps speech, and I had to help get the Kennedy children through the crowds, a bruising business—Fred Dutton, Bill Barry, and I did the blocking. The crowds delayed us, and as I had feared we got to Lincoln's mother's grave too late to have enough light for television. But Bob seemed to enjoy it, the place was quiet, and as he walked around he said to me, "It's a nice place, isn't it?"

Next day we motorcaded all morning through the north-central factory towns. At the courthouse stops I hung around the edge of the crowds. Indiana people just stand there, hands in pockets, listening, as though to say, "Go on—I dare you to make me clap." Bob followed the line I'd given him. When he emphasized that violence could not be tolerated, he got big applause; when he went on to say injustice could not be tolerated either, everybody was entitled to jobs and schools, they didn't applaud but they didn't mind—they'd heard what they wanted to hear, that he was against violence in the streets, and that was enough. It worked.

That afternoon we boarded the *Wabash Cannonball* and whistle-stopped from Logansport to Fort Wayne, and it was terrific—a hill-billy guitar band aboard playing an old song called "The Wabash Cannonball" and a Kennedy song Ted Sorensen had written to the tune of "This Land Is Your Land," big friendly crowds, good back-platform speeches pitched at each town, great TV, and a mood aboard the train among press and staff that was happy. After each stop Bob would sit down beside Fred Dutton or me, bend his head forward a little, and look up from beneath the lock of hair, a quizzical mocking smile on his face. The *Cannonball* made good network evening news. As we rode, Milt Gwirtzman gave me the evening speech for Fort Wayne and said Bob wanted me to touch it up and give it some class. I put in a quotation from Pericles and sharpened some of the applause lines.

He delivered it in a college gym to a friendly audience of townsfolk. He came upon the Pericles passage unexpectedly and stumbled through it—it *was* hard to read—and while he was stumbling a baby started to cry in the audience. Its parents tried to hush it but couldn't. Bob involuntarily looked at it in annoyance, and then went back to his speech, and its parents took it out. He turned toward them and put out his arms and pleaded, "Please don't leave," then turned back to the crowd and made a face, then back to the parents with another plea, then to the audience, "You see how ruthless I am—I've just thrown a baby out of the hall." Often during the campaign he kidded himself about being ruthless, as he had at the end of his 1964 campaign for senator when he said, "I'm glad this campaign is almost over, because then I can go back to being ruthless." He just about killed the ruthlessness issue in the 1968 spring primaries. After his formal speech on education at Fort Wayne, which he plowed through and which was listened to quietly, he took questions on all subjects for at least a half hour, and he was at his very best. He finally announced he would take only one more question, and did, and the crowd stood and clapped, thinking it was all over, as did I; but Bob hesitated, then motioned for silence, then said quietly, "Camus once said there will always be suffering children in this world but perhaps we can make it a little less suffering and if you and I don't help them, who will?" Then he added very quietly, "Help us," amid dead silence and walked off. It was, like Stevenson's welcoming speech to the 1952 convention, one of the most moving political moments of my life.

Later, looking back, I thought those two days, the history day on Monday and the factory towns and the *Cannonball* on Tuesday, were the days when Bob Kennedy turned the corner in Indiana (though perhaps I'm biased). Before then, his campaign had not been in tune with the Indiana voters. On those days, it was—he felt at home with them, and they with him. He knew it, and so did the newspapermen. His brother Ted and Larry O'Brien thought we were doing it just right. Bob told me the briefing sheets were a life-saver. Fred Dutton did too—they gave Bob a sense of security coming before a strange audience.

Not everybody was pleased with the new Bob Kennedy. Bob himself had misgivings—once he asked plaintively when he could have a liberal day. Fred Dutton and I told him we would get him a labor audience for that purpose but he'd have to remember they were red-necks and nigger haters as well as workingmen. Once he asked why he had ever entered the Indiana primary in the first place. I said nothing but the fact is that had I been consulted I would have advised him against it—Indiana is just not Kennedy country. Once when I wrote something conservative, Fred Dutton vetoed it, laughing, saying, "I understand what you're trying to do, turn him around, and that's okay, but don't turn him around too fast." *The New York Times* said that Dick Goodwin and I had turned Kennedy around and made his speeches sound like old George Romney speeches on free enterprise. (Dick Goodwin was innocent; I did it.) Arthur Schlesinger called me from New York and asked what the hell we were up to, and I told him, and he said, "Well, maybe, but it makes very curious reading in the East." No doubt it did, But Bob Kennedy couldn't have won in Indiana by making speeches that pleased eastern liberals (which Arthur understood better than many). Adam Walinsky and Jeff Greenfield were hurt—they, especially Walinsky, thought they had turned Bob into a liberal and now I was turning him back into a conservative. They conceived all this as a struggle for the soul of Bob Kennedy. I conceived of it as an effort to win the Indiana election. They were quite funny about it. One night I found them making up limericks about how Robert Kennedy came to Indiana and joined the Ku Klux Klan. By this time they had all but abandoned the Indiana campaign.

Actually, Bob had been a liberal when they were children, and indeed he was by instinct and conviction a good deal more liberal than his brother Jack had been—he had a real passion for the disadvantaged, the Negroes and poor Appalachian whites, the starving American Indians and Mexican migrant workers, for *los de abajo.* These people knew he cared. He was the only white man in America that Negroes trusted. They didn't care if he talked backlash to the

Kokomo autoworkers. They knew that in his heart he was for them. Once during the Indiana primary he went into black Gary and white-backlash Hammond and Whiting all on the same day, something no other candidate in America would have dared to do that terrible spring. But never in Indiana did he simply declare that violence and rioting cannot be tolerated and let it go at that; always he followed it by saying that neither can injustice be tolerated. At least, that was true every time I heard him speak, and I was watching him closely and would have picked him up quickly if he had missed a beat, because I knew the press would crucify him. This may be viewed as a cynical effort to have it both ways; it may also be viewed as an effort to heal the country's wounds, to bring us together again. God knows we needed it, after Vietnam and the murder of Martin Luther King. And no one would maintain, indeed, that Negroes could go on tearing the cities to pieces—or be expected to endure forever the injustice of poverty and second-class citizenship. Bob said nothing in Indiana he would have to take back if elected, nothing he would have to disavow in other states.

I spent a good deal of time briefing newspapermen and TV people on Indiana, explaining why this was not Kennedy country—redneck conservative voters who supported Governor George Wallace of Georgia, Governor Branigin's machine, business against Bob, labor too, and the growing suburbs, all the other reasons he would do badly. I could do this better than Bob's press secretaries, Frank Mankiewicz and Pierre Salinger, because I knew Indiana, I myself was a journalist known to the national press, and, furthermore, I believed what I was saying. I told the reporters where to check what I was saying. For example, I steered John Steele of *Time* to Kokomo, and he came back with a briefcase full of Ku Klux Klan literature.

Bob got along well with the press. He usually ended a whistlestop speech with a quotation from George Bernard Shaw, "Some people see things as they are and ask why? I dream things that never were and say why not." (I doubt that half his crowd understood it, but he delivered it well and it always worked.) When he came to the start of that line, the words "George Bernard Shaw," the newspapermen traveling with us started moving to the buses. Once, for a joke, he omitted it and left quickly, almost stranding them. Aboard the plane, at the end of a day, he would leave the back of the Electra where Ethel and we staffers rode with him and go mingle with the press. The effect was curious. They liked him. But some of them wrote nasty stories—they were afraid they were being taken in by him and bent over backward to be "objective." (His brother Jack had been far less free with them.) Roger Mudd, the television broadcaster, was given all kinds of breaks to do a special show on Bob, but it turned out to be just short of a hatchet job. Bob got even: In California, Mudd interviewed him, and Bob kept telling him to watch his language, throwing him off balance.

Once I told Bob he was weak with suburbanites and businessmen; he ought to quit talking to Negroes and students. He said, "But those are the audiences I like to talk to. I feel at home with them." It was true. He had no feel for the petite bourgeoisie, the suburbanites. It would have been his gravest weakness as a national candidate, particularly in such states as Illinois and California. In Indiana he simply did nothing about it. In California, he had to try, though he hated it. It probably cost him Oregon, a state of petite bourgeoisie, pseudointellectual college professors, righteous good-government people. Once Bob said to me, "Who else could have put together the combination against me—business, labor, and the South?" I added, "And the Jews." It was true. Big business feared him; President Johnson had told big labor to oppose him; the South hated him for implementing desegregation. (Why Jews opposed him I never clearly understood.*)

*Various writers, including Arthur Schlesinger, Adam Yarmolinsky, William Vanden Heuvel and Milt Gwirtzman, V. O. Key, and Richard Dawson Kahlenberg, in pieces published and unpublished, have referred to Jews' unfavorable opinion of Bob. As its sources, they have suggested his father's reputation, his own Catholicism, his tough shanty-Irish demeanor, his six months as assistant counsel to Senator Joe McCarthy's witch-hunting committee, his "ruthless" pursuit of Jimmy Hoffa and other witnesses later before his Rackets Committee, his very 1968 campaign style—mingling with the sweaty crowds, while Eugene McCarthy campaigned in television studios and suburban ladies' teas, both elements more congenial to suburban Jewish voters. Schlesinger has written, "Labor, the party regulars and the south brought [Hubert] Humphrey great strength. [Humphrey] also had a long record of service to Jewish causes. . . . McCarthy too had strong Jewish support. The Jewish community saw him, said Adam Yarmolinsky, as 'the professor who gave your bright son an A, and Bobby Kennedy was the tough kid on the block who beat up your son on his way to school.' When Kennedy came to New York the day after Indiana [Vanden Heuvel and Gwirtzman reported], a group of rabbis waited on him. 'Why do I have so much trouble with the Jews?' he asked. 'I don't understand it. Nobody has been more outspoken than I have. . . . Is it because of my father when he was in England? *That was thirty years ago.*' One of his visitors said that, after the Six Days' War, American Jews needed 'continual

When Bob had decided to enter the primaries, his brother-in-law Steve Smith, who managed the Kennedy family money, said, "This is going to cost us four million dollars and we're not going to get a damn thing for it." In every state the opposition constantly accused the Kennedys of buying the election. Actually, in Indiana, Eugene McCarthy and the Kennedys spent about the same amount of money; in Oregon, McCarthy spent more; in California, the Kennedys more. McCarthy's main sources, Steve Smith said to me in California, were the AFL-CIO's COPE and the Teamsters union. Smith said, "What the hell do Robert Kennedy's relatives want of him for their money except that he be a good president? What do George Meany and Jimmy Hoffa want from McCarthy?" This rankled all the more because McCarthy was so sanctimonious about his ineffable children's crusade. Walt Sheridan, the investigator from the old Rackets Committee who was now on Bob's staff, told me that the Hoffa money was being channeled through a man in Chicago.* I offered to ask Emil Smicklas to investigate it if Steve Smith and Sheridan thought it important. They did. I would move on it right after California.

Bob wanted to do sidewalk campaigning in an Indianapolis blue-collar white neighborhood. I remember East Tenth Street not far from my old home on Brookside Avenue, with a movie house where I used to watch my aunt play the piano on Saturdays as a kid. Bob motorcaded it with several stops. He toured factories, shaking hands; and watching, I thought him, surprisingly, not so good at it as Stevenson. Stevenson had liked to stop and talk for a long time with two or three men. Kennedy shook more hands, but it was more

---

reassurance' about Israel; Kennedy wearily said he would make his position clear again on the west coast."

My own Jewish friends supported Bob. But they were sophisticated political people; perhaps other Jews were put off by things like Irish toughness. The problem must have been more atmospheric than substantive. Certainly Bob was aware of it the day he and I discussed it.

*Allen Dorfman, an insurance man. Earlier Bob's Senate Rackets Committee had investigated whether Dorfman and his father had loaned Teamsters pension money, which they handled, to leaders of organized crime. Years later, in 1982, Dorfman was convicted, together with the new head of the Teamsters and a gangster and two others, of conspiring to bribe a U.S. senator from Nevada. While Dorfman was out on bond awaiting sentencing, a sentence that seemed likely to be long, the Syndicate became suspicious that he might talk freely to the FBI about organized crime in return for a lighter sentence, and one day in 1983, in a suburban shopping-mall parking lot, he was assassinated in the manner favored by gangsters.

mechanical, and he did not give the impression he was genuinely interested in the men, as Stevenson had. As part of my Indiana's-past-greatness notion, I wanted him to visit the old home of James Whitcomb Riley, the poet, in Indianapolis. Fran and I visited it—we had once taken our kids there—and near it we found a day nursery. Bob resisted going but, on my urging, went, and at the nursery, while he was speaking briefly, two little Negro children laid their heads in his lap, and he patted them and went on speaking. A photograph of it was printed in *The Saturday Evening Post* with some such caption as "How could anybody hate Robert Kennedy?"

The problem of most politicians is how to get crowds. Bob's that spring was how to avoid them. Eugene McCarthy, and even Governor Branigin, with his machine, spoke to half-empty halls. Not Bob—he could not even stroll along a sidewalk quietly without getting mobbed. He was kinetic. Once he ventured into Monument Circle, the heart of Indianapolis, and his crowd was the biggest I ever saw there; he could not speak, and I got separated from him somehow and had to climb over three or four cars to get back to him. The crowds in the cities were almost frightening. Few things anywhere contain the frenzy, the drama, the unbelievable tensions and pressures of an American presidential campaign. Often, exhausted, Bob would say, "There must be some better way to pick a president." It was worse than that, though. It was a cruel, bloody, and bloodthirsty spectacle. Yet there was a fascination and an exhilaration in it too. And we were winning. We were beating the terrible local press, the suspicious national press, the sanctimonious McCarthy, the dull governor, the skeptical parochial narrow-minded Hoosiers themselves. Were beating them all. Or, rather, Bob Kennedy was. More than most candidates, despite his big staff, he seemed alone. He took advice but he would turn a speech line and make it his own. He went yammering around Indiana about the poor whites of Appalachia and the starving Indians who committed suicide on the reservations and the jobless Negroes in the distant great cities, and half the Hoosiers didn't have any idea what he was talking about; but he plodded ahead stubbornly, making them listen, maybe even making some of them care, by the sheer power of his own caring. Indiana people are not generous nor sympathetic; they are hardhearted, not warm and generous; but he must have touched something in them, pushed a button somewhere. He alone did it. He always looked so alone too, standing up there by himself on the trunk of his convertible—so alone, so vulnerable, so fragile, you feared he might break. He was thin. He did not chop the air with his hands as his brother Jack had; instead he had a little gesture with his right hand, the fist closed, the thumb sticking up a little, and he would jab with it to make a point. When he got applause, he did not smile at the crowd, pleased; instead he looked down, down at the ground or at his speech, and waited till they had finished, then went on. He could take a bland generality and deliver it with such depth of feeling that it cut like a knife.

Eugene McCarthy, by contrast, could say startling things and nobody noticed. He had a low-keyed easygoing manner that suggested a professor—or a preacher without conviction. He never cut, except when he campaigned in New Hampshire against Vietnam, and even then it was the issue, not the candidate, that cut. Bob always cut. He pushed buttons no one else pushed; he aroused wild enthusiasm and love and equally wild hate. Nobody hated McCarthy. Nobody hated Humphrey. But a lot of people in this country hated Kennedys. Bob Kennedy was no more comfortable with professional politicians than with small businessmen. His people were the disadvantaged. Somehow, all this came through, to both his followers and his enemies. For a politician, Bob had an off-trail personality. There seems to be something in the American electorate that cuts down the off trail, the best, the truly good—Stevenson, Jack and Bob Kennedy—and turns instead to the ordinary, the second rate, the Johnsons and Nixons, Carters and Reagans. Maybe the country deserves a hollow man like Nixon.

Before Bob entered the primaries, Jacqueline Kennedy, the president's widow, had told Arthur Schlesinger, "If he gets in, they'll kill him, just as they did Jack." All this spring he rode in motorcades on the back of a convertible, completely exposed. I never rode in a motorcade or went into a crowd with him that I did not watch the windows of surrounding buildings and watch people in the crowds. Once in a town in California a few days before he was shot, while we were whistlestopping the Central Valley, I saw a man close to the train's rear platform ask a hostile question with a look of sheer hate on his face; and all through Bob's speech, I stood close behind Bob and I watched the man, and if he had made any move like reaching in his pocket I would have knocked Bob down. This was on all our minds all spring. He had only one bodyguard, Bill Barry. I talked to Barry and Fred Dutton, but it was no use—Bob had a fatalistic view that if he was going to get killed he was going to get killed and there was nothing to be done about it. I still told Barry and Dutton that you could at least cut the odds—put him in a closed car in motorcades, get more police out to precede the motorcades and search the buildings, not publicize the motorcade route in advance. It was no use. They were for it but they knew he wasn't, so nothing was done.

It was partly for this reason that I came to despise McCarthy. The weekend before the Oregon primary, with California another week away, McCarthy said publicly that rumors would undoubtedly be spread the final weekend that an attempt would be made to assassinate Robert Kennedy. It was a terrible thing to say.

Fran compared Bob with Manolete, the bullfighter. Monument Circle and the other mob scenes were a little like a bullfight. The populace came to see people tearing Bob Kennedy to pieces. They pulled his clothes off him, tore his suits, ripped off his cuff links and necktie. A book about Manolete said that the crowd kept demanding more and more of him, and he kept giving it, until there was nothing left to give but his life, and he gave them that.

The Indiana primary was May 7. On Monday and Tuesday I tried to educate the TV people on Indiana. They weren't listening. One of them showed Larry O'Brien and me his network's tabulation of delegate strength state by state—*including Indiana*—and said they were going on the air with it twenty minutes after the polls closed in Indiana. I wondered why we bothered to have elections at all. Fran and I watched the returns on television with Bob and the others in his suite. It soon became clear we were winning and pretty big. After a while McCarthy went on TV and said he didn't think it made much difference if one came in first or second or third. Bob grinned and said, "That's not what I was taught." He came in first, Branigin second, McCarthy third. He had not only beaten McCarthy; he had beaten an incumbent governor in his home state. That was a great night. Going home to my mother's house, Fran and I said it was nice to win one. It seemed so long since we had. Indeed, the five years since Jack Kennedy's death had been dreary and bleak ones for the country. Now for the first time since 1963, during these weeks of the Indiana spring primary of 1968, Fran and I had felt hope. We had been doing something we thought important, doing it together, and it had worked and we'd won; we were on our way now, for the first time in five years. This was, really, what Robert Kennedy had to offer the people—hope.

I went out to California for Bob. I wasn't sure I needed to, Fred Dutton knew it well, but he and Bob thought I should do the briefing sheets for his stops. Fran and Marian Schlesinger went to Oregon to do their sister act with faculty wives.

Bob won the Nebraska primary. I thought that after Indiana, McCarthy had decided to let Nebraska go, to put everything he had into winning Oregon, and to hope that a victory there might propel him to a victory in California. Bob had to win California. The press was discounting Indiana because it was small, atypical, and full of Negroes. California was a truer test, big and diverse, a nation and an empire in itself. And early polls had shown Bob in trouble there. California is, probably, the hardest state in the nation to campaign in. The suburbs around Los Angeles reach for unbelievable miles and miles and miles. It is a scheduler's and an advance man's nightmare. I'd been through it all before, but the others hadn't, and it floored them.

The reports from Oregon were bad. Fran told me she and Marian couldn't move votes, the campaign was disorganized, scheduling and advance were poor, nobody seemed to know Oregon, she was uneasy. On my way back west from my weekly trip to teach my seminar in New York, I stopped in Portland, and from Fran's room at the Benson Hotel looked down on Bob, walking back to the hotel from a street rally. Somebody said it'd been a good rally but it didn't look good to me; he shouldn't be able to walk down a street in the center of town without anybody paying attention. In his room he asked if I'd been doing the briefing sheets. He liked them. He wished I'd write major speeches too because "I haven't really had a speech since Bloomington." He said it almost plaintively. He really was pulling these campaigns out of his guts, and he looked it, drawn, nervous. I asked if he wanted me to stay with him in Oregon or go back to California. He thought about it a long time. Finally he said,

"I don't know. I guess it's too late in Oregon. But I'll leave it to you." It wasn't like him. I went back to California.

I asked Arthur Schlesinger to come out and help with speeches. The day before he arrived, Bob lost Oregon to McCarthy. Bob took it very hard. We saw him for a long time that Wednesday night in Los Angeles at the Ambassador Hotel and urged him strongly not to say—as he had intimated—that he would drop out of the race entirely if he lost California. Only a week to go. Next day, Thursday, May 30, Arthur and I went with him to Fresno. On the plane I got Bob to do his homework—read his day's briefing sheets. He was distracted. We began talking about making news. Bob asked why he didn't send a telegram to Hubert Humphrey challenging him to join his debate Saturday night with McCarthy, and Arthur drafted one. At the Fresno airport he read his Humphrey telegram, then began kidding the crowd. The crowd was small and unresponsive, and Bob wasn't good. I noticed his legs were trembling. We went whistle-stopping up the San Joaquin Valley, and I told him to turn the speech around—kid the crowd first, then go into the issues, including the telegram. He used the telegram all day. He kept losing it, several times started to read it, couldn't find it, turned to me and asked for it, once saying to me, "Where's that damn telegram?" but saying it into the microphone so the crowd heard it. The next time I gave him a copy as he went to speak; I told him it was the last I had and if he lost it this time he was on his own. He kept losing his briefing sheets too, so didn't know what crop was grown at each stop, and Fred Dutton or I had to write it out in big block letters at the last minute. I had dug up a good story for him about Mexican migrant workers but he didn't use it. Indeed, he gave the Mexicans small comfort that day in the valley. Previously he had been identified with Caesar Chavez, the radical organizer of Mexican migrants. Now Fred Dutton was turning him around, as I had in Indiana, fearing he was becoming too closely identified with Mexicans and Negroes in California. As the day went on, the crowds got bigger and more responsive, and Bob got better. He knew how to work a crowd. At one stop he began:

"Has Senator McCarthy been here to Turlock?"

Crowd roar: "NO."

"He hasn't? I'm shocked. Well then, surely Vice-President Humphrey has been here?"

"NO."

"No? I can hardly believe it. You mean Senator McCarthy and the vice-president don't care about Turlock?"

"NO."

"Are you going to vote for somebody who doesn't care about Turlock?"

"NO."

"Who are you going to vote for?"

"KENNEDY."

"I don't believe it. On election day, you'll forget how to spell my name."

"NO."

"You'll forget all about me."

"NO."

"Do you promise?"

"YES."

"Do you know what my family and I had for breakfast this morning?"

"NO."

"Turlock turkey. [Turlock called itself the Turkey Capital of the World.] We have Turlock turkey every day for breakfast. Do you believe that?"

That was the way he used the crops from the briefing sheets. He had another routine:

"Are you going to help me?"

"YES."

"Are you going to vote for me?"

"YES."

"Have you read my book?"

"YES."

"You lie."

Earlier in his campaign he had used the rather strident closing that his brother Jack had used: Give me your heart, give me your hand, your help in this election; but by now he had shifted to kidding the audience, much more in character for him. They were very different men. John F. Kennedy was more the politician, saying things publicly that he privately scoffed at. Bobby Kennedy was himself. Campaigning, Jack gave the impression of decisive leadership, the man with all the answers. Bob seemed less sure he was right, more tentative, more questioning, and completely honest about it. Leadership he showed; but it had a different quality, an off-trail unorthodox quality, to some extent a searching for answers to hard questions in company with his audience.

I do not mean to extend this into what the McCarthy people kept calling "the politics of participation" or "the new politics." There was a great deal of talk that spring—and later too—about "the new politics" and most of it was baloney. We campaigned the old-politics way—Negroes, blue collar, white collar, ethnic groups, Mexican-Americans, Catholics, pitching the speeches straight at his audiences. The idea of "new politics" arises periodically, as it did in 1952 when Stevenson attracted volunteers, including Lake Forest Republicans, or in 1968, when McCarthy's Vietnam stand attracted the kids, or, at its zenith, in 1972, when George McGovern attracted kids and homosexuals and "women's liberation" women and anti-political-boss people and all manner of zealots. All three—Stevenson, McCarthy, and McGovern—lost. And lost to the practitioners of the old politics. And the day after the voting, everybody forgot about "the new politics."

In Indiana, looking ahead, I had worried about the California crowds—the Indiana crowds were mobs, but I knew how volatile California crowds could be and was afraid Bob might get hurt. He found that if we used police in a California crowd the police shoved and the crowd shoved back. But if we just used Bill Barry and a couple of us, the crowd gave way. Nevertheless, we often wondered what would happen if one of those crowds turned hostile. In California, we ran into more zealous and hostile McCarthy hecklers than in Indiana—they sometimes drove their cars in and out of our motorcade on a Los Angeles freeway, trying to break up our motorcade, a dangerous business. John Siegenthaler asked my advice about scheduling Bob into Berkeley, the epicenter of student radicalism in America. I was for it provided he had security. I thought most Californians didn't like Berkeley, and if student radicals prevented him from speaking, it would help him with other Californians—he could afterward tell the press that if allowed to speak he would have told the students, "You remind me of the Hitler Youth movement." While we were discussing it, hecklers booed Bob down at another college, and he sent word: No more colleges in California. Watching his final TV debate with McCarthy in San Francisco, Fran and I thought Bob at least held his own. After the debate we went with Bob and the others to a fund-raising gala at the city auditorium where Hollywood stars performed and, since we arrived with the candidate, we wound up in the front row. One beautiful performer, Raquel Welch, announced she was for John F. Kennedy, meaning Bob. Jerry Lewis, the comedian, doing his heckling act, took the microphone to, of all people, Arthur Schlesinger and told him to sing "Shine On, Harvest Moon." I was probably the only person in the United States with a worse voice than Arthur and the only one more discomfited by such a spotlight. Arthur manfully croaked. Lewis stopped him. Lewis tried three or four others, including me. All either collapsed in laughter or screeched off key. Then he took the microphone to Fran, and she, who had a good voice, sang it perfectly, and the house cheered, five thousand people, she stopped the show. A good night.

On Sunday we all went to Los Angeles. I spent Monday and election day at the Ambassador Hotel working on a memo titled "Beyond California"—what Bob should do between the California election and the Democratic National Convention. I also wrote California election night victory and defeat statements for Bob. I thought if he won California, he had a pretty good chance of being nominated; if nominated, I felt sure he'd be elected president.

Election day was nervous. I'd thought we'd been ahead in California but that McCarthy was catching us during the last week. It depended now on whether our poor people voted. Fran and I went to Bob's suite in the Ambassador shortly before the polls closed, and it began to fill up. Bob wasn't there. The South Dakota primary was the same day, and Bob won. At about eight Bob stuck his head in the door and said to everybody. "You want me to tell you about the Indians? In one county in South Dakota, there were eight hundred sixty-eight votes and I got eight hundred sixty-six and Humphrey got two and McCarthy got none." Then he disappeared.

We were watching NBC, Huntley-Brinkley. They were not "projecting" a California winner. But their actual returns showed us losing. We couldn't find out where the votes came from or what they meant. On CBS, Cronkite was "projecting" Bob the big winner, but his returns were small and kept fluctuating wildly. Worried, I went to try to persuade Bob not to withdraw if he lost. I found him in a small room across the hall with Fred Dutton, Ted Sorensen, Dick Goodwin, and Jesse Unruh of California. Bob seemed out of sorts, distant, withdrawn within himself. Goodwin was urging him to go on TV and claim victory on the basis of the CBS projection. Unruh opposed it. Bob told Steve Smith to do it. We tried to talk to Bob about what he would say; I drifted back and forth between the little room and the suite, Fran with me, and gave him my "Beyond California" memo and he started to read it but I told him to put it in his pocket and read it tomorrow; and Fran gave him a memo he'd asked for analyzing the Oregon defeat, and he put that in his pocket too. Pressures mounted from reporters and TV directors for him to go down to the Ambassador ballroom and speak. Finally he did, followed by the photographers and reporters, one of whom asked if I wasn't going down with him "into the burning pit," or something like that, and I said no, I'd been there before, I'd wait here. We watched TV in the little room. He came on and was very good, bantering with the audience. I must have quit watching and wandered out into the hall to get some air. Jeff Greenfield came running by, saying something that ended with "shot," and I ran after him, saying, "What did you say?" and he said angrily, "You heard me," and kept running and I followed saying, "No I didn't," and he said, "There's a rumor Kennedy has been shot." I went back to the little room. Sorensen, Goodwin, and somebody else were watching television. On TV the ballroom downstairs was a madhouse. Steve Smith was asking people to leave, somebody was asking for a doctor in the house, the announcer was saying that nobody knew for sure but it was thought that several people had been shot and one of them was Bob. But he thought Bob had been shot in the hip. Fran put her arm around Ted Sorensen. We kept watching the horror. Then the announcer said it was said that Bob had been shot and in the head. Every one of us said, "Oh no." Ted got up and walked to a window, and Fran went with him. Then somehow Fran disappeared, one or two young staffers came in, then somehow all the staffers, young and old, began to hurry to the elevator—outside we could hear sirens, they were taking him to the hospital—and I started running with them, it was a natural impulse to go where your candidate was, but as we turned a corner I stopped and thought, What the hell am I going there for? He needs a doctor, not a writer. If I can do anything for anybody it's for Fran. I remembered that when President Kennedy had been shot I'd stayed alone in Washington and not had Fran come to me, and later this had hurt us both; so I let the others go and went back to Fran and we sat watching television and grieving. About 4 A.M. we went to bed. I kept wondering if I could have helped if I'd gone down with him.

Next morning we had thought to go to New York but instead we watched television and missed our plane. We went to get something to eat. The hotel seemed empty. Fran wanted to see Ethel, she said she couldn't leave without seeing her or getting word to her. I felt helpless. A *Look* photographer who'd been with us throughout Indiana helped us make calls to find out how to get into the hospital. We went there, to the intensive care unit. We talked a little to John McCone and his wife; from California himself, he had been President Kennedy's director of the CIA and was a close friend of Bob's. Ted Kennedy came in and we talked to him a few minutes and I scribbled out a note to Ethel and gave it to him, something like "Dear Ethel, we are praying. God bless you and yours. Fran and John," and asked if Ted would give it to Ethel, and he read it and said, "I sure will." The McCones took us back to the hotel. The rest of the day we watched TV and made plans, called Dan and Fred and my mother. (Dan had been dating one of Bob's daughters at Putney.) Adlai Stevenson III called, as did Newt Minow and others from Chicago. When we went to bed past midnight Bob was still alive. We thought if he could just make it through the night he might be all right. Early in the morning Newt Minow called and wakened me: Bob had died in the night.

We walked around the hotel, looking for somebody or something. I bought a black necktie. We found Walt Sheridan making lists of people to go on Air Force One, which President Johnson was sending, to take Bob's body back to New York for the funeral, and they had us on the list, but we decided not to go—we had to get to our children. Fran and I took a plane to Boston, rented a car, picked up Fred at Exeter and Dan at Putney, both crying, then went to New York and rejoined the campaign party at the Commodore. Ed Guthman asked me to stand vigil, and Fran and I walked to St. Patrick's Cathedral, and I stood vigil from 12:30 to 12:45 beside the casket in the cathedral with Burke Marshall and Jacqueline Kennedy and Dick Goodwin and others. Late as it was, there must have been a million people on the streets just standing and staring toward the cathedral. In the morning we took the boys and went to the funeral service in the cathedral, where Bob's brother Ted so bravely spoke, then we got on one of the buses and went to the train. The locomotive was freshly painted black. The train ride to Washington took forever. The train was at once terrible and great. He had loved whistlestopping by train. The crowds were astonishing. They lined the railroad right-of-way. Trains run through poor parts of town. Negroes and factory workers. They were his people. The disadvantaged. Old men stood with their hats over their hearts. Young women held babies. Factory workers stopped work and leaned out of windows and climbed up on roofs. Aboard the train, people, Bob's family, the staff, press, kept moving around, people we'd been with all spring. Fred told Paul Douglas, who had recommended him for Exeter, about the project he started after Martin Luther King had been killed to get Exeter boys to help paint apartments of Negroes in the Boston slums. We reached Washington in dark and rain and went in buses to Arlington National Cemetery. So it really was all over. Fran and I took Dan and Fred and fled to Michigan.

THIRTEEN

AS TIME GOES BY

1.

Up in Michigan, I seemed able to accomplish little. I did manage to say no to George Ball, who called to ask me to help Hubert Humphrey, the probable Democratic candidate for president. I had said after Bob Kennedy's death I was through with politics. Fran had said the same thing and to this day she has shunned all public deeds. I took up the Stevenson manuscript, put it down, tried to read leftover student papers, put them down. I could think of little but Bob. Finally, to exorcise it, for writing has always been my salvation, I began writing a journal of the Indiana and California campaigns, writing about him, the Bobby Kennedy I had loved.

Early in August the Republican National Convention nominated Richard Nixon for president, and that galvanized Democrats. I began getting more calls asking me to help Hubert Humphrey and to go to the Democratic National Convention in Chicago. Adlai Stevenson III was a delegate and thought I would be. There would be a ceremony honoring his father.

The Democratic National Convention of 1968—God help us! Lyndon Johnson was in many ways an admirable president who pushed through Congress more progressive social legislation than

any other president since FDR. Mayor Richard J. Daley was, as I
have suggested, almost surely the best mayor Chicago ever had.
Both understood power better than anyone else. Their behavior at
the 1968 convention was therefore inexplicable. As Daley's police
beat the kids in the streets, and as Johnson's political operatives
smothered the convention, one could only feel that two stubborn old
men were destroying any chance the Democratic party had to keep
the unspeakable Richard Nixon out of the White House. The real
victim of the convention was Vice-President Humphrey, now helpless heir to Johnson's Vietnam War. One day as I was walking down
Michigan Avenue, a limousine pulled to the curb, and the vice-
president stuck his head out and called, "John!" We shook hands,
and he said, grinning but his jaw thrust out at the same time (something no other man can do), "I'm going to get it and I want you to
help me in the fall." I said I would. He was always direct, he never
hesitated to ask help.

The rest of the convention was far less cheerful. One night I sat in
a room at the Chicago Club with Ralph Bellamy, the actor—he and
Dore Schary had taken part in the memorial to Adlai Stevenson—
looking out the window at Michigan Avenue, where a wave of
young Vietnam War protesters pursued by police swept down the
street, tear gas bombs smoking among them. Disheartened, we
called Fran up at Three Lakes. She reported that she had just returned from Smith Lake and that, as she was driving the Jeep out of
the turnaround at Smith Lake, she had seen a black fox. Bellamy
could hardly believe that anywhere in the United States one could
still see a black fox in one's own driveway.

I went to Washington September 29 to help Hubert Humphrey.
Hubert Humphrey ran for president on courage alone. His party,
torn by the primaries and convention, was shattered by the revolt of
the black and young against Vietnam and racial injustice, by the
counterrevolt of blue-collar workers. His campaign was floundering.
He had little staff, few good writers, no position papers; no direction.
My first weekend in Washington I met with him and his other advisers in his apartment. They began to show him advertising materials they had prepared but he interrupted, "Wait a minute. I want to
ask some questions." He said he had spent last week in the West and
South, and the crowds had been good, but when people asked for

bumper stickers and buttons, there were none. Nor any TV or radio spots. He said, "Where the hell is the campaign?" The others tried to evade. Finally Larry O'Brien told him the truth: The Democratic National Committee was broke. Contributors thought this a lost cause. The people who make buttons and bumper stickers had shut off the national committee's credit. The committee could not pay the fuel bill for the vice-president's airplane—it might not take off Monday.

Humphrey sat silent a moment. Then, thrusting out his jaw, "All right. I see. Well, I can raise money," and all fall he did, seeing people he shouldn't, and never complained. His was a brave campaign.

I had no great heart for it but I admired Humphrey and I did not want to have in the White House Richard Nixon. I thought Nixon a thoroughgoing scoundrel, a hollow man, a master of deceit, and, considering his and Joe McCarthy's campaign against Stevenson in 1952, a real menace to civil liberties. When my liberal friends like Arthur Schlesinger refused to help Humphrey, considering him an apologist for Johnson's war, I told them, "All right—you can abstain if you want to, but you're going to help elect Richard Nixon." Similarly, on an October afternoon when Humphrey mounted a loading platform at a factory and took off his coat and harangued the workingmen, some of whom heckled him and held up George Wallace signs, Humphrey leaned forward and told them, "All right, vote for Wallace if you want to—you'll get Richard Nixon for president and you'll get a recession and you'll lose your jobs." I was proud of him.

I spent two weeks in the Washington headquarters, writing speeches, then went to California to find out what we ought to do there. But in San Francisco I ran into Ted Sorensen's brother, also working for Humphrey, and, talking, we realized that California issues didn't matter, the only thing that mattered was Vietnam: Humphrey had to break at last with President Johnson on the war. We did not think he could repudiate the administration wholly—he had been its vice-president for four years—but we devised a formula, details of which I now forget, that would avoid an open break yet free him from the fatal Johnson embrace. The election was only about two weeks away. I flew all night from San Francisco to Hartford, Connecticut, where Humphrey was campaigning, missed him there, chased his motorcade all day through whistlestops, and finally that night on his plane to New York made my presentation. He said he would think about it. I kept other people away so he could. As the plane was descending, he said, "I'll do it. But I'll have to see him first."

His chief aide, Ted Van Dyk, arranged for Humphrey to see President Johnson privately the next day, a Sunday. But when Humphrey got to the White House, a presidential aide told him the appointment was canceled. (News of the appointment had leaked to the press; Johnson would never do what the press predicted.) Humphrey, for once, was speechless. The aide said, "Maybe you can see him Monday." Humphrey told him to tell the president where he could shove the appointment.

During the last week Humphrey did move some distance away from Johnson on the war—not so far as we had hoped, but far enough to help. I went with him around the country—Los Angeles, Ohio, Pennsylvania, New York, Baltimore, Michigan, Illinois, Ohio again, Texas, Los Angeles again, a frantic campaign, big speeches and a murderous schedule everywhere. Despite everything, he never lost his boyish bubbly enthusiasm. Once on the plane, reading a speech I had drafted for him, he looked up and said, "God—he makes me sound like Stevenson." Kidding himself—he always did. We knew Humphrey was closing the gap. Fast enough? The poll takers and TV anchormen kept predicting a Nixon landslide. Right up to the end, Walter Cronkite on CBS kept "projecting" that Humphrey would carry only two states and the District of Columbia. (How would you like to raise money for such a candidacy?) We knew it would be far closer than that and after all, we had been in national politics before, Ted Van Dyk and I and Jim Rowe, who campaigned with us. It turned out to be one of the closest elections in American history. I have always thought that if the terrible Chicago convention had not torn the party to pieces, Hubert Humphrey would have been president of the United States and Richard Nixon never would have. What that would have saved the country!

On November 20 that year, 1968, Fran and I went home to Highland Park and, after six years, dating from the time we had gone to the Dominican Republic, we retrieved from tenants our old Victorian house on Maple Avenue. That day was her birthday, and it was also Bob Kennedy's birthday, and when we arrived we found, too late, a telegram from Ethel asking us to come to a memorial service that day.

2.

On Maple Avenue, we dug in to finish the Stevenson book. On June 5, 1970, three and a half years after I had begun writing, I finished the rough draft—more than sixteen thousand pages, some two and a half million words. I spent another year and a half cutting and rewriting it into a semifinal draft, still enormous, then I began clearing it with young Adlai, a difficult sometimes almost painful process that stretched over three more years. He raised numerous objections, but we never were forced to arbitration. Most of his objections related to my account of his father's relations with his lady friends, his remarks about Jews, and his feelings toward Negroes. I must say I thought young Adlai behaved well; I am not sure I would want to read a candid biography of my own father. In any case, he did not gut the book, nor did I falsify it. I also now think, upon reflection, that when I wrote the first draft I had been too keenly aware that I was a partisan of Stevenson and so, trying to be "objective," had been hypercritical of him; young Adlai's objections helped restore balance.

I had also promised to show parts of the book to various people in return for their cooperation, such as George Ball, who had given me access to State Department files. And I had to get permission to quote from letters other people had written to Stevenson. (If you write a letter to me, I own the leter and I can sell it, burn it, do anything except publish it—you have a common-law copyright in it.) Most biographers, I am told, paraphrase letters written to their subject—too much trouble to seek permissions. But I wanted to quote from many verbatim, especially those from his lady friends, in order to preserve the flavor of his friendships. In certain cases, obtaining permission resembled diplomacy far more than literary endeavor. Nearly every one of his friends was extremely generous, not to say courageous, in giving permission even when their letters did not show them at their best. All this stretched on through 1976. And so did final editing—Sam Vaughan at Doubleday was, rightly, determined to publish the book as one volume. But we could not cut it enough, and it had to be published as two volumes, each eight hundred or nine hundred pages. The two taken together were entitled *The Life of Adlai E. Stevenson*. The first, covering his life through his first presidential campaign, was called *Adlai Stevenson of Illinois*. The second was called *Adlai Stevenson and the World*. Doubleday launched the first in 1976 with fanfare in Chicago, the second a year later in New York at the United Nations. More than ever before, I made speeches and television appearances around the country, that dubious effort to publicize a book that has become so much a part of publishing. The book was widely and favorably reviewed. It sold only moderately well. Perhaps most disappointing to Fran and me, it won neither a Pulitzer Prize nor a National Book Award. I came to feel that if I had written it fast and published it as only one volume soon after his death, it would probably have been best-seller and won a major award. On the other hand, it would have been a very different book. The enormous amount of documentation made it so long. The material did not overwhelm me. But I was always conscious that I alone had free access to all of Stevenson's papers and I felt an obligation to history. In any case, for better or worse, the biography of Stevenson is done, it exists, and nobody needs do it again.

After it was published, I was often asked three things: What will Stevenson's place in history be? And did I admire him as much when I finished as when I began? And would he have made a good president? As to the first, his place in history probably depends upon what direction history takes. If it moves in the direction he hoped, toward world order through international organization, he probably will rank high, but if it goes as it has seemed to be going, toward a world of competing or even warring nation-states, he may be seen as nothing but a failed prophet. The last is really unanswerable—we never know what kind of president a man will make until he becomes president, during the election of 1860 few people would have predicted that the plain lanky man from rustic Illinois would make our greatest president, nor would many have said in 1945 that the failed haberdasher from Missouri would also make a great president. That was the answer I usually made in public. Actually, I think from his record, we can conclude that the prognosis for Stevenson's presidency was good. When he was governor, nearly all his appointments were good, he was able to get his program through the balky legislature, and he elevated the tone of Illinois government and led the people. As a presidential candidate, he attracted some of the ablest people in the country to help him and he could have put them into his administration. In domestic policy, he was a centrist, often less liberal than I myself might have preferred but perhaps that was apposite to his times, and in any case, his real interest lay not in domestic affairs but in foreign policy, a trait that in a president is not bad. At the United Nations he made little policy—policy was made in Washington, not in New York—but he was an able advocate of America's cause and, moreover, by his own prestige he enhanced the UN's prestige: Never since he was there, nor for that matter before, has the UN stood so high with the American people. He was in a sense the ambassador of the UN to the United States, not the other way around, and as president one could expect he would have used the UN well. And finally as president he would have understood the power of the presidency and coupled it with his own eloquence to rally the people to his purposes. As to whether I admired him as much when I finished writing his life as I had when I began, the answer is clearly that I admired him even more. I had always known he possessed great political courage, as when he stood almost alone against Senator Joe McCarthy. But what I had not been fully aware of was his personal courage. For I had not realized what a horror his private life had been. He had an unhappy and on one occasion traumatic, childhood, a foolish father, a pretentious and suffocating mother, a domineering older sister, a disastrous marriage, and, despite all the friends and comings and goings, an essentially lonely life. He never complained about it; it was as though he simply assumed that one's private life was torture.

Adlai Stevenson was one of the most important figures in my life. In life, he gave me a great deal, and I like to think I helped him. After he died, he remained important to me because of the biography. Its second volume was published just twenty-five years after I first met him.

3.

In 1969, to help support us while I finished the Stevenson book, I resumed teaching, this time at the Medill School of Journalism at Northwestern University in Evanston, just a thirty-five minute drive from our house. For a year I was a visiting lecturer, then Dean I. W.

Cole appointed me a full professor, complete with tenure and Blue Cross. I taught there ten years. In the main, I taught two graduate seminars, one the seminar on the limits of American power that I'd previously taught in the East, the other a seminar on magazine writing.

Writing cannot be taught (and I told my students so). If, however, they could write a decent English sentence, I could perhaps teach them to write a better one, with help from Strunk and White and from Fowler, and I could also perhaps teach them something about how to do legwork for a magazine article, how to structure their material in a way suitable for magazines, and how to cut and shape a rewrite—what I'd learned. Most of them had had no experience at anything but a spot news story. Each was required to submit an outline of a proposed piece, then to report and write and rewrite a story of from fourteen to eighteen and a half pages. They wrote on all sorts of subjects—Alcoholics Anonymous, a plane crash, a solar-heated house, a Chicago slum, the American Nazi party, a murder case (but I soon learned that a murder case was beyond most of them). The class rarely met as a group. Instead, I met individually with each student at various stages of his project. Wearying of marking up their drafts in longhand, I devised a set of rubber stamps saying such things as "awkward," "loose, wordy," "not entirely clear," "says little," "what mean?" On some pages I stamped as many words as they had written. I also wrote critical memos to each student. And I tried to discourage them from certain fashionable but erroneous usages, such as "media" for "television" and "image" for "reputation," as well as "impact" as a verb for "affect" and "input" for "suggestion."

When I started teaching, I was, by and large, on the students' side. But after a few years, after all the unmet deadlines and broken appointments, after all the superficial interviews and sloppy drafts dashed off at the last minute, I found myself approaching each new student somewhat warily. The Northwestern students seemed to be of about the same caliber as those I'd known in the East. Some found magazine writing all but impossible. Some could not do penetrating interviewing, many had trouble conceptualizing the story, nearly all had trouble organizing their material. Most of their writing was disappointing. Grade schools and high schools, apparently, no longer teach English. I taught my course to fifty-four students each year; if I found one or two who had a chance of making it as a writer, I counted it a good year. And a few of them did—I still occasionally hear from one.

I was troubled by Northwestern's "affirmative action" program. Under it, admissions officers were obliged to give preference to Negro applicants. Since many of them came from slums with terrible public schools, they were simply not equipped to do college work. It was not their fault—they had been short-changed in the lower grades. I thought it laudable that we try to redress the injustice done for so many years to Negroes by giving them preference for higher education but it did create problems for us teachers and sometimes for them too. I had one Negro student in his late twenties who had been working as a television reporter and who came to us on a scholarship provided by his employer. He simply could not do what my course required, and I had to give him a C. That same term he received Cs in his other two writing courses. So he was obliged to leave us (he needed a yearlong B average to graduate). We had done him no favor by accepting him and then sending him home a failure to the employer who had thought him so promising. And yet on principle I see no alternative to affirmative action.

What I found most disheartening about my students, however, was that so many were careerist. They—mistakenly—regarded a graduate diploma from Medill as a union card that would guarantee them a job on a newspaper. They were not interested in the pursuit of knowledge or of excellence. They wanted a degree and a job. (But, then, so had I when I was their age.)

When I began teaching, American campuses, even conservative Northwestern, were aflame with the Negro revolution and antiwar protest. More than once our campus was closed by student strikes and demonstrations. Students wore long hair and beards, sandals and chains. "Wow," they said, and they would "trash" something and "get stoned" on narcotics. Some insulted and harassed their professors, though for some reason not me. Those were the years of the Kent State massacre, of President Nixon calling young people "bums," of the Weathermen and the Black Panthers, of what in Chicago were called the Days of Rage—Fran and I happened to be in the Loop just a couple of blocks away the day the violent young men and women fought the police on the street and broke a city official's neck. It was a hard time to be a student, a hard time to be a parent, and even a rather hard time to be a teacher. Yet I preferred all that to the inertia and careerism that replaced it. Students were at least alive.

Teaching made me reflect on my own work. What does a writer need? Well, he needs to read good writing. He needs to write. And he needs to rewrite, and rewrite, and rewrite his own sentences until they say as precisely and as economically as he can make them what he intends them to say. He needs to acquire respect, even reverence, for the English language. And while he is working, he cannot be conscious of any of this. I myself write all the time. For example, I don't know what my hunting and fishing partners think about during the long hours of silence while we're together, waiting for the fish or the game to appear, but I know what I do: I write. Almost automatically, in my mind I form sentences, an idea or a snatch of description; then rearrange the words, then revise them inside my head again and again.

What does a good reporter need? Well, he needs first of all an inquiring mind. He needs skepticism but he also needs humility—when his probing shows him that his initial skepticism was wrong, he needs enough humility to admit it and report what he originally doubted. He must be fair. He needs a deep sense of responsibility, responsibility not only to his readers and to society in general but also to the people he is writing about. He must not become so bemused by "scoring a scoop" or publishing a sensational exposé that he does irreparable damage to human beings. Always he must have doubts, not certitudes, about his own impressions. He needs, of course, to see all—not just "both"—sides of every question. He must realize that the hardest thing of all is to discover the truth and that many men do not want to hear the truth—they kill the messenger that brings it. (How many times in my own writing have I been denounced for bringing it.) And of course at bottom he needs to be able to inspire trust, for without that nobody will confide in him, and he will get no story.

Early in my career, it took me three weeks to do a story—one week to get it, a week to write the rough draft, and another week to

and McCarthy's so-called patriotic anti-Communist crusade. "Patriotism [is sometimes] the last refuge of scoundrels. . . . Patriotism with us is not the hatred of Russia; it is the love of this Republic and of the ideal of liberty of man and mind in which it was born." I did it for Hubert Humphrey in 1968, when I thought he needed to do something courageous—I conceived a speech in the South attacking the South's racist hero, George Wallace. These are both creative ideas. And often within a speech is a small creative bit. When in 1960 Kennedy agreed to address the Greater Houston Ministerial Conference on the subject of his Catholicism, Ted Sorensen knew the speech could not deal only with Kennedy's religious beliefs; it must at least include local references. I suspect his thinking went like this: Where is the candidate going? To Texas. What happened in Texas? The Alamo. Did any Catholics fight at the Alamo? He called our researcher, Myer Feldman; Feldman came up with a string of Irish names of men who had fought at the Alamo but he could not find out whether they were actually Catholic; and so Sorensen wrote, "Side by side with Bowie and Crockett died McCafferty and Bailey and Carey, but no one knows whether they were Catholics or not. For there was no religious test at the Alamo." Politics? Yes. But creative thinking too. In my own magazine and book writing, I often similarly conceptualized a story. The Centralia mine disaster story, as I have suggested, wasn't there till I conceived it. So with "Why Did They Kill?" about the three boys in Ann Arbor who murdered the nurse. So with others. Over the years, I must have poured a good deal of creative energy into political speeches for candidates. Who know what novels, what *War and Peace*, I might have written? (And might not have.) But then I would not have been an ambassador nor would I have learned to care so deeply about certain public issues nor come to understand so fully the importance of serious politics to the life of our democracy. No regrets. (But I warned Fred.)

4.

Odds and ends—in these years, I was making an occasional speech and writing an occasional opinion piece for a magazine or newspaper, *The New York Times, Washington Post, Chicago Tribune, Philadelphia Inquirer, USA Today*, often on politics or on U.S. policy in the Caribbean. Magazine editors and book publishers wanted me to go back to doing heavy fact, crime in its social context. But I'd be repeating myself. I received honorary degrees from Indiana University and Knox College, gave my papers to the Library of Congress, four and a half tons of them. For several months I wrote a column for *Life*, and the editors began to negotiate a contract, through Dorothy Olding, making me a permanent contributor. At that point, however, the editors were fired; my career at *Life* ended (and so, for a time, did *Life*). The editors of *Look* asked me to do a piece, but about the time I finished it, those editors were fired; soon *Look* too folded. In the '70s and '80s, the magazine market was hardly the stable haven it had been in the 1950s.

Newt Minow was chairman of a task force established by the Twentieth Century Fund on political campaign television and asked me to write the final report. This led to a new project—he and I, together with Lee M. Mitchell, a young Washington lawyer, wrote a book for the fund, *Presidential Television*, discussing the problems raised by the awesome power of the president to simultaneously command the attention of virtually the entire nation.

I next did a book for the Twentieth Century Fund, *U.S. Policy in the Caribbean*. It seemed to me that the United States had had no real policy toward the Caribbean since President Kennedy's Alliance for Progress. Roxane Eberlein did the historical research; I did interviewing in Washington, New York, and the Caribbean basin. In the book, I discussed recent revolutionary changes that had caused the Caribbean nations to drift away from us. I argued that the United States had important strategic, economic, and political interests in the Caribbean. But we remained indifferent to it. We were the only great power that did not take its near neighbors seriously. We should, I argued, take a national decision that the development of the Caribbean societies was in the vital interest of the United States and we should place that interest high on our list of priorities, perhaps in fourth or fifth place, or right after the survival of Israel. I offered some twenty-nine specific recommendations, such as normalizing relations with Cuba. The book was respectfully received but it had only marginal effects on policy. We will no doubt see little real change until we elect a president with a real interest in the Caribbean. We have not had one since President Kennedy.

5.

To succeed, a politician needs not only to be articulate, attractive, and a leader, he needs even more to be lucky. Adlai Stevenson had been lucky for a time, had hit a rising curve that carried him to the Governor's Mansion and propelled him toward the White House. But then his luck went bad—he was obliged to run against Eisenhower, was overtaken by Kennedy. His son, Adlai III, had the good luck to run in Illinois for state representative in a year when he could run at large and could lead the ticket statewide; he was handy when Dick Daley's Democratic machine needed a clean candidate for state treasurer; and then one September day in 1969 lightning struck: In the midst of a political rally at his father's old house in Libertyville, word came that the incumbent U.S. senator from Illinois had just died. Instantly young Adlai, at thirty-nine, became the leading candidate for the Democratic nomination for the Senate the next year, 1970. Throughout that fall and winter, I went down to the Loop nearly every Saturday to meet with him and a small group of advisers as he maneuvered, like his father, to win the support of the Daley machine yet to maintain too an independent stance. Nominated, he went to call on Mayor Daley and asked, as he was leaving, "Do you have any final advice for me?" The mayor pondered a moment then said, "Yes. Don't change your name." "Name recognition"—the Stevenson name was indeed known all over Illinois. In the fall campaign of 1970, I wrote speeches in his Loop headquarters. Since it was a small staff and since he was accessible, I was able once more to coordinate speeches, scheduling, and campaign strategy. Young Adlai campaigned well and was again in luck: His opponent was a downstate courthouse politician who made nearly every mistake possible. To try to save the hapless Republican candidate, President Nixon and Vice-President Agnew—remember Agnew?—came repeatedly into Illinois; every time they did they handed us about six thousand dollars worth of television time free, for the stations felt obliged to give Adlai free time equal to theirs. (How all-absorbing are such tactics during a campaign—and how quickly forgotten.) Young Adlai was less eloquent and less dazzling than his father, but he gave the impression of great solidity, of trustworthiness, and the time was right for that too. It was one of those rare campaigns where we did everything right. He won big. He was later reelected and in the Senate he worked hard. But he was not happy there, for reasons I never fully understood, and when his second term expired, did not run for reelection.*

While he was in the Senate, I saw young Adlai frequently and from time to time sent him memos or speech drafts on issues I felt strongly about. I did the same with Ted Kennedy. I regarded those small private contributions to public policy as more important than the writing I was doing.

In 1972, I became involved in a presidential campaign for the last time. Before the early primaries, I tried to help Senator Edmund Muskie, whom I had long admired and who, in the beginning, was the front runner for the nomination. I traveled with him a little and I went a good many times to Washington to meet in Clark Clifford's quiet office with Clifford and Muskie's other senior advisers, Senator Albert Gore, Sol Linowitz, and Jim Rowe—a useful exercise.†
Muskie, however, proved to be a surprisingly weak candidate, and he was overwhelmed by the sudden surge of revolt and fragmentation that swept the Democratic party. The unthinkable climax came when the young rebels actually threw Dick Daley and his delegates out of the national convention. And nominated Senator George McGovern, a thoroughly nice man, but surely not a president.

Nonetheless, that fall I went to live at the Hay-Adams in Washington and to write speeches for McGovern. A number of people asked me to, and he was after all running against Richard Nixon. I could do little for him. His cocksure young staff, Gary Hart and the others aboard his plane, guarded him too jealously. Some of them were given to noisily and publicly resigning every few days and to

---

*Instead, he ran in 1982 for governor. Here his luck ran out. Given the circumstances of that time, he should have won rather easily. Instead, he lost (by about five thousand votes out of about three and a half million cast). His excellent political sense seemed to desert him. He beat himself. And he lost many of his and his father's old friends.
†Clifford had played a similar role in Jack Kennedy's 1960 campaign and now, since he had served quietly on intelligence panels and had been for a time President Johnson's secretary of defense, was considered not only one of Washington's most powerful lawyers, but also an elder statesman. He was also an expensive lawyer—a story, probably apocryphal, was told that he once conferred at some length with a voluble client, then sent him his advice in a one-sentence letter, "Do and say nothing," along with a bill for five thousand dollars, then huge, and when the client expostulated and at some length demanded to know precisely why he should do and say nothing, sent him a second one-sentence letter, "Because I said so," together with a bill for another five thousand dollars.

talking freely to the press, bewildering to anyone who had known the anonymous staffs of FDR and Truman and Stevenson. I worked at the Washington headquarters. I had written speeches and done editorial advance work in the fall campaign of every Democratic candidate for president in the last twenty years, starting with Stevenson in 1952, and in presidential primaries and senatorial campaigns as well, but I had never seen any campaign so poor as the McGovern campaign. Ted Van Dyk and Milt Gwirtzman, whom I had worked with before, now nominally in charge of issues for McGovern, were able professionals; but nobody else on McGovern's staff seemed ever to have worked in a national campaign before. I told Fran my arrival had raised the average age of the staff to thirteen and a half. The headquarters had the uproarious atmosphere of a college dormitory—scores of barefoot girls in blue jeans and boys in long hair and beads racing about mindlessly, taping up funny signs in the corridors. Over the door to one office hung a sign WAR ROOM, and inside, a half-dozen youngsters were always lounging about in broken chairs, playing with maps, and denouncing the Vietnam War—to each other. The chief fund-raiser was named Kimmelman; a woman's liberationist changed his name on the door to KIMMELPERSON. I should have realized that this campaign was not for me when I found that one of my speechwriter colleagues was Stephen Schlesinger, the son of Arthur. (Stephen, I should add, was a serious and effective young writer, as uncomfortable as I with the silly children surrounding us.) If you left your desk unguarded to get a cup of coffee, when you returned your pens and paper and sometimes even your typewriter would be gone. I was grateful when I was assigned to write the major speech of the campaign, the one on Vietnam, and could withdraw to Clark Clifford's quiet law office to discuss and write it with him. We produced a passable speech that was at least carefully drafted, but the staff on the plane rewrote and fussed over it so long and amid such frenzy that sloppy drafting crept in, with the result that the press, not unjustly, accused McGovern of shifting his position.

McGovern himself made mistake after foolish mistake. A friend of mine who had investigated Jimmy Hoffa for Bob Kennedy was investigating the Watergate burglary, new that fall, and when from time to time I ran into him he told me he was sure Watergate led straight to the White House and was deadly serious; but McGovern persisted in referring to it, in the cant of that strange time, as "the Watergate caper." He, who was supposed to be a plain man of integrity, anything but slick, fell into the trap of performing for the television cameras, as when he journeyed all the way to Superior, Wisconsin, in order to read a statement on wheat while standing in front of a grain elevator for the benefit of television cameras—a "television event," his youthful staff called it; a stunt. On Columbus Day, he made a speech praising Americans of Italian descent as the most law-abiding of all Americans—doing clumsily what Dick Daley had done skillfully for years: ethnic politics. I used to dread the morning paper; it was almost sure to recount another blunder. Near the end, Ted Van Dyk said, "John, if he wins we're going to have to work harder than we ever worked in our lives." None of us thought he would. Never before had I worked for a candidate I didn't believe in. I was pleased, however, when in later years he became a sort of elder statesman of the Democratic party.

In 1976, the mad proliferating primaries gave us Democrats a presidential candidate who was a caucus politician from a southern state, with no national experience. Fran and I watched the convention on television with dismay. For us, it hit a maudlin low point when the father of Martin Luther King, Jr., shouted to the convention that he had "talked to all three of them up there" (President Kennedy, Robert F. Kennedy, and Martin Luther King, Jr., presumably in heaven). After the convention I composed a song lyric to be sung to the tune of "Rock of Ages":

Jimmy Carter is our boy
He will bring eternal joy.
Never lies, oh never sins,
Never loses, always wins.

Take the even, take the odd,
He will lead us back to God.
No more whiskey, no more gin,
He will save us all from sin.

Jimmy Carter and his sis,
They will bring eternal bliss.
He the master, I the clod,
On my stumbling way to God.

Smite the heathen, praise the Lord,
Cleanse the evil Gerald Ford.
Send us manna, send us joy.
Give us peanuts, Jimmy boy.

Peanuts, popcorn, Cracker Jack,
Jesus Christ—our Jimmy's back.

It may seem unfair to poke fun at a man's religion, but when a man uses his religion to win public office, it is fair game.

For the first time in twenty-four years, I had no part in the campaign. Not to be part of a presidential campaign is liberating. If you're on the plane and the candidate blunders, you forgive it, he's *your* candidate, sitting only a few seats away; but if you're on the outside, you see him for what he is, a blunderer. I couldn't bring myself to vote for either Carter or Ford; I wrote in Ted Kennedy. In the fall of 1979, I thought Carter could not be reelected and suggested, as did others, that Ted Kennedy consider running against him in the 1980 primaries, and he did, but Iran and Afghanistan saved Carter, and Ted failed. And we got Ronald Reagan, an amiable actor who after a short while stopped seeming to me even amiable. Adlai Stevenson and President Kennedy—oh to live in such a time again!

My malaise during the McGovern campaign was not, of course, all his fault. In part it was my own. The country was changing, and I wasn't. After President Kennedy's death, President Johnson had pressed forward in the FDR-Truman-Stevenson-Kennedy tradition; but all the while, the ground was shifting beneath his feet, and it collapsed in 1968—the year of the Tet offensive, the Bob Kennedy and Eugene McCarthy primaries, campus revolt, and the Chicago convention. Out of all this came somehow a new style in politics. The "New Liberalism" and the "New Politics" arose, as I have said. Young people were in revolt. They declared they wanted to "open up" the party—no more boss-controlled conventions, let the people through the primaries decide. What they did not realize was that they were handing control of politics over not to the people but to the poll takers and the television anchormen. And control through a handful of small unrepresentative states—it is absurd that a few farmers in Iowa and New Hampshire should choose the leader of the Western world. When in 1972 the press and television announced that Ed Muskie should get 50 percent of the vote in New Hampshire, and when he got 46 percent, far more than any other candidate, they announced he'd lost. Later they discovered he'd actually gotten 49.9 percent—but that was long after they'd driven him out of the primaries. As for issues, forget unemployment and inflation, nuclear arms control—what mattered to these young people were such issues as "women's liberation," "gay liberation," abortion, legalization of marijuana. *Those* were, to them, the questions by which the Republic would live or die. The rebels demanded proportionate representation among convention delegates for women, Negroes, and Hispanic Americans, which, of course, could only lead to the odious quota system long ago abandoned as racist. Even Richard Nixon—he of the Watergate cover-up—talked about an "open" government. New leaders arose who spoke in the idiom of populism and seemed bent on dismantling the government. All these changes were said to be destroying big-city machines, making national conventions obsolete, and creating something on the order of a New National Democracy. It struck me, however, that if we want a New National Democracy, more than the usual 20 percent of us will have to vote in the primaries; and the press, especially television, will have to stop covering the primaries like a series of baseball games—will have to stop predicting who will win and start telling us what we may expect the candidates to do if they do win. Time was when reporters told us what the candidates thought about issues—Lincoln on slavery, Bryan on silver, Stevenson on Korea. Nowadays each night during the primaries they tell us who will win by what percentage next Tuesday and why they were wrong last Tuesday about who would win by what percentage. At least since ancient Athens, men have heeded soothsayers' predictions. Yet *who will win* is a question of no importance whatsoever to the voter (he will know anyway on election day), though it may help the gambler place his bet and the candidate plan his strategy and raise money. ("When the polls go good for me," Richard Nixon once said, "the cash register really rings.") And what if we awake some morning to learn that a member of the press—not, probably, a leading television commentator, but one of his anonymous writers—or a poll taker has been corrupted by a politician? What if the Watergate conspirators, instead of merely hating the members of the press, had bought a few?

Some advocates of the "New Politics" maintained it was new be-cause it brought mass popular protest movements, such as the civil rights and anti–Vietnam War movements, into the mainstream of politics. But this is precisely what the old politics has always done. The farmers' protest movement beginning in the 1870s, for example, was taken up by the Populist party, and that in turn was absorbed into the Democratic party and remained for many years a powerful force in the Democratic Party. It is the genius of the American polit-ical system that the two parties have historically acted as sponges, soaking up conflicting pressures in society by the very process of bringing them into the mainstream and making them heard. The only time the system broke down, the Civil War resulted.

In taking our politics away from the professional politicians, we have handed it over to television and poll taking and advertising. So powerful is television that it takes over whatever it becomes in-volved in. When it covers a professional football game, not the weariness of the players decides when time out will be called; in-stead, television decides. A little man with a little red hat stands down on the sidelines; he works for television, and when he lifts his little red hat, time is called, for that signals it is time for a television commercial. Even baseball, virtually our only remaining national innocence, plays most of the World Series not on golden afternoons but at night, "in prime time." During political campaigns, hired "television consultants" not only school their candidates in words and gestures; they chart strategy and select issues. They are prima donnas and behave during campaigns as if *their* fate were being de-cided. And indeed it is—a television consultant with a string of los-ing candidates will not find his services in demand. The star system; once again, winning, not governing, is the object. Having schooled their candidate in words and gestures and issues, they put him on TV display then send forth their poll takers and await the verdict; and if the poll takers' computer spits out an unfavorable verdict, they change the words and gestures and issues. Television converts serious political questions into theater; thirty-second spot commer-cials may take over entirely. Television killed magazines; it has also killed serious political speeches.

During the 1976 campaign, President Ford's staff offered him up to a live TV interview in Chicago provided the questions were easy. The interviewers, whom television likes to call "electronic journalists," asked him only whether winning Illinois was important, what kind of weather he would like on election day, and his views on the Michigan–Ohio State football game. This is journalism? The Ford campaign bought television time to broadcast half-hour "documentaries." The broadcasts showed Ford appearing at rallies during the day, reproduced the crowd's roar—or some other crowd's roar dubbed in at the studio—and showed a running commentary by a sports announcer who supported Ford. They showed Ford speaking, but one did not hear a word he said. Instead, one saw and heard the sports announcer comment, "The response from the people was tremendous, overwhelming." The sports announcer then "interviewed" Ford, asking, "How many leaders have you dealt with, Mr. President?" "One hundred and twenty-four leaders of countries around the world, Joe."

TV news broadcasters themselves often undermine our political system. Some local anchormen, straining to attract attention to themselves in order to raise their ratings, affect to hold in contempt all politicians and parties. They cover serious politics as gossip columnists cover divorce rumors. They degrade politics. Some anchormen, both network and local, who become well known pretend modestly to be simple reporters while presenting what is actually nothing but their own opinions. Some become oracular, presenting their opinions as final judgments; people see it and believe it.

As is well known, broadcasters and their partners, the poll takers, devised a technique called exit polling—asking voters leaving the polls how they voted—and early on election night they use those polls to "project" who is winning, often doing so with east coast results hours before the polls have closed in California, thus, probably, causing some west coast voters to stay home—why bother to vote for someone who's already lost? Moreover, serious students of politics tend to take exit polls as definitive. But they are no more reliable than any other poll.

In 1984, virtually every work and every act of both the Republican and Democratic candidates was aimed at nothing but the evening TV news. Their staff poll takers and TV writers strove single-mindedly for, in their strange vocabulary, "the sound bite"—

the fragment of a candidate's speech that gets on the network evening news. Issues, smissues. Reduce the complexity to bumper stickers. Mondale's poll taker, who virtually took over his campaign, in preparing him for his first "debate" with President Reagan instructed him not to come out fighting, as the president's staff expected, but to treat the president with respect, to praise him for his good intentions, to appear to regret that such a kindly nice old man could not seem to remember the facts of the issues—what reporters called the gold watch speech, one given at the dinner honoring a faithful, grandfatherly employee upon his retirement. Along with a pat on the head. Nevertheless, the poll taker, worried by the movement in his polls of young white men toward Reagan, and fearing it might be reinforced by Reagan's height and actor's dominance of the platform, instructed Mondale to assert his own manhood—to turn to face Reagan, to take one step toward him, and only then to return to his lectern and speak to the people. Mondale did it, and with considerable help from the befuddled president, "won" the debate. (Mondale did not, however, as the poll taker also suggested, plant the idea that the president's hearing was poor by lowering his own voice or turning away from Reagan while speaking.)

Newspapers and TV networks alike covered the two debates as though nothing else happened during the campaign. Indeed, nothing else did, for those two debates were nationally broadcast live on all three networks. Yet debating is one of the few things a sitting president is never called upon to do.

It may well be that by now the evening TV news has acquired more influence over the electorate than the president or Congress. But nobody elected these anchormen to anything, and they are responsible for nothing and accountable to no one. Political parties are responsible and they are accountable; they have to listen; if they don't, their candidates will be voted out. They meet the people's needs through negotiation and compromise; they determine who gets what. Who weakens the party system weakens democracy. TV is no substitute at all.

When television and poll taking were new, candidates and their staffs relied on George Gallup's periodic poll and paid little more than passing attention even to it. Today every candidate has his own poll taker. In 1984, each actually took a poll every day. "Tracking polls," they called them, and they decided the candidates' policy positions, his campaign strategy, his travels, his speeches, his money raising, his mannerisms and dress and gestures. And in a sense, our future.

Yet polling is notoriously unreliable. As I discovered years ago, while reporting on opinion in Muncie, people often will not tell even a reporter what they really think, as I have said, though they may tell him what they "hear people saying." And polling is not done by experienced reporters with plenty of time; it is done by young clerks holding a clipboard. Or even done by telephone. People lie to poll takers. Or they refuse to talk to them. (I myself have been approached by three poll takers, one face to face, two by telephone; I refused to say anything except that I don't like polling.) In constructing their "voter profiles," poll takers can be reasonably sure of some things—they can, for example, verify by objective fact that a man is a Negro, either by checking his address (in most cases) or visually (in most cases). But other data they cannot verify—his income bracket, for example, or how long he went to school, or his age, or his religion, or, except in some primaries, whether he is a Democrat, Republican, or "independent." For these and other "facts" they have only his word. How do they know he is telling the truth?

How good is "scientific random sampling"? I am not statistician enough—or numerologist enough—to know. But I do know there is no magic in numbers. Yet numbers seem to increasingly run our lives. Figures on population, the economy, money, unemployment, arms control, politics, the numbers of poll takers, the numbers of TV ratings—it is not really things but numbers that are in the saddle. People believe numbers, believe them just because they are numbers. This is a mistake. "I still think," Joseph Wood Krutch wrote, "that a familiarity with the best that has been thought and said by men of letters is more helpful than all the sociologists' statistics."

When I worked on presidential campaign staffs, my colleagues included such men as Carl McGowen, Ken Galbraith, Arthur Schlesinger, Bob Tufts, Dave Bell, Bill Wirtz, Bill Blair, Ted Sorensen, Kenny O'Donnell, Fred Dutton, Larry O'Brien, Jerry Bruno, Ted Van Dyk, Milt Gwirtzman. Not one of them ever imagined that he was "molding the candidate's image"; not one talked to the press much or leaked anything to the press that harmed the candidate; not one ever imagined that he was himself the candidate. One of them, the late Jim Rowe, liked to relate how, when he was on President Roosevelt's White House staff and insisted that FDR do something his way, the president ended the discussion: "I do not have to do it your way," the president said, "and I will tell you the reason why. The reason is that, although they may have made a mistake, the people of the United States elected me president, not you."*

Today, young poll takers for hire and young television consultants for hire infest Washington. They are paid and well paid. They completely dominate campaigns. Some intend to remain in their profession; others see a campaign as a step up to an even higher paying job. They advance their own cause, not their candidates', by talking freely to the press. Sometimes they favor correspondents with their unfavorable opinions of their candidates. They feud endlessly among themselves; they go public with their feuds. Every now and then they resign, publicly and noisily. To me, they seem to be monsters. Some seem hysterical, even heartless. Mondale's own manager, two weeks before the election, flew from the cool computerized Washington office to the sweaty campaign plane in Milwaukee to tell Mondale that their polls and other "evidence" showed a Reagan landslide. Mondale had just come in from a triumphal bus trip through his own Mississippi Valley heartland, ablaze in golden October glory, and his crowds had been big and warm, even hot. He was campaigning his heart out; he'd felt that maybe at last he was turning it around. To his manager he protested piteously that he'd thought his crowds had been good lately. No matter—he was twenty points down in their polls. After that they left him alone, and for the first time he came alive. He did it all alone.

We have always been a wasteful people, never more than in the late 1960s and 1970s and 1980s, when we wasted all our politics on appearance. While our "young activities" were loudly debating their nonissues, the rest of the world was facing issues of a wholly new order. Nearly half the two billion people living in poor countries are starving. The poor countries no longer look to us or to Moscow—they are on to both of us; that game is over—they look to themselves

* Arthur related this in his fond memorial to Jim Rowe in the annual report of the Twentieth Century Fund, of which Jim had long been a director.

and to each other. And in each poor country, the poor eye the rich hungrily, the rich the poor warily. The Law of the Sea goes unsigned by us, yet the deep seabed may shape our future more than the moon and Mars. Energy is an issue containing all others; we have not begun to face it. Such issues are of a wholly new magnitude, for they are planetary. Almost nobody talks about them. The arms race is all but out of control. Nuclear proliferation is not a threat, it is a fact: The bomb will reach desperate hands. We know now that nuclear war will likely mean the end of man.

One of the books that impressed me most when I was in college was written by another Indiana author (and ambassador), Claude Bowers. *The Tragic Era* recounted the history of the period of Reconstruction after the Civil War. It seems to me, unhappily, that our country has during the twenty-odd years since the death of President Kennedy passed through another tragic era. Since then, it has been all downhill. My privilege was to live during the time when Roosevelt, Truman, and Kennedy were president—times when the United States under their leadership was behaving like a great nation. Since President Kennedy we have had a succession of failed presidents. And it is almost as if the country itself, buffeted by assassination and Vietnam and Watergate, became unhinged. Dismayed as I have been for these past twenty years, I cannot believe that the country, given a true leader, will not pull itself together and once more regain its rightful place as the leader of the Western world and the model of a good society that cares for its own disadvantaged. I have no patent on patriotism. But anybody who has written about this country all his life and ached to see it better cannot help but thrill when it does something right; anybody who has occupied high public office cannot watch without emotion as the flag goes by. My faith in this country is unashamed.

6.

Of late, young senators have been declaring that the "old liberalism" of the 1950s and 1960s (and earlier) will not do in the '80s (and beyond)—we need, they say, "neoliberalism" (though I have yet to see a clear explanation of what "neoliberalism" means). Nonsense. True, the economy must be adjusted from smokestack industry to high-technology industry, as the young senators keep saying.

But the human needs are the same for a man on a computer assembly line as for a man on an auto assembly line—his wife gets sick, he is laid off, his kids get in trouble, and he gets old. A generation of conservative yammering about "big spenders," plus the yelping of George Wallace *et al.* about sending a message and getting the government off somebody's back, plus pseudosociological notions about a combined blue-collar and white-collar middle-class new majority, have scared some liberals. The 1980 election of Ronald Reagan was called a basic political realignment, and after his re-election landslide in 1984, it was said that the Democratic party's old coalition had fallen apart and the party was intellectually bankrupt, devoid of new ideas. But the truth was that the party's problem was not ideas, it was leadership. We Democrats had not had a truly presidential leader since Robert Kennedy and Hubert Humphrey. In 1972 not McGovern, in 1976 and 1980 not Carter, in 1984 not Mondale—as national leader, not one measured up to FDR or Harry Truman or John F. Kennedy. Or, for that matter, to Dwight Eisenhower.

After the Reagan victories too the notion arose that the country was "turning conservative," and many Democrats thought their party ought to follow that trend, at least tactically. To my mind, it would be as suicidal for the Democratic party to abandon its traditional liberalism in 1988 as it was in 1972 to surrender to the then-fashionable young people's New Politics. The Democratic party, as Dean Acheson once said of it, is my party because it has always been the party not of one interest alone, the business interest, but of the many interests.

The conservatives crusaded against "Big Government" and swore to "get the government off the back" of their beloved free enterprise. Deregulation. How did that turn out? In Arizona and a dozen other states, the legislatue deregulated interest rates on consumer loans. According to *The Wall Street Journal,* an elderly Navajo woman in Arizona with a family of twelve, who had won a land dispute and been given a house in town by the government, left the reservation and moved to town, though she knew little English and knew little of the ways of town. She earned five hundred dollars a month. Soon her son needed money for clothes, and she borrowed seven hundred dollars from a loan company; she put up her new house as collateral.

The loan company charged her 127 percent in interest and "points." (Often the interest rate itself was advertised as "only" 28 percent; points—one point equals 1 percent—for administrative costs and so on ran the bill up. Borrowers don't read the fine print.) A South Carolina used-car dealer claimed the right to charge 500 percent. Some of these lenders were huge national finance companies.

But they were not alone. In the new atmosphere of deregulated free enterprise—and unrestrained greed—not only loan sharks but also executives of some of the nation's big banks and other financial institutions were caught conniving against the rest of us for profit, and so were mighty defense contractors as well as the manufacturers of defective and dangerous automobiles. These were not fly-by-night loan sharks; these were big, respected, famous corporations. How did they get so famous? By advertising their respectability on TV. How so respected? By getting big. How did they get so big? By screwing the little guy. And who was to protect the little guy if not the government? Nobody. And who chooses the government? The political parties. The Navajo woman can survive in such an unregulated jungle only if some political party looks after her "special interest" in her house.

None of this is a "new idea." Farmers in the last century restrained the railroad's greed only through the new government regulatory agency, the Interstate Commerce Commission. Theodore Roosevelt carried on with his trust-busting, and so did Woodrow Wilson, and the whole reform movement came to a thundering climax under Franklin D. Roosevelt. "A new deal for the American people" and "malefactors of great wealth," "one-third of a nation ill-housed and ill-clothed and ill-fed" and "the forgotten man" were far more than slogans; they were the pledges and the protests of a leader of a people that had had enough of greed and injustice. Any young senator worrying today about "population transfers" and "structural unemployment" during the transition to "high tech" would do well to worry instead about injustice—the wrongs of our society today and tomorrow. That, not electronic chips, is still the test of our society. Things may be in the saddle but they cannot ride mankind. Our Democratic party need not worry about new ideas if it keeps its eye on the old idea, the idea of a just society. That requires a leader.

national product. It is, at bottom, measured by the well-being of its citizens, especially its lowliest citizens. When they dwell in misery, the whole society rots. The well-being, the very security, of the highest depends upon the well-being of the lowest. Political stability and national security come from all, not from a few. From the improvement of the condition of the weakest comes the nation's strength.

Foreign Policy: Here I lack both the information and the wisdom to state the liberals' view (if there is one) of America's proper role in the world, much less to discuss the budgetary implications of foreign policy alternatives or to recommend one of those apocalypic revisions of our role, such as disengaging from NATO or declaring "no first use" of nuclear weapons, which appear, fortunately, in learned journals. I simply don't know enough. Rather I will merely put forward a few ideas in areas I have studied or had some firsthand experience in.

We liberals would hope that other nations establish elected democratic governments, since we believe that their peoples will fare best under that system; but we think it is really none of our business how they choose to organize their societies, and if one of them goes under to a dictatorship of the left or right, we pity its people but we will not intervene so long as that dictatorship's policy does not threaten our own vital interests. This does not mean that we should shut our eyes to repression. We should make it clear by our words, but even clearer by our diplomatic deeds, that we prefer freedom to repression. Small things count—we can invite the representative of, say, democratic Costa Rica, but not the representative of a dictator, to White House receptions; we can send the vice-president to ceremonies in the democracies; more tangibly, we can give the representatives of democracies access to high levels of the State Department. And even more, we can deal promptly and sympathetically with whatever problems they wish to take up with us, including their loan applications and the terms of their trade. Yet we liberals resist those who would put our policies into an ideological straitjacket—we oppose a mindless anti-Communist crusade, for example, or, for another example, human rights as a rigid policy, for while we think we Americans should always stoutly uphold the principle of human rights as we conceive them, to attach the word "policy" to them may be dangerous, since to do so might lead to a crusade to impose our view on other nations—some of which have different views, such as the Soviets' view that the right to a job is a basic human right—and might ultimately lead us to try to police the world. What we favor instead might be called a policy of live and let live. Or, as President Kennedy said, "make the world safe for diversity."

We liberals believe the United States should develop a truly special relationship with Mexico, Canada, and the nations of the Caribbean basin. We would strengthen the OAS, and we would revive the principles of the Alliance for Progress throughout the Americas. We believe that, worldwide, we and the other developed nations should work for North-South accommodations. We wish to promote the development of underdeveloped nations and underdeveloped peoples, not only because it is just but because it is in our own interest. We would stop or virtually stop selling arms, especially to poor countries, sales that are an obscenity; arms do not develop, arms kill. We favor an all-out effort at arms control and, ultimately, at disarmament, especially nuclear arms control and if ever possible nuclear disarmament by the United States and the USSR. We know that every arms race in history has led but to war.

Finally, we would work to strengthen the peacekeeping ability of the United Nations and to use the UN more. In recent years, as small new nations have flooded the United Nations and swamped the United States in vote after vote in the General Assembly, U.S. presidents have tended to bypass the UN and our ambassadors there have even publicly denounced it. But before we adopt that long-ago slogan of Barry Goldwater, "Get the UN out of the U.S., and get the U.S. out of the UN," we should pause and ask ourselves: Do we really want to go back to the world we had before the UN existed? After World War I, we did indeed keep the League of Nations out of the U.S. and the U.S. out of the League. The League collapsed; we and the rest of the world lived in a jungle and ended up in World War II. Out of that came the determination "Never again," and we built the UN. Its flaws are all too apparent. In the General Assembly, often the Third World countries are indeed exasperating, irresponsible, and ridiculous. The Security Council is impotent in big-power confrontations. Yet it has dealt successfully with other disputes. Time and again the UN has served as a fireman to put out

public sector and in Washington. Cindy, trained as a social worker, settled into working with Cambodian refugees. Dan, after succumbing briefly to the upheavals of the late 1960s, graduated from college, worked as an advance man in a couple of Illinois campaigns and for Ted Kennedy, then went to work for the Inter-American Development Bank. Fred did well at Exeter and Harvard—at commencement Fran and I sat in the sunlit Harvard Yard and watched him deliver the student speech—and, after his graduate work in history led to a book on Democratic party liberalism, went to work for Mondale, as I have said, and for Geraldine Ferraro and then for New York Governor Mario Cuomo. All three kids have been a great satisfaction to us. When they were growing up, the times were difficult and we were lucky. They avoided the shattering disasters I'd done so much writing about—no violence, no prisons, no real problems. We have friends who to this day don't know where their children are, for in the 1960s they went underground, as the saying went, with some radical student movement.

Fran and I were traveling a good deal during these years. For several years we took to going south in the winter. One year we went to Puerto Rico, another to Key West (mainly to visit the Dick Roveres). And we finally went back to the Dominican Republic. We had long since sold our beach house there—Sosúa was filling up with tourists—and so we rented a house in Cabarete, a remote coastal hamlet. We saw old Dominican friends from Santiago; to avoid Dominican politics we kept out of Santo Domingo. We stayed three or four months, taking with us our cat, named Miss Prettyface, and making her plane reservations when we made our own. (She got us through customs rapidly; everyone was too busy admiring her to pay heed to us. Fran said what a wonderful cover for a CIA agent— to arrive in a country elderly and carrying a cat in a cage.)

But after several years of winters in a Dominican hamlet and long summers at Smith Lake, we realized we had too little time, only two months in the spring and two in the fall, in our old house in Highland Park, with its spacious lawn and its lilacs and honeysuckle, with our books and records, pictures and Ben Shahn drawings, and *things,* familiar things we had accumulated over more than forty years together; and so we took to staying home winters, harsh as the climate is. The climate bothered us little; we simply stayed in the house, arguing with the cat and watching old movies on television, especially W. C. Fields, Laurel and Hardy, and *Casablanca.* And it was nice to live in the Chicago milieu. I was heartened to observe that Chicagoans had lost none of their side-of-the-mouth humor. When jogging became a national craze, the Chicago saying was "The only trouble with jogging is, you can't hit anybody." And when the Cubs, playing on the distant shores of San Diego in 1984, seemed—and were—on the verge of kicking away their first chance in nearly forty years at winning the National League championship, one of their loyal long-suffering fans said, watching it on TV in a bar across the street from Wrigley Field, "The goddam Cubs—they oughta name a disease after 'um."

Smith Lake became increasingly important to us. After we had spent several full summers there and found that the place worked, we sold the old camp at Three Lakes and moved to Smith Lake for good. For several months a year, we'd rather be there than any other place on earth. No television, no telephone, once a week to town for mail. We made improvements—built a big screened porch onto the camp, built a log sauna, built a separate guest house that also contained a carpentry shop for me and a room for me to write in. The great addition was the porch. We cantilevered it out over the cliff beyond the camp among the high pines, almost overhanging the lake, and there, when I am not fishing or writing, we sit together and stare out at the loons on the lake. One day we watched a moose swim the length of the lake. Once a doe with two fawns came and nuzzled against the screen wire. A fierce mink chased our cat. Once a bear came to the porch; Fran and Dan chased it away; it returned; they chased it again; and when it came back a third time Dan shot it. Fran kept saying, "If I sit here on this porch long enough and stare at the lake and the trees, some day I'm going to see an eagle in the tallest pine near camp," and one day she did.

8.

Once more the little personal things mattered, not great affairs of state or writing to improve society. Things like sitting on the porch and seeing an eagle, an unexpected call from an old friend, Miss Pretyface's digestion, her devotion too, and the scilla suddenly ablaze in spring. Too bad, though, how many of the little things are irritating—unctuous doctors and imperious nurses, "new improved" plastic packaging that cannot be opened, incomprehensible Medicare forms, putting up with a cowboy taxi driver because you can no longer see well enough to drive, forgetting. You resist too allowing nothing to matter but health and money. And the magnification of disaster—what would not long ago have been only a serious concern, like your wife's surgery, becomes a consuming, paralyzing nightmare.

I have always been greatly bothered by Leon Trotsky's death. Not that he was murdered but the manner in which he was murdered—a man crept up behind him while he was writing at his desk and drove an ice pick into his brain. That brain—it had learned so much, remembered so much. Shattered, destroyed, in one instant. Now somebody would have to learn all that over again. I've said earlier that any elderly man retired from public life, observing his young successor's moves, wants to shout out, "Don't take that road; we almost took it, and it leads to the precipice." Yet if all the old men lived forever they would go on making the same mistakes that have produced the muddle we're in now. Well, so far I've been lucky: I can read. And so I've been writing, and, chance permitting, I intend to write till I drop.

My writing, however, has taken a perilous course. Many years ago, when I began my freelance career, I wrote on speculation; but I quickly learned to write magazine pieces only on assignment and books only on contract. When you write for a living, you cannot afford to write on speculation. But now, blessed with an income first from teaching then from retirement, I was ending as I had begun—I wrote on speculation. It is liberating—you can write whatever you wish. But it is dangerous—the writing itself can become undisciplined and even self-indulgent.

I first wrote a book about Smith Lake and called it *Sometimes in the Summer*. (The title comes from a line out of an early book by my Michigan writer friend John Voelker, one of the loveliest English sentences I ever read: "Sometimes in the Summer in the nighttime, when there was a moon there was a mist, so that the fields looked like a lake.") Never have I rewritten a manuscript so many times, changing not mere sentences but the whole concept. Having nearly always avoided writing in the first person, I found doing so extremely difficult, the hardest writing I ever did (till now). When I finally got it the way I wanted it, I loved it. Publishers hated it, and it remains unpublished. I still think it one of the best pieces of writing I have ever done. But, then, ever since my first book, I've had trouble writing about, or getting people to read about, Upper Michigan. In that respect, it resembles the old saying about Latin America—the people of the United States will do anything for Latin America except read about it.

Having finished *Sometimes in the Summer,* I turned next to something I had secretly wanted to do all my life: write a novel. I had never been able to afford the luxury of trying. Now I did. For some years I had been bothered by political television and poll taking. But I didn't see a factual piece in it—once you've said, "Television and poll taking are corrupting American democracy," there is little more to say. (John Voelker once conceived a short story entitled "Lost All Night Alone in a Swamp with a Bear," then realized he'd told the whole story in the title.) It occurred to me, however, that one could take the television-polling theme and elaborate it through the characters of a novel. So I wrote a novel. To feel comfortable in attempting it, I made the work as close as possible to writing heavy fact (as, earlier, I had done in writing a screen treatment for a movie). I wrote an outline of the plot—a U.S. senator from Illinois running for reelection sees his campaign faltering and brings in a Washington television consultant, and the television consultant, taking over the campaign, bribes the leading TV poll taker to predict a landslide victory for the senator, thereby shutting off his opponent's campaign contributions; exposure of the bribery causes the senator's downfall. I invented characters—the senator, his frigid wife, his loyal chief of staff who hates television, the chief of staff's wife and a beautiful girl TV reporter with whom he has an affair, the TV consultant as villain, the professional poll taker. I sketched a biography of each. I constructed a detailed campaign schedule and wrote notes about places—the uproarious campaign headquarters, rallies, a TV studio, the campaign plane, and so on. Only then did I start writing the rough draft.

I had always known that magazines like the *Post* used up a great amount of material—about eight pieces of heavy fact a week, fifty-two weeks a year. And that television chewed up even more. What I had not known was how much material a novel chews up. Into this novel I put pieces of a score of people I'd known plus more that I invented in order to make a handful of characters. Into it I put a dozen political campaigns. Into it I put a lifetime of living. It was all packed down—a novel deals in essences. When I finished, I thought I could never write another novel—I'd put into this one everything I knew.

Doubleday published it with a terrible title, *The Televising of Heller.* Arthur Schlesinger and Ken Galbraith liked it and gave it great jacket blurbs. (Ken told me privately as a joke that Arthur was miffed because both Ken and I had now written novels but Arthur hadn't.) John Houseman took it to CBS and proposed a movie, and CBS concurred, and Houseman bought an option on the screen rights and was ready to go into production. CBS at that time fed scripts it was considering into a computer, and if the computer declared that the show would get a low audience rating, CBS turned it down. The computer hated *Heller;* CBS dropped it. The final irony—a computer bars from TV a novel denouncing poll taking and TV.

Thus encouraged, I started another novel, an autobiographical one called *Farewell to Indianapolis;* but it kept sounding like Eugene O'Neill's *Long Day's Journey into Night* or Thomas Wolfe's *Look Homeward, Angel,* and after a time I put it aside and started a third novel. This one, it will come as no surprise, was about an ambassador to a small Caribbean country; I called it *Your Excellency,* and my agent Dorothy Olding submitted a rough draft, and publisher after publisher turned it down. But writing it and *Farewell to Indianapolis* made me realize what I really wanted to do: write my memoirs. And so I have. On speculation.

ACKNOWLEDGMENTS

As Maureen Stapleton said when she won an Academy Award, "I wish to thank everybody I have known in my entire life."